AIG AN OIR

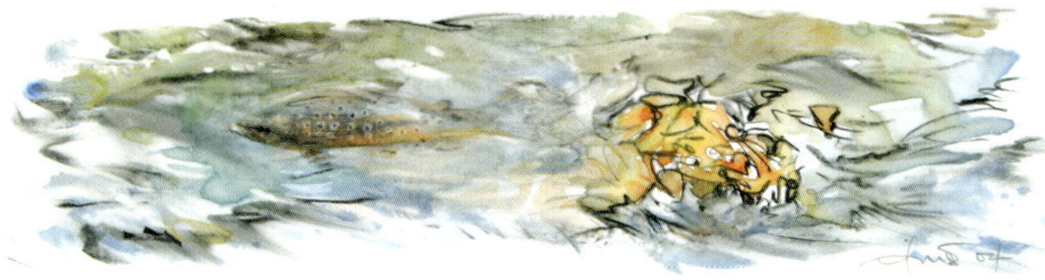

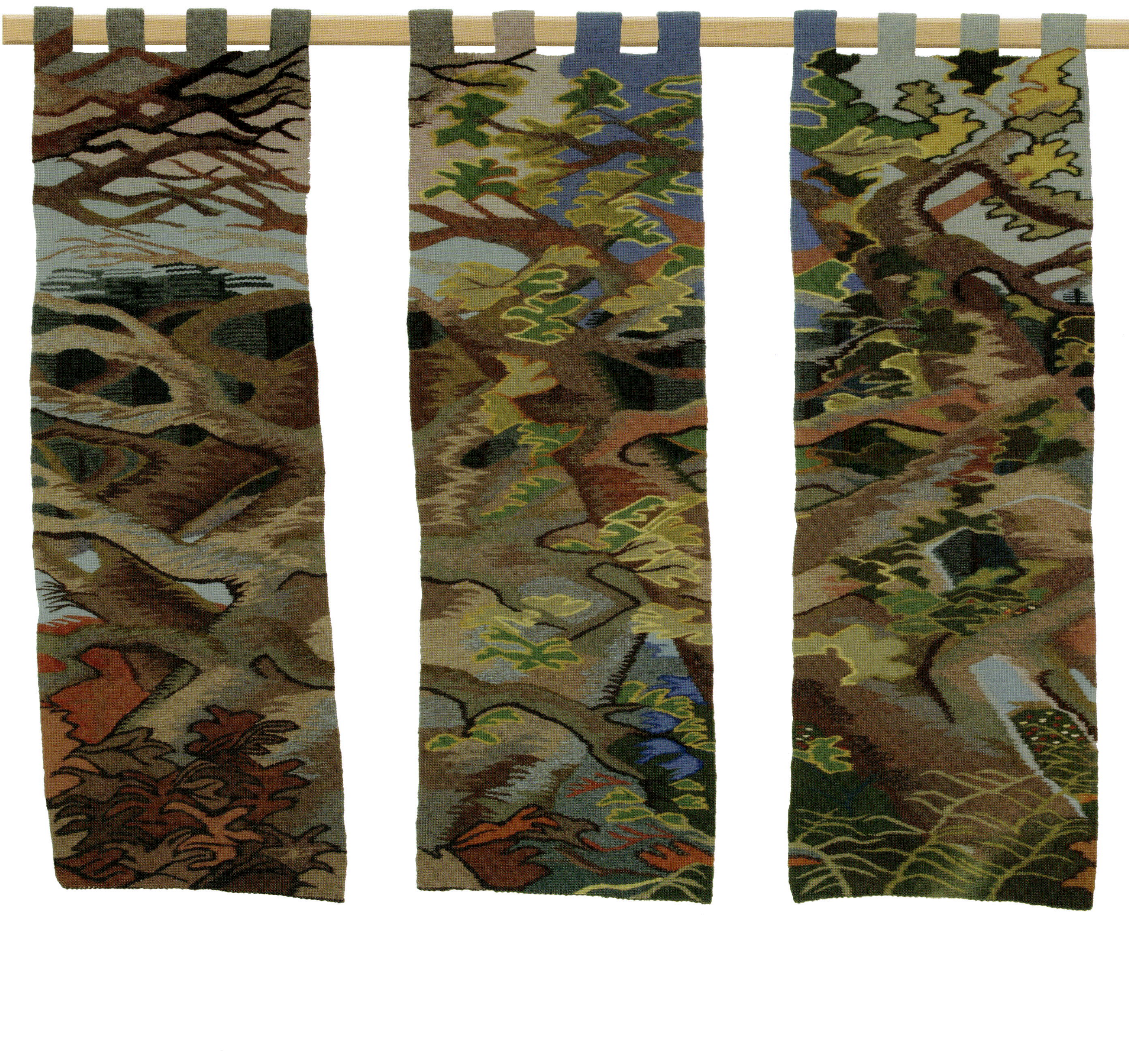

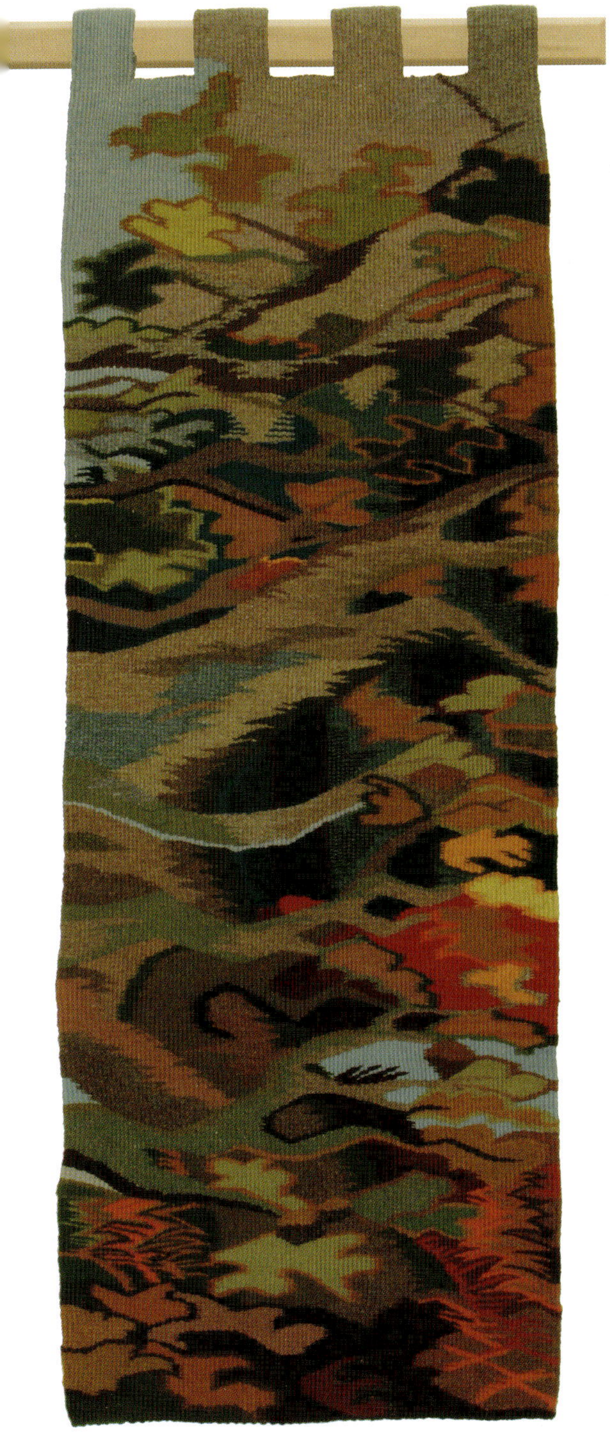

Aig an Oir

At the Edge – Scotland's Atlantic Oakwoods

Text by Robert Burton

THE SOCIETY OF WILDLIFE ARTISTS
LANGFORD PRESS · 2005

Langford Press, 10 New Road, Langtoft,
Peterborough, PE6 9LE
Telephone/Fax 01778 341132
www.langford-press.co.uk
Email sales@langford-press.co.uk

Designed and typeset in Arepo, Cycles and Frutiger
by Nye Hughes, Dalrymple, Edinburgh
Printed and bound in Singapore under the supervision
of MRM Graphics Ltd, Winslow
Photography by Chris Christenson of Coldwells Art
Company Limited, Dalkeith
Eadar-theangachadh bho Bheurla le Uilleam MacNeacail
Gaelic Translation by William Nicolson

A CIP Record for this book is available from the
British Library

ISBN 1-904078-18-4

Half-title: Carl Ellis *Brown trout*
Frontispiece: Louise Oppenheimer *Seasons at Barnluasgan,* handwoven wool wallhanging
Below: John Paige *Golden-ringed dragonfly emerging*
Opposite: John Paige *Midges*
Contents: Jane Smith *Oak leaf print*
Forewords: Carry Akroyd *Sessile* (p.8) *and pedunculate* (p. 9) *oak leaf studies*

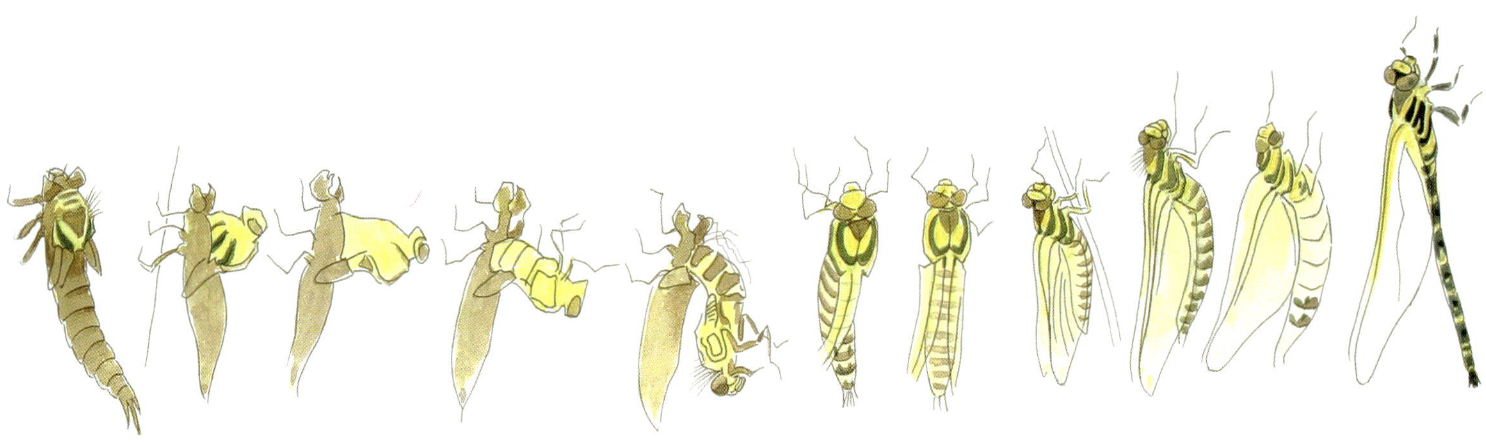

ACKNOWLEDGEMENTS

The artists, author and publisher would all like to express their heartfelt gratitude to Moira Baptie and Roland Stiven for administering the Aig an Oir project so expertly and for their help in this publication. Without their hard work and dedication the project would not have been such a great success. Thanks also to Forest Enterprise Scotland staff Margaret MacCallum, Jamie McIntyre and Chris Marsh for showing Robert Burton around the study areas and for their part in organising the artists' residencies.

The project partners would like to thank Allan MacColl and Moira Hunter for kindly granting their permission to reproduce part of their father Donald MacColl's poem, *Beside Loch Shiel*. Our thanks also to Michael Schmidt of Carcanet Press for granting us licence to reproduce part of *Woods of Raasay* by Sorley MacLean.

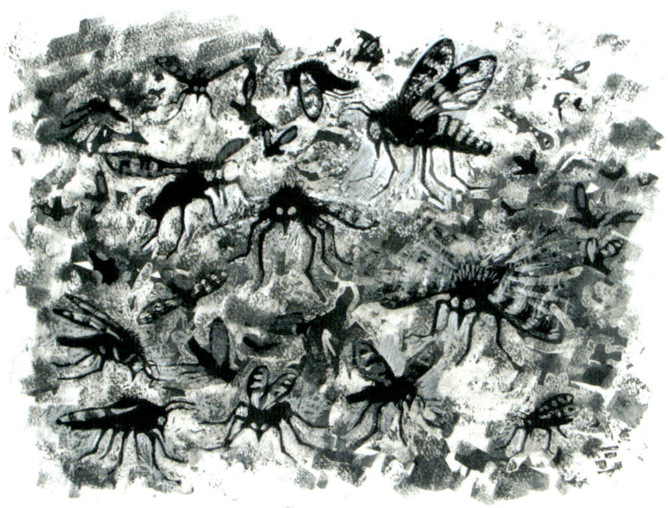

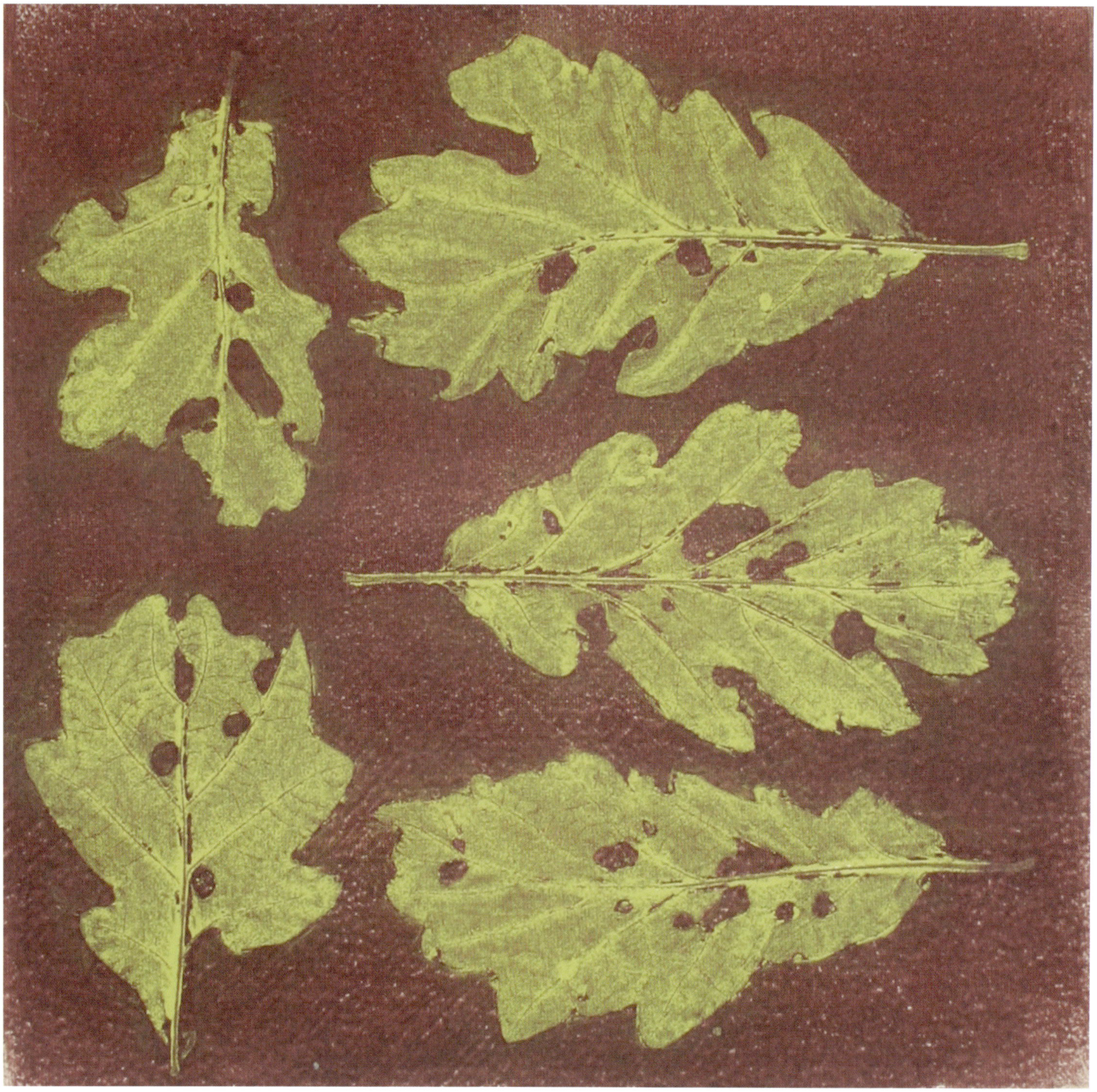

Contents

Forewords

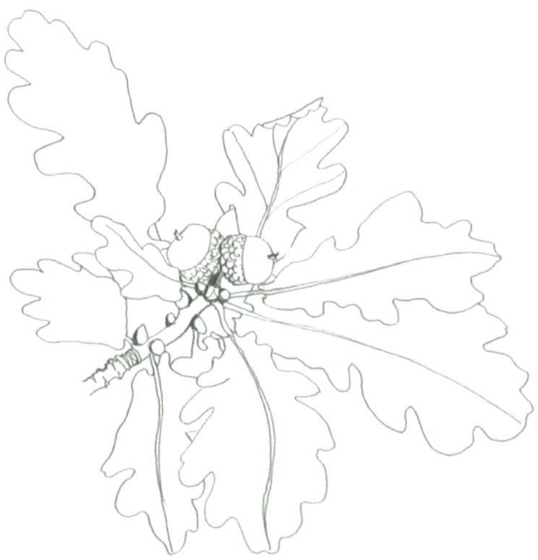

By the nature of what they do, artists who take wildlife and the natural world as their starting point spend hours on their own. It might be out in the field, head down, hunched over a sketchpad or at an easel, often with a telescope or binoculars, trying to realize their observations or record sensations. Or else it's in the studio, working to shape ideas and raw material from the field into some kind of meaningful creative end.

Occasionally, however, there are opportunities to work alongside other artists and as a group share a focus on a specific place or kind of habitat. This adds an air of excitement and collective enthusiasm, as experiences are compared, observations contrasted, and sometimes new techniques acquired or working materials swapped. Someone finds a great spot for butterflies on the wing; another is absorbed by the plants; one artist tells of a good site for singing warblers; or two or three together are inspired by the same aspect of the wider landscape. Someone has an interesting range of papers to work on, and another artist has brought their woodcutting materials.

It was exactly these kinds of individual and shared experiences that lay at the heart of the Aig an Oir project. Three groups of eight artists – SWLA members and artists from the local community – gathered for a week in each of the project areas, and through the year there were further visits by SWLA members, local artists and bursary winners, who visited the sites either on their own or in groups of two or three.

Whatever the nature and timing of the artists' visits, their output was prolific and incisive, and a varied selection graces the pages of this book. The result is a beautiful and powerful portrait of the oakwoods, which, together with the text, reveals their essential character and also brings to life broader concepts and principles, such as biodiversity, ecology, habitat management and sustainability, as well as their historical and cultural heritage, all of which are fundamental to understanding and appreciating the woods.

I would like to thank all the artists who volunteered to participate and enthusiastically contributed their creativity and time. Their effort was skillfully managed and sensitively administered by Moira Baptie of FCS and Roland Stiven, the overall project manager, and we are extremely grateful to both of them. The artists are also very grateful to all the FCS staff and rangers from the three project areas, who offered so much advice and local knowledge. From the very beginning, Hugh Insley, Chief Executive, Forest Enterprise Scotland, was determined to see the Aig an Oir project happen. Now that it is successfully concluded we would like to thank him particularly.

It is said that a work of art is never finished, it just stops in interesting places. In a sense, that is also true of the native Atlantic oakwoods and the story of their restoration – a work in progress with a wealth of interesting places to stop and observe their natural history and understand their place in the economic and cultural history of the west coast of Scotland, and places to just simply appreciate their beauty.

Bruce Pearson
Vice President, Society of Wildlife Artists

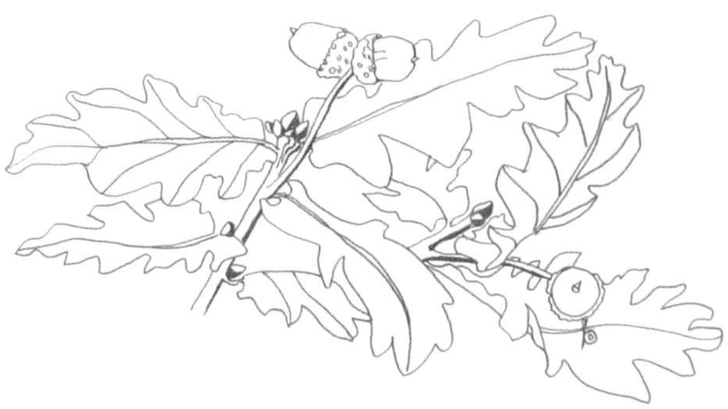

The Atlantic Woodlands, scattered along the extreme western fringe of the continent, are one of the most important and scarce habitats in Europe. Scotland can be considered very fortunate in having the largest and most intact share of this unique ecosystem, and yet, among the general population, knowledge of the presence and significance of these relicts is abysmally low. This magnificent book and accompanying exhibition will undoubtedly help raise awareness and appreciation of these national treasures, as well as generating concern for their continued survival.

Throughout the country 'the rainforest' appears to be an essential part of the curriculum in virtually every primary school. As a result we have raised a generation of young people who know more about the tropical forests of the Amazon basin or Borneo than they do of the woodlands in their own country. When I tell audiences that Scotland has its own rainforests, I am treated to scepticism or disbelief. Yet ecologists recognise the Atlantic Woodlands as part of the Temperate Rainforest Biome, which spreads from New Zealand to Chile, and is even more fragmented and threatened than its tropical equivalent.

If scientists have yet to convince us of the value of our Atlantic Woodlands perhaps artists will succeed? Artists, with their intuitive sympathy for atmosphere, nuance and detail, seem to have the ability to connect closely with this intricate and intensely complex environment of weather-shaped trees and blankets of bryophytes. In the eighties, in a parallel project to Aig an Or, a group of Canadian artists, under the auspices of the Western Canada Wilderness Society, produced an exhibition and book on the Carmanah temperate rainforest of Vancouver Island that changed the hearts and minds of the local population and eventually led to the creation of a new Provincial Park. In the same area, scientists had been struggling for years to get the authorities to listen to their arguments for protecting biodiversity.

Now, in Scotland, we finally have an exhibition and publication – the result of an exemplary level of community involvement – that does justice to our beautiful Atlantic Woodlands in all their many guises. Without doubt it will have a similar impact in strengthening our commitment, at all levels, to protecting these scarce remnants from any further degradation and encourage the regeneration of former forested areas on the West Coast.

The Royal Botanic Garden Edinburgh, with its deep commitment to both Scotland's natural heritage and the study of biodiversity, especially among the less well-known mosses, liverworts and lichens that thrive in the Atlantic Woodlands, is keen to raise awareness of conservation issues among all levels of society. Our experience has also been that a combination of art and science can be a powerful medium. In the recent past we have been involved in a number of successful projects in this area, including the Scottish Rare Plants project and the Millennium Forest exhibition Return of the Natives. We are equally proud to be associated with Aig an Or and congratulate the team that turned this exciting vision into a reality through hard work and dedication. I would now encourage you, while enjoying the many beautiful images in this publication, to take the underlying message concerning the future of these precious places into your heart.

Ian D. Edwards
Royal Botanic Garden Edinburgh

THA AN LEABHAR THA SEO A TOIRT taghadh dh'en ealain a chruthaich buill comunn nam Fiadh-Bheatha, agus a ghabh pàirt 'sa phrosceit seo 'Aig an Oir' 'sa bhliadhna 2004.

'S ann ri linn 'Aig an Oir' a dh'eirich an iarrtas air fiosrachadh fhaotainn air obair Coimmisean na Coille, comhla ris na coimhearsnachan a's na sgirean a leanas mar

tha Ceannloch san eilean Sgitheanach, Sunart, A' Mhorairne agus Cnàpadal, na tri ma dheireadh an Earra-Ghaidheal.

Chaidh an sgrùdadh seo air adhart gus ath-bheothachadh thoirt air doireachan daraich an taobh siar.

Than a coilltean seo prìseal airson an cumadh, is mar a tha iad sgaoilte fosgailte air a' ghrùnnd, a leigeal le solus na greine cead fàs thoirt air fluraichean beaga nadurach, is eile mar cròtal is corcuir. Tha an cuspair seo air fhoillseachadh gu ealanta air na làrich chaidh ainmeachadh.

Ged a bhuineas na craobhan dhan àite, se glé bheag a tha nàdurach mu'n timchioll.

Dh'eirich an suidheachadh seo mar thorradh air cleachaidhean, agus feumalachd muintir na sgìre fad linntean, mar a tha Rob Burton ga mhineachadh sa leabhar.

Tha gu leor 'sa làtha ann a faotinn coire dh'an phoileasaidh a bha ann nuair nach robh am beachd an riaghladh ach fàs math a thoirt air fiodh ann an aithgearrachd, agus canaidh moran gu robh e cearr craobhan coigreach a' chur as ùr fo sgàil na seann deidhinn, ach 's math gu robh an seann stòc calma fallainn, chos a nis gun gabh car a chur 'sa ghnothach.

Tha e na adhbhar molaidh gu bheil na coilltean iomallach seo, chaidh air di-chuimhne, a nis a' faotinn taic bho na coimhearsnachan airson an cumail beò, agus dochas gu 'm bi e chum buanachd do'n linn ri teachd.

Tha eachdraidh na coilltean seo a' dearbhadh cho cugallach sa bha iad, coltach ris an tuath bha nabachd riuthe. 'S en gealltanas is fhearr againn gum mair agus gu meudaich na craobhan seo, an dòchas gum bi sin chum math muintir na sgìrean 'sa bheil iad air oir a h-Alba.

Chaneil sinn idir a deanamh leisgeul iomradh a' thoirt ann an Gàidhlig air a leabhar agus air a phroiseact. Tha an canain coltach ris na doireachan, an cunnart a dhol a bith. Chunnaic mise na craobhan seo an toiseach air latha briagha samhraidh san Og- Mhios sa bhliadhna 1972. Air an t-slighe tilleadh a Ard na Murchan, stad mi feòrach do dhuine nach do thuig mo chainnt, ach stiùir an nighean aige mi air an rathad cheart gu aiseig Chorrain Ard Ghobhar.

'Se taic chaich chur am proseict seo air adhart, gu araidh na fir seo:

Rob Livingston-Hi Arts, Bruce Pearson agus Chris Rose, le cheile a Fiadh Beatha nan Ealain. Cheart cho feumail bha an taic airgiod a fhuaradh bho Iomart Lochaber, Whelk Eorpach, North Highland Leader + 2000–2006 Programme. 'Se n uidh a bh'aig na coimhearsnachan, agus luchd ealain fad às, comhla ri feadhainn faisg air laimh san tri coimhearsnachan, gun a shoirbhich cho math leis a ghnothach. Chuidich e gun d'fhuair sinn cead feum a dheanamh dhe'n na tallaichean agus na cailearaidhean, ach chan fheum sinn di-chuimhne dheanamh air oifeagearan na proseict agus sgiobean a Chomisean fhein.

Bha luchd ealainn a sealltainn torradh an cuid obrach aig An Tuireann am Portrigh, Taigh Tasgaidh Cille Mhàrtainn faisg air Cnàpadal, Studio Resipol Suinart agus Taigh Bàn Lochalin 'sa Mhorairne (aite bithidh).

Bha na cruinnichean bha sin air leth taitneach agus cairdeil; chur sluagh an àite eolas air urrachan a Chomumm Ealain. Chord sin ris na h-uile. Bithidh an taisbeanadh ri fhaicinn anns na Botanics an Dun Eidean san t-Sultain 2005 far am bi Rob Burton fhein a bha uaireigen a fuireach an Earra-Ghaidheal. Ma tha buanachd re tighinn an cois na h-obrach seo, bithidh duil gun cuidich e na coimhearsnachan ri tìde.

Uisdean Insley
Ard Runaire, Iomart Coilltearachd na h-Alba

THIS BOOK BRINGS TOGETHER A selection of the art created by members of the Society of Wildlife Artists who took part in the Aig an Oir (At the Edge) project during 2004.

Aig an Oir grew out of a desire to gain recognition for the work of Forestry Commission Scotland and its partners, including the local communities on Skye, in Sunart and Morven, and at Knapdale, to restore the native Atlantic oakwoods in the west of Scotland.

These woods have a magical quality, which derives from the shape and distribution of the trees, their open ground flora, the epiphytes that cover the trees and, most of all, the special light within them. The essence of this has been captured brilliantly by the Society's artists during the three Aig an Oir residencies.

Although they are native woodlands, little about them is natural. The very quality that everyone appreciates has been created by man's intervention over the centuries, as Robert Burton describes in this book.

Leaving these woods alone and trying to preserve them is not an option. This approach will surely lead to their eventual extinction. And yet our past attempts to regenerate them have produced something very different to the desired end product. Open space allows a thick tangle of many species, few of which are oak trees. This brings a realisation that the future management of these woods and the re-creation of these attractive open woodlands with their almost lawn-like ground flora is going to take time, patience and probably the use of techniques with which foresters have lost familiarity, such as controlled grazing.

With the wisdom of hindsight everyone now recognises that the overzealous pursuit of wood production under earlier forestry policies was a mistake. Native woodlands such as these never should have been underplanted with exotic conifers, and it is lucky that they have been robust enough to survive sufficiently well for us to be able to reverse the process.

The project has been a celebration of these remote and often overlooked woods and of those individuals and communities who have contributed not only to their survival and return from the brink but also to ensuring that they are secured for future generations.

The history of these woods has proved to be as fragile, and yet at the same time as enduring, as the communities living among them. The strongest guarantee for their future existence is that they contribute to, and are understood to be of value to, the communities of these places at the edge of Scotland.

We make no apology for promoting Gaelic through this project and book. As the native language of the area, it is even more threatened than the oakwoods. The first time I saw these beautiful woods was on one of those special west-coast days in June 1972, when sun from a cloudless day shone through the freshly opened leaves. Returning from a visit to Ardnamurchan Point, I stopped at an isolated house to ask the way back to Corran Ferry. The old man working in his garden looked at me, shook his head, and went indoors to find his daughter, who was more comfortable speaking English.

Aig an Oir would not have happened if it hadn't been for the support and help from our partners, Robert Livingston of HI~ARTS and Bruce Pearson and Chris Rose from the Society of Wildlife Artists, and, importantly, the funding received from Lochaber Enterprise and the European WHELK and North Highland LEADER+ 2000–2006 Programmes. However, it is the enthusiasm of the local communities, the artists from far afield and from within the three communities, the local studios and art galleries, the Project Officers, and the local Forestry Commission teams that has really made it truly special.

The evening 'hangings' when the Society's artists presented the initial results of their work at the An Tuireann Arts Centre on Skye, Kilmartin Museum near Knapdale, Resipole Studios in Sunart and Whitehouse Restaurant in Lochaline were exciting, vibrant and happy occasions, bringing the nation's top wildlife artists into direct contact with communities seldom in the limelight. That alone was a huge reward and success.

The exhibition at the Royal Botanic Gardens in Edinburgh in September 2005 and this book, skilfully penned by Robert Burton, himself once a resident of rural Argyll, continue this success. As products of Aig an Oir, all of these outputs will help to secure the future of both Scotland's Atlantic oakwoods and the communities who care for and depend upon them.

Hugh Insley
Chief Executive, Forest Enterprise Scotland

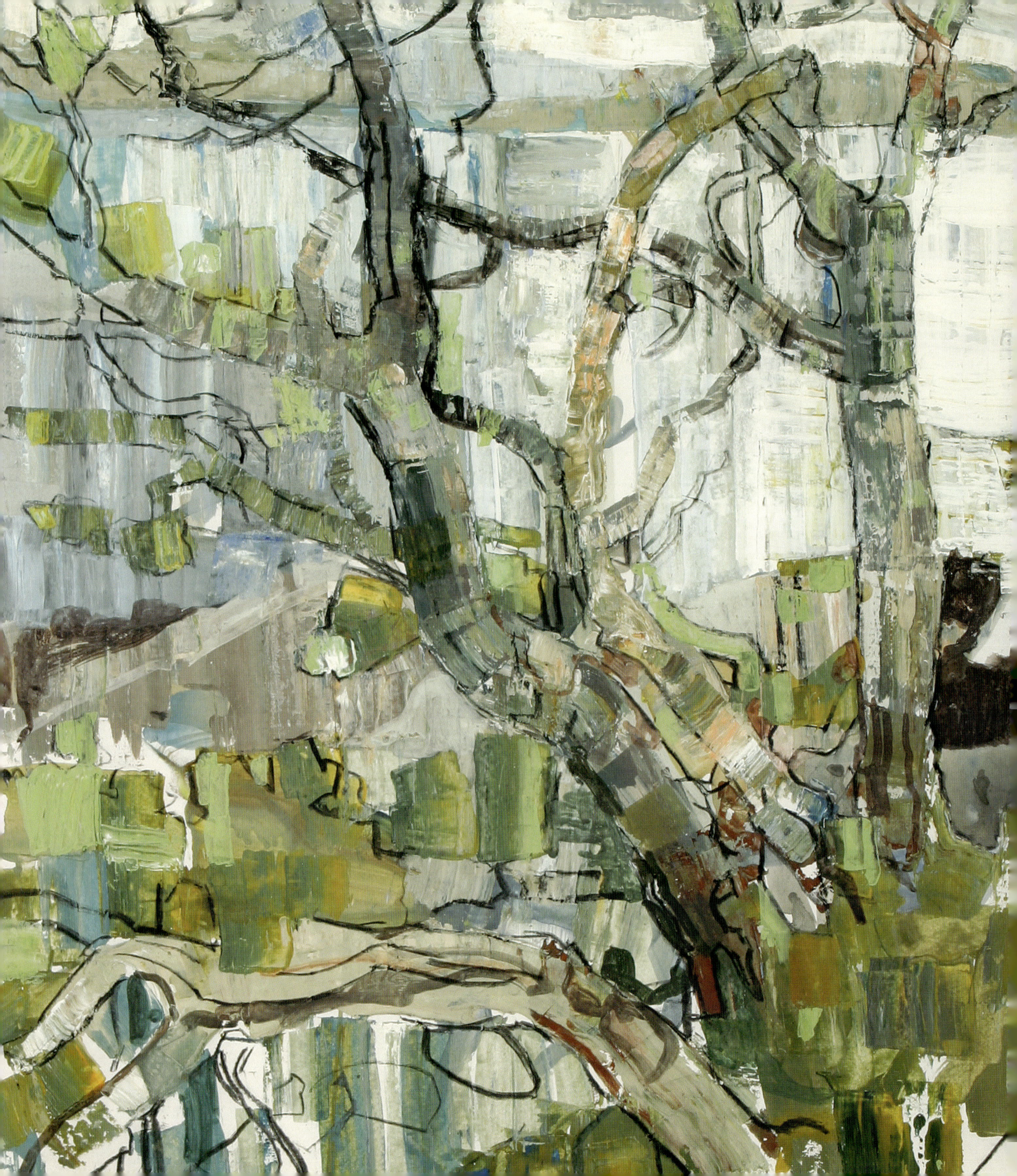

1

At the edge

Bi gach creutair d'a laigead
Dol le suigeart do 'n choill

There's no creature so feeble
But goes with joy to the woods

FROM THE SONG OF SUMMER
BY ALEXANDER MACDONALD

If you drive into the western Highlands of Scotland, turning off and heading west from Loch Ness perhaps, or coming up directly from the south via Loch Lomond, you enter one of the wildest and most remote parts of Britain. The human population is small and scattered, and you can go for miles without seeing a building or another human. The landscape is breathtaking, but although the steep, rugged hills impart a grandeur to the scene, they are bare. Along the valley below, the terrain is softer. It is clothed with patches of deciduous, broadleaved woodland: a few acres here and there, perhaps a larger spread covering miles of the valley floor, or just a ribbon of trees following a burn up the hillside.

These woods go unremarked; they are not what visitors come to the Highlands to see. Yet they are part of the once-great Caledonian Forest, which is better known for its stands of dramatic ancient Scots pines, familiar to visitors to Speyside in the central Highlands. They are the remains of a special habitat known as the Atlantic oakwoods. Within the Highlands, the oakwoods range from Sutherland in the north to Loch Lomond in the south. Elsewhere, they can be found along the length of the Atlantic seaboard: in south-west Scotland, the west coast of Ireland, the English Lake District, West Wales and Cornwall, and thence to Brittany in France and Galicia in Spain.

With good reason the Atlantic oakwoods are sometimes described as a temperate rainforest. The Highlands are famous for their wet climate, and with nearly 2000 mm of rain falling every year on Fort William, this is well within the range of rainfall in tropical rainforests. We think of tropical rainforests as thronging with life: monkeys, hummingbirds, bizarre insects and garish orchids. We are told that saving rainforests is vital for preserving 'biodiversity'. We know this from television programmes and books, but the rainforest on our doorstep has been woefully neglected. It turns out that 'the Celtic rainforest' is unexpectedly rich in animal and plant species, with thirty-four species regarded as priorities for conservation in a British context. They are not so dramatic as the flamboyant wildlife of the tropics, but the remnants of their woodland home are national treasures and are worthy of preservation for their own sakes.

Thirty years ago, I lived in Argyll. It was the time when the Forestry Commission was planting vast tracts of country on the west coast with exotic conifers. Rows of fast-growing Sitka spruce were sprouting all over open moors, and, to my distress, they were also being planted under the native oaks and birches. The oaks and birches initially acted as sheltering nurses but would later be crowded out as the conifers overtook them. How silent and barren would be the new forests when they crowded out the native vegetation! Exotic conifers were not the only problem. On land that was still farmed, I noticed that nothing grew under stands of deciduous trees except a sward of grass. The sheep were eating out any tree seedlings that tried to sprout. What would be left after the current stands of trees died, I wondered.

In the years since, there has been a serious change of heart, and the native woods are being restored. The Atlantic oakwoods have been identified as a

Matt Underwood
Across the sound from Kinloch woods, Skye (detail)
gouache · 84 x 55 cm

threatened habitat in a European context, and Forestry Commission Scotland, together with private woodland owners, is making strenuous efforts to save them. The future of the woods is now much more secure. Restoration of existing woods by natural regeneration bolstered by new plantings, although a slow process, is bringing back the woods' former ecological structure and diversity, and will make them safer and more viable in the future. Hand in hand with woodland restoration goes the conservation of the rare and endangered species that are restricted to the Atlantic oakwood ecosystem.

In 2004, Forestry Commission Scotland arranged for members of the Society of Wildlife Artists to visit the western Highlands and record their impressions of the oakwoods as part of a campaign to draw attention to the importance of the woods and the efforts to preserve them. Through the medium of the artists' work, which is shown on these pages, it is hoped that the beauty and wildlife values of the oakwood habitat will be better appreciated. The project was dubbed *Aig an Oir*.

We were particularly interested in the concept of these woods being 'at the edge' – *aig an oir* in Gaelic. The Atlantic oakwoods are at the edge in several important ways. Geographically, they are at the edge of Europe (and those of the west Highlands are on the edge of Scotland), and they are at the edge of the land, where it meets the sea. The wet but mild 'oceanic' climate generated by the Gulf Stream sweeping in from the Atlantic is the key to the woods' unique ecological value. The woodland is also at the edge because it was nearly destroyed by centuries of climate change, grazing by domestic stock, timber extraction and, more recently, the planting of conifer trees and the spread of other exotics such as rhododendron. Today the once-wide sweep of woods across the Highlands is represented

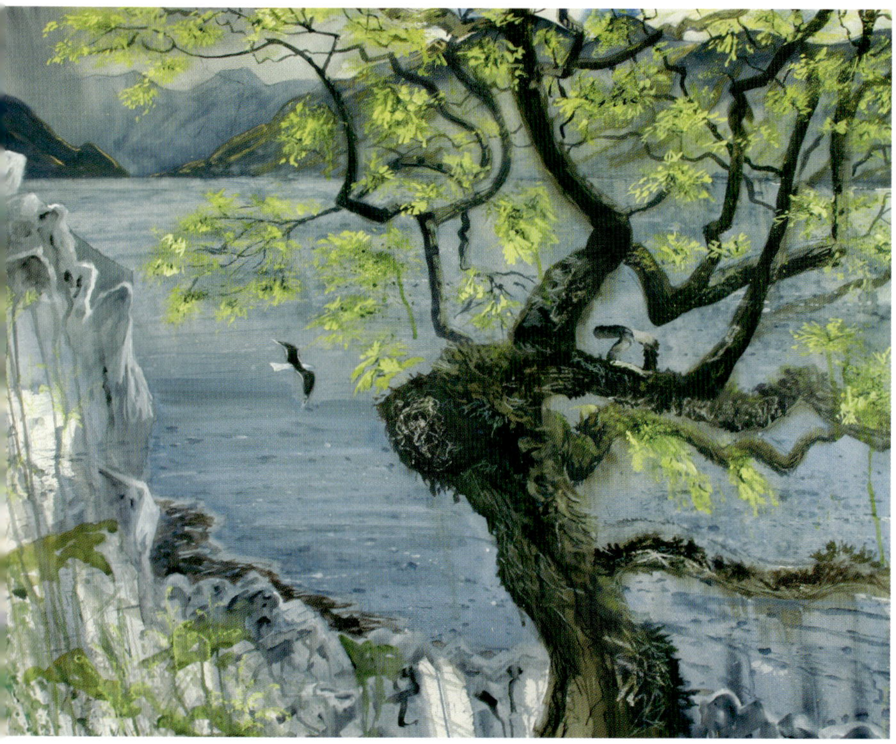

1

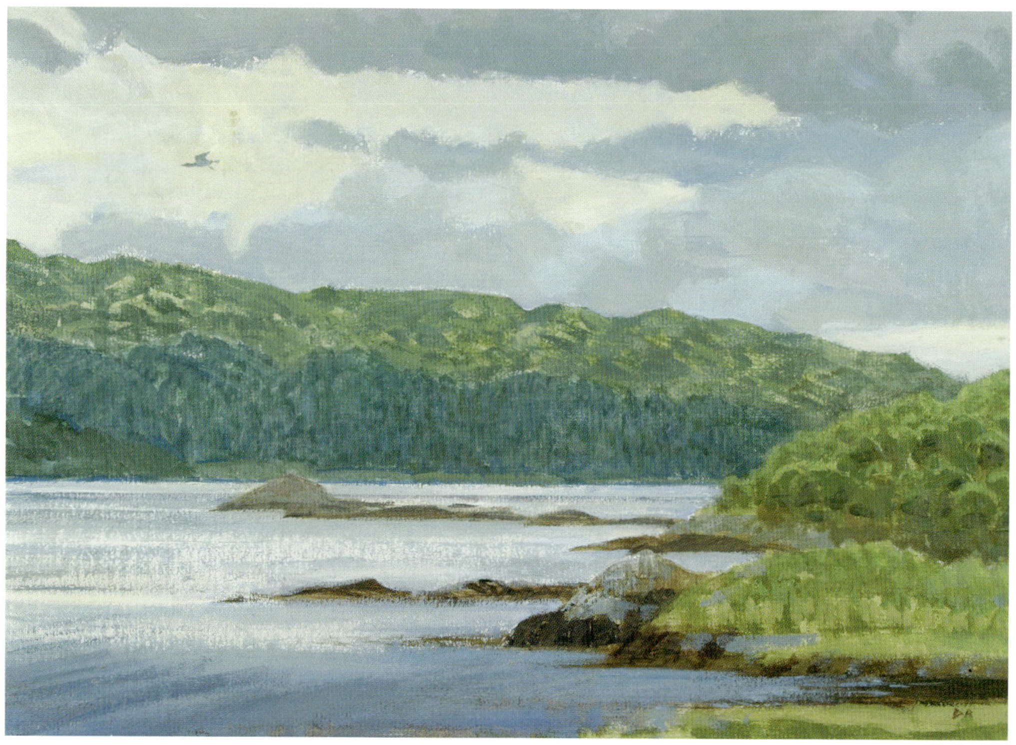

2

by no more than scattered scraps.

We visited three places: the Kinloch Hills on Skye, Ardnamurchan and Morvern on each side of Loch Sunart, and Knapdale and Taynish in mid-Argyll. They contain some of the largest and best-preserved areas of Atlantic oakwood and they are home for a number of rare species. All three areas are designated as Special Areas of Conservation (SAC). SACs form a network of large protected areas across the European Union called 'Natura 2000', which is designed to conserve the most important sites for habitat and species conservation across Europe.

If you have not been to the Atlantic oakwoods before, and even if you are familiar with the natural history of woods elsewhere, I urge you to take advantage of any guided tours on offer or at least acquire a colour leaflet. Otherwise you will miss some of the fascinating features they have to offer.

1. Paul Henery *Atlantic oak, Leitir Fura, Skye*
   mixed media · 96 x 116 cm

   I spent all day painting a windswept oak on the shore below Leitir Fura. The trunk was covered in lichens, which appeared ancient, while the newly emerged oak leaves were bright and fresh. I stood next to an otter holt and looked across to Knoydart, watching the great black-backed gulls patrolling the coastline constantly.

2. Darren Rees *Loch Sunart from Ceol na Mara*
   acrylic · 26.5 x 35.5 cm

3. Darren Rees *Rubha an Daimh, Loch Sunart*
   watercolour · 26.5 x 35.5 cm

4. Darren Rees *West along Loch Sunart*
   acrylic · 29 x 39 cm

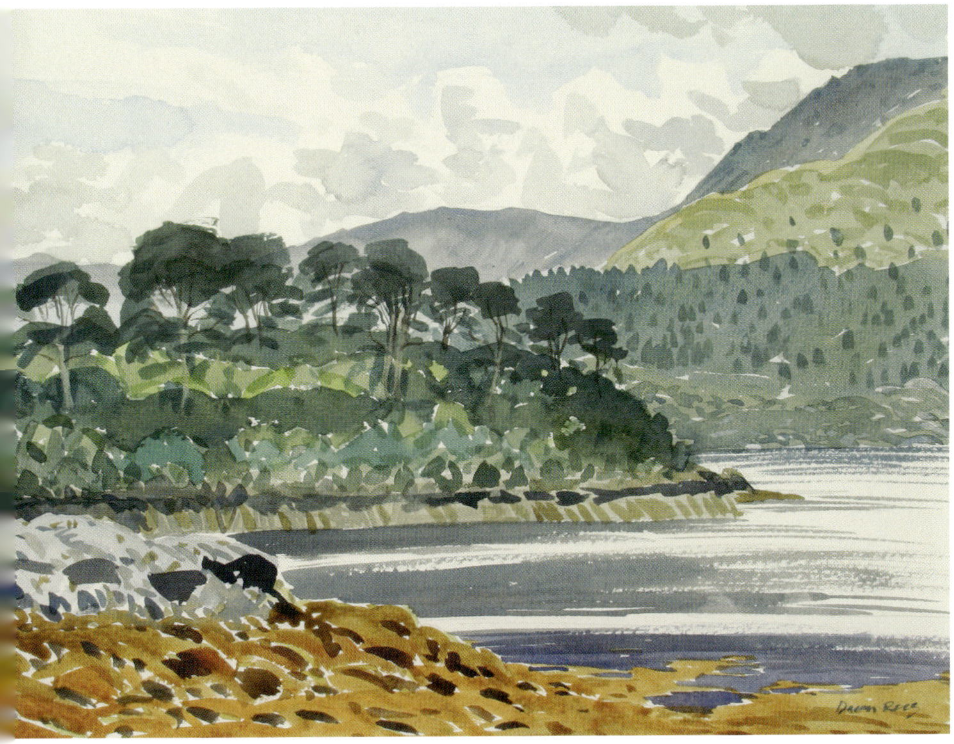

3

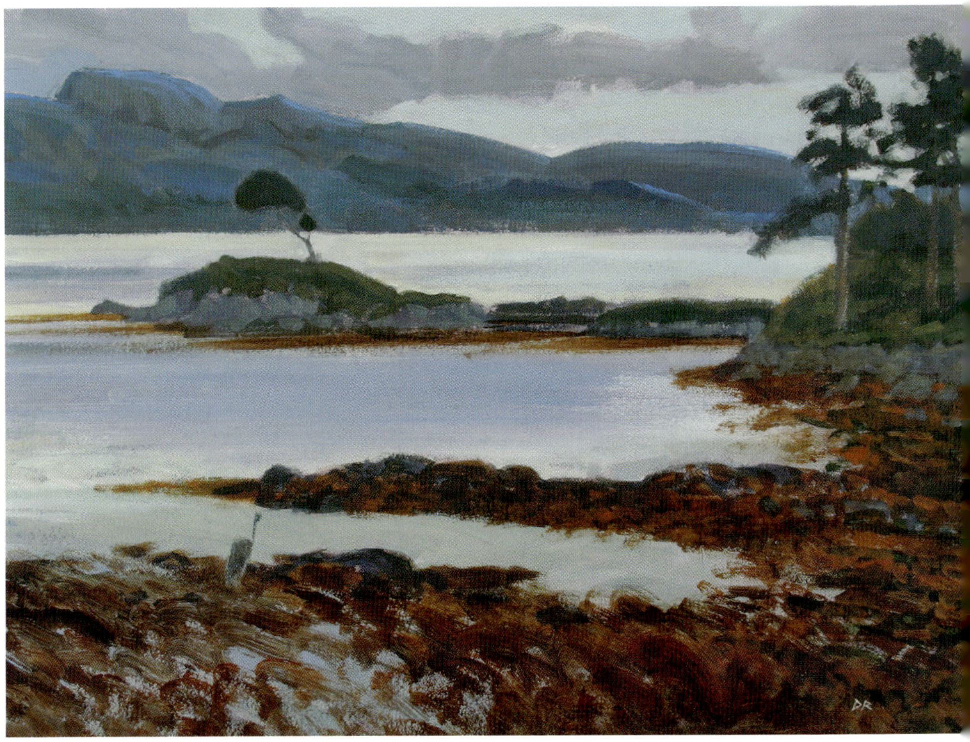

4

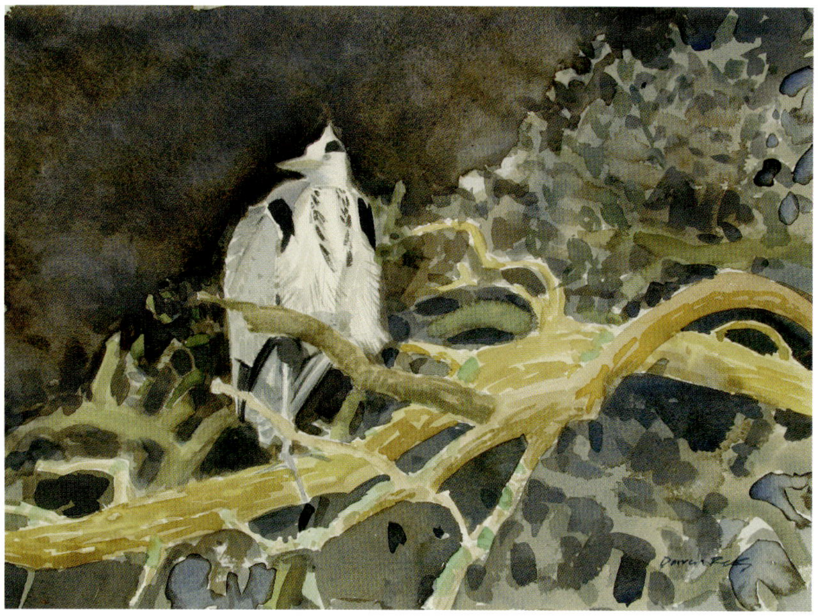

1

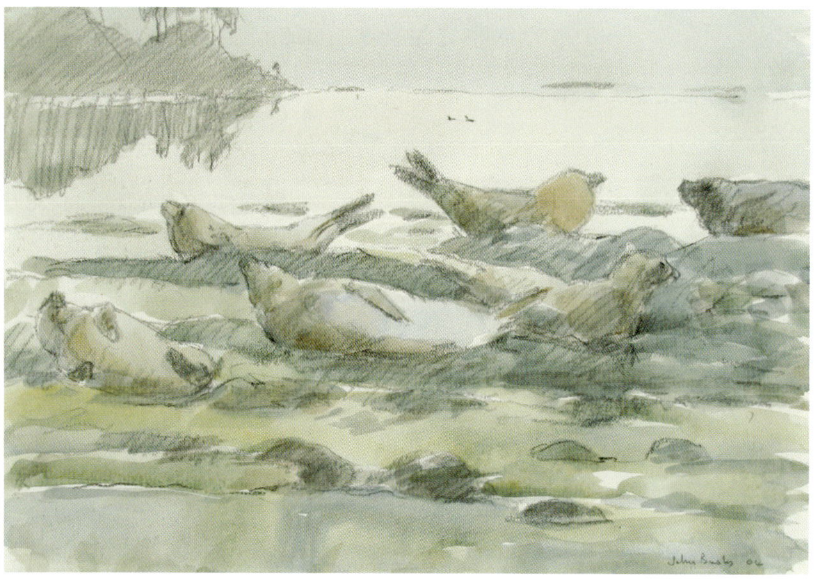

4

1. Darren Rees *Resting heron*
   acrylic · 25 x 36 cm
2. John Davis *Common Seals, Faery Isles*
   watercolour · 15 x 22 cm
3. Robert Greenhalf *Sheep on the beach, Kentra Bay*
   watercolour · 28 x 38 cm
4. John Busby *Resting seals*
   watercolour · 19 x 27 cm
5. Dafila Scott *Seals hauled out, Loch Sunart*
   oil on paper · 38 x 51 cm
6. Robert Greenhalf *Herons – Rubha an Daimh*
   watercolour · 28 x 38 cm

Dafila Scott *Seals hauled out, Loch Sunart*

The upper reaches of Loch Sunart feel quite landlocked, so it was somehow surprising to find the seals hauled out on the rocks at Garbh Eilean. They looked so comfortable! Being dry in parts and wet in parts, they caught the morning light in different ways, and it made interesting effects on their coats. Sometimes it wasn't obvious where seal ended and rock or weed began.

Robert Greenhalf *Sheep on the beach, Kentra Bay*

At low tide, Kentra Bay becomes a wide expanse of sand and mud, with only a shallow river meandering to the sea. There are a few small islands – little more than rocks topped by grasses and other salt-tolerant plants – and there are areas of saltings around the head of the bay. The local sheep moved with the tides, visiting the islands and saltings at low water and retreating to the higher areas with the turning tide.

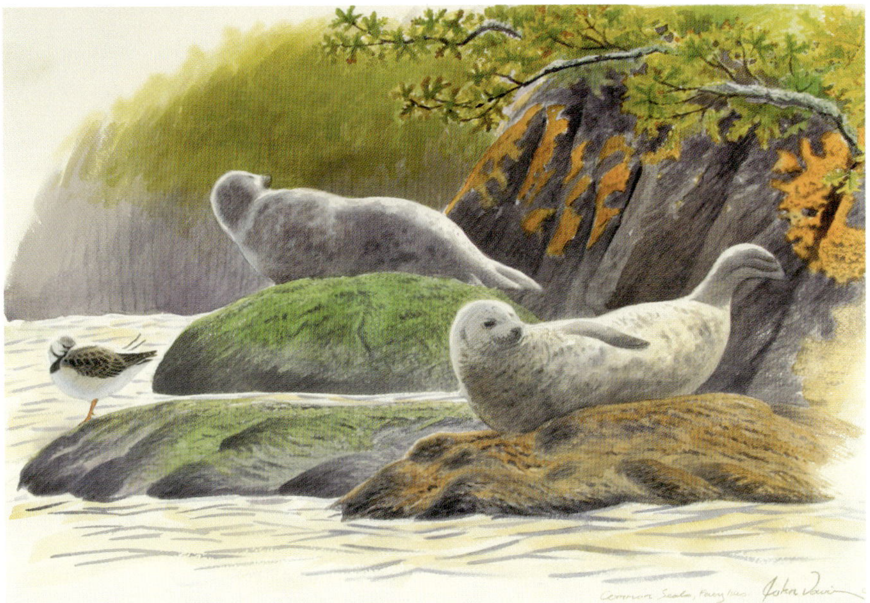

2

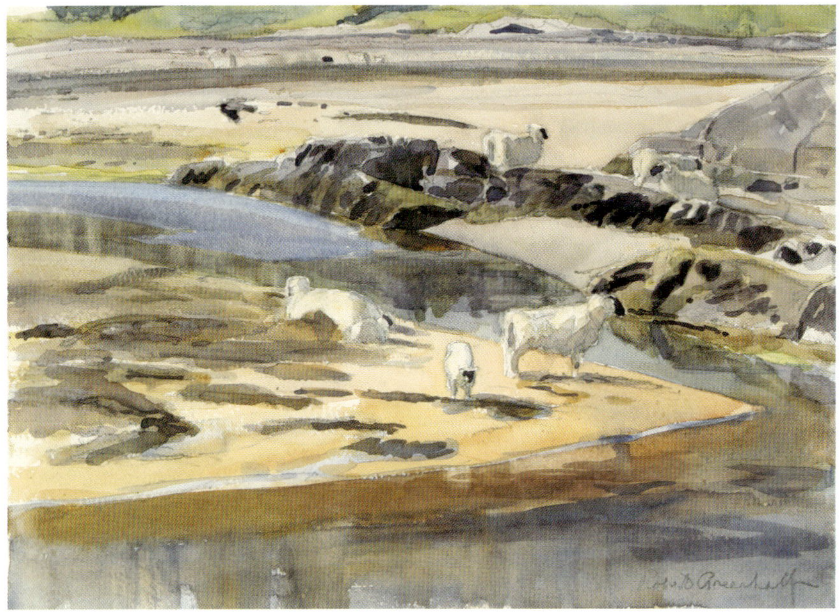

3

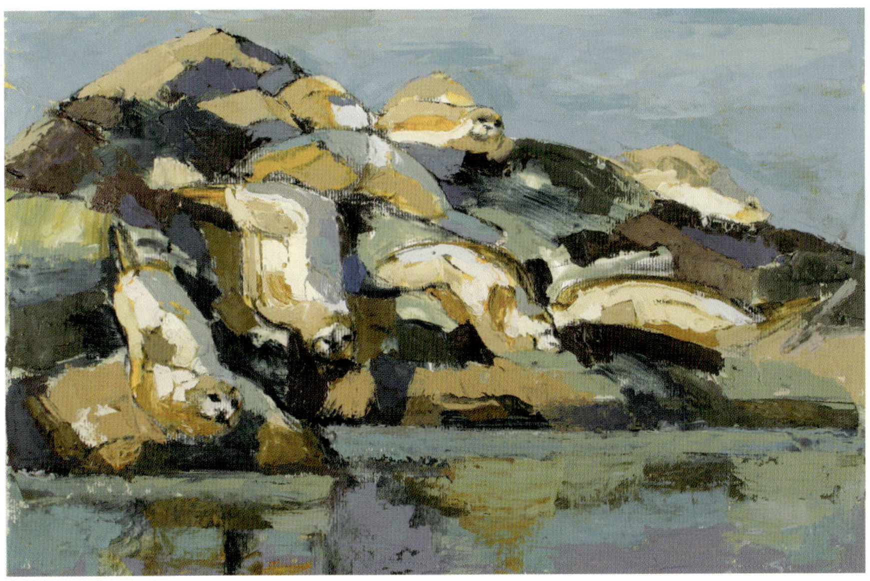

5

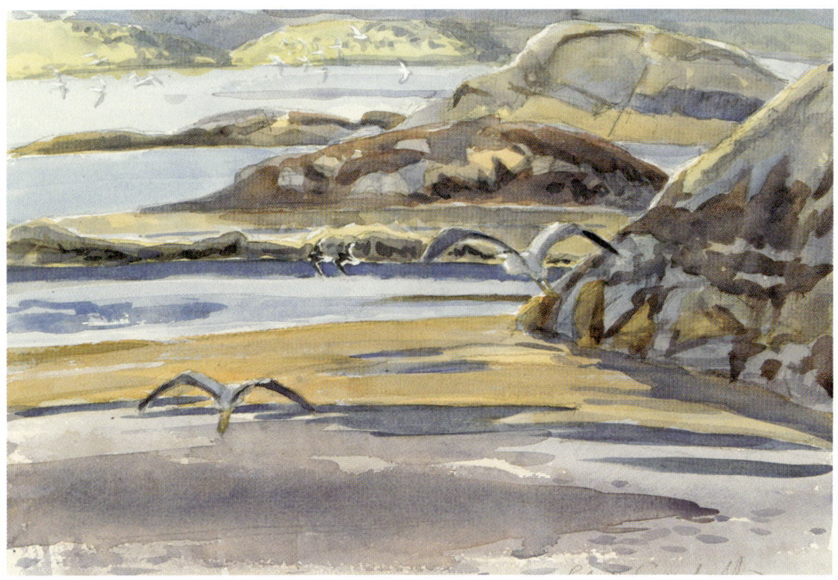

6

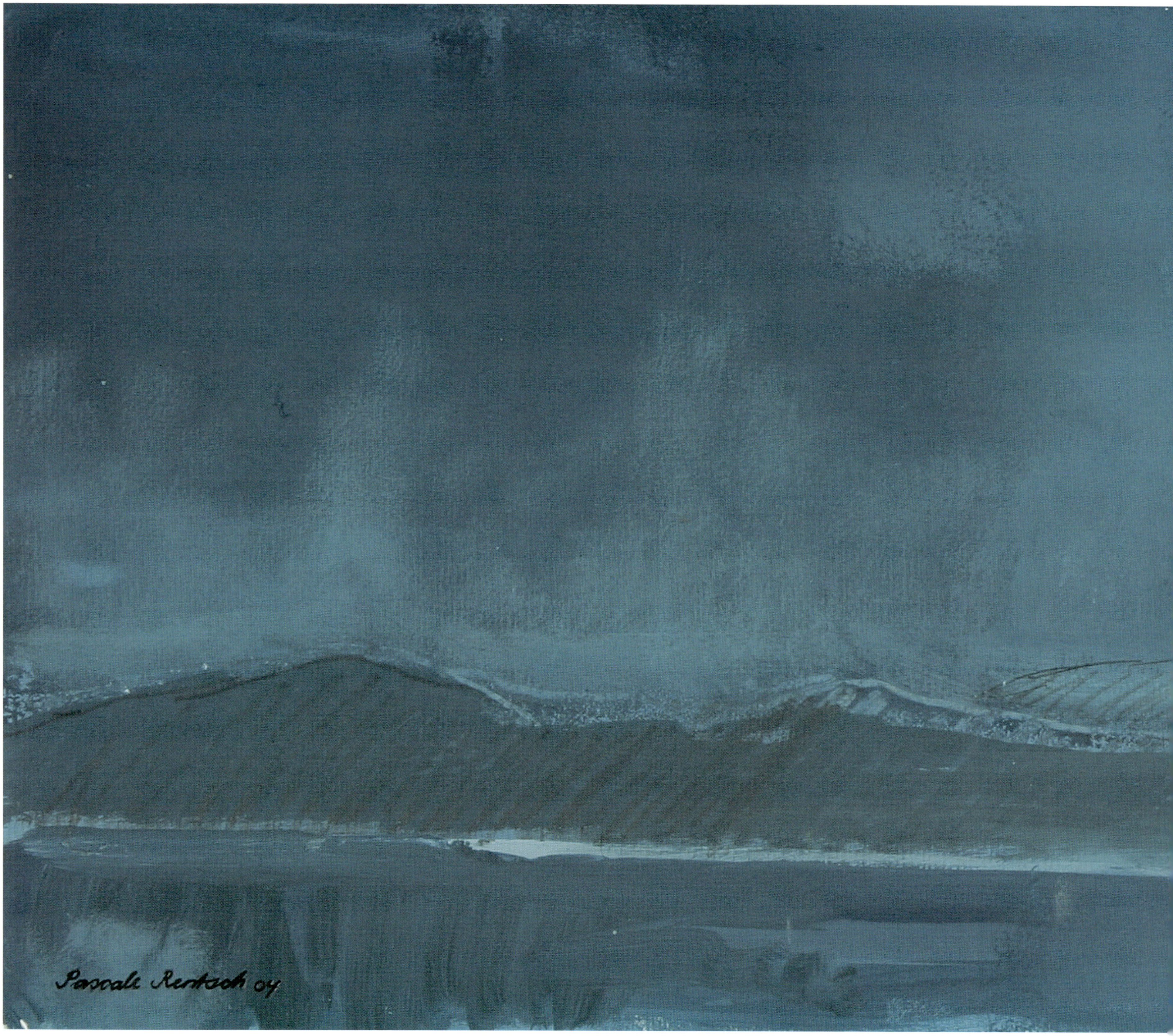

Pascale Rentsch *Sound of Mull, Sunart*
emulsion and acrylic · 20.5 x 48.5 cm

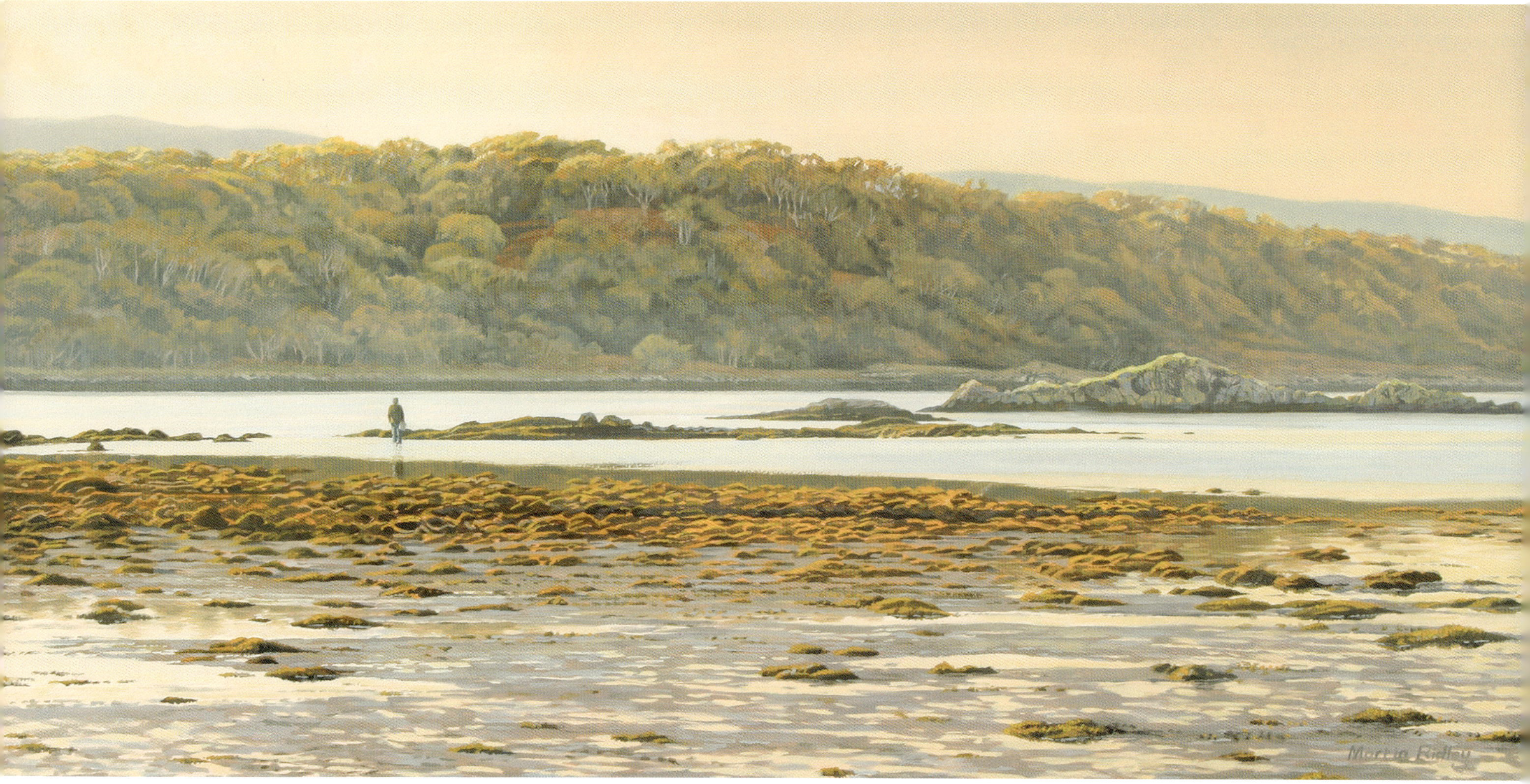

1

1. Martin Ridley *The bait digger, Taynish*
   oils · 30 x 60 cm
2. Martin Ridley *Two crows later I, Loch Sunart*
   oils · 39.5 x 48 cm
3. Martin Ridley *Two crows later II, Loch Sunart*
   oils · 39.5 x 48 cm

Martin Ridley *Two crows later*

I wanted a title to suggest a brief passage of time, the time it takes for an autumn squall to blow through. Frequent showers funnelling down the loch is one of the ingredients that make the Sunart oakwoods so special. The vista is ever changing, often dramatically, and sorties of hooded crows seemed to mark the passing showers perfectly.

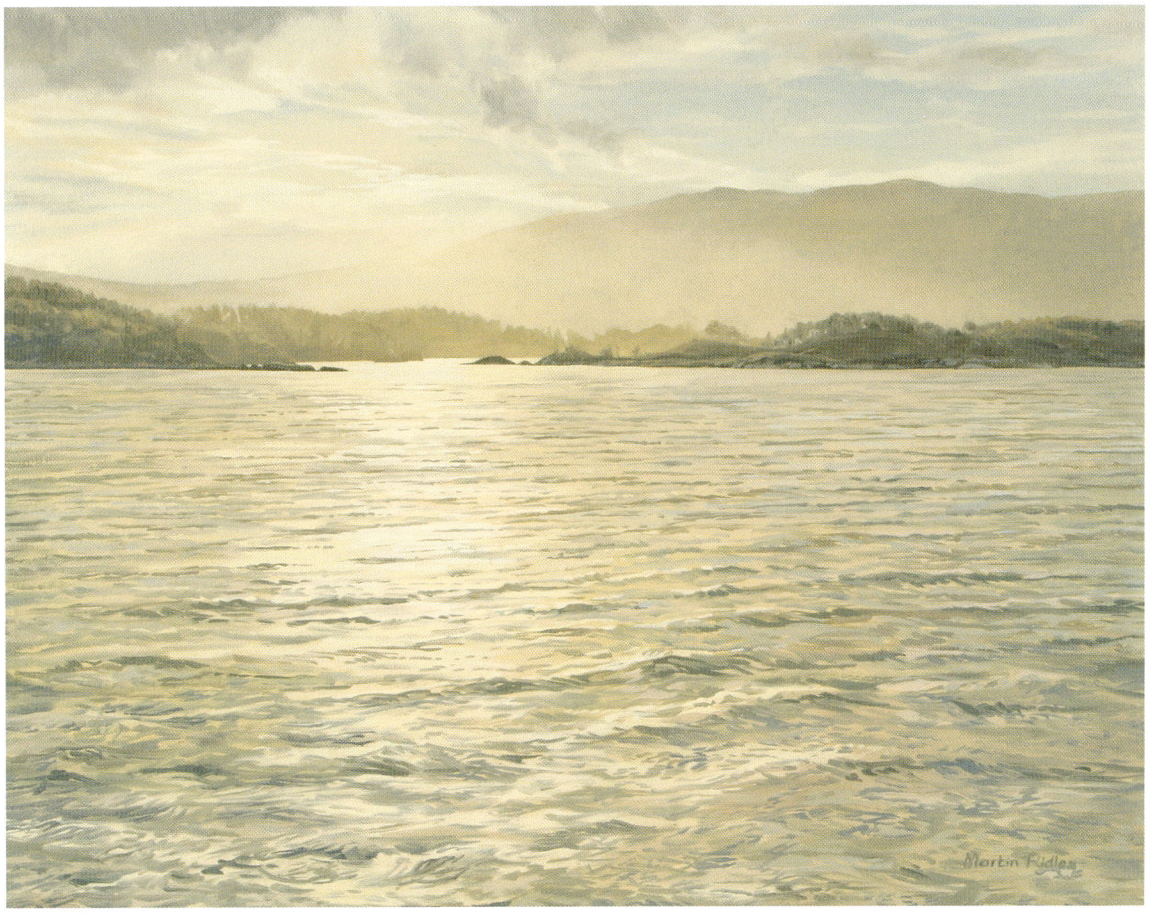

2

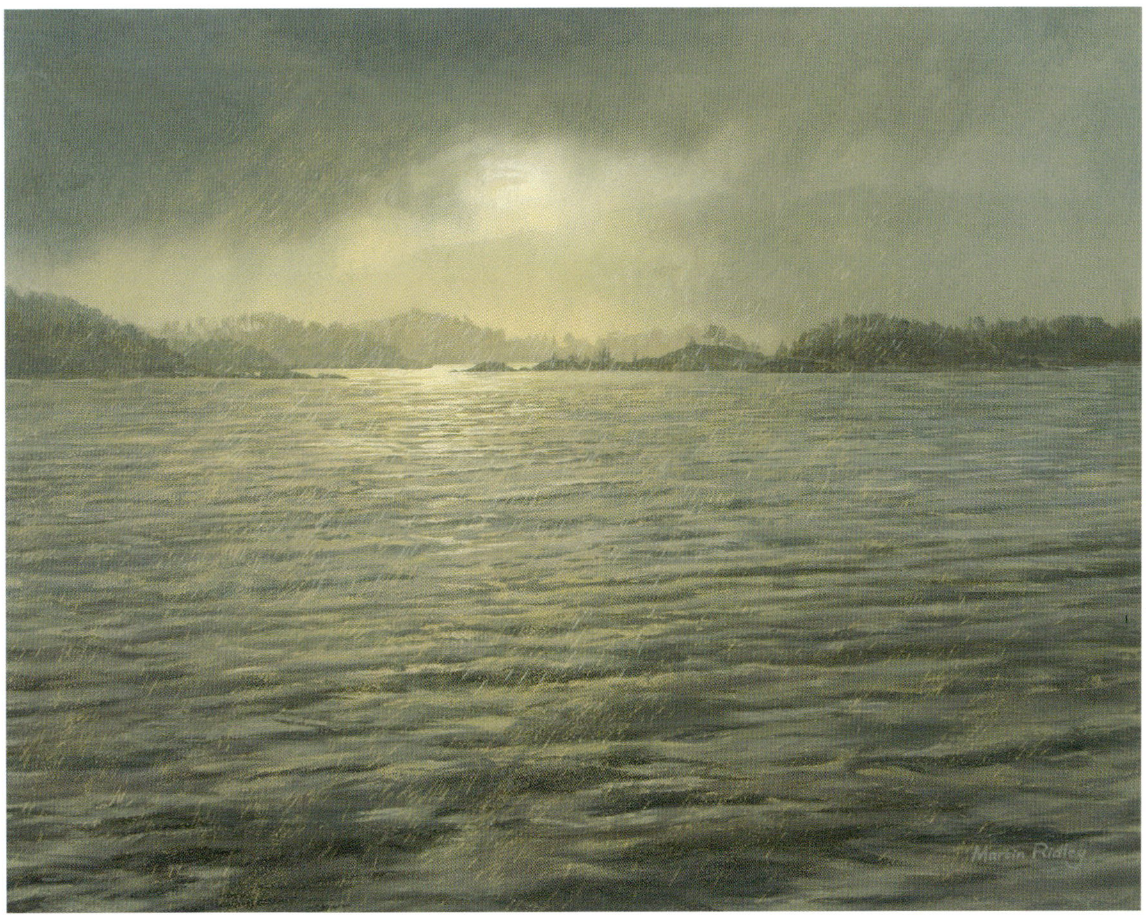

3

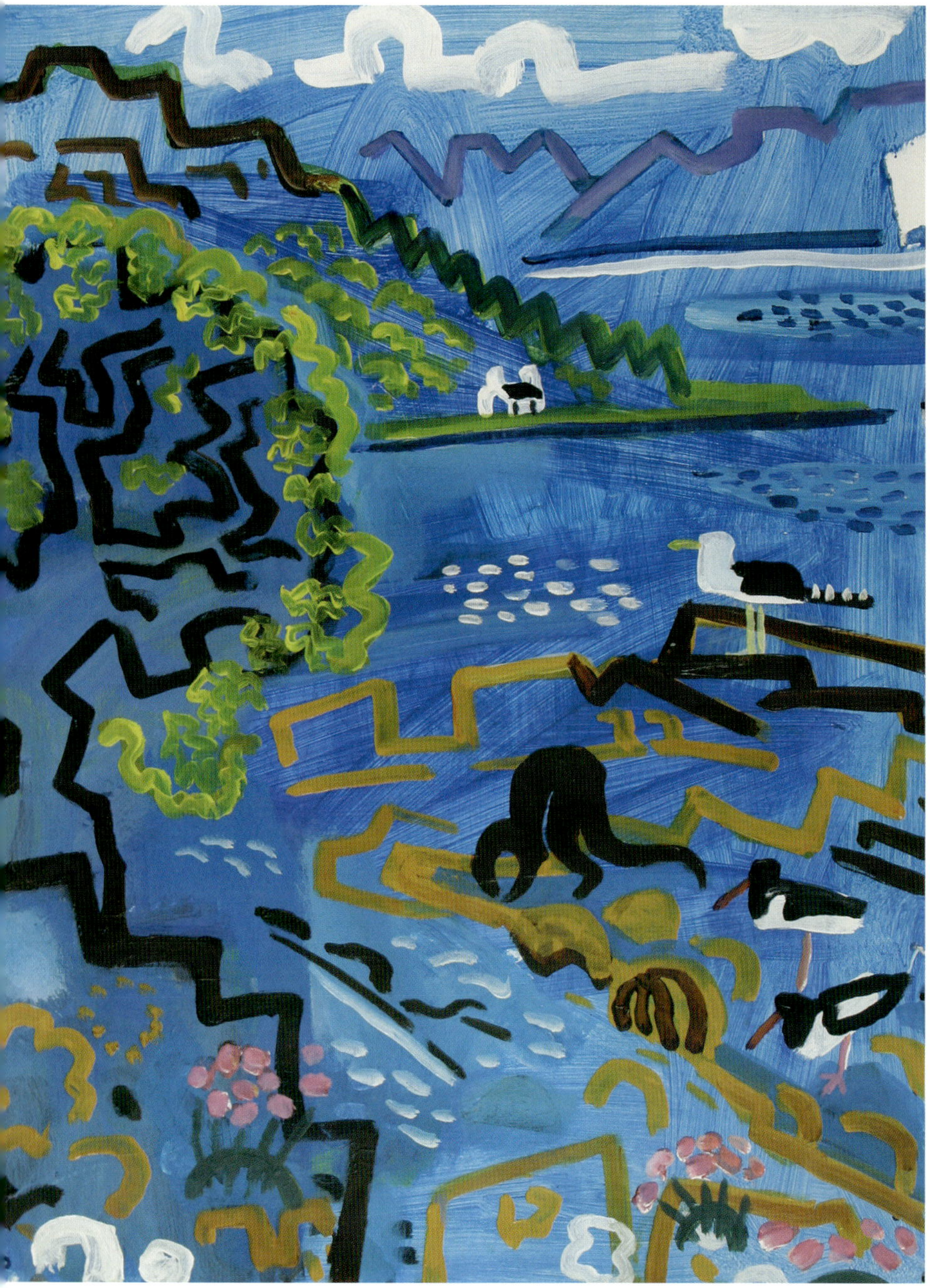

1

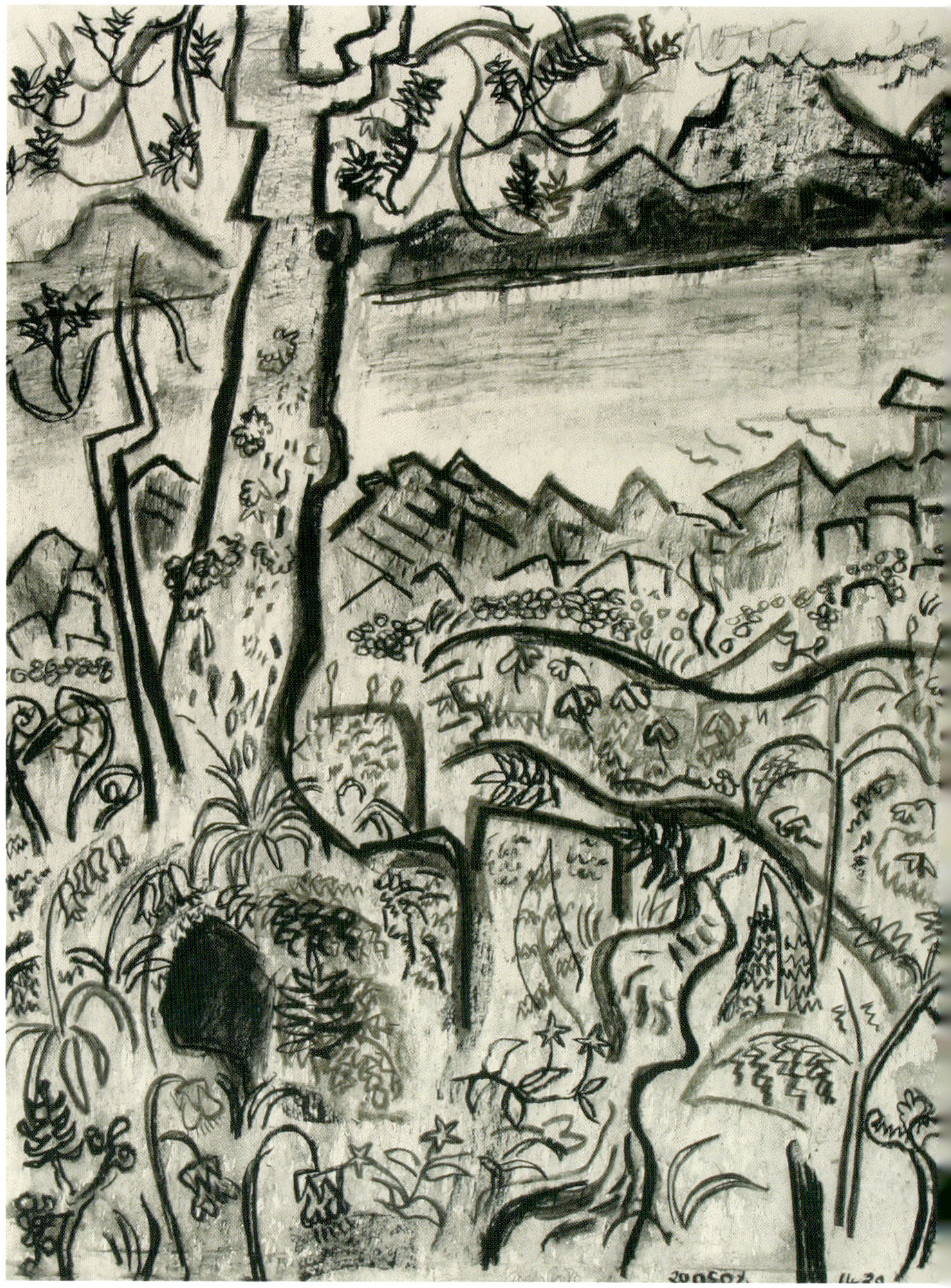

2

1. Greg Poole *Across from Kinloch Woods*
acrylic on paper · 75 x 55 cm

Across from Kinloch woods I get the long view. A small oak perched below me on a rocky outcrop, sweetshop-coloured with thrift and orange lichen circles. Great black-backed gull stands guard on an islet. Oystercatchers are only temporarily alarmed when an otter climbs ashore, lollops, poking around before seamlessly taking to water again.

2. Greg Poole *Burn meets the shore , Kinloch Woods*
charcoal · 73 x 59 cm

Where the burn leaves the shelter of the woods to cut across the rocky shore, I made two charcoal sketches in pouring rain. Redstart singing right at the top of the aged ash overhead, invisible.

The ash a worn grey bark, its upturned branches sleeved with lichens, ending in feathered, yellow spearlet clusters of new leaves. The burn has carved itself a channel with sides softened with moss, wood sorrel, creeping yellow pimpernel, ferns and water avens.

3. Greg Poole *Tattooed oak*
acrylic on paper · 78 x 55 cm

Oak with newly opened, translucent, yellow-ochre leaves against the light. Trunk crusted and tattooed with lichens. Looking through to sound and mountains beyond, a rent in the cloud gleams silver in the royal-blue waters.

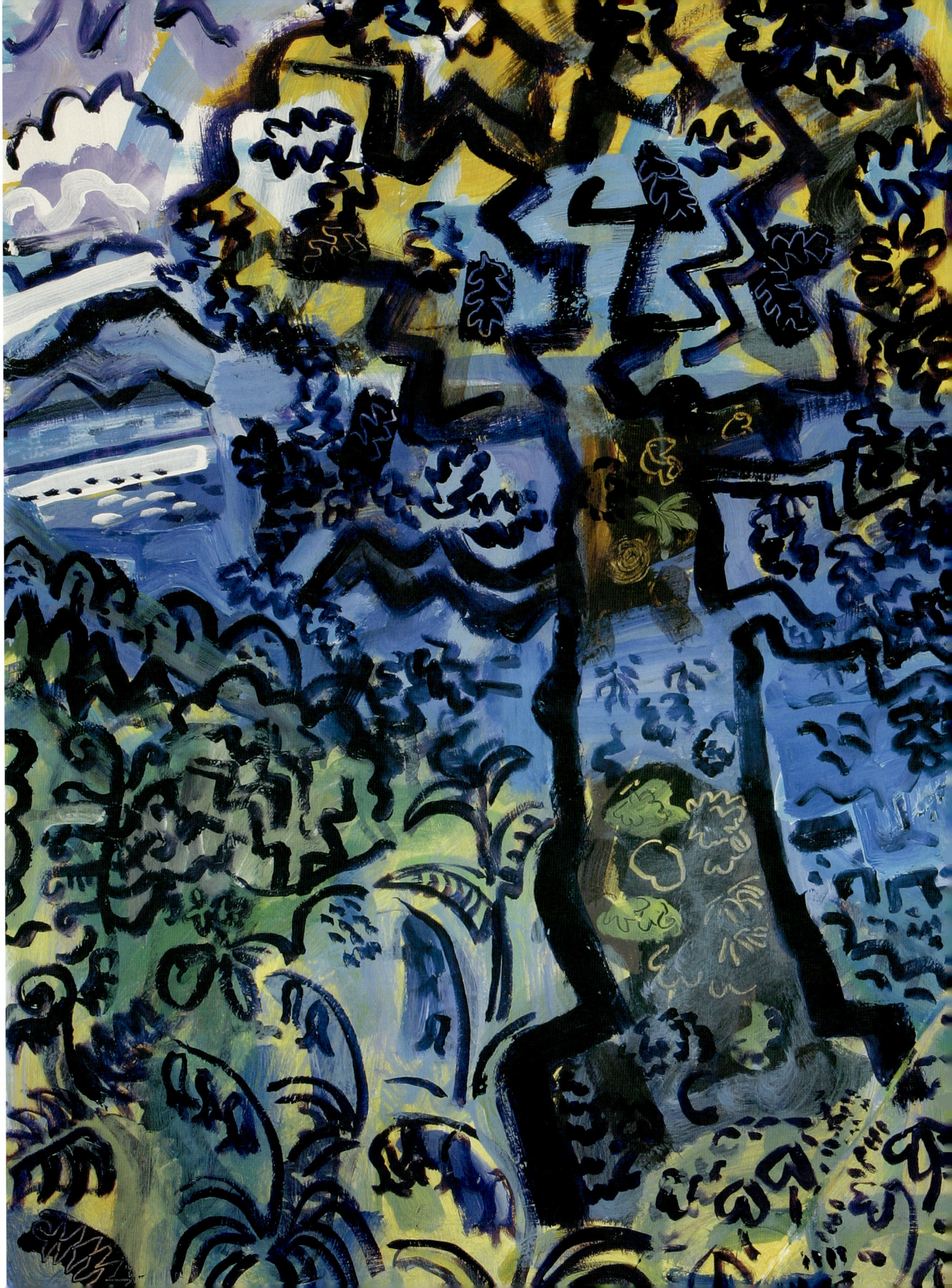

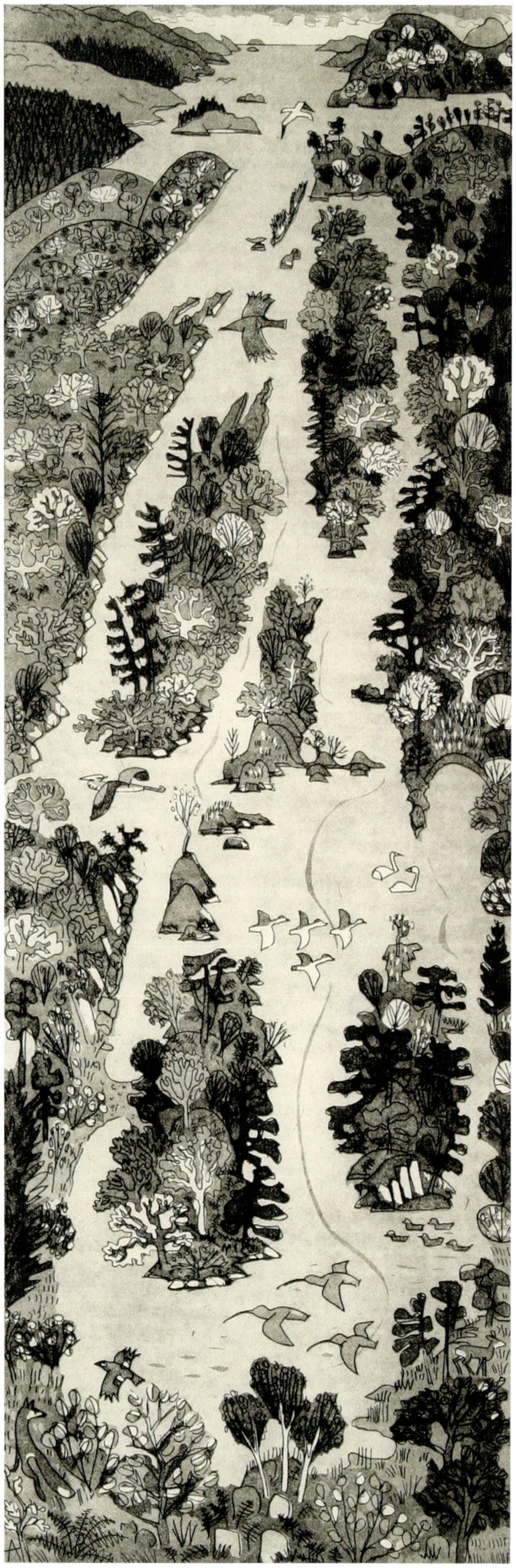

1

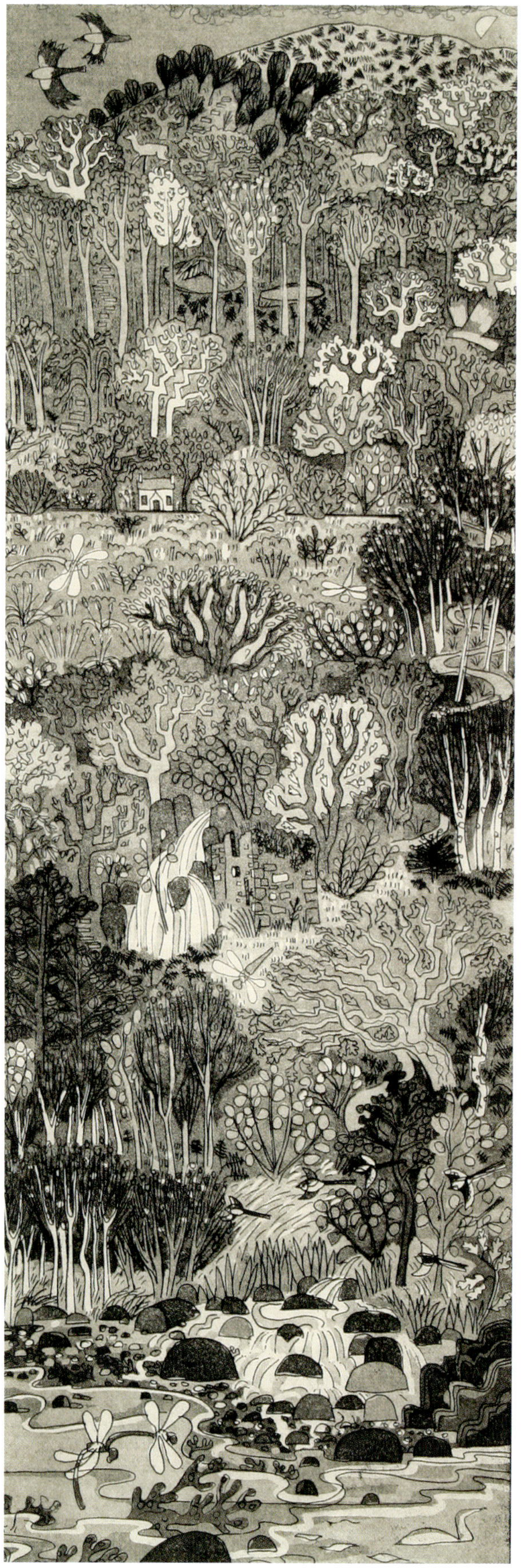

2

1. Carry Akroyd *Faery Isles*
aquatint · 60 x 20 cm

I walked around the area, climbing up on to rocks and peering through branches to get a sense of the whole magical place. Very still, quiet and secret, full of birds coming and going. Fox, squirrel, deer and signs of an otter restaurant, with footprints.

2. Carry Akroyd *A walk at Taynish*
aquatint · 60 x 20 cm

This is the walk, on reserve footpaths, from the shore of Loch Sween up to the top of Barr Mòr (bald top). It includes many dragonflies, the old mill and waterfall, the bog, the gatehouse, and the charcoal platforms with plantation oaks, then twisty oaks and birch opening to the bracken summit.

3. Peter Partington *Disputing territory – grey herons, Sunart*
watercolour · 49 x 37 cm

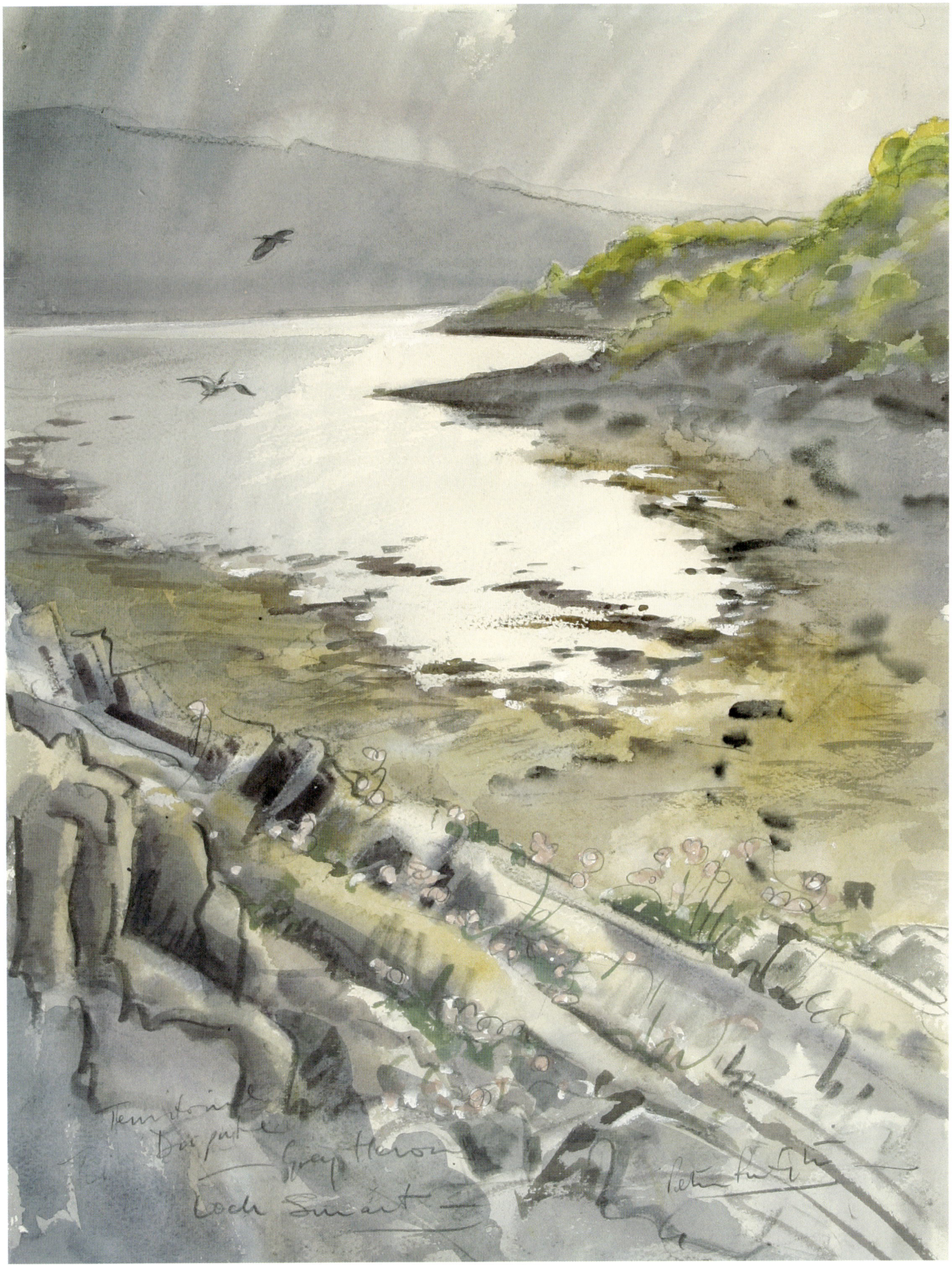

3

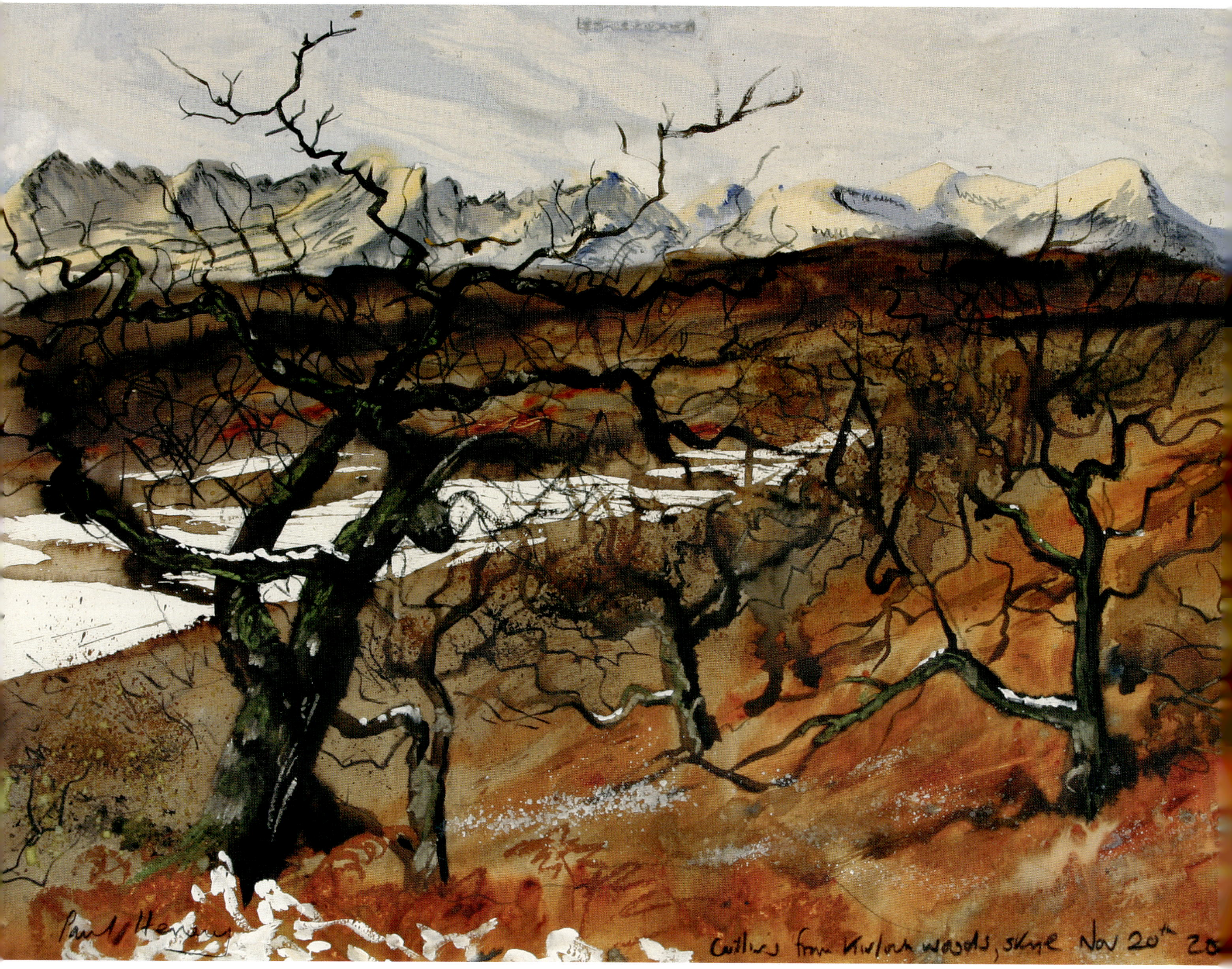

1

1. Paul Henery *Cuillins from Kinloch woods, Skye*
watercolour · 43 x 56 cm

The bluebells have gone,
Shadows are faint,
Treecreepers search alone,
Only the dark, skeletal oaks remain.
Above the woods, above the loch,
First snows have covered the Cuillins,
A buzzard passes over,
Woodland colours are rich.

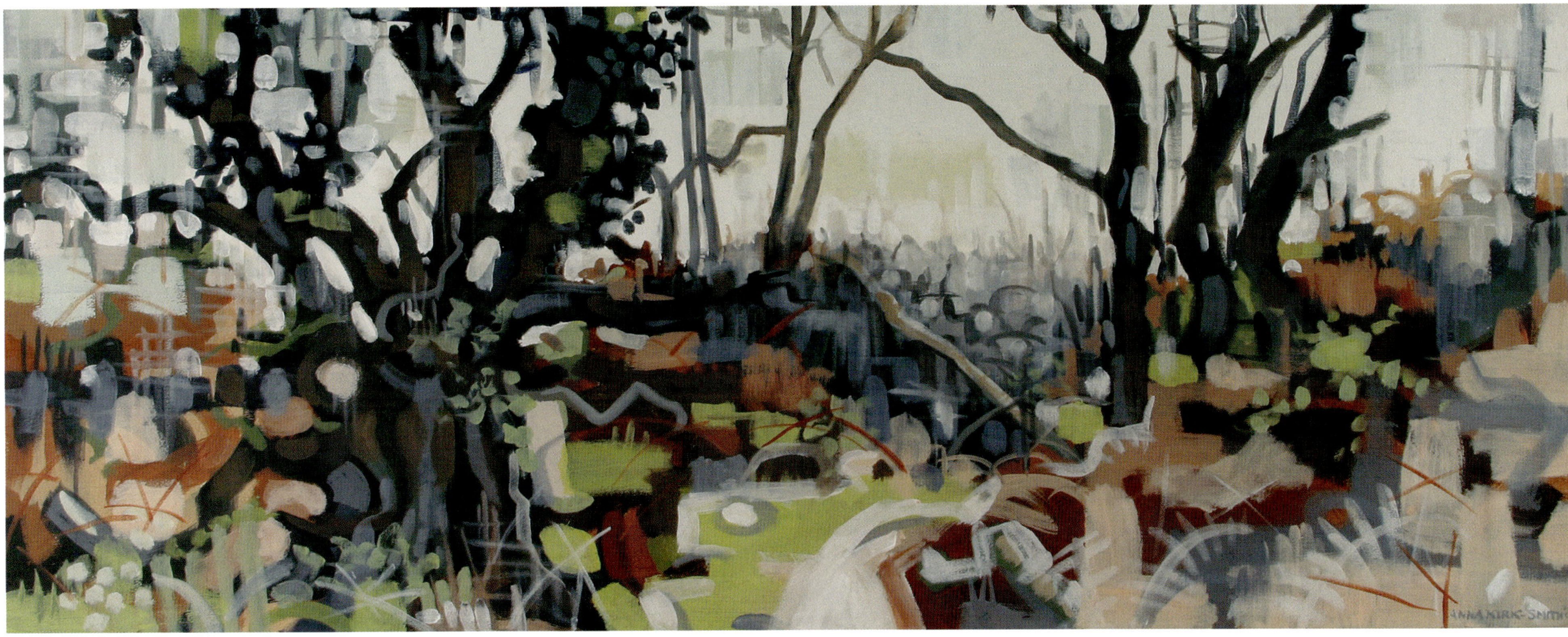

2

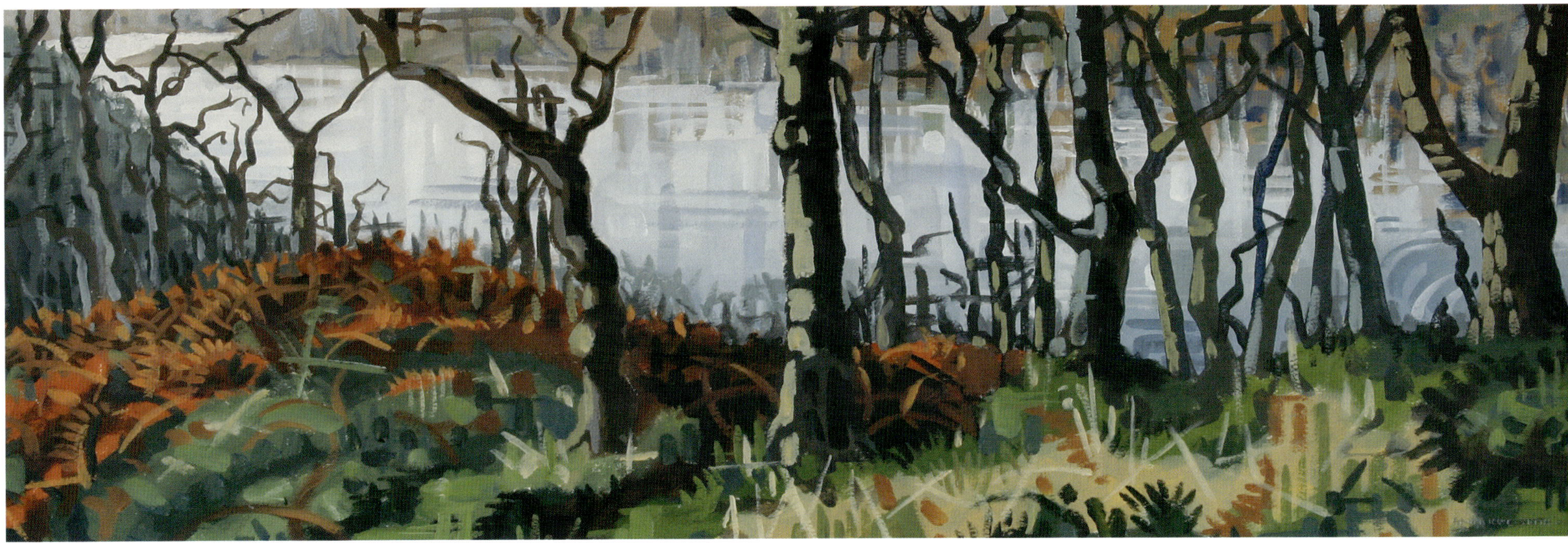

3

2. Anna Kirk-Smith *After the rain, Taynish*
acrylic on canvas · 61 x 152 cm

The cold winter light filtering through an old oak overgrown with ivy and lichens.

3. Anna Kirk-Smith *Fleeting light, Taynish*
acrylic · 27 x 96 cm

A brief break in the clouds allowed the waters of Linne Mhuirich to silver through winter trees. The light and hues change fast: glassy and clear here, grey and rain-soaked within minutes.

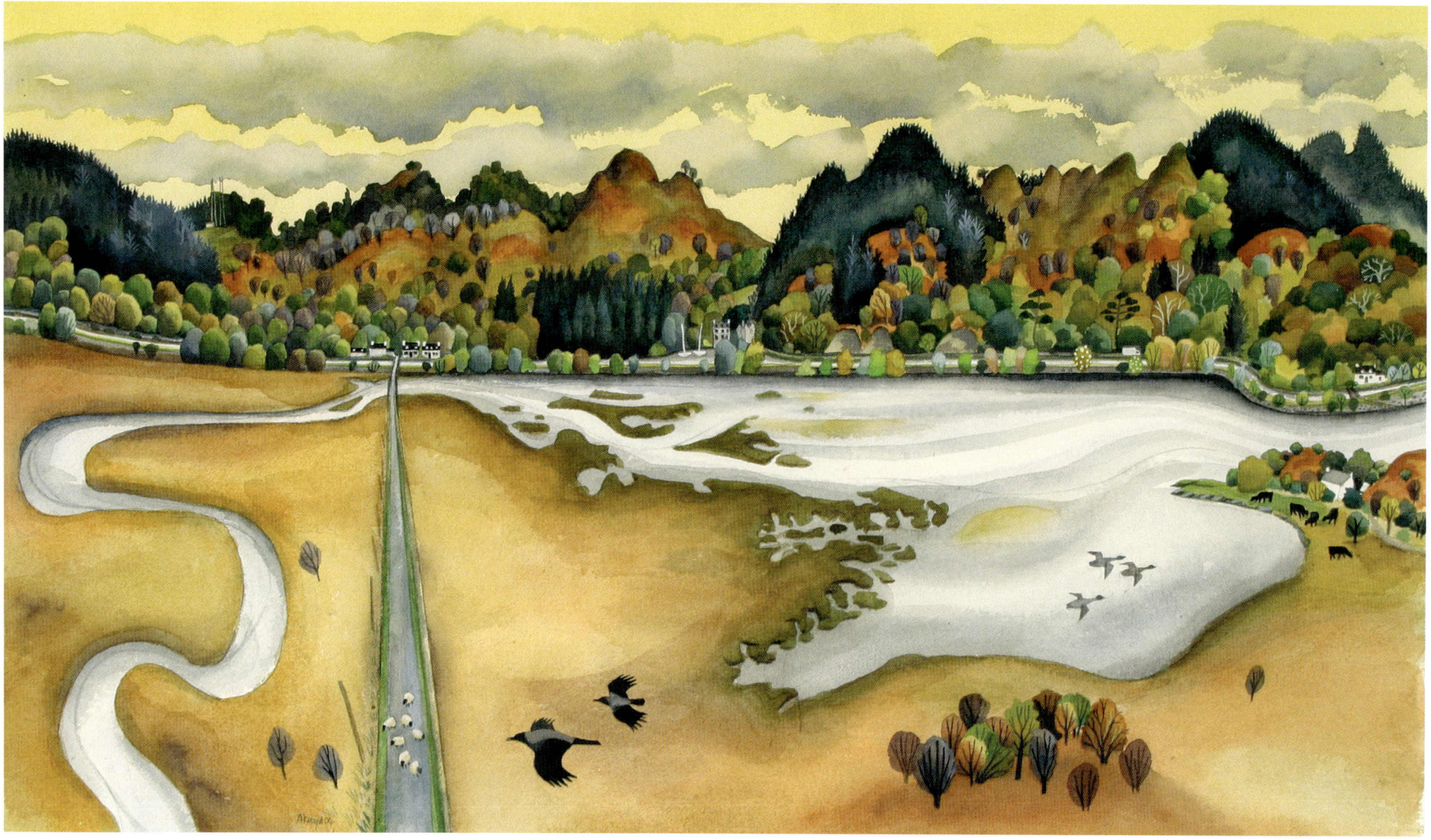

1

1. Carry Akroyd *Knapdale skyline*
watercolour · 48 x 76 cm

This is a condensed impression of the northern escarpment, showing the characteristic knaps and dales. It is from an imagined viewpoint, and the information for it was gathered from Crinan Ferry, the road to Islandadd Bridge, and along the canal from the swing-bridge. The painting shows areas where plantation spruce has been cleared, and the vestigial border oaks and pioneer birch are encroaching on the bare slopes.

2. Carry Akroyd *By Crinan*
watercolour · 60 x 60 cm

I made a number of sketches from Crinan woods, hanging on to my drawing book through wind and rain. Looking down, the road and canal squeeze between the estuary and the abrupt rise of Knapdale. Cleared hillsides contrast with plantations, and the oak and birch persist in inaccessible corners, ready to come back. Ravens honk and float about.

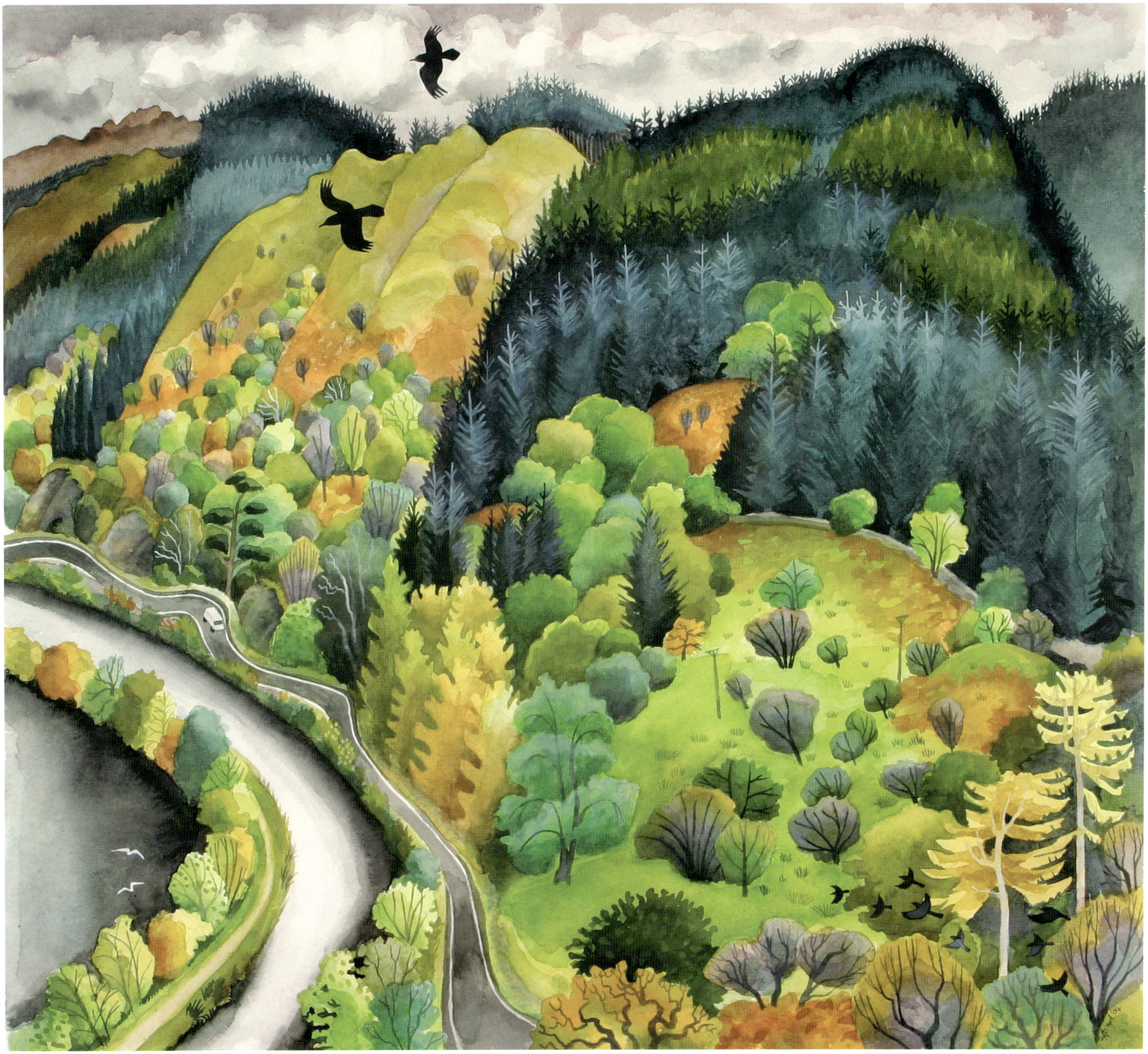

2

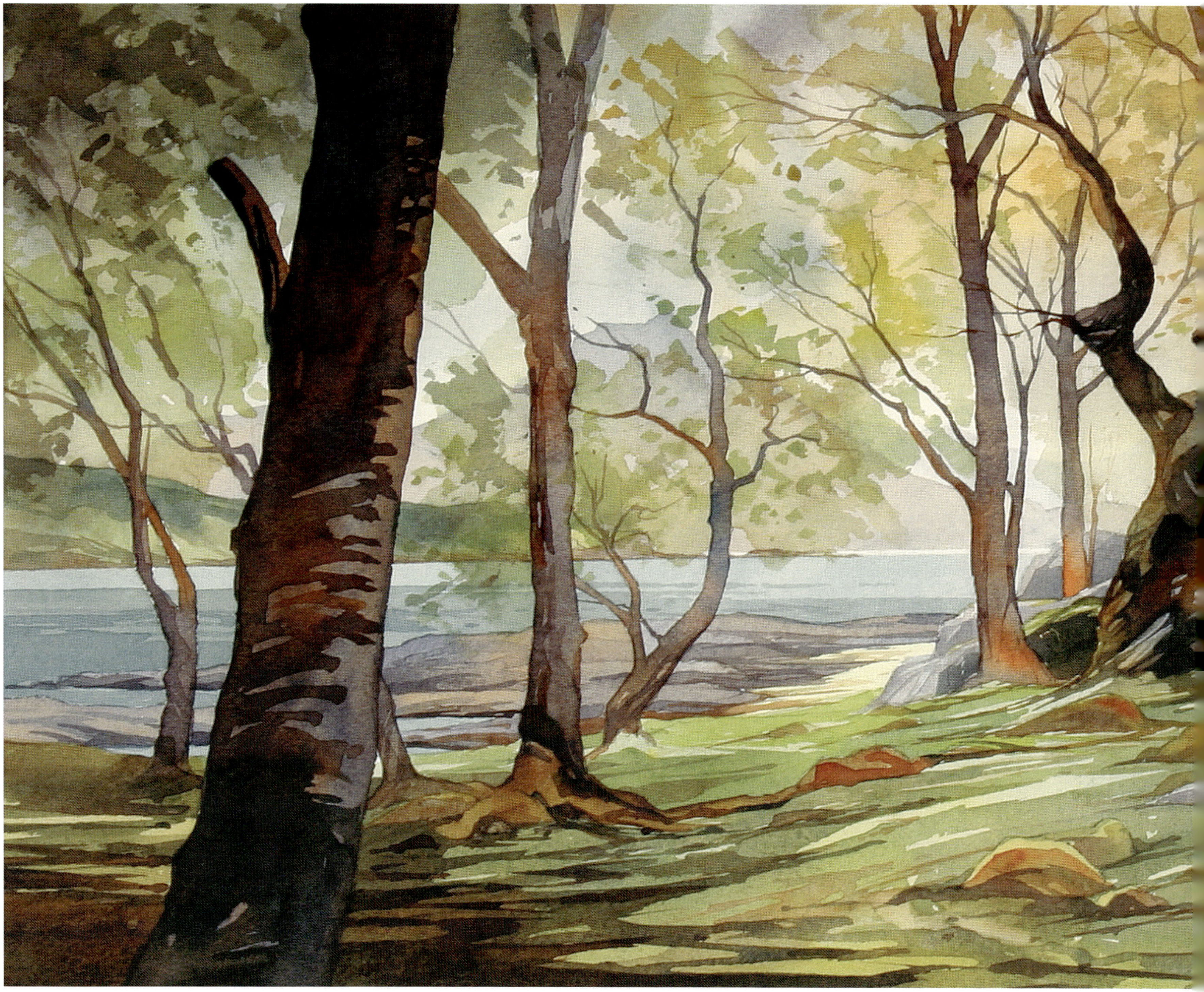

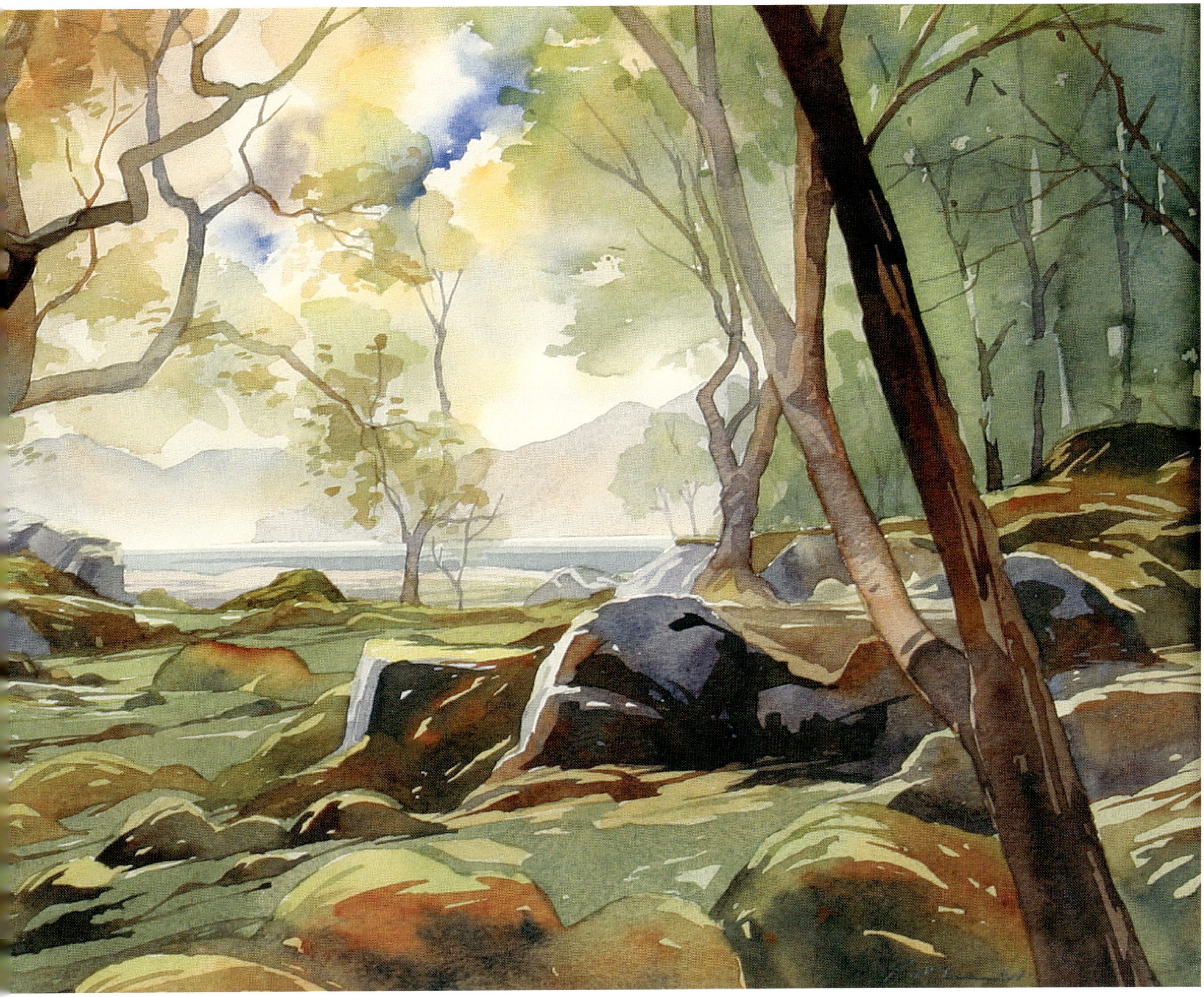

Peter McDermott *Ancient oak – dappled light, Kinloch*
watercolour · 26.5 x 65 cm

Like some aged grandfather surrounded by younger members of the family, this old retainer silently bears testimony to new generations of seed and sapling.

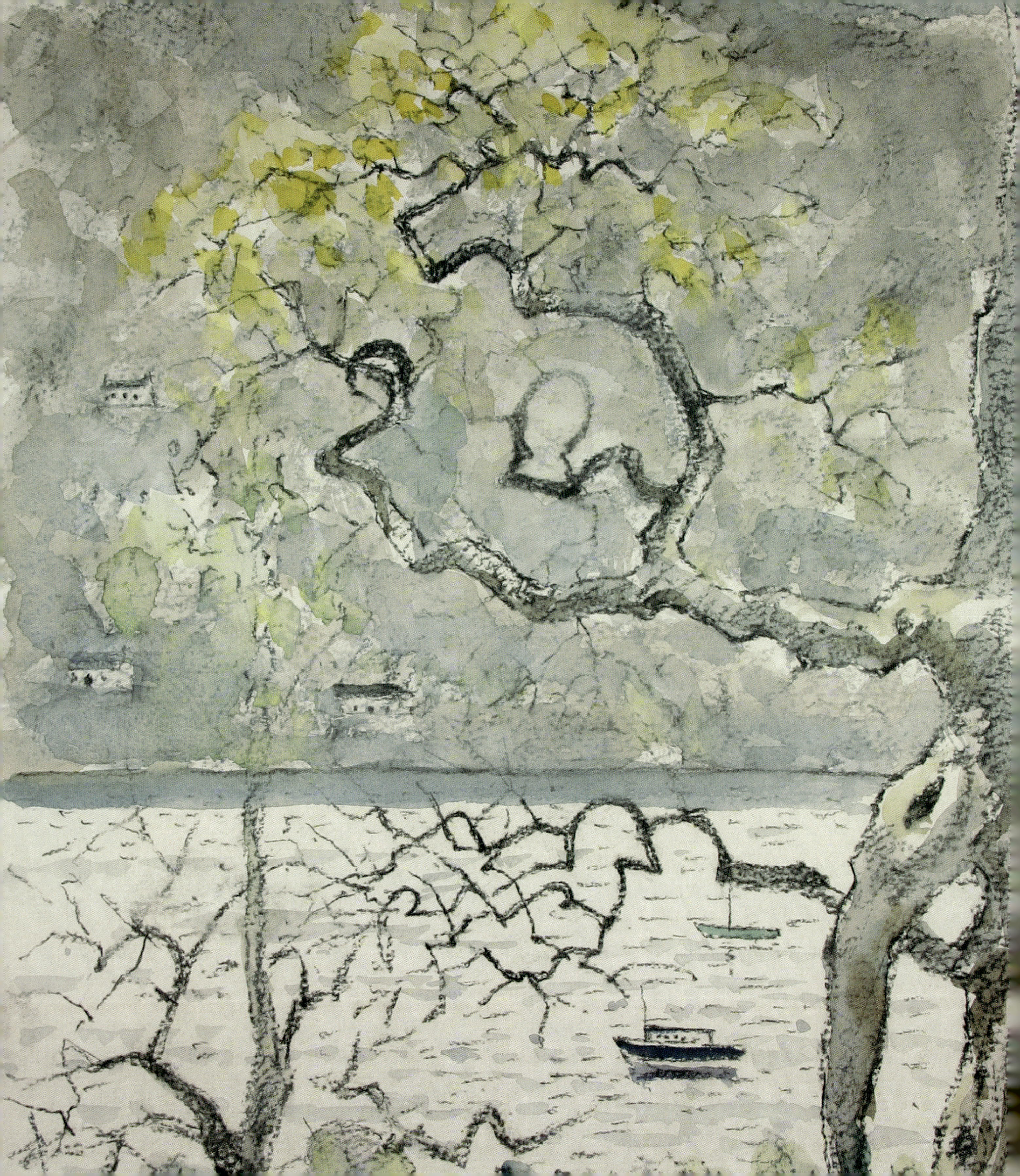

2

Looking around the woods

John Busby *A maze of oak branches, Salen woods, Sunart*
conté drawing and watercolour
38 x 27.5 cm

I was intrigued by the way the oak branches twisted back on each other and formed an intricate pattern against the hillside and loch. First leaves showing as delicate warm yellows.

The narrow roads that wind through the western Highlands are often uncomfortably wedged between sea and hillside. The water on one side holds the attention of passengers in the cars and buses that pick their way around the bends. There are boats, seabirds, seals and perhaps even dolphins to exclaim at; and the trees pass in a blur. Even with footpaths and signs as guides, I suspect few visitors, or even residents, will find the time to go beyond the special observation points and take a walk through the woods. Even those that do may not realise that they are in a treasure house of natural wonders, laced with relics that point to human occupation through distant centuries.

I am lucky because I have been shown around some of the best examples of the Atlantic oakwoods by people who know them well. I have seen things that I would never have noticed or appreciated if I had been on my own. My guides interpreted the broad canvas – the ecology of the woods and the history of management that has determined how the woods look as they do – and the fine detail – the presence of a moss or an insect. Armed with these introductions to the woods, I went out to observe for myself. So I wandered among the trees, taking pleasure in simply being there and looking for anything of interest. I would pause to watch and record, and then try to explain to myself what I was seeing. Sometimes I accompanied the artists, and I found that our ways of working were not dissimilar.

My first visit was to Ariundle, a National Nature Reserve in Strontian Glen, and my guide was Eilidh-Ann Madden, the local ranger, born locally and delighted to have found such a job near home. Ariundle comes from the Gaelic *Àirigh Fhionndail*, meaning 'shieling of the white meadow'. A shieling was a hill pasture. The Norse name for Strontian Glen is more appropriate: Egadale – oak valley.

The outstanding impression on entering Ariundle, and other Atlantic oakwoods, is a feeling of space among tall trees set in a sea of mosses. The mosses blanket the woodland floor, smother boulders, climb the tree trunks and spread out to festoon the branches in many shades of green. The outlines of the woodland floor are softened and rounded by the thick layer of moss. Large boulders make comfortable seats with 15-cm cushions of soft, springy greenery. Ancient stone walls look like closely trimmed hedges.

The lush growth of mosses is one of the signs of the environmental basis of the Atlantic oakwoods. There is an unusually high degree of 'oceanicity' – a combination of high humidity, frequent rain, cloud cover and mild climate, which comes from the proximity of the Gulf Stream. Only the west coast of Ireland has a greater oceanicity than this part of western Scotland. Once you are aware of the mosses, you will be struck by the exuberance of their growth wherever you look. The moss carpet absorbs huge amounts of rainwater, which evaporates slowly during dry spells, maintaining the level of humidity and the growth of other lower plants – the liverworts and ferns, and the many-hued lichens. The mosses are at their best in darker parts of the woods, on northern slopes and under a dense canopy. In lighter situations, on sunny slopes and along the edges of the woods, there are patchworks of tree lungwort and other lichens, which are one of

SMEÒRACH CHLANN RAGHNUILL

Eċin bhuchullach, bhreac na coille,
Le 'n òrganan òrdail mar-ruinn,
'S feadag ghlan am beul gach coilich
'S binn feadail air geugan barraich.
'S mise 'n t-eanan beag le m' f'headan,
Am madainn-dhriùchd am bàrr gach badain,
Sheinneadh na puirt ghrinn gun sgreadan –
'S ionmhuinn m' fheadan feadh gach lagain.

THE MAVIS OF CLANRANALD

The spotted woodland birds their lay
With their well tuned organs play;
The cock's loud clarion, shrill and clear,
On high-tapped boughs is sweet to hear.
A little bird with my reed I rove,
Each dewy morn from grove to grove;
I sing not harshly my sweet song,
Strains that to lowly dells belong.

BY ALEXANDER MACDONALD

the glories of these woods. Eilidh-Ann also showed me the fern called polypody, which grows along the branches of the trees. It relies on continual dampness, and she told me that a frazzling of its fronds is an indicator of a dry summer.

THE OAKWOODS

Some woods, although classified as 'Atlantic oakwood' habitat, have precious few, if any, oak trees. Oaks may be replaced by birches, both downy birch and silver birch, which are pioneering species that quickly colonise open ground where the trees have been cleared. Where the soil is alkaline, often in damp hollows, ash and wych elm form the canopy, and there may be a ground layer with dog's mercury, enchanter's nightshade and ramsons – the strong-smelling wild garlic. Alder and goat willow also like wet places, and they spring from mats of *Sphagnum* bogmosses in places where it is too soggy to walk. Here, too, are yellow flag iris, meadowsweet and angelica. There may be some exotic trees planted among the natives, but no one knows if the Scots pines in Ariundle are naturally occurring or planted.

The oaks in these woods are mostly sessile oaks

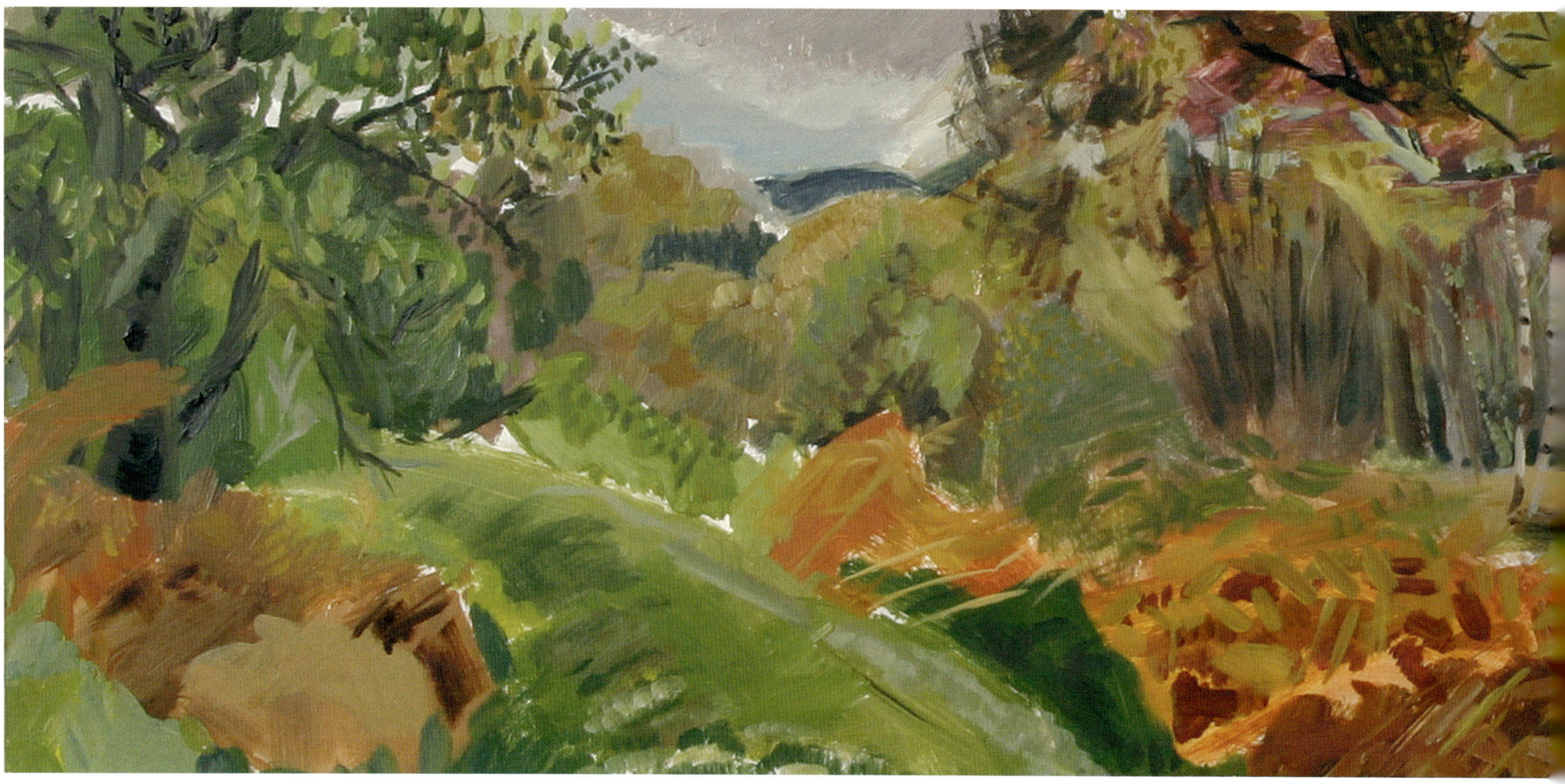

1

Quercus petraea, which are more characteristic of the thin, acid soils of highland Britain, but there may be pedunculate oaks *Quercus robur*, which are the dominant oaks in the richer soils of lowland Britain. The sessile oak is so named because its flowers and acorns do not have stalks like the pedunculate oak. The leaves are the other way round and the sessile oak is the one with stalked leaves. Just to confuse matters the two species hybridise, so identification can be a matter for the expert.

The ecosystem of an oakwood, at its simplest, consists of three layers. The main storey consists of large trees of oak and birch, and sometimes elm and ash, which provide a canopy of branches and leaves. The understorey consists of smaller trees, especially hazel but also holly, rowan, gean, juniper and hawthorn. The ground layer is made up of grasses, bracken and other ferns, blaeberry and heather, mosses and many kinds of flowers. But this simple scheme is infinitely variable. The details of the composition of species and the height of the layers vary according to soil, exposure and wetness. Shade is important for the lower layers. A dense canopy shuts out the light, stifling the ground layer and preventing the growth of a new generation of trees. When an old tree falls, light is let in and seedlings sprout from dormant seeds around it.

1. Nik Pollard *Path through Barnluasgan III*
   acrylic on board · 30 x 122 cm
2. Matt Underwood
   Linear study
   conté · 58 x 41 cm

   I passed this oak tree every day and admired the lichen all over the trunk, up into the lower branches; its tattooed appearance made it visible within the wood from the shore.

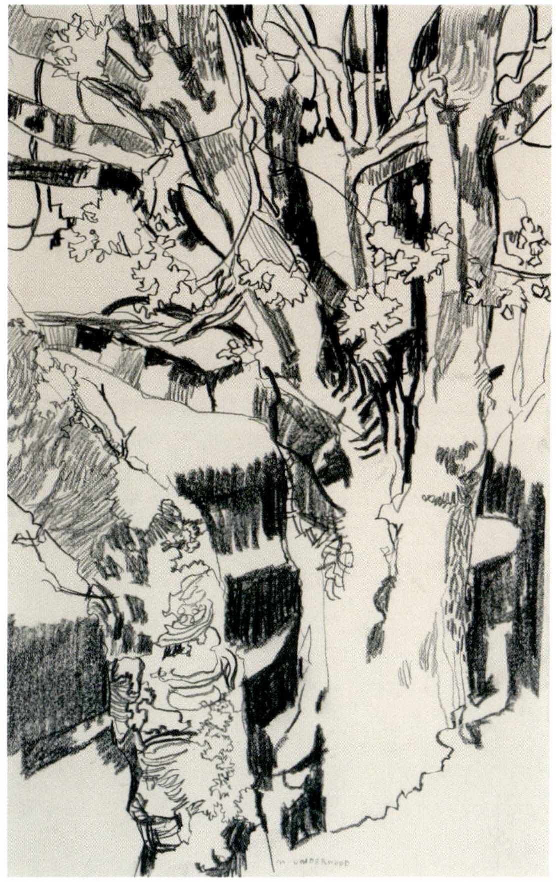

2

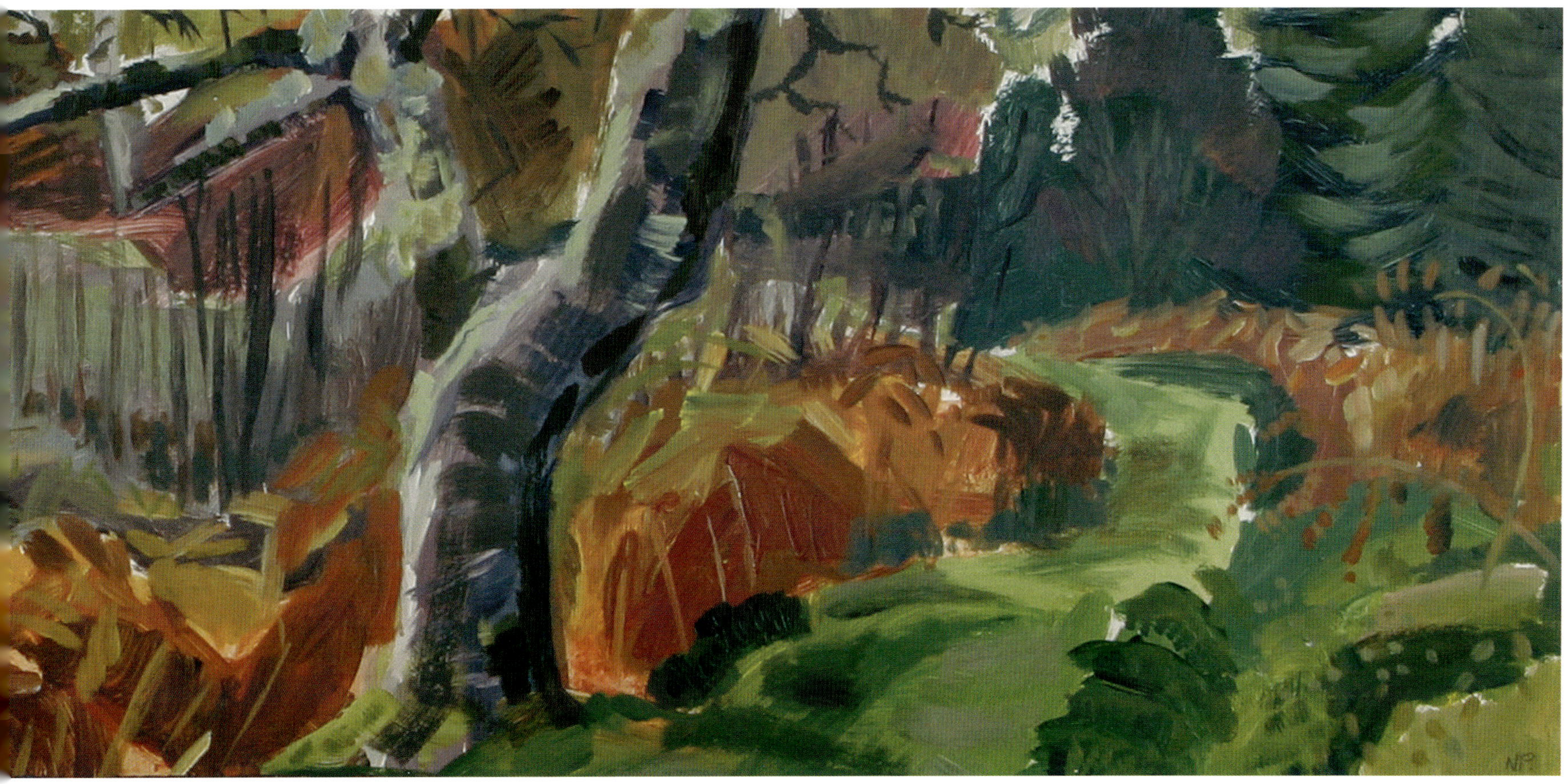

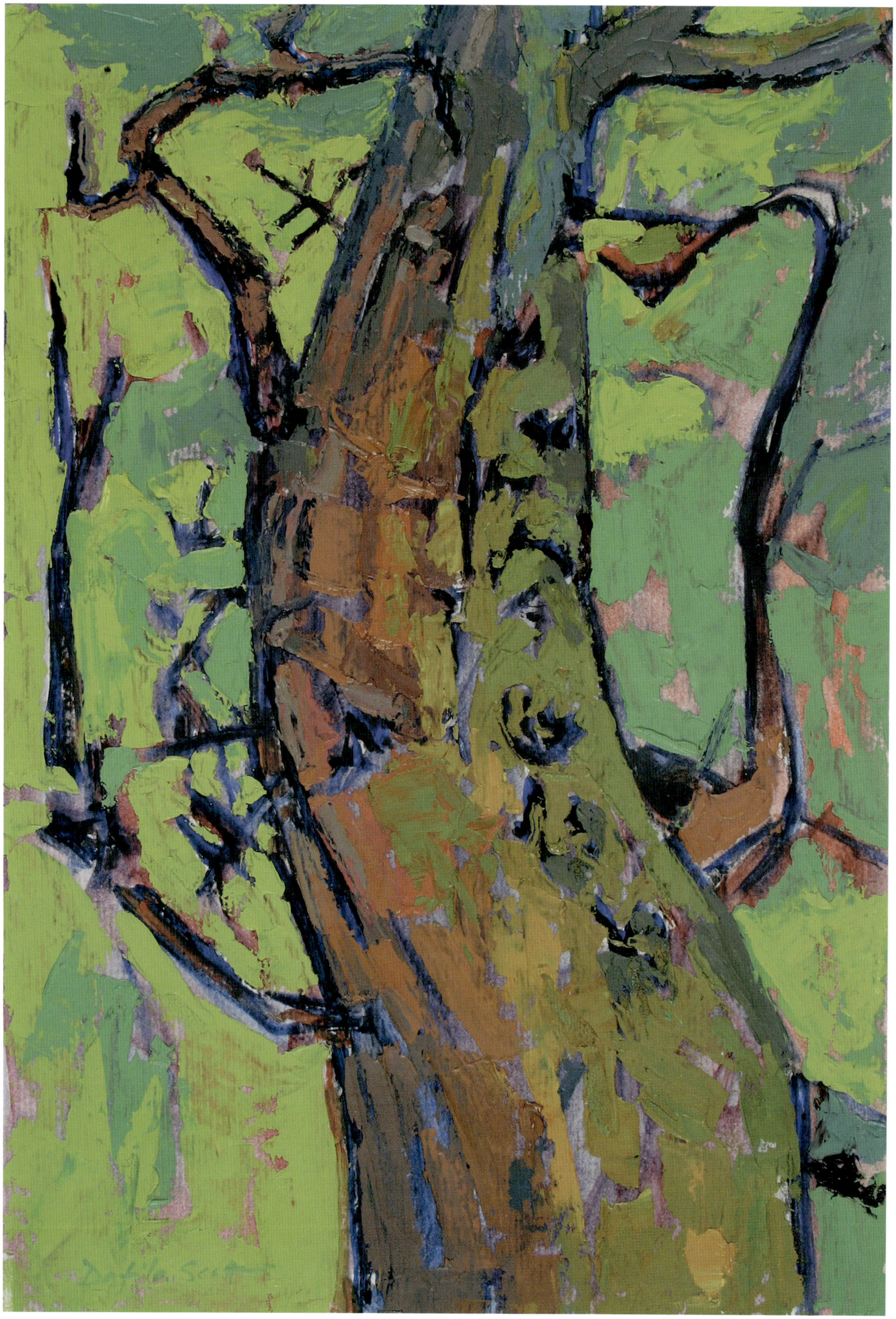

1

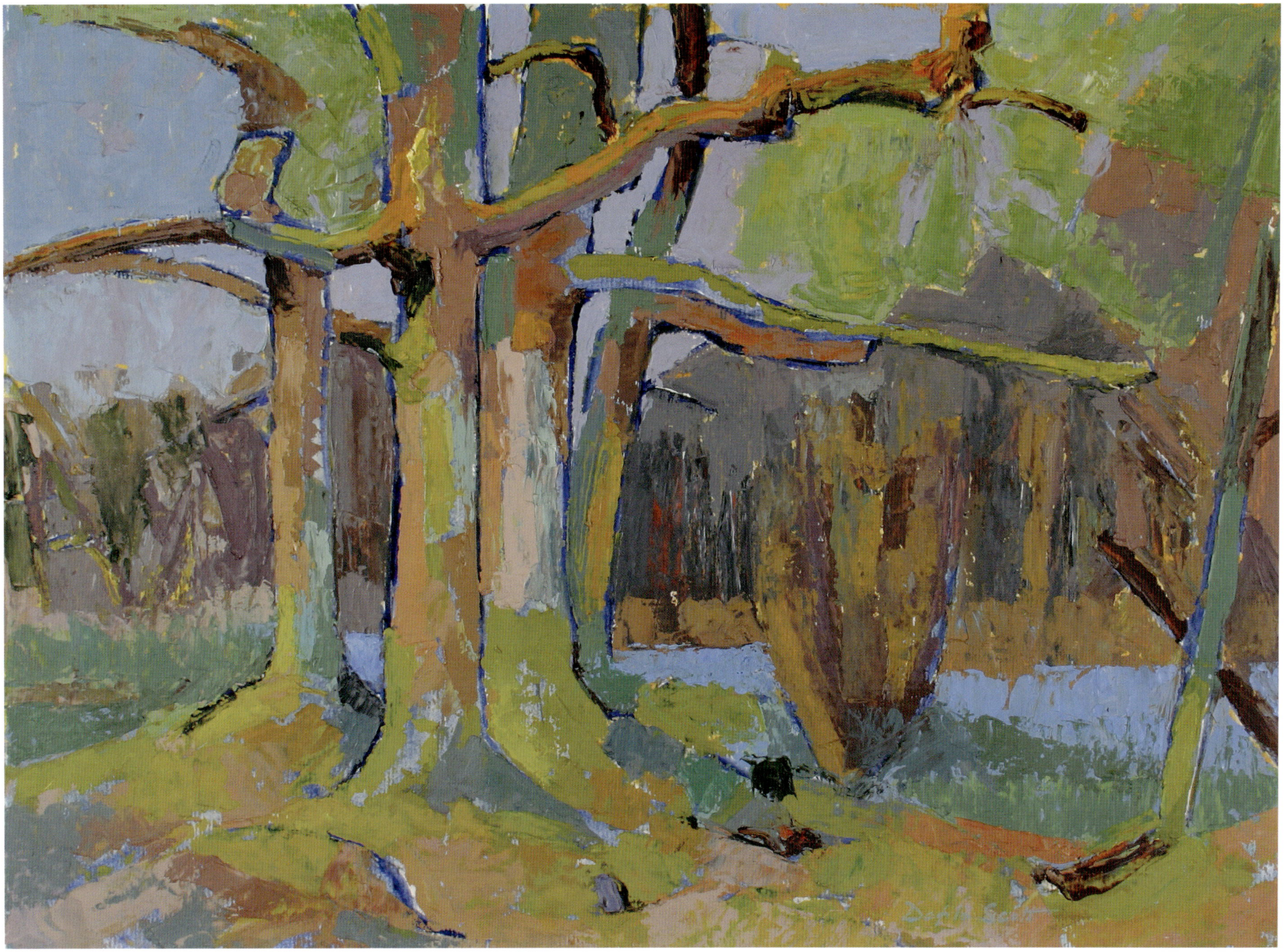

2

1. Dafila Scott *Oak trunk with epiphytes*
   oil on paper · 38 x 25.5 cm

   This was a particularly spectacular oak, with strongly orange and reddish lichens growing on it, as well as lots of moss, liverworts and ferns, going way up in to the canopy.

2. Dafila Scott *Oakwood and bluebells*
   oil on paper · 25.5 x 38 cm

   Going into the woods at Ariundle was like going into a magical ancient woodland, even though most of the trees are not that old. For me the most striking thing was the moss everywhere – on the ground, on the boulders and up the trees. It reminded me of all sorts of stories from childhood and gave me a feeling of being enclosed, at first comfortably so but later rather less comfortably so.

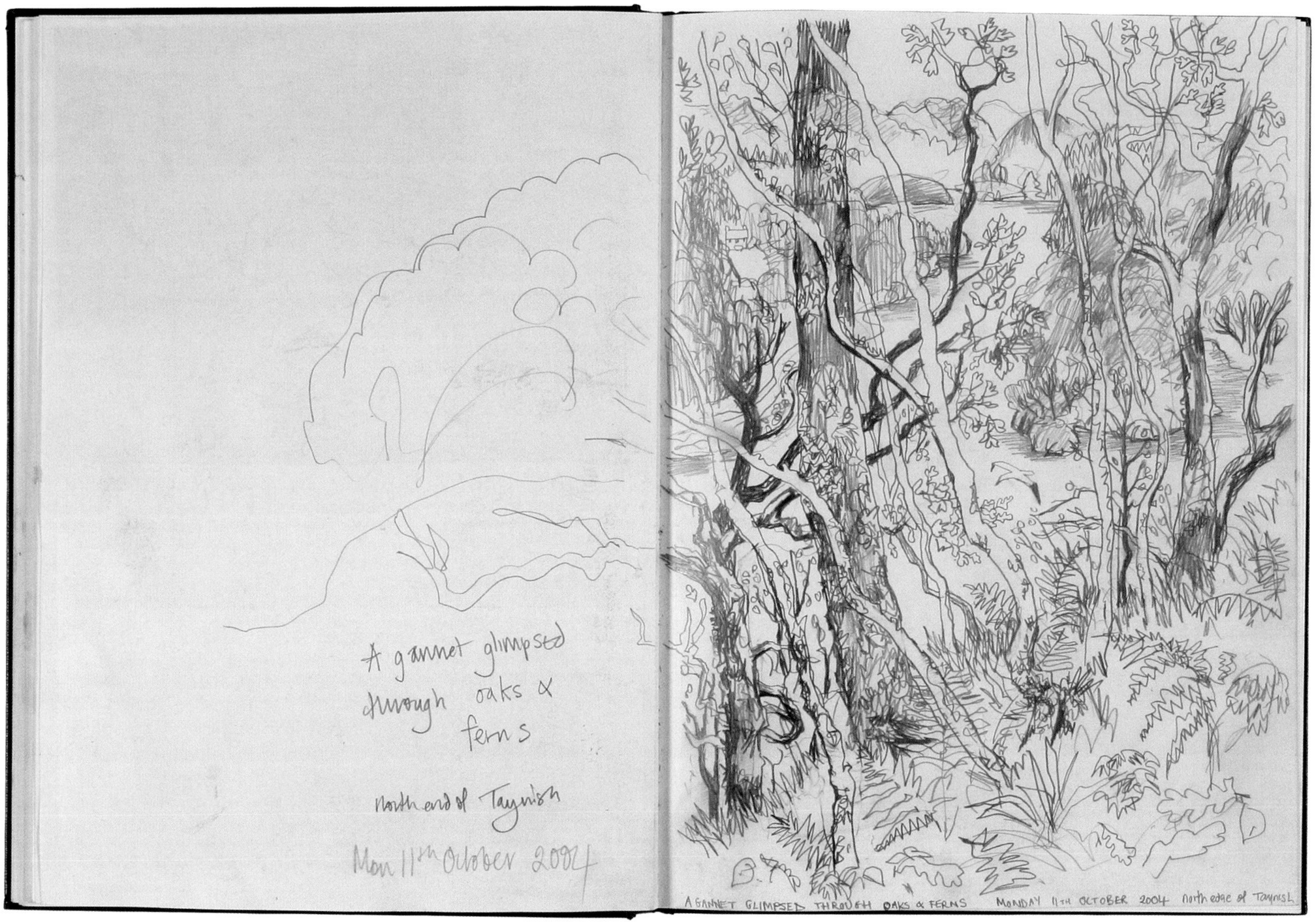

1

1. Carry Akroyd *A gannet glimpsed through oaks and ferns*
   pencil sketch · 29 x 21 cm
2. Carry Akroyd *Rain passing Barnluasgan ridge*
   watercolour · 40 x 57 cm
3. Carry Akroyd *From Barnluasgan to the Paps*
   watercolour · 40 x 57 cm

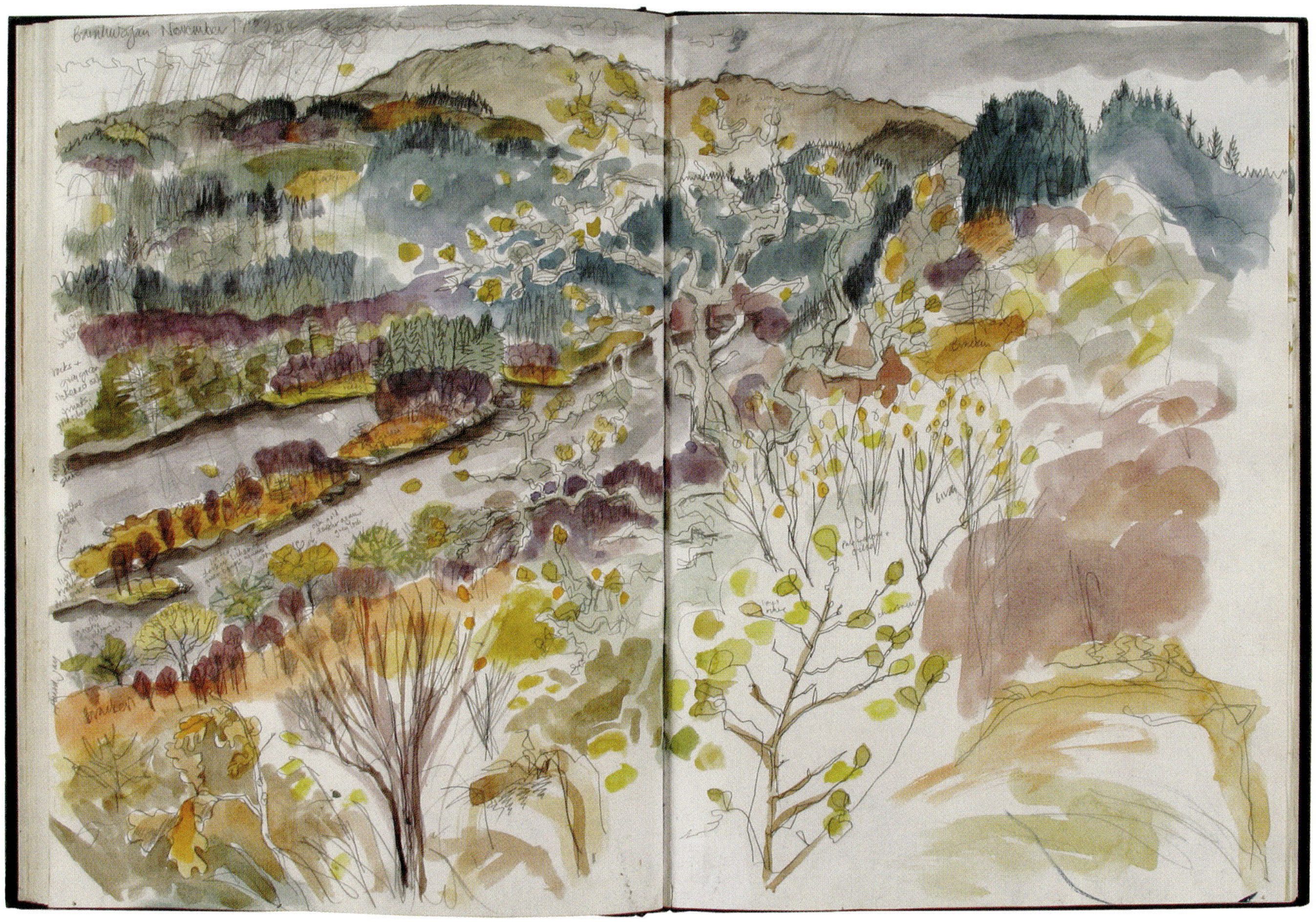

2

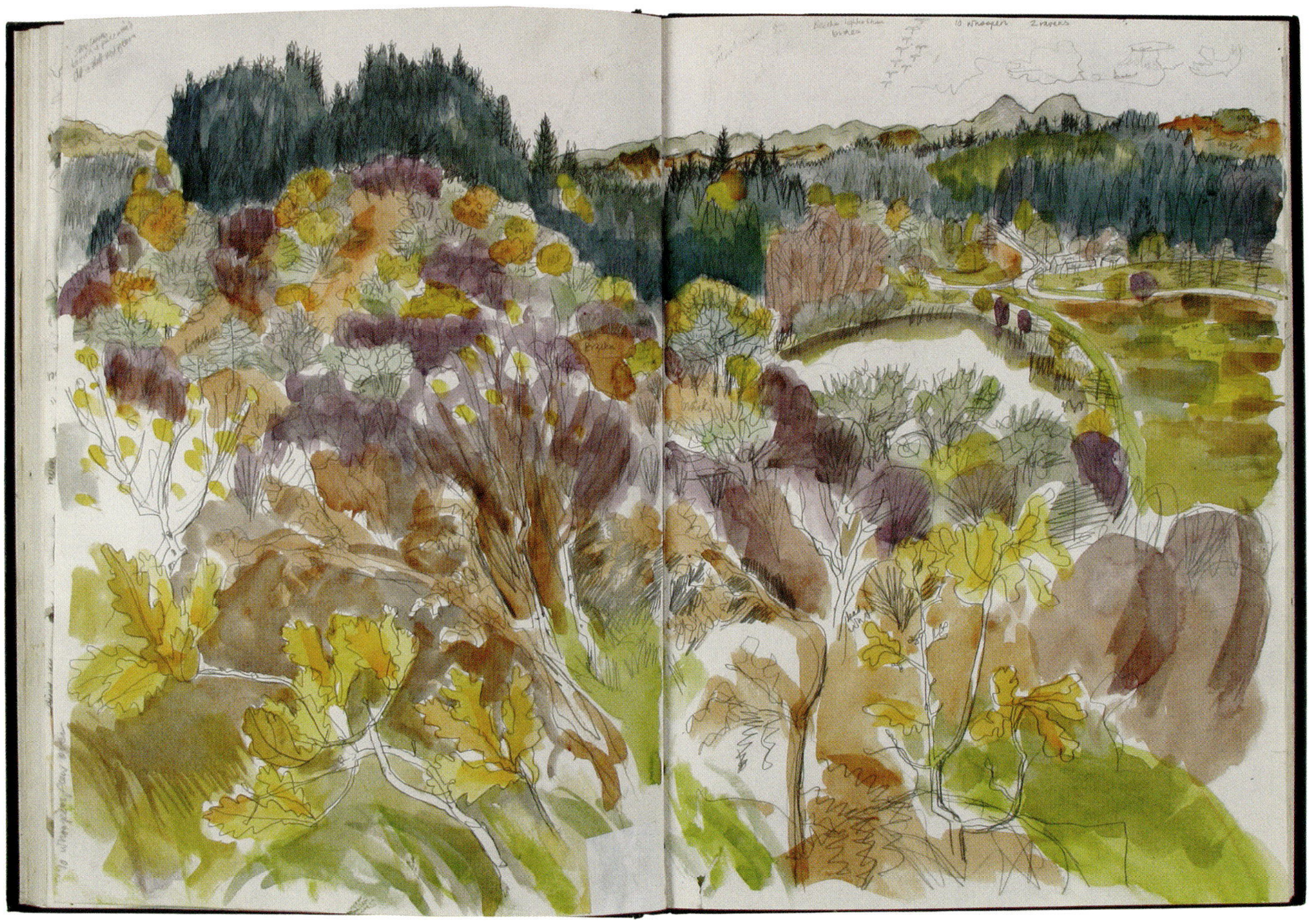

3

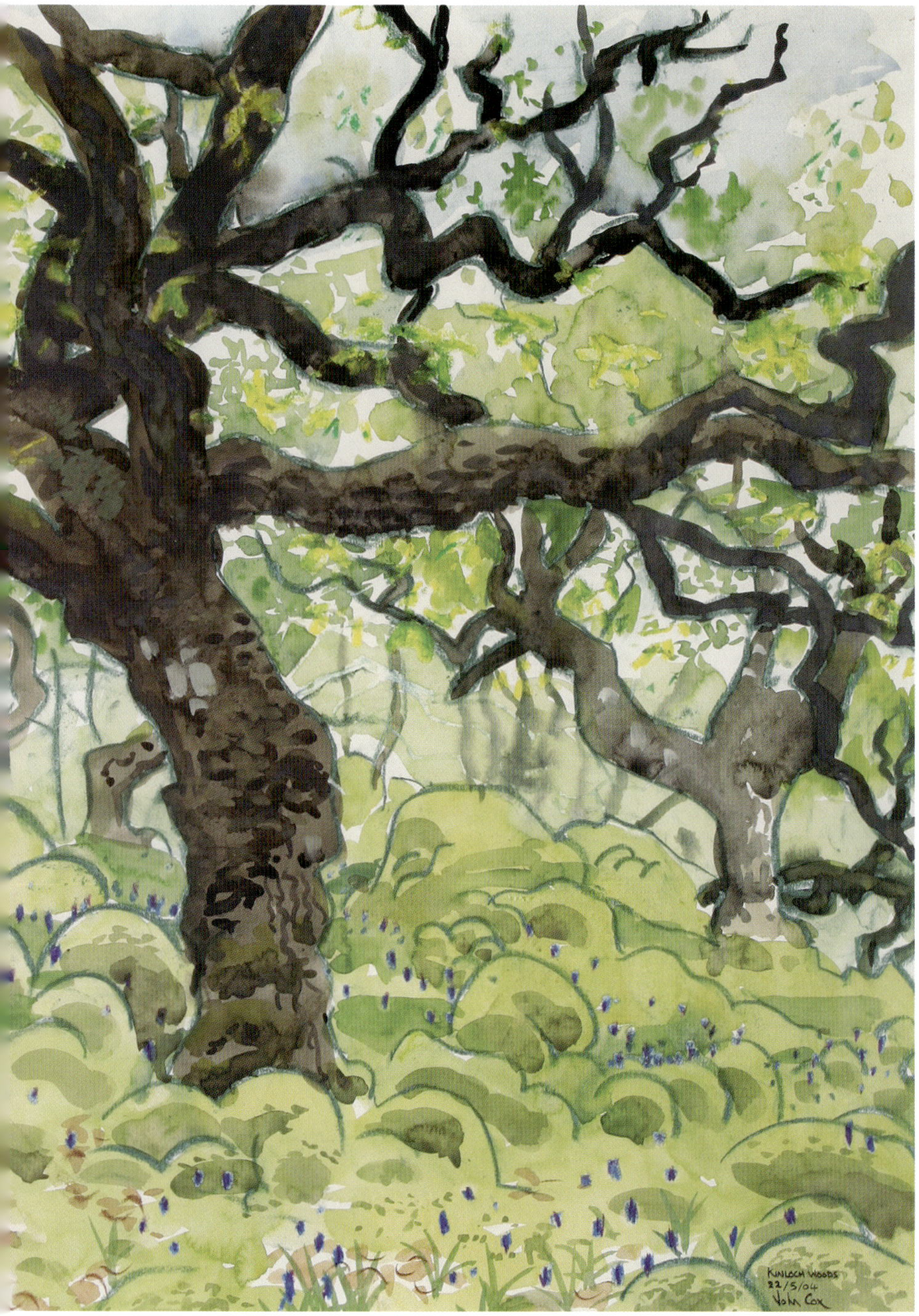

1

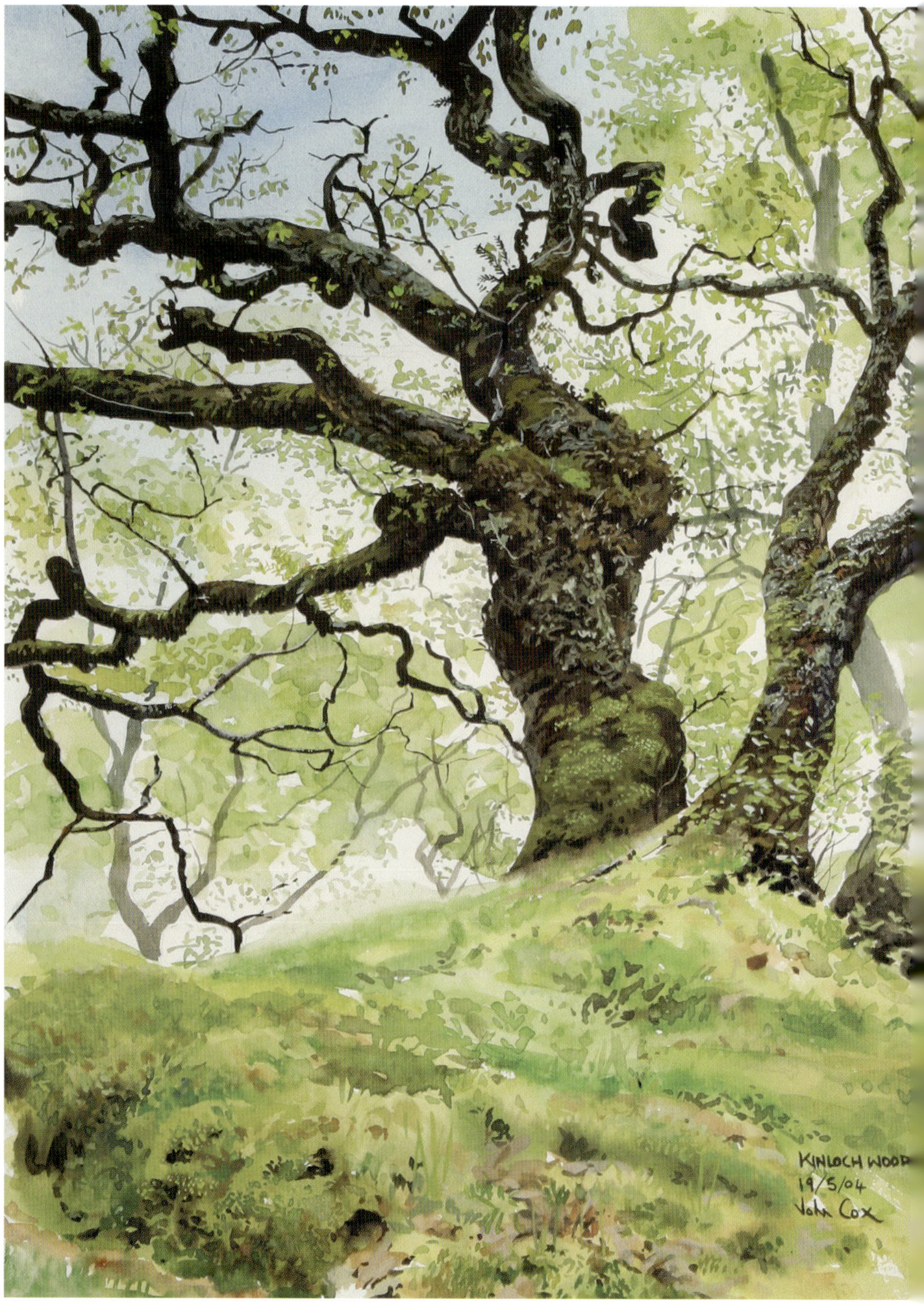

2

1. John Cox *Mossy hummocks and bluebells*
   pastel, crayon and watercolour · 59 x 41 cm
2. John Cox *A well-lichened oak*
   watercolour and gouache · 40 x 30 cm
3. John Cox *Raven family over Leitir Fura*
   watercolour · 41 x 28 cm

   Even when we were first shown round the ruins of Leiter Fura in the pouring rain, the place was fascinating. When I went back, the rugged, bleak and desolate atmosphere had gone. The sun was blazing down. A couple of adders were sunning themselves on the broken-down rocky walls, and a family of ravens played around in the air as I painted; but it was the ruins themselves and their history that really interested me.

Following spread

4. Nik Pollard *Path through Barnluasgan I*
   acrylic on board · 30 x 122 cm
5. Nik Pollard *Path through Barnluasgan II*
   acrylic on board · 30 x 122 cm

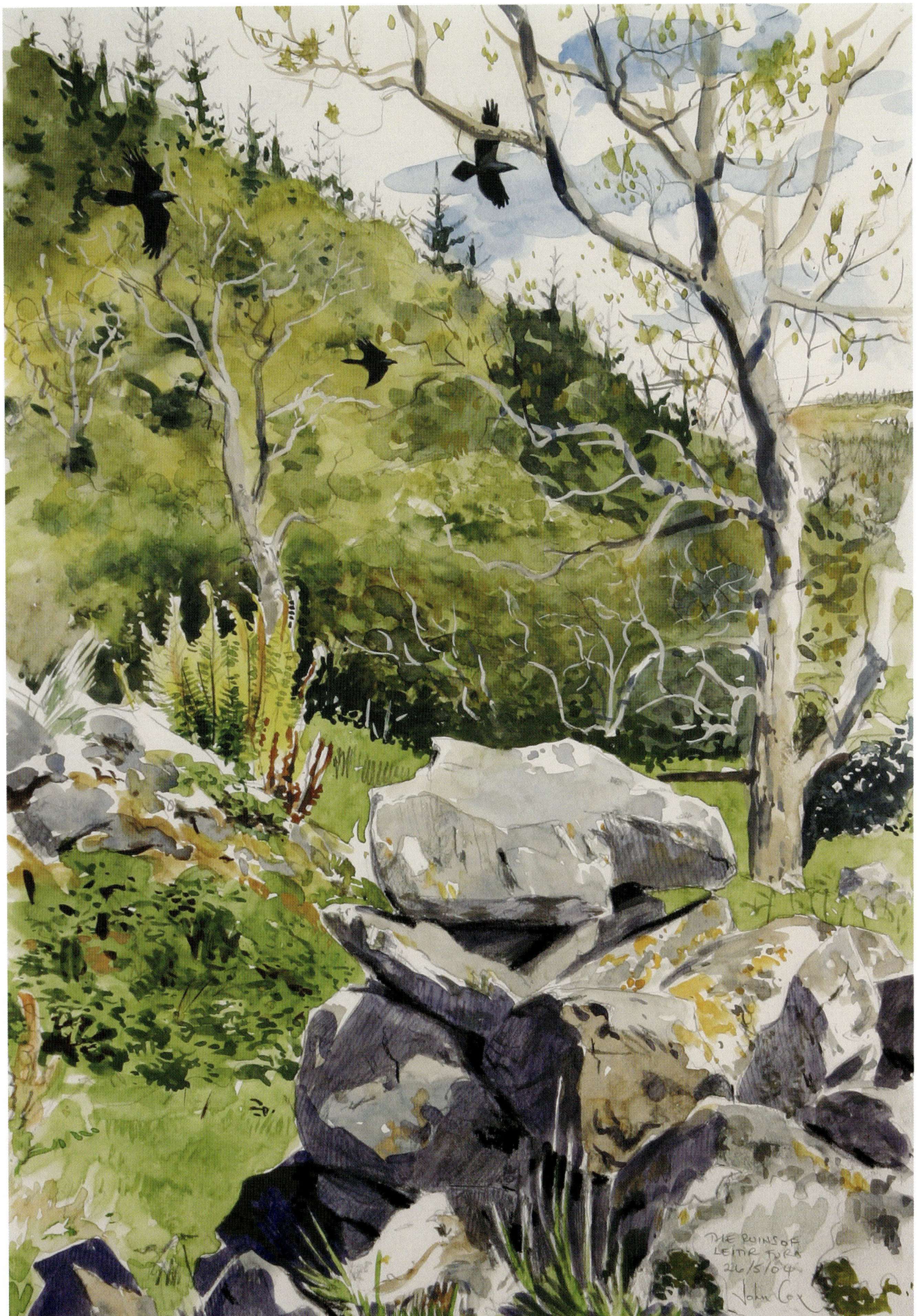

3

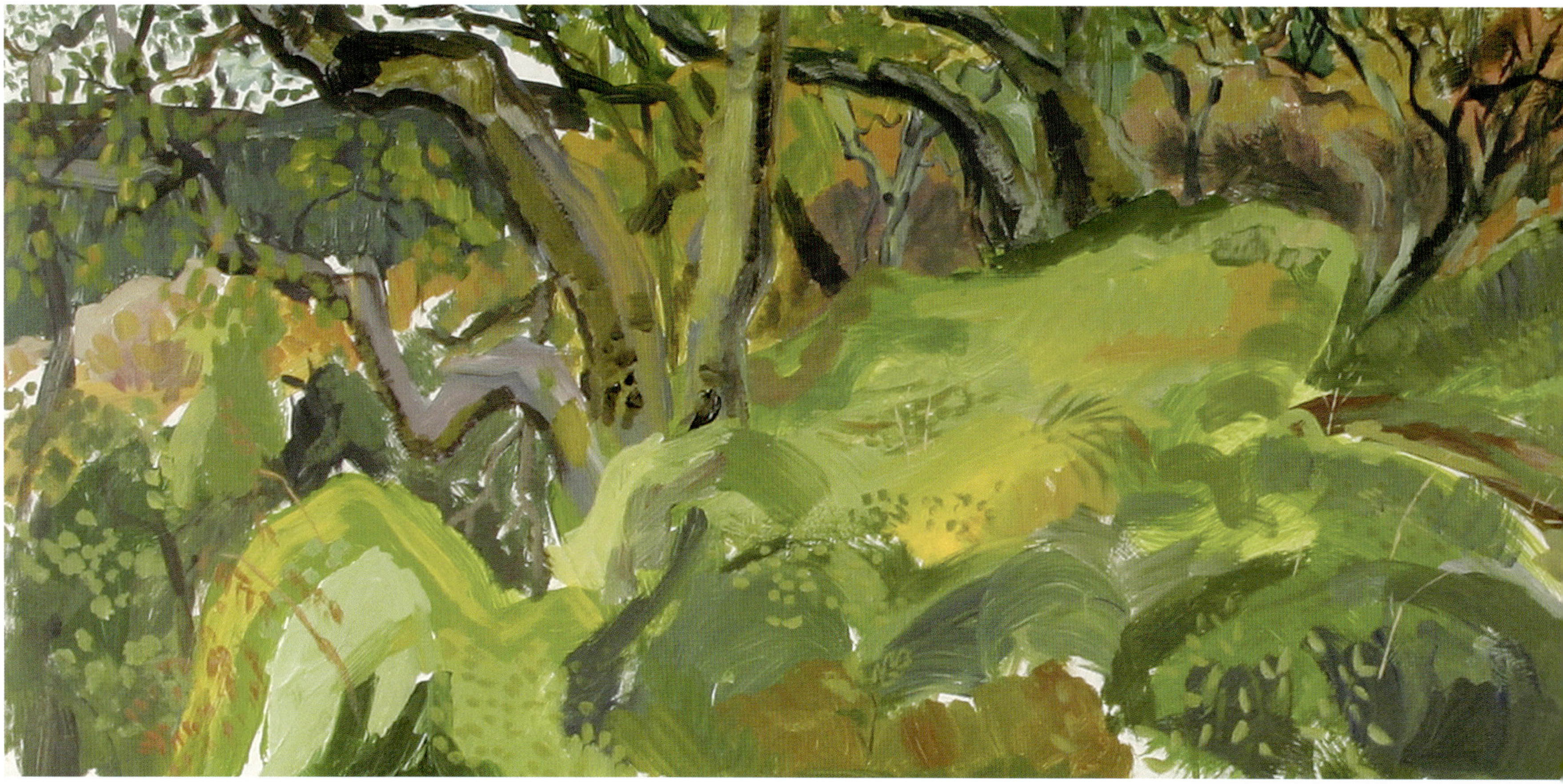

4

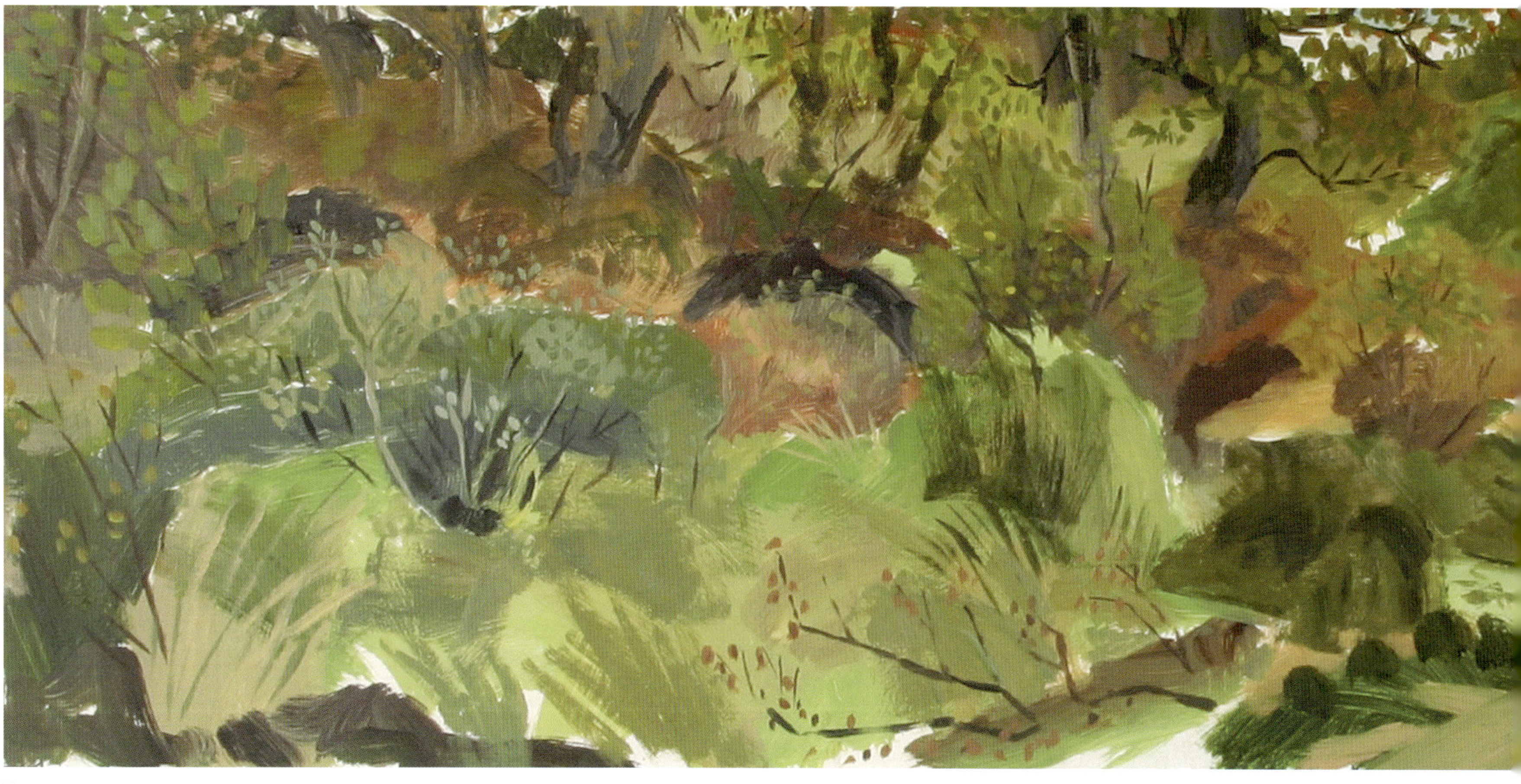

5

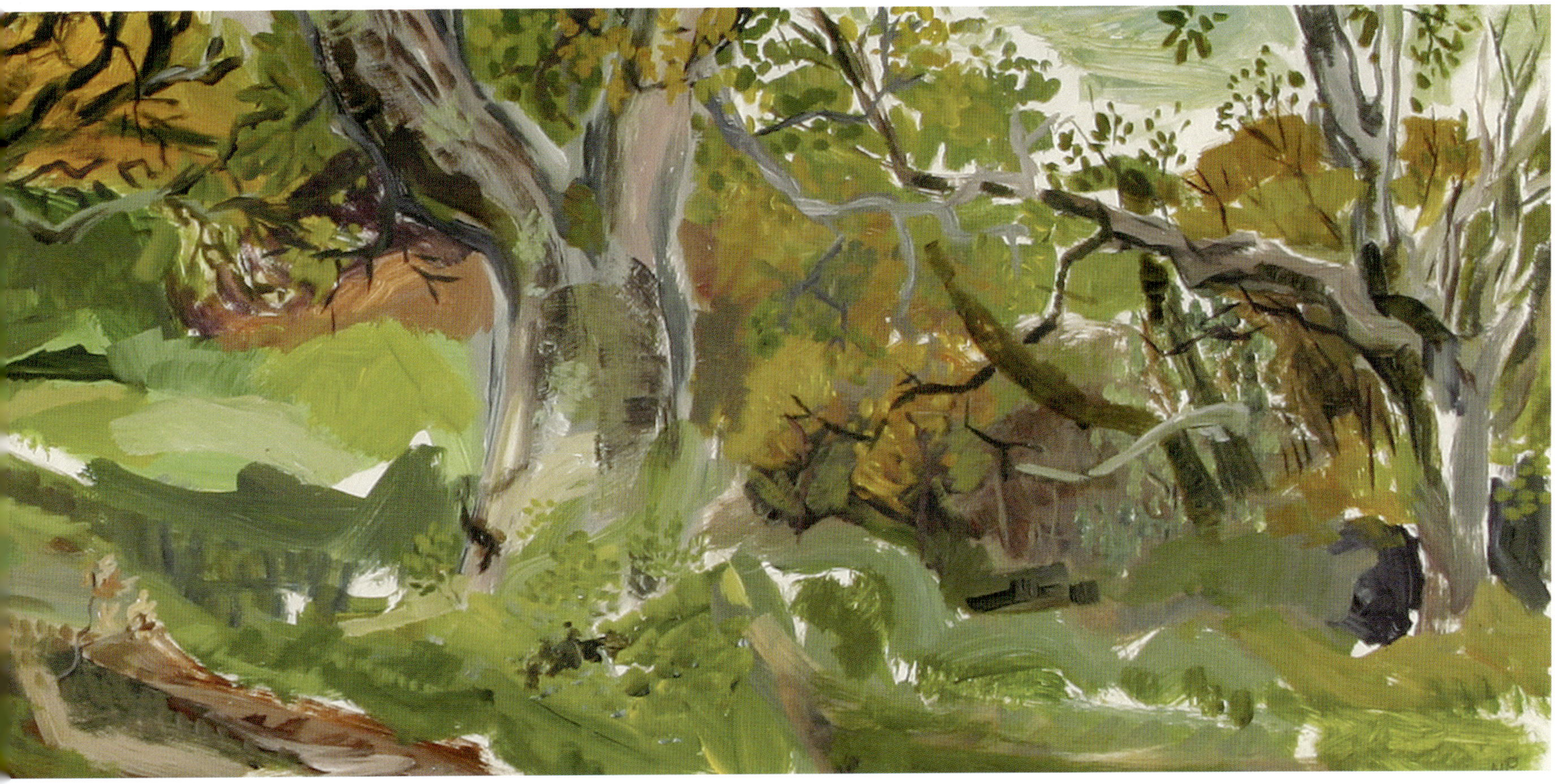

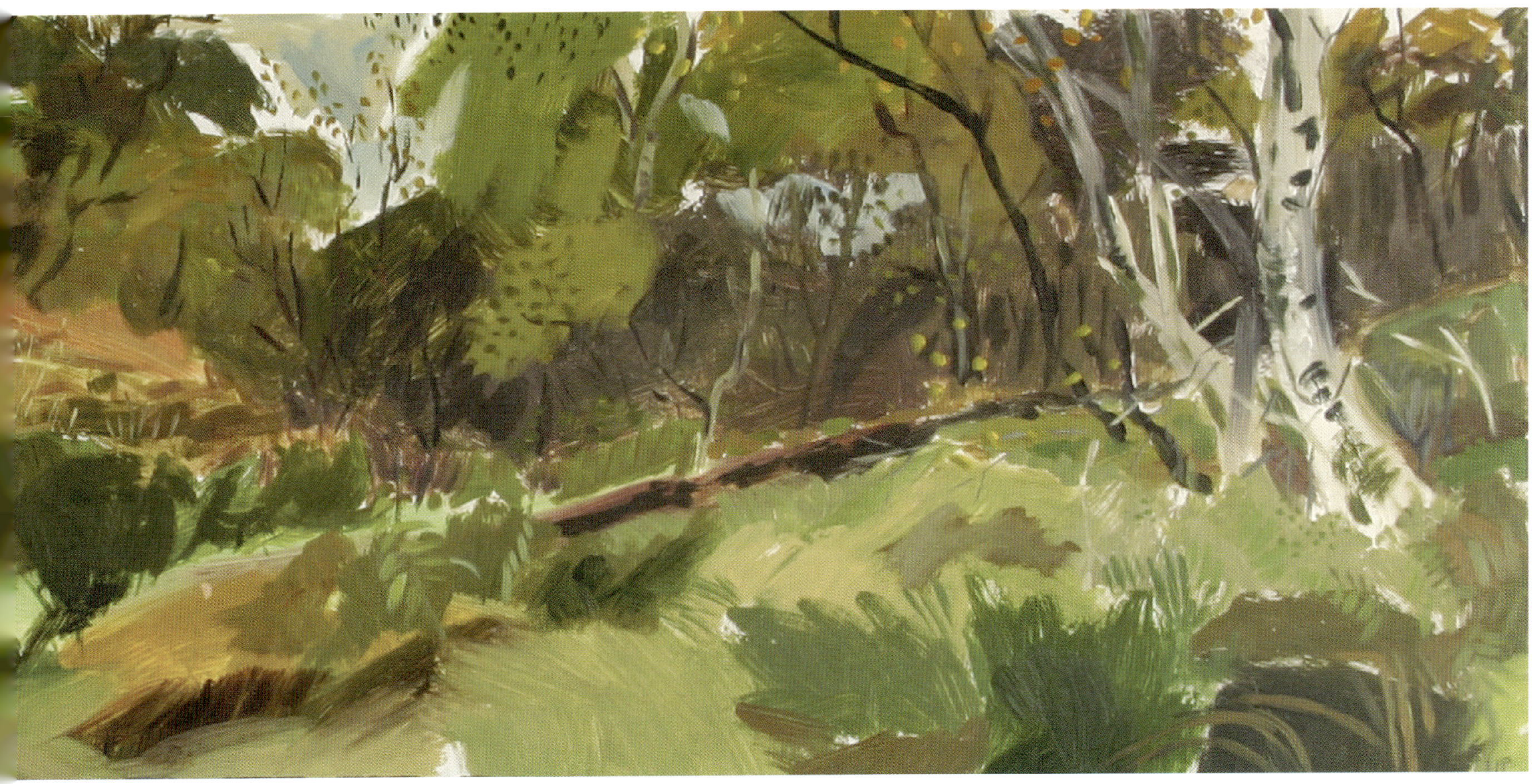

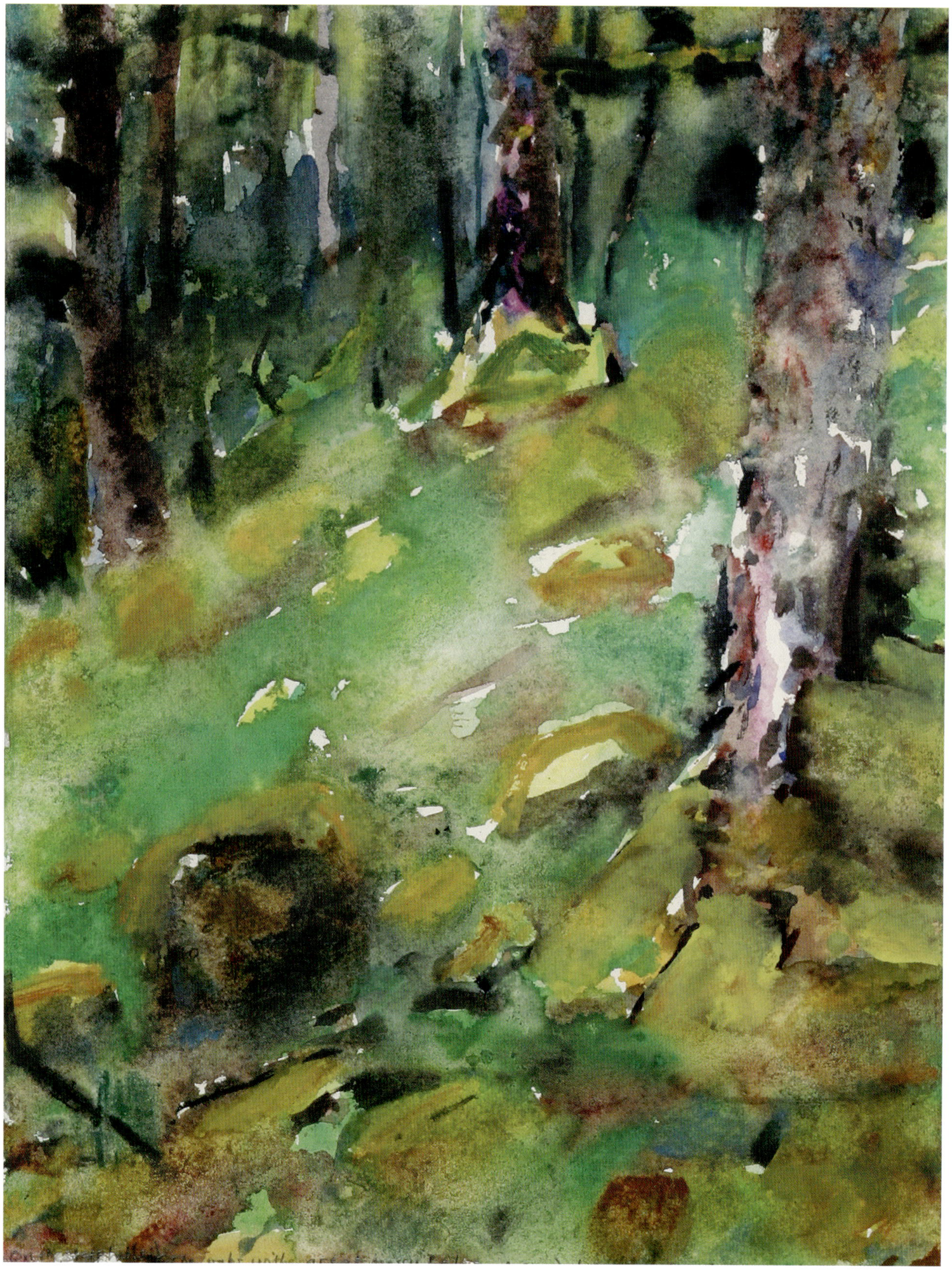

1

1. David Guy Measures *Oaks amidst the boulders with great mossy boles*
watercolour · 38 x 28.5 cm
2. David Guy Measures *An isolated oak on the shore of Loch Sunart*
watercolour · 28.5 x 22 cm

Because of morning rain, I set up to paint from the back window of the caravan, whereupon the rain ceased and the sun appeared.

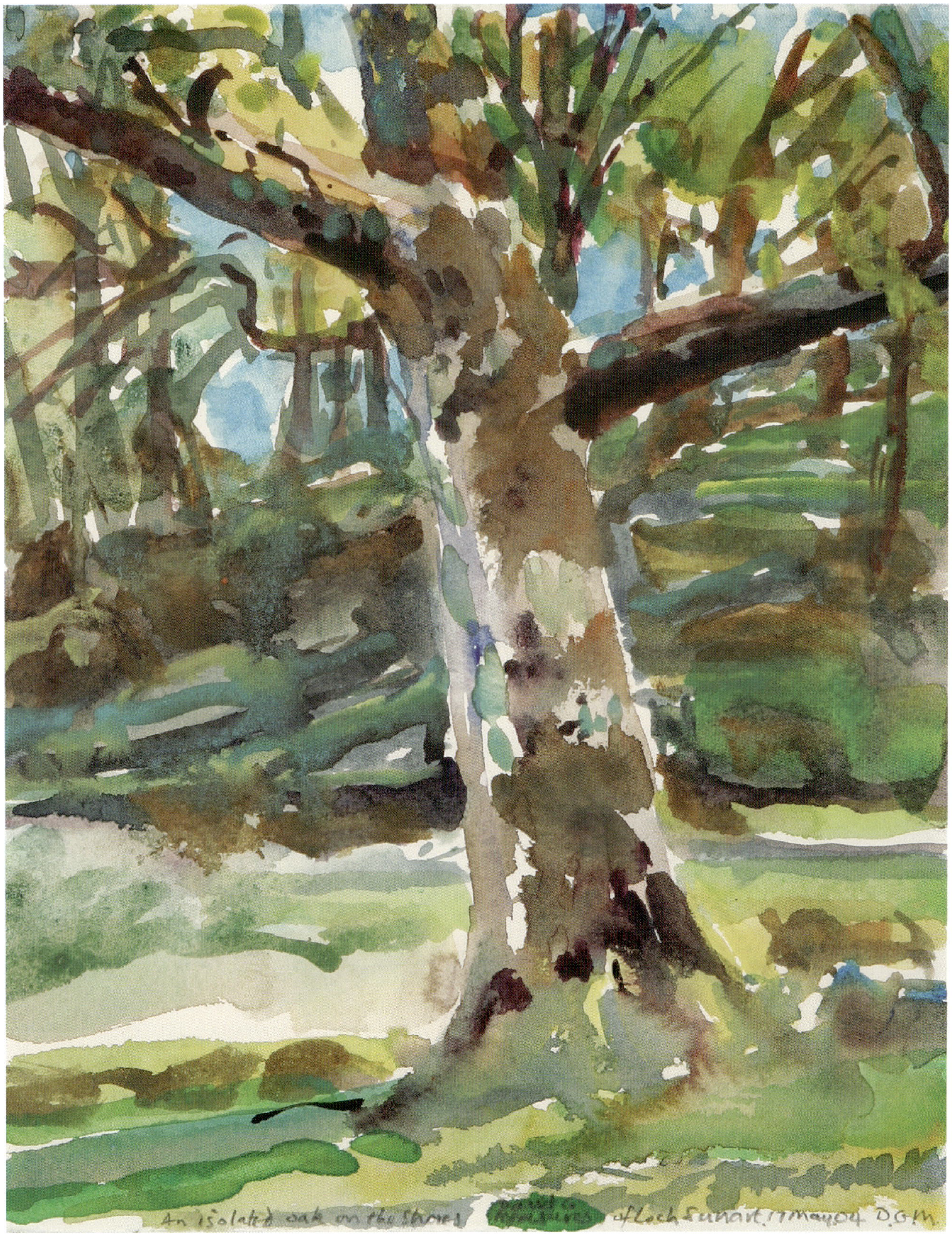

2

1

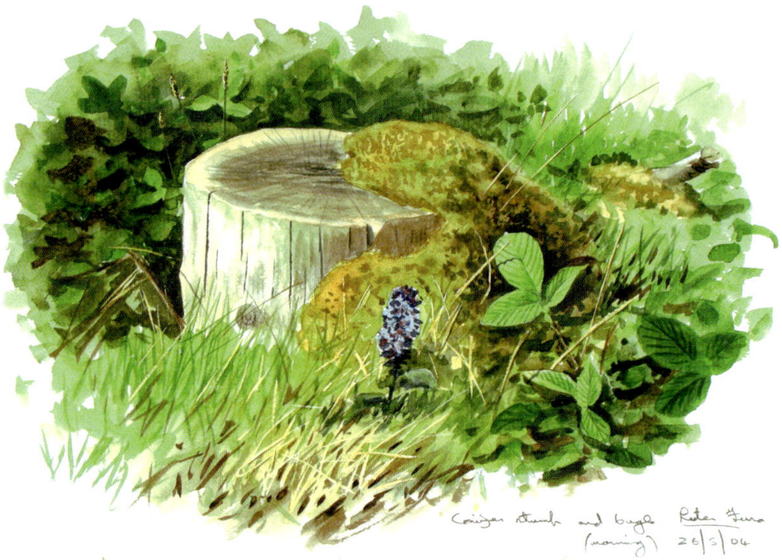

2

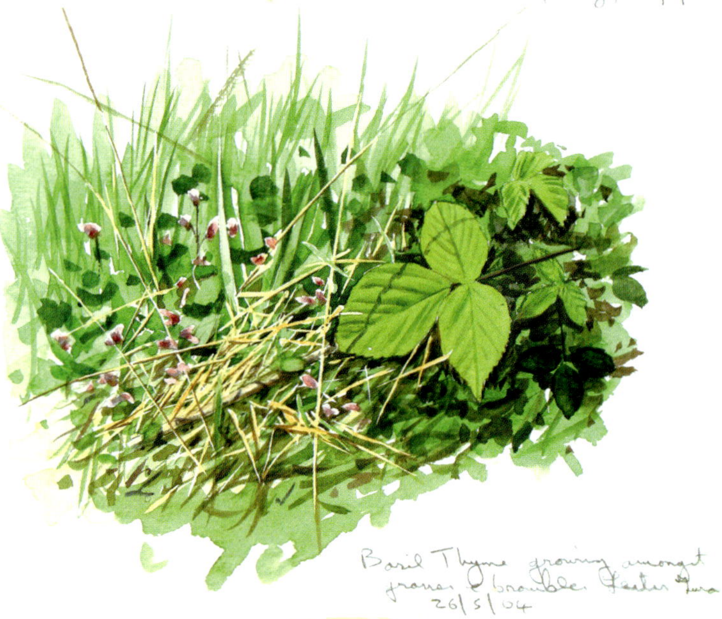

3

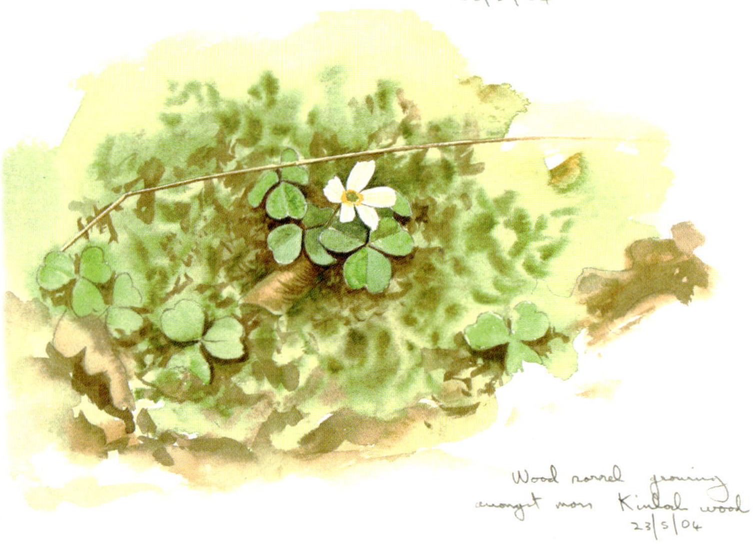

SPRING FLOWERS

Spring is the best time to visit these woods, just before the foliage of the trees unfurls into the pale green tracery overhead and the midges put in an appearance. The flowers are at their brightest and the bracken has yet to spread its fronds and smother the woodland floor. Some of the flowers can be found in any deciduous wood, as their names suggest: wood sorrel and wood anemone. I saw blue bugle and violet, yellow celandine, cow-wheat and yellow pimpernel, and many more. When I visited Ariundle in late May, it was primrose time; on later visits, there were eye-catching swards of bluebells, and a careful search revealed common spotted and other orchids. At Knapdale there is rare narrow-leaved helleborine. This orchid is found on calcareous soils, in open woods where it gets plenty of sunlight. The decline of woodland management and the replacement of the old woods by dense conifers have led to shading, which has driven the helleborine out of many of its old haunts (although recent restoration work and removal of conifers are allowing it to spread again).

On sunny days, the interest of woodland flowers is doubled by the butterflies, bees and other insects visiting them for nectar to sip and places to lay their eggs. Violets attract pearl-bordered, small pearl-bordered and dark green fritillaries; lady's smock is the food plant of orange tips; and the various grasses that make up much of the ground layer are important for speckled woods and chequered skippers. The chequered skipper is a speciality of these woods. It has been in decline for half a century and is now extinct in England. Its British stronghold is about fifty sites in the western woods of Scotland. It needs damp glades with good growths of purple moor grass, its favourite caterpillar food plant, and bugle, marsh thistle and bluebells to provide nectar for the adults. Long swathes of suitable habitat are created by the clearings under power lines, which makes it easy to find good places to search for this butterfly!

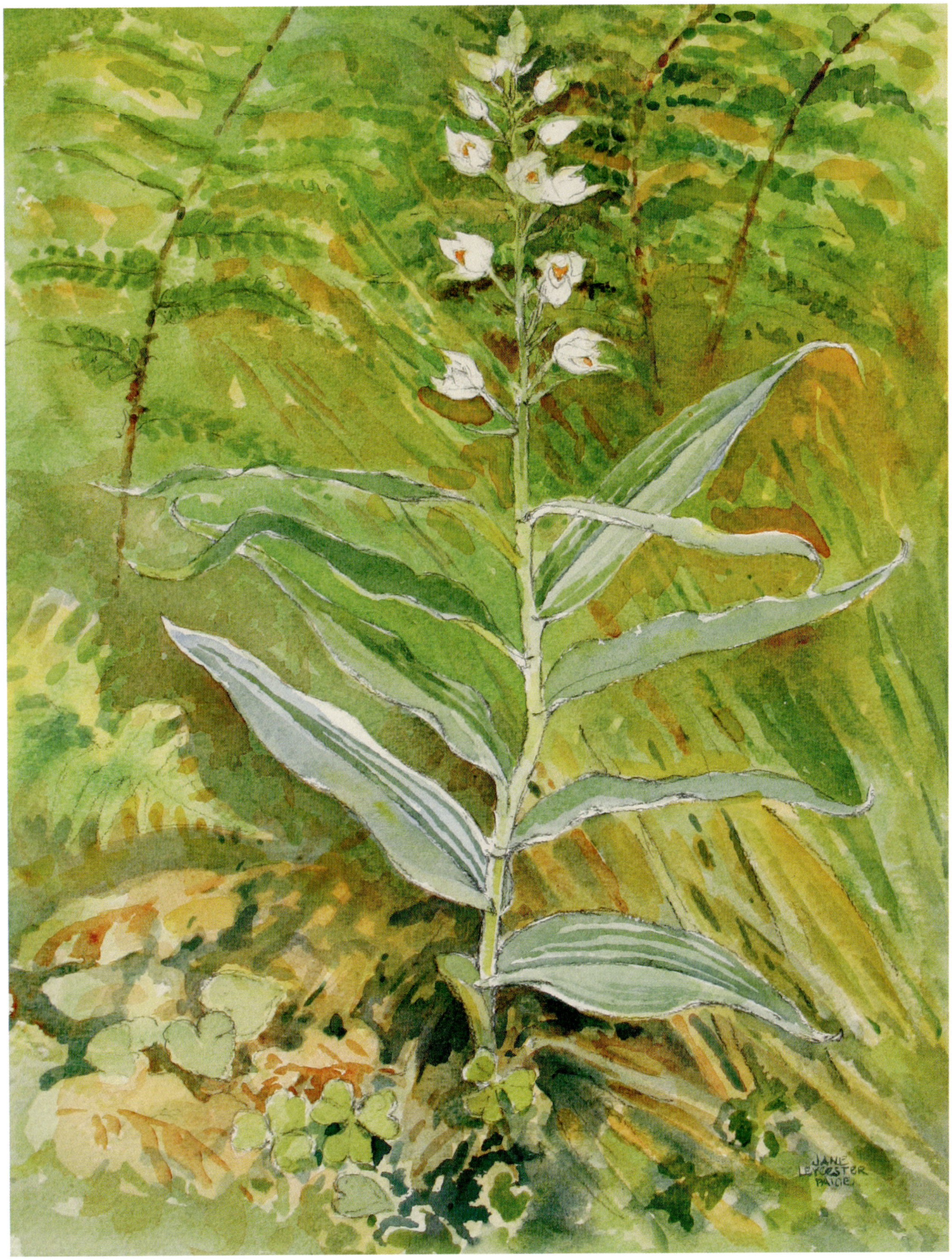

4

1. Alastair Proud *Conifer stump and bugle*
   watercolour · 30.5 x 39.5 cm
2. Alastair Proud *Basil thyme growing amongst grasses and brambles*
   watercolour · 18 x 24 cm
3. Alastair Proud *Wood sorrel, Kinloch woods*
   watercolour · 18 x 24 cm
4. Jane Leycester Paige *Narrow-leaved helleborine,* Cephalanthera longifolia
   watercolour · 31 x 24 cm

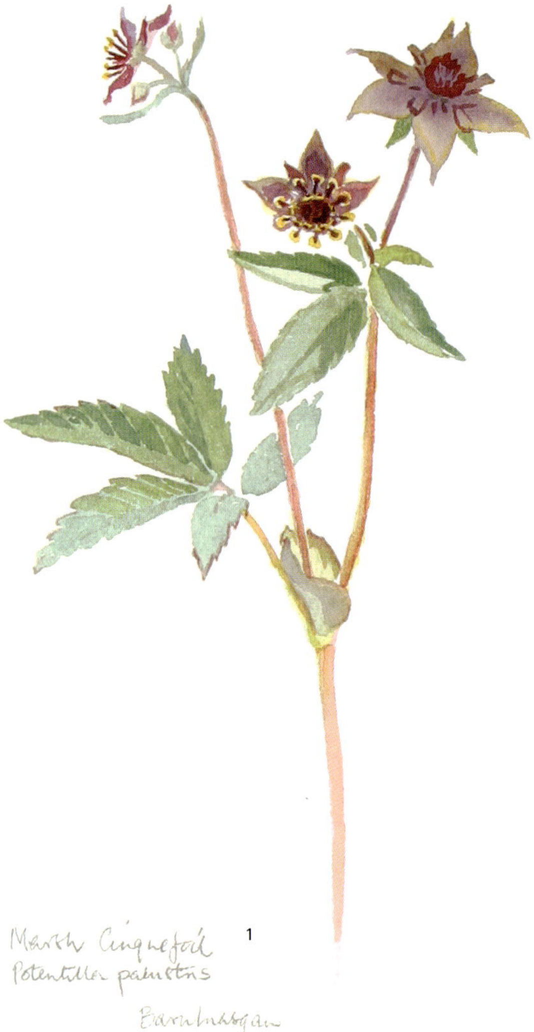

1

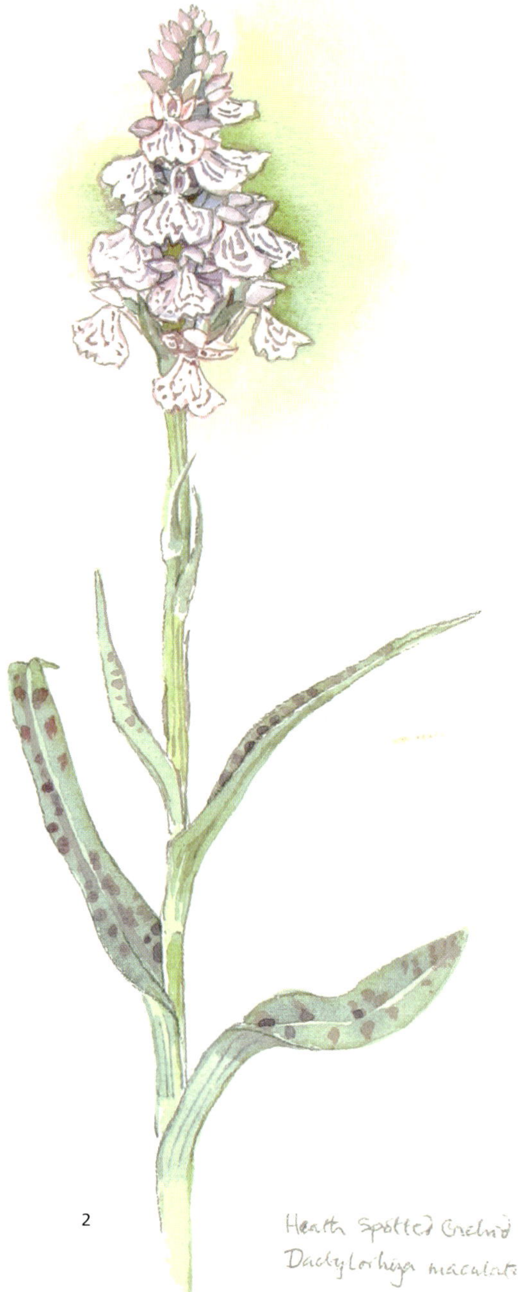

2

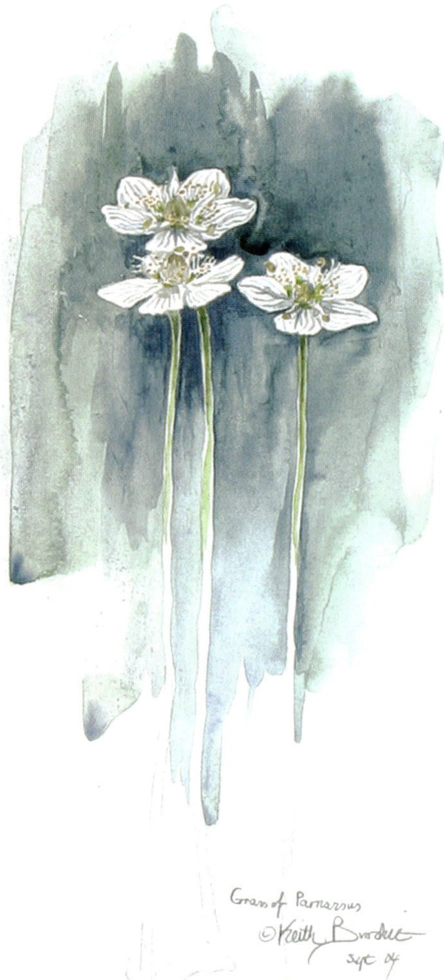

3

1,2 Jane Leycester Paige *Marsh cinquefoil,* Potentilla palustris*, and heath spotted orchid,* Dactylorhiza maculata
watercolour studies · 31 x 24 cm

Both of these flowers are found around Loch Barnluasgan. The heath spotted orchid is easily recognised, when compared with the common spotted orchid, by the wide, frilly labellum and small 'tooth', giving the flower a 'crinoline lady' look.

3. Keith Brockie *Grass of Parnassus*
watercolour · 19 x 9 cm

4. Darren Woodhead *Butterfly studies I*
watercolour · 28 x 38 cm

5. Darren Woodhead *Butterfly studies II*
watercolour · 28 x 38 cm

After a brief warm spell days before we arrived, chequered skipper and speckled wood butterflies were out in their droves. Often feeding on bugle and bluebells, the skippers were always defensive of their territories, darting off at the sight of other passing insects.

4
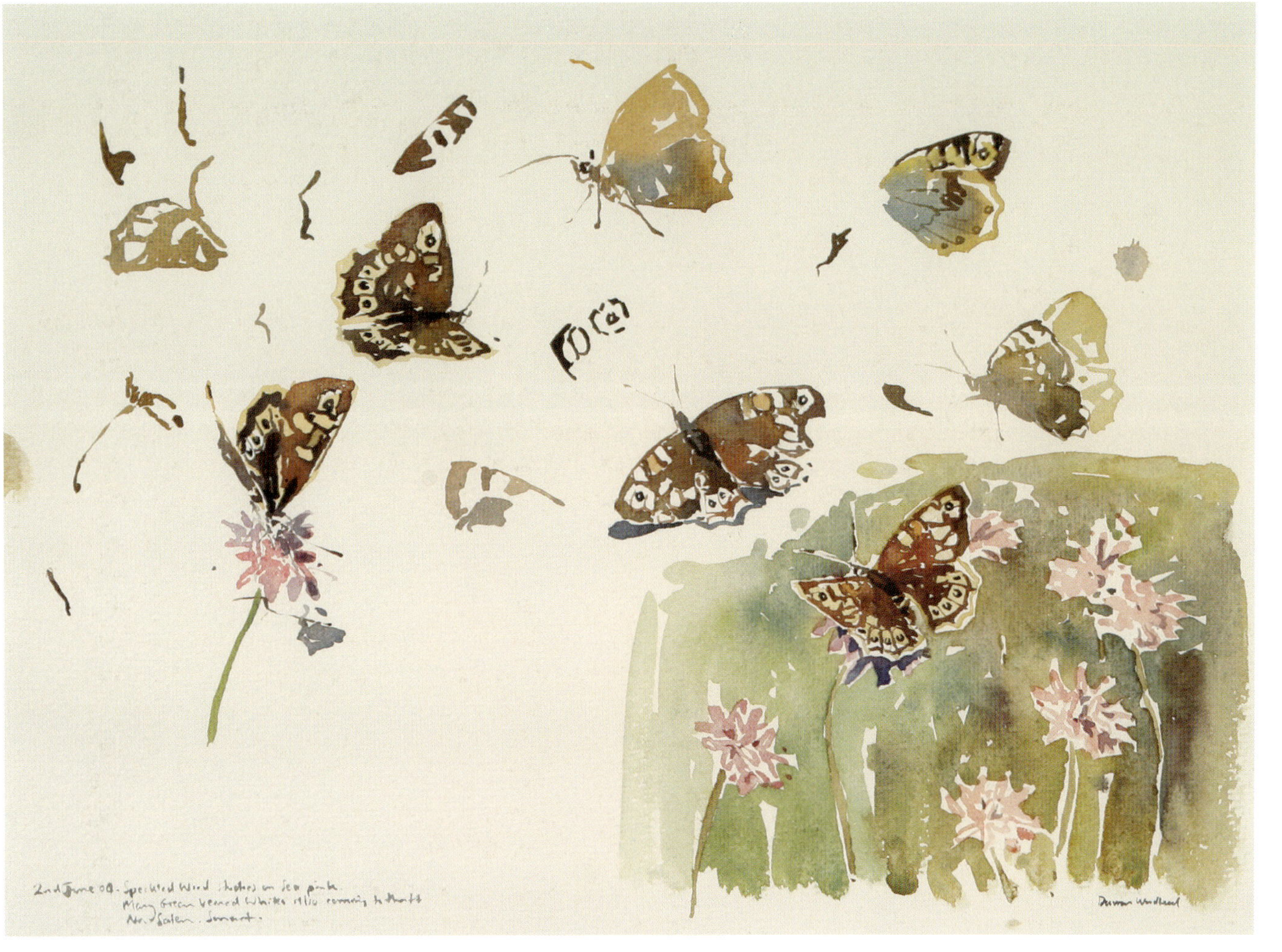

5
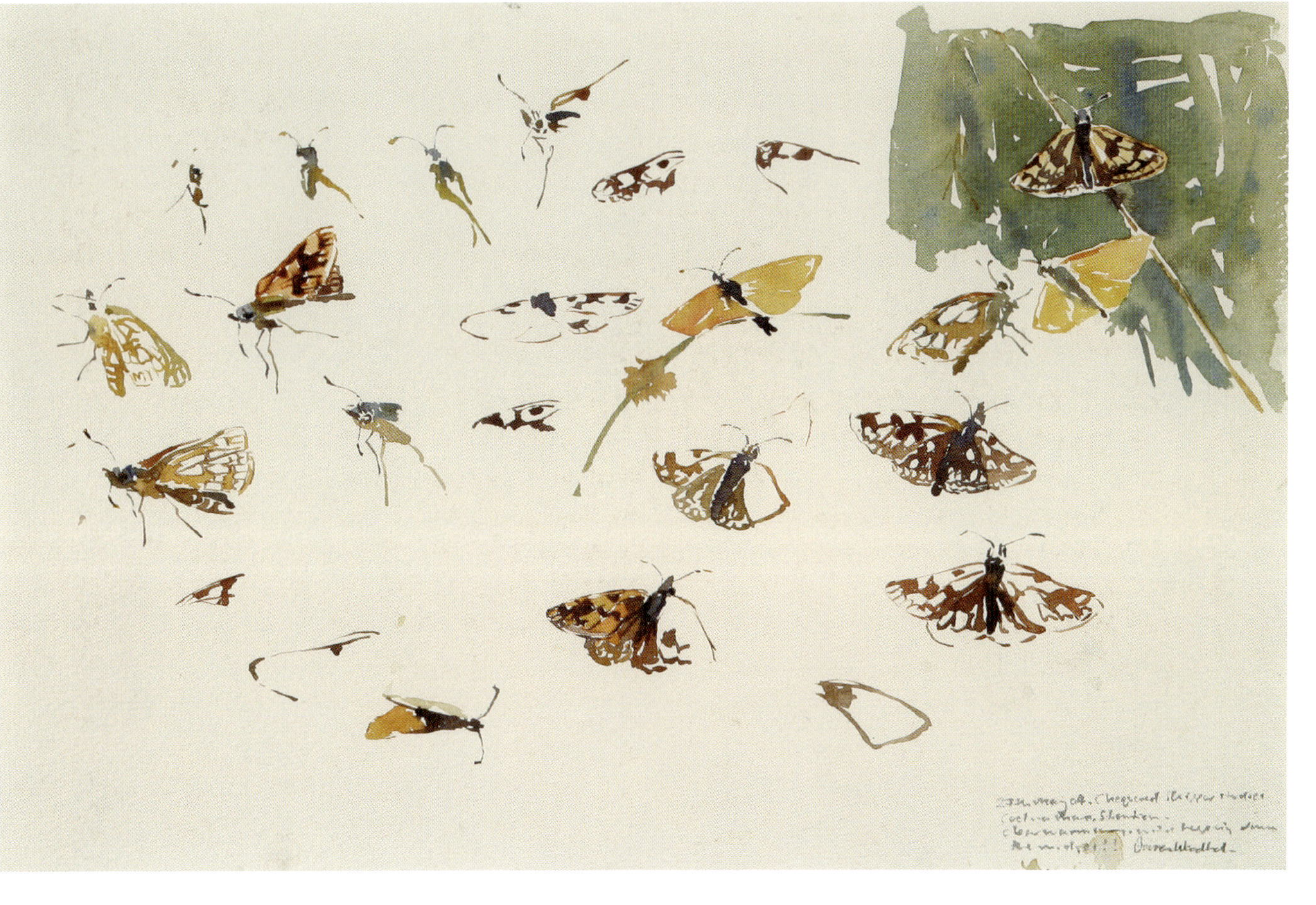

1. Richard Tratt *Chequered skipper butterfly*
oil sketch · 15 x 20.5 cm
2. Richard Tratt *Small pearl-bordered fritillary*
watercolour · 15 x 20 cm
3. John Cox *Green hairstreak*
watercolour · 12 x 10 cm
4. Richard Tratt *Chequered skippers*
oil on board · 25.5 x 25.5 cm

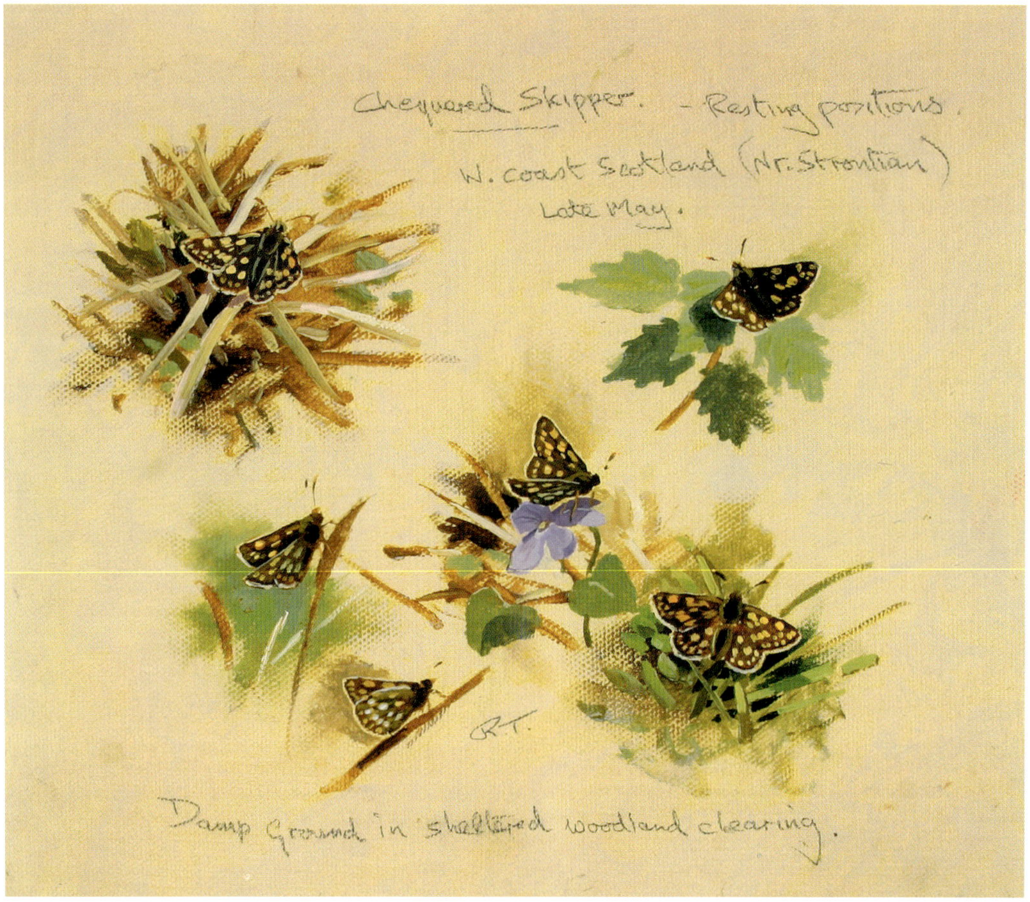

1

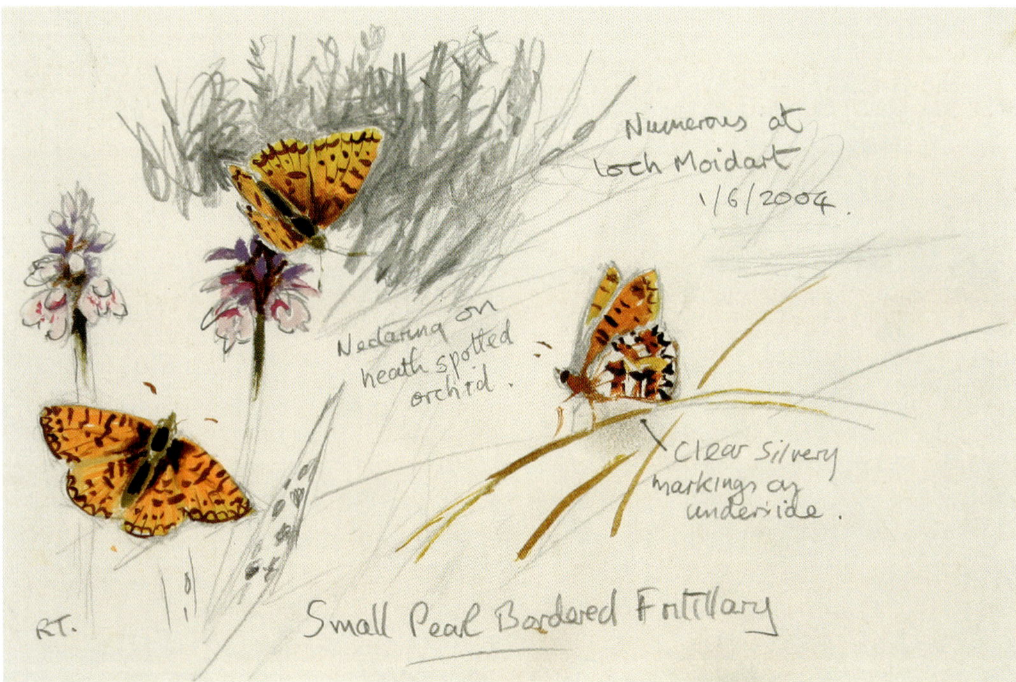

2

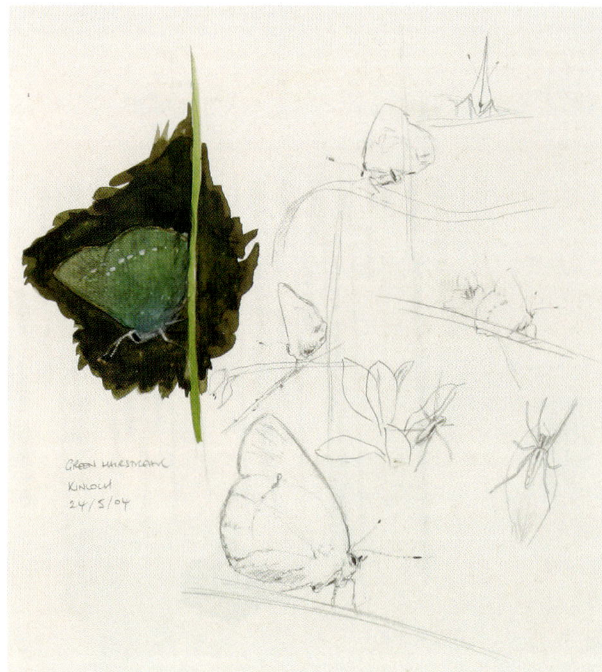

3

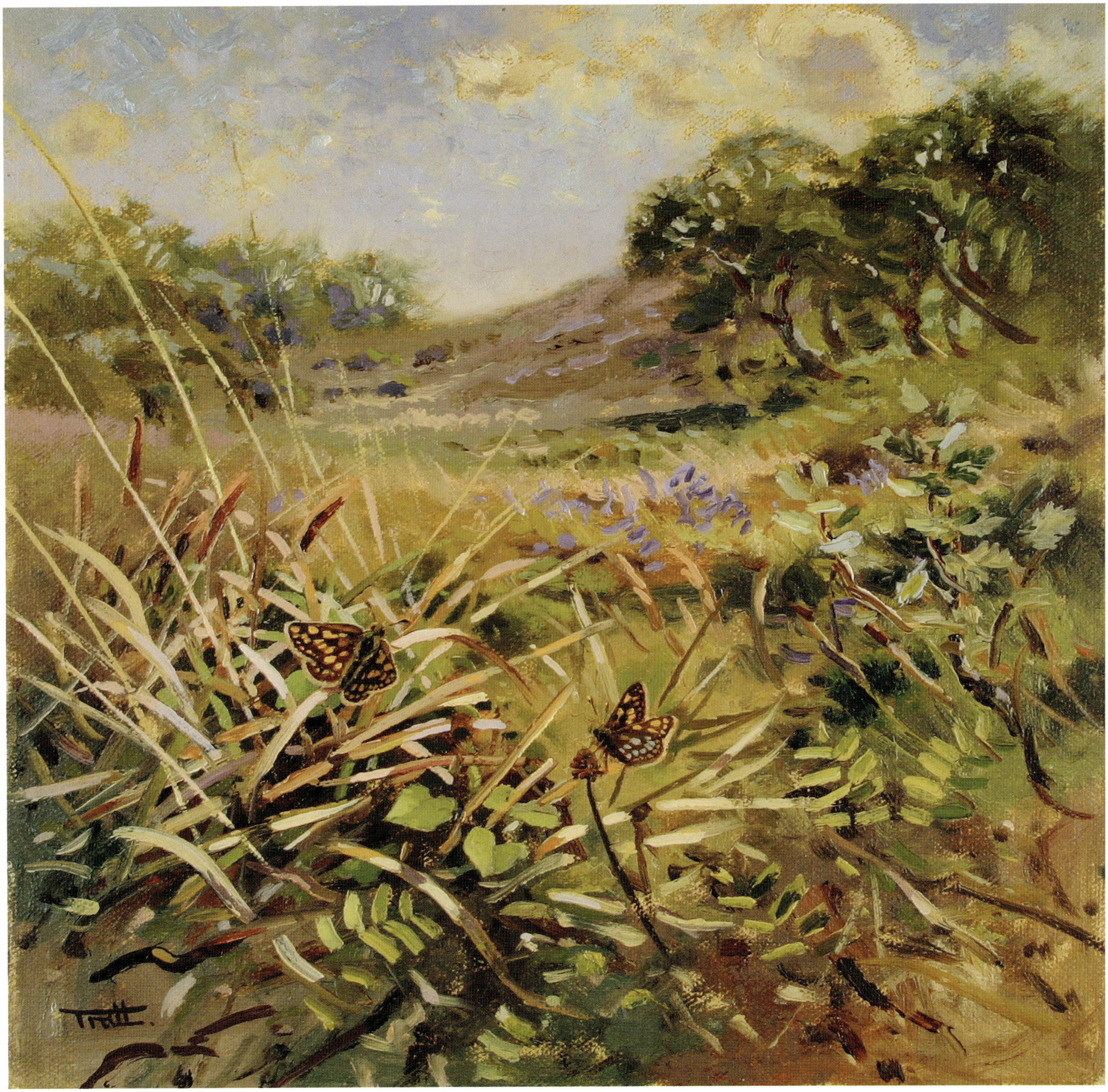

4

When the leaves are still not fully spread, it is easy to spot small birds flitting and perching in the canopy as they sing. A few weeks later, they will be disembodied voices and shadowy figures flitting among the leaves, so focusing binoculars to match the bird with the song will not be easy. Yet birdwatching visits should not be too early in the year because some of the best birds associated with oakwoods are migrants and reach the Highlands about a month after they appear in the south of England. They, like the resident species, subsist on the insects living on tree leaves, and successful nesting for some birds depends on the abundance of caterpillars. By July, nesting and song are over, but even in winter a wood may suddenly become alive with a band of birds passing by through the trees. Mostly they are tits, often with goldcrests and treecreepers, and occasionally great spotted woodpeckers, foraging together.

The most abundant birds are chaffinches, robins and blue tits, but the woods can be surprisingly devoid of birds where there are stands of single-age oak and little understorey. This habitat lacks variety and may not contain the succession of abundant food supplies needed for rearing broods of baby birds. There may also be a shortage of nesting places. Young trees do not have the holes required by tits and redstarts, while blackbirds and robins do not like open woods without an understorey.

The melancholy song of the willow warbler is, for me, the most distinctive sound of these woods. At times their incessant complaining songs seem to be everywhere. The visually almost identical, but vocally very distinct, chiffchaff is nothing like as common as it is in the south; but the bird that got the most attention from the artists, as well as me, was the wood warbler. We liked it because it sang from low perches, where it was easy to watch and paint. We could sit comfortably in one place while the bird performed in a circuit around us, singing from one perch, then a few minutes later flying, still singing, to another perch and so on. A poet has described the song as 'little waves of pearls dropped and scattered and shivered on a shore of pearls'. More prosaically, the song starts with a stuttering *tip-tip-tip*, which accelerates into a trill, but confusingly the trills are mixed with bursts of plaintive notes, so it sounds as if there are two birds singing.

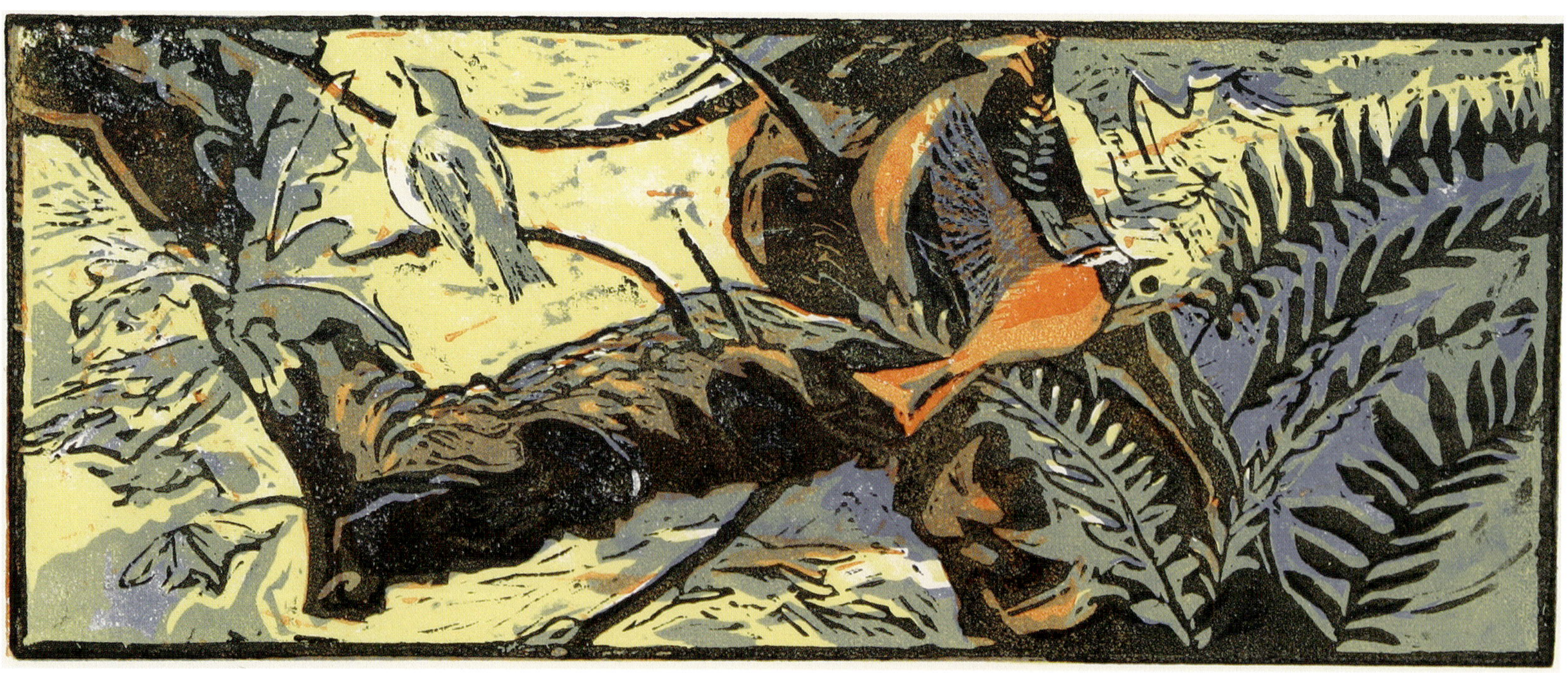

1

Three other songbirds are typical of western oakwoods, and two of these are frequently met in the Highlands. I watched a pair of tree pipits carrying food for their young, but I must have been too near the nest because they flew from perch to perch, refusing to deliver to the waiting nestlings, so I moved on. The redstart nests in holes in trunks and stumps, and has eye-catching plumage. The name is Old English for 'red tail' and the Gaelic is, contrarily and oddly, *cean-dearg* – 'red head'! We did not find any of the third species, the pied flycatcher. It is common in the west of England and Wales but something of a rarity in western Scottish woods. Nestboxes have been put up in several woods to encourage it, with some success.

Elusive woodland birds to look for include treecreepers swarming jerkily up tree trunks and spotted flycatchers darting out from perches to snap up insects (but watch out for chaffinches, which also do this), but the woodcock is the prize. You may catch sight of it flying away silently through the trees when it is disturbed, but it draws attention to itself in the long summer evenings by flying up and down woodland edges, uttering a very distinctive croaking. This is its territorial display, called 'roding'.

2

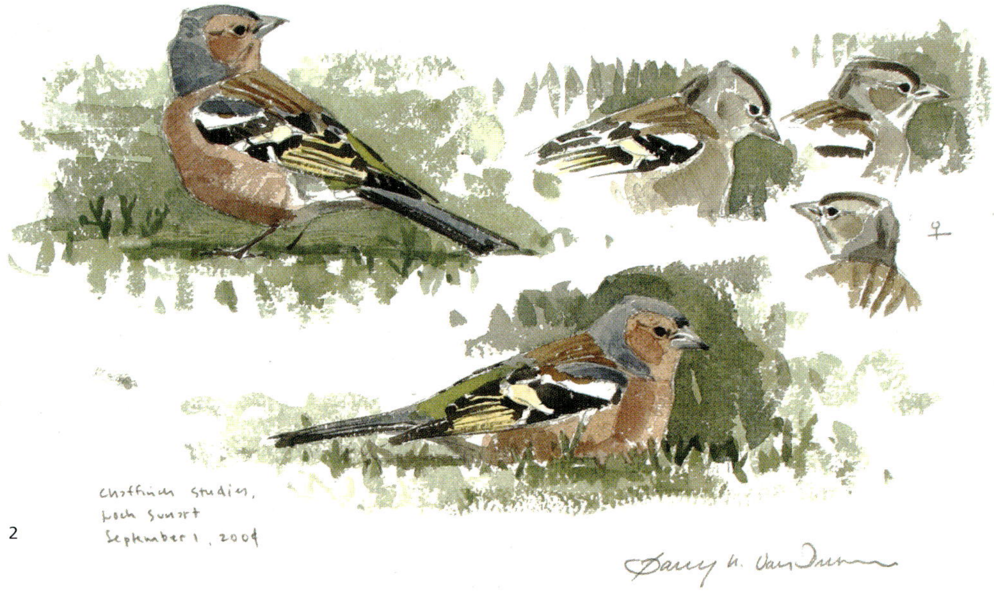

3

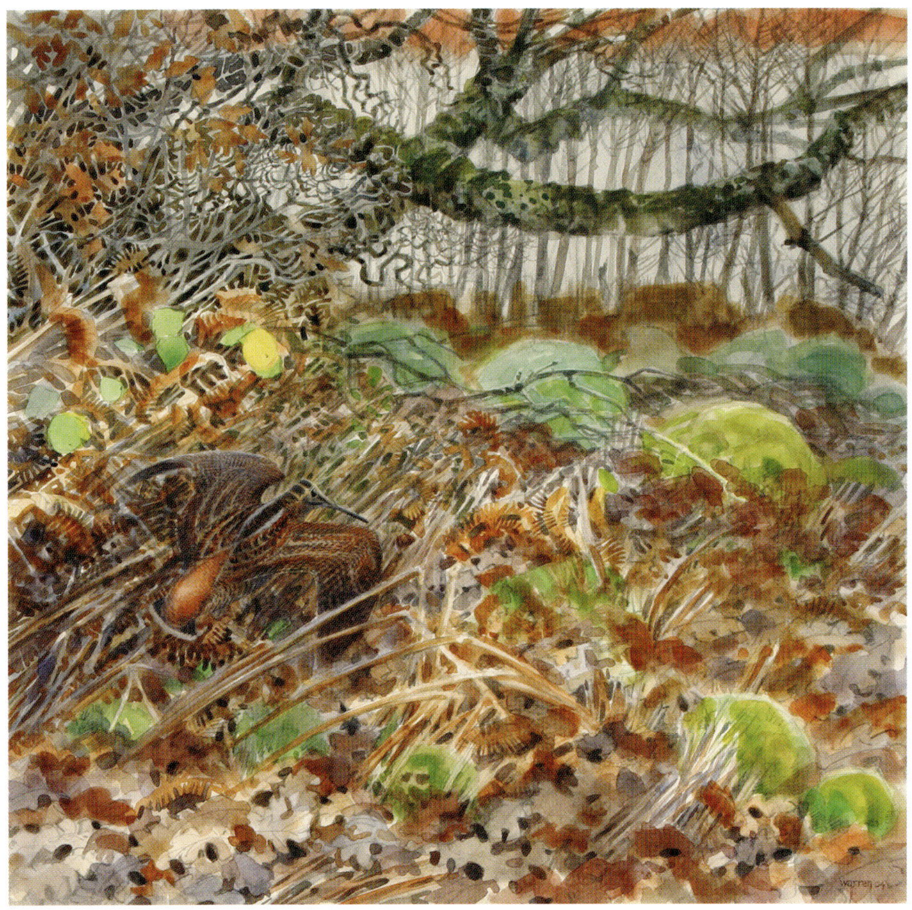

1. Robert Greenhalf *Redstart and wood warbler*
   four-colour woodcut · 16 x 39 cm

   The oakwoods along the north shore of Loch Sunart were alive with the 'ticking and trilling' of wood warblers. Hyperactive and sticking to the canopy, where the yellows and greens of their plumage echoed those of the oak leaves, they were initially difficult to locate. By climbing the steep, boulder-and-moss-strewn hillside, I found that I could often get level with, or even above, the birds in the trees at the foot of the hill. From this vantage point I looked down through a mosaic of lemons and greens, light and shade, often with a glimpse of dark blue sea beyond. Redstarts were much less numerous and surprisingly elusive, allowing only a few tantalising glimpses.

2. Barry W. Van Dusen *Chaffinch studies, Loch Sunart*
   watercolour · 30 x 39.5 cm

3. Michael Warren *Woodcock*
   watercolour · 40 x 40 cm

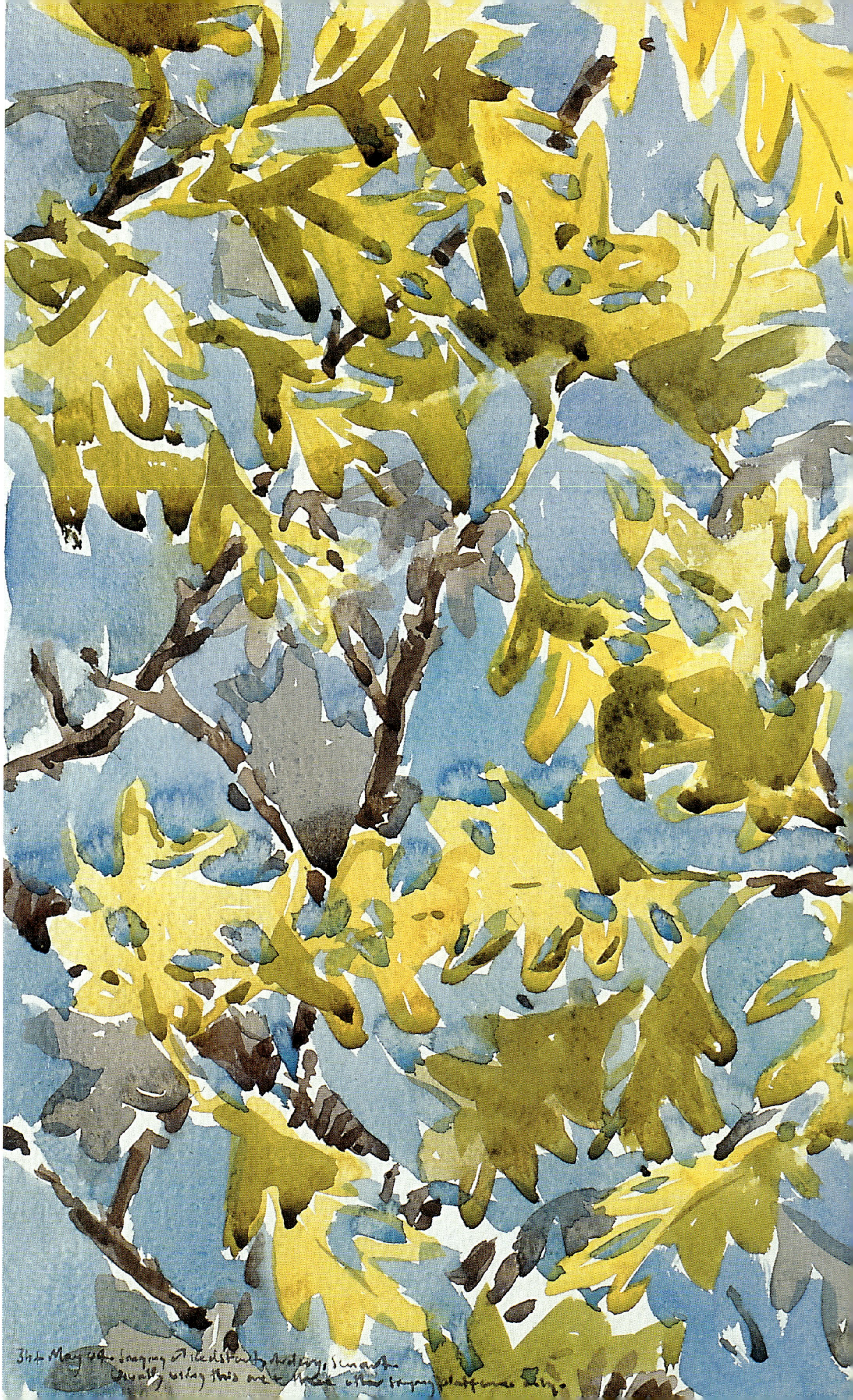

Darren Woodhead ***Singing male redstart, Sunart, 31 May.***
watercolour · 38 x 58 cm

Males were elusive in these woodlands, singing from perches high in the crown of tall oaks.

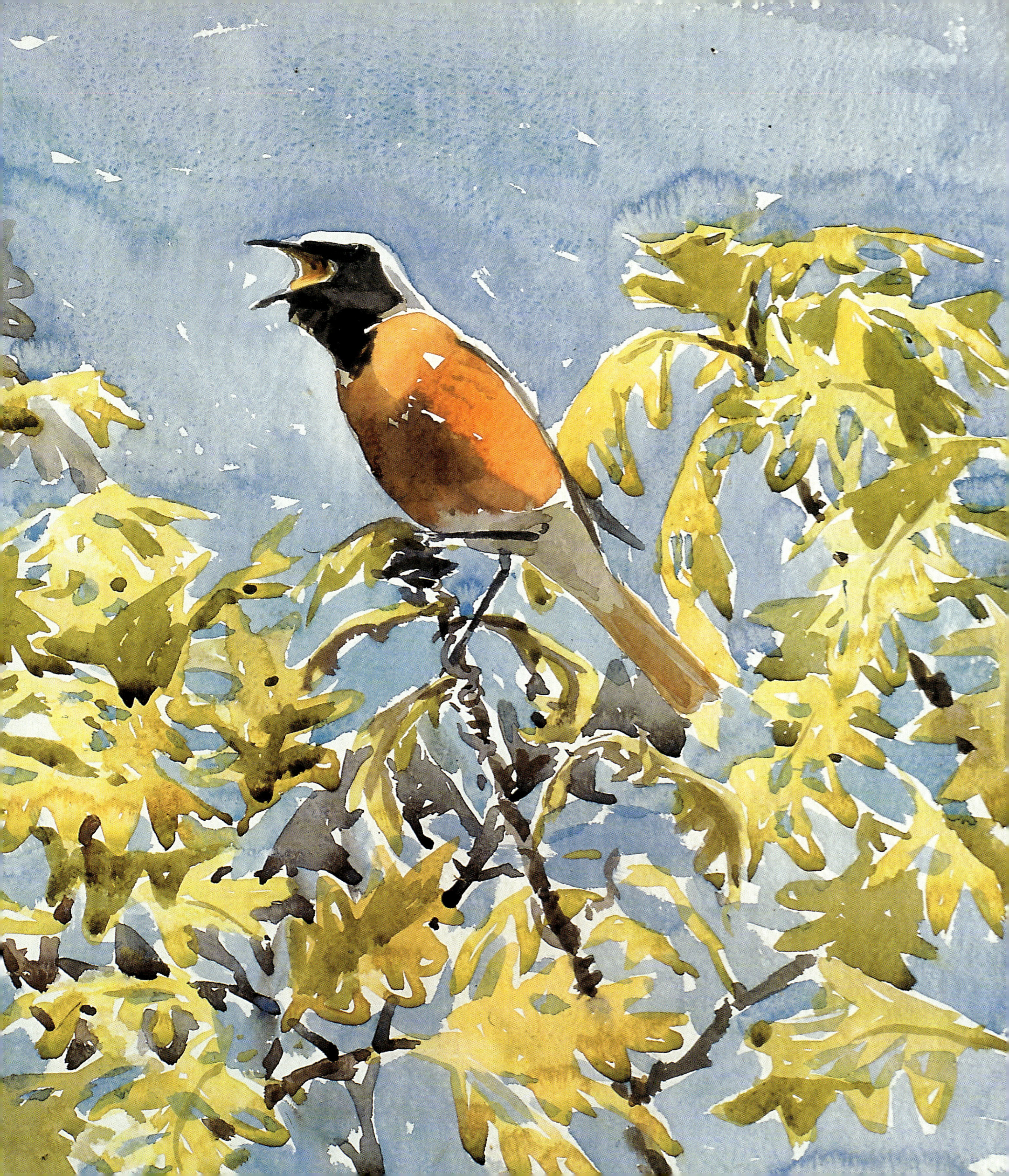

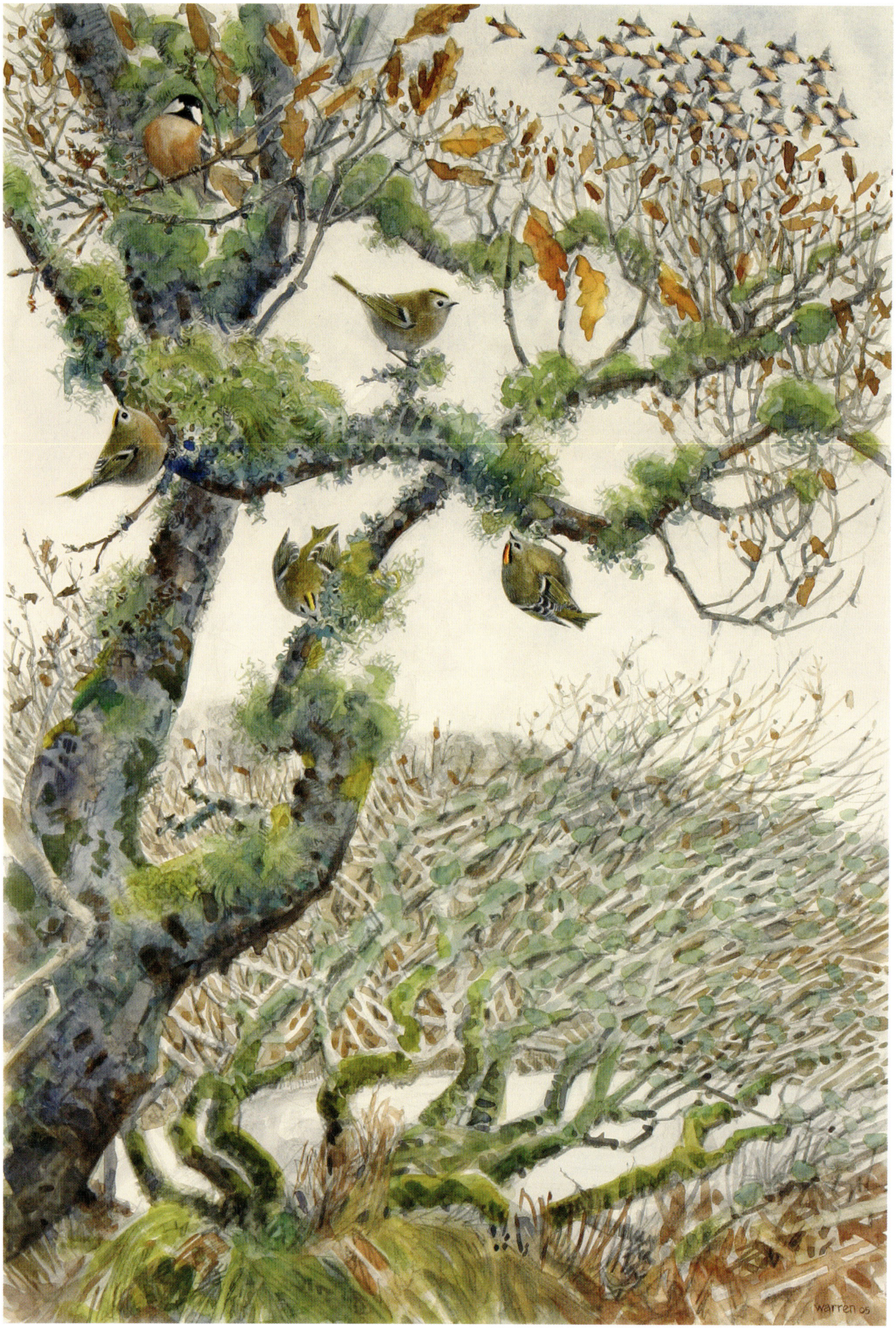

1

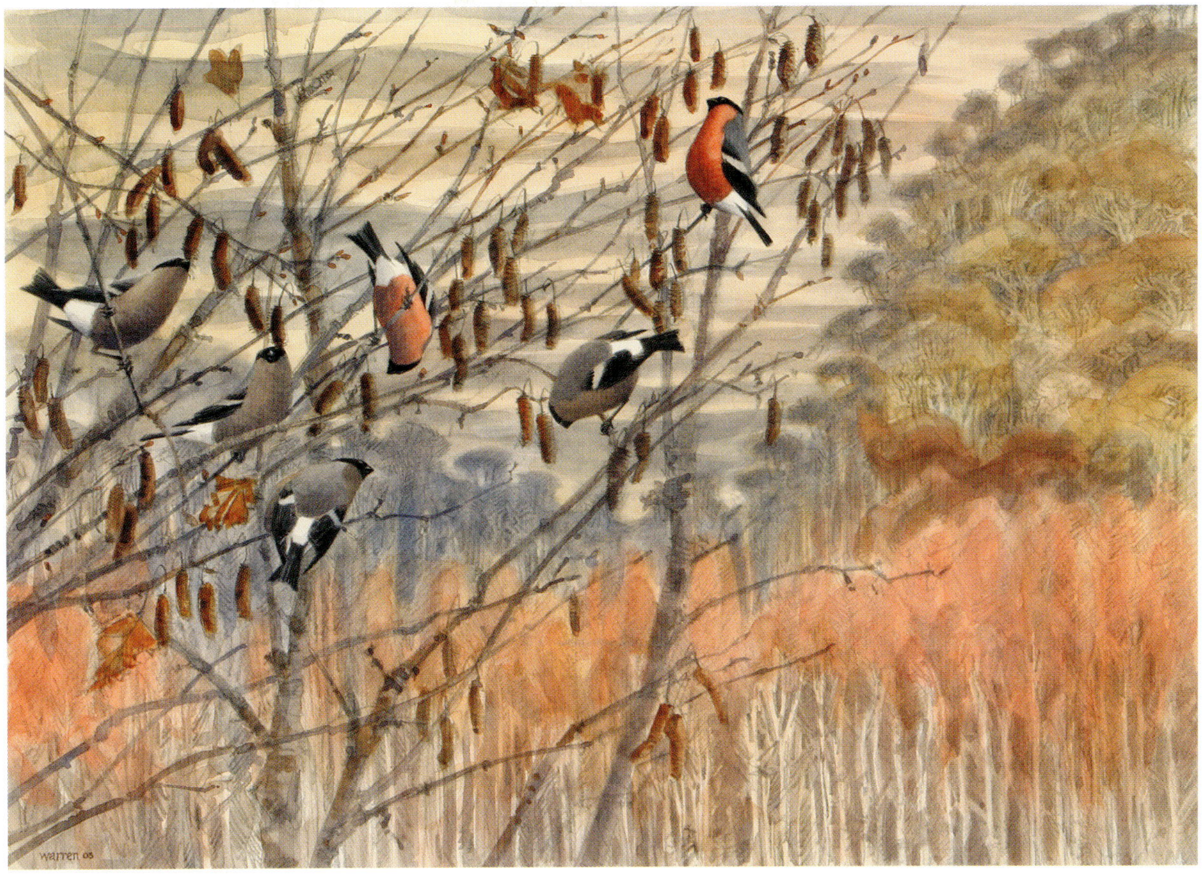

2

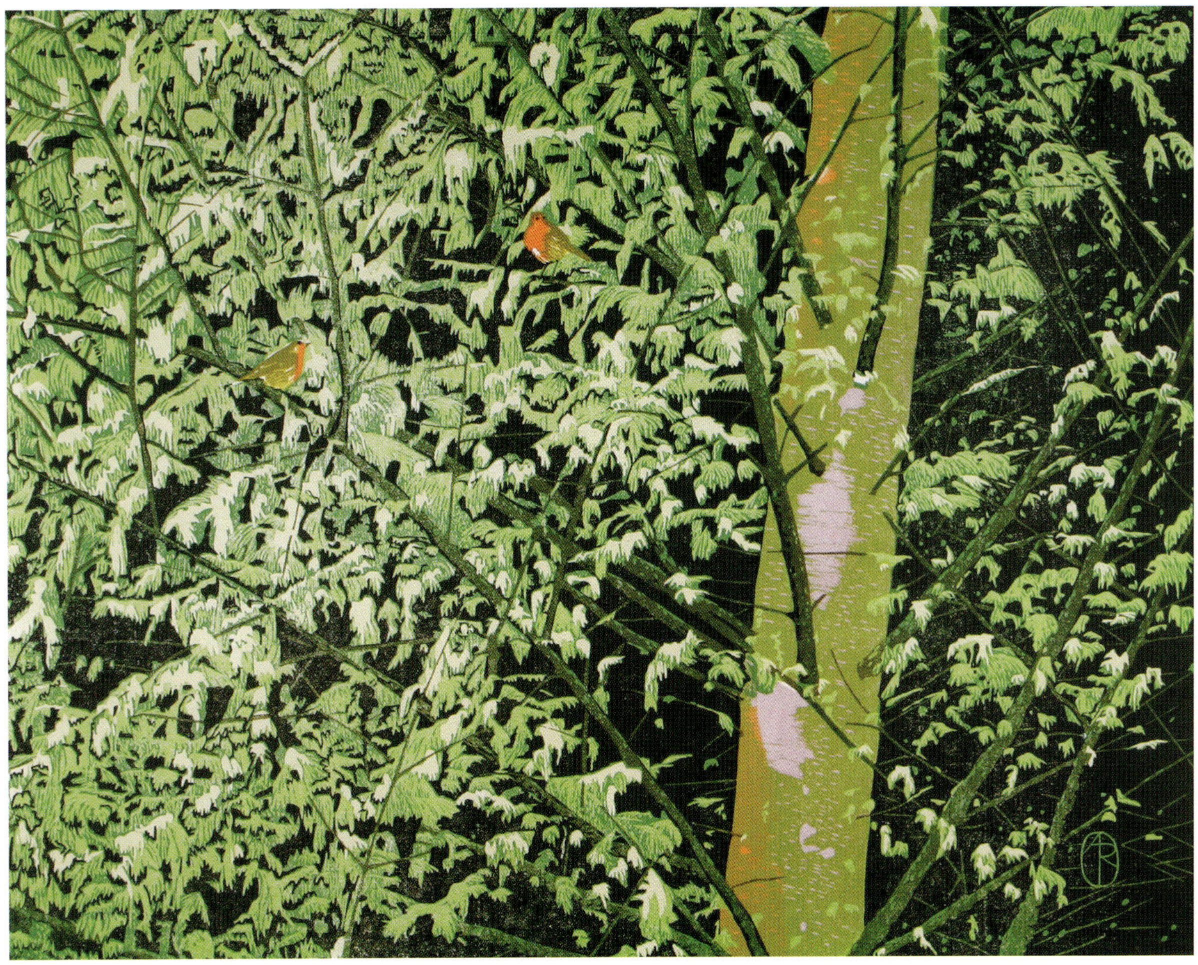

3

1. Michael Warren *Coal tit, goldcrests and waxwings*
   graphite and watercolour · 52.5 x 35 cm

   The woods were very quiet. Then a group of birds appeared, a coal tit with a small party of goldcrests. As I sat painting and sketching, I heard waxwings. A party of about thirty flew low overhead. There was a large irruption of this species into Scotland in autumn.

2. Michael Warren *Bullfinches*
   graphite and watercolour · 35 x 47.5 cm

3. Andrea Rich *Bearded*
   woodcut on Hosho paper · 40 x 51 cm

   I have named this print after the tree. I believe it was an old birch, almost completely covered in moss and lichen. I was in Knapdale and hiking on the Faery Isles on an overcast and drizzling morning. The sky would clear and the sun would shine through from time to time. When the light reached this beauty, its bark shone violet and the moss glistened. I remember thinking that the isles could have been named for this tree alone. It looked enchanted. It was late in the year and I hadn't seen many birds, but these robins were curious and obliging and made fine ornaments in the branches.

1 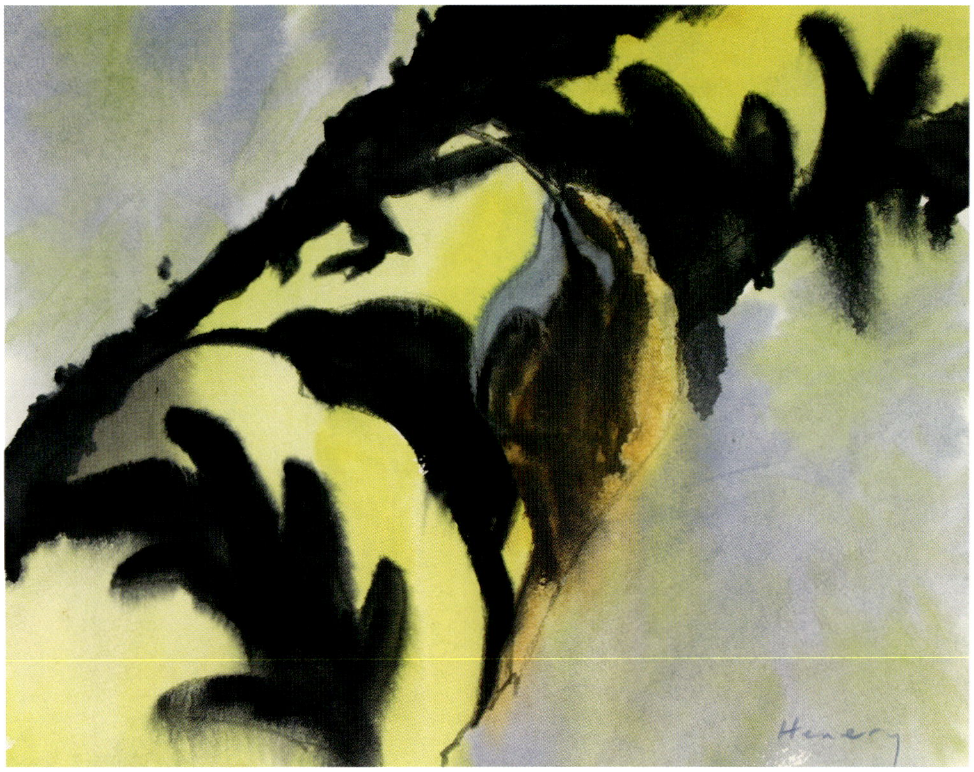

2 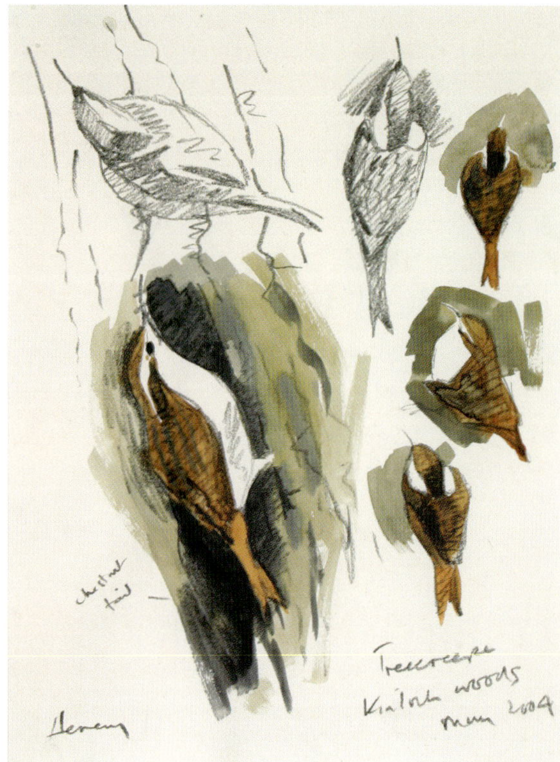

1. Paul Henery *Sunlit treecreeper*
   watercolour · 27 x 33 cm

   As the treecreepers search the trunks and branches, broken sunlight casts oak leaf shadows, against a backdrop of bluebells.

2. Paul Henery *Treecreeper sketches*
   watercolour · 29 x 21 cm

3. William Neill *Coal tit*
   watercolour · 41.5 x 51 cm

   Some of these old oaks have suffered impressive damage during their lives, huge branches broken off, no doubt in winter gales. These are sometimes still bedded in the tree, but more often, as in this case, the branch lies below and becomes the source of new life. Despite the damage there is always evidence of the ability to resurrect and grow again from the ruin. On a warm summer's day, this seemed almost as prolific as any tropical rainforest.

4. William Neill *Great spotted woodpecker*
   watercolour · 35.5 x 41 cm

   When I found this nest there was much activity, with the adults coming and going regularly. Both birds were happy once I had settled down some distance away with my telescope, and their hard work was non-stop. It was extraordinary just how much food they could find and how quickly they could find it. This was not so surprising when I returned the next day and found that the birds had flown. Fledged chicks must be quite demanding!

3 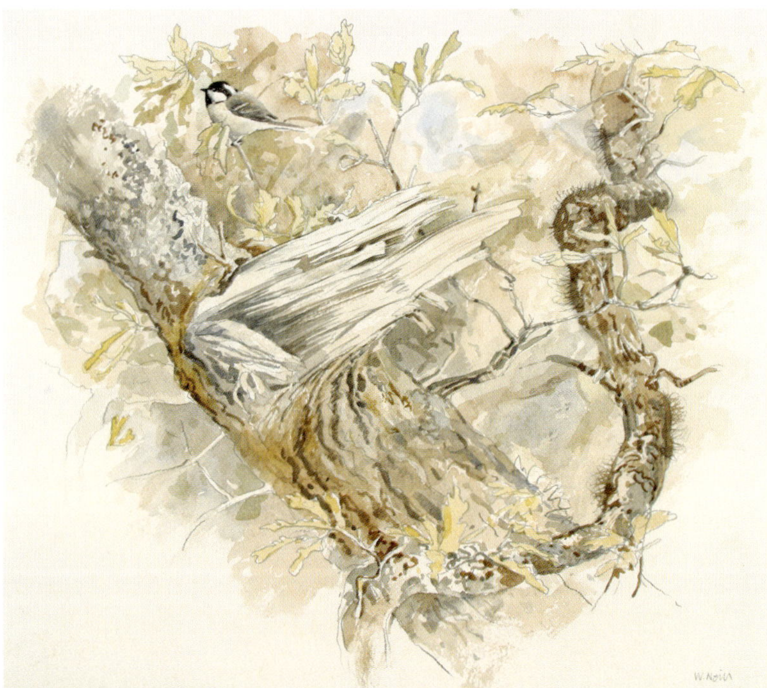

4 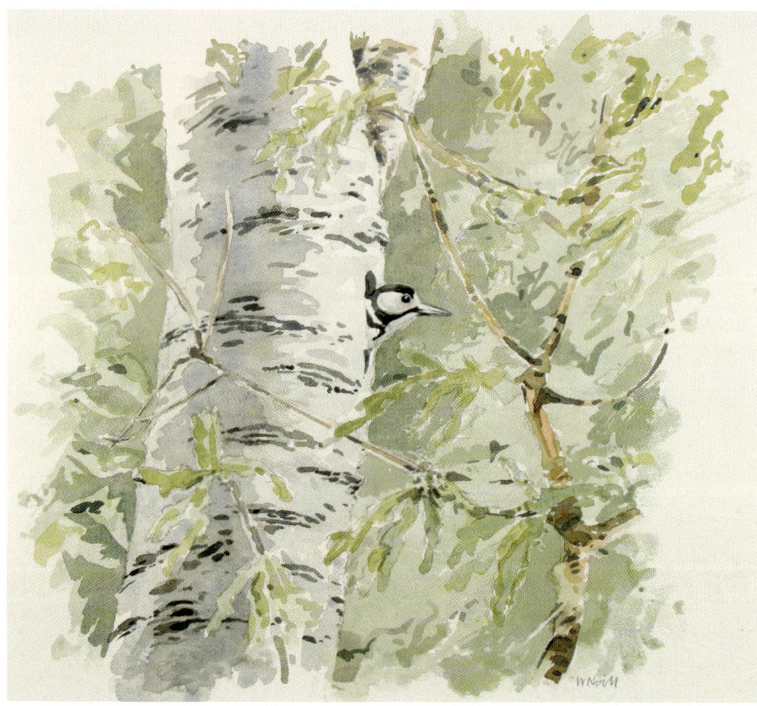

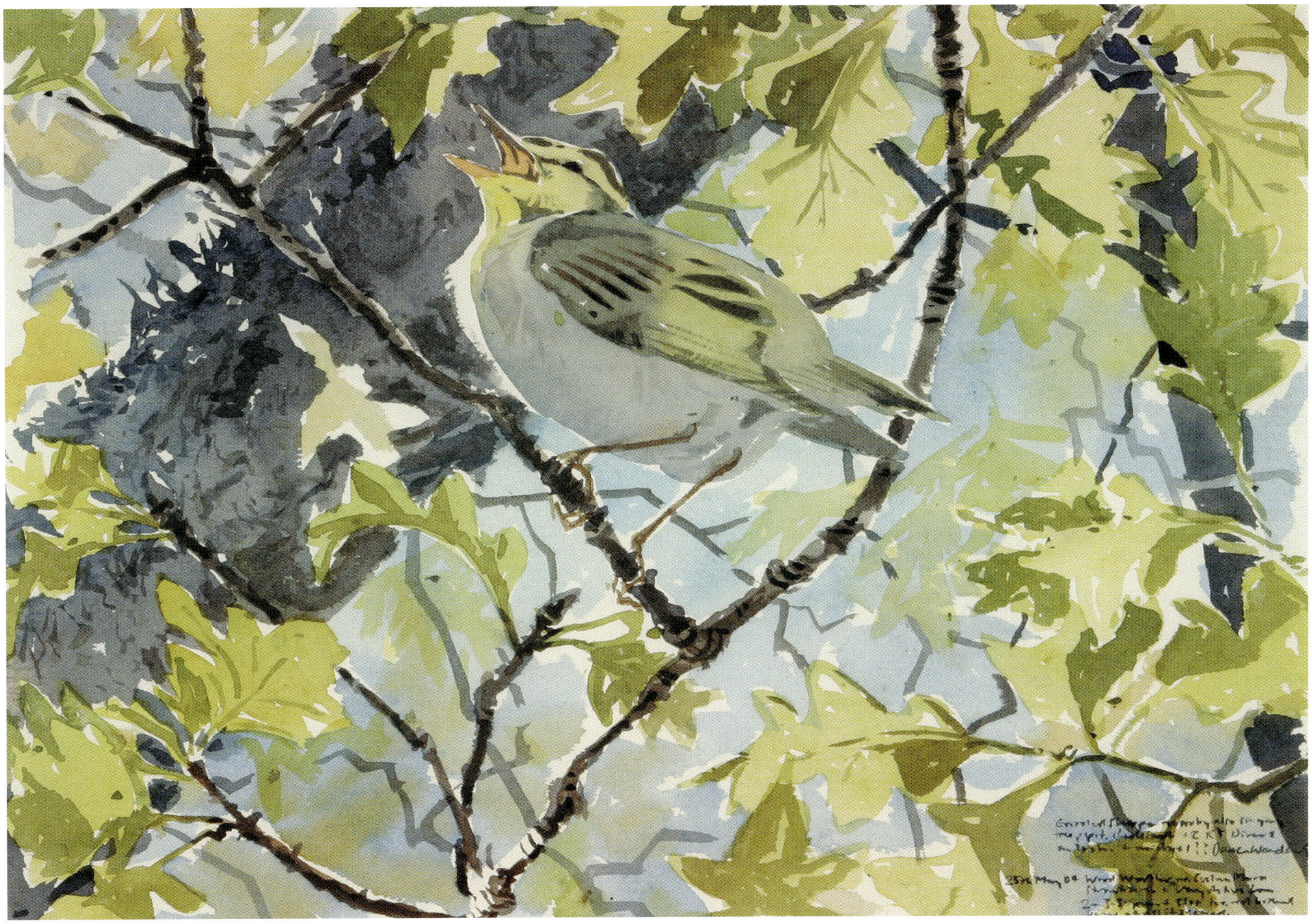

5

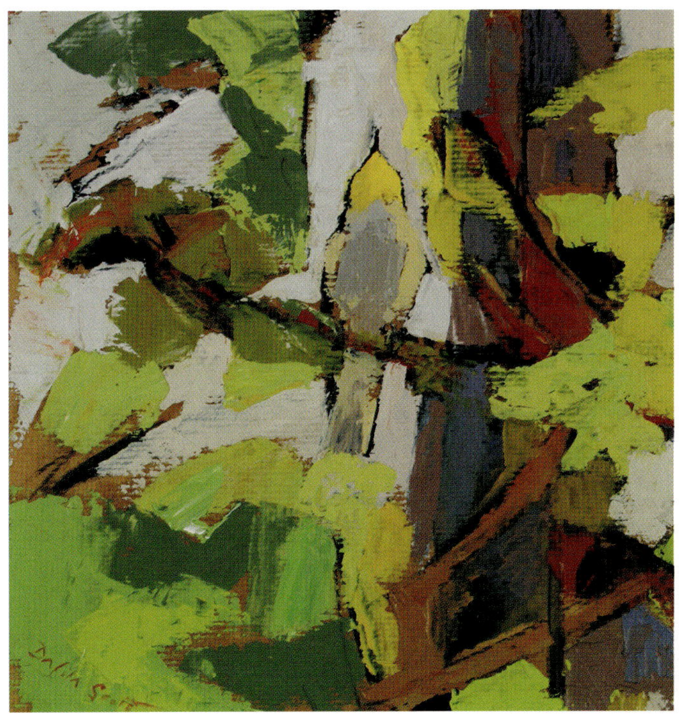

6

5. Darren Woodhead *Singing wood warbler*
watercolour · 28 x 38 cm

Lemon-yellow oakwoods hold a variety of singing birds and none more vocal than trilling wood warblers. This male held a territory in a shallow bowl on the lee side of a hill. He sang continuously until midday, with a short break before his afternoon activities began, performing song flights and vociferously proclaiming his territory.

6. Dafila Scott *Wood warbler, Ariundle*
oil on paper · 25.5 x 20.5 cm

During an afternoon and a morning at Ariundle in mid-May, it was impossible to walk in the woodland without seeing and hearing wood warblers. From underneath, the yellow throat was well set off by the early leaves of the oaks.

RAVINES

The hillsides above the oakwoods are drained by burns that, over the millennia, have cut their way into the underlying rock. The channels where they now flow are damp, dark reservoirs of humidity, where the vegetation has escaped the ravages of grazing animals and is lush even by the standards of the west coast. Where a footpath crosses a ravine by a bridge, stop to look up and down, or, even better, find a larger stream which has cut a wide gorge and walk up between the vertical faces. You enter a place that is the nearest thing in these woods to the rainforest of popular imagination.

At Resipole, I picked my way up an amazing ravine that is famous for its epiphytic growths. The ravine is deep, steep-sided and, entering it, you are cut off from the outside. It is a 'lost world', very different from the airy woods and pastures beyond the rim. Stepping gingerly over boulders and skirting still pools linked by shallow riffles and cascades, my route was sometimes barred by eroded, bare skeletons of trees that had toppled into the ravine long ago. Their gnarled successors still hung over the rim on each side, intermingled with smaller hazels and hollies. On the flat bottom of the ravine, green islands are dotted with primroses and violets, water avens and yellow pimpernel, and arrays of freshly unfurled ferns.

The biggest interest was the rock faces on each side of the ravine. There are swards of thick moss growing on the walls, wringing wet with water dripping off the tips. Liverworts cover the flat rock faces, with tiny ferns, wood rush and a few flowers nestling in cracks. Tangled ropes of honeysuckle hang down like lianas, heightening the rainforest effect. Sometimes I thought I had spotted a plant I had not seen before, only to find it was only a large, ebullient version of something common growing in a particularly favourable niche of dampness, light or fertility. In this ravine, there is one lichen, *Parmentaria chilensis*, that is found nowhere else on the mainland of Britain but is widely distributed in Central and South America. I would have liked to find it because a photograph shows that it lives up to the description of 'blackberries floating in custard'.

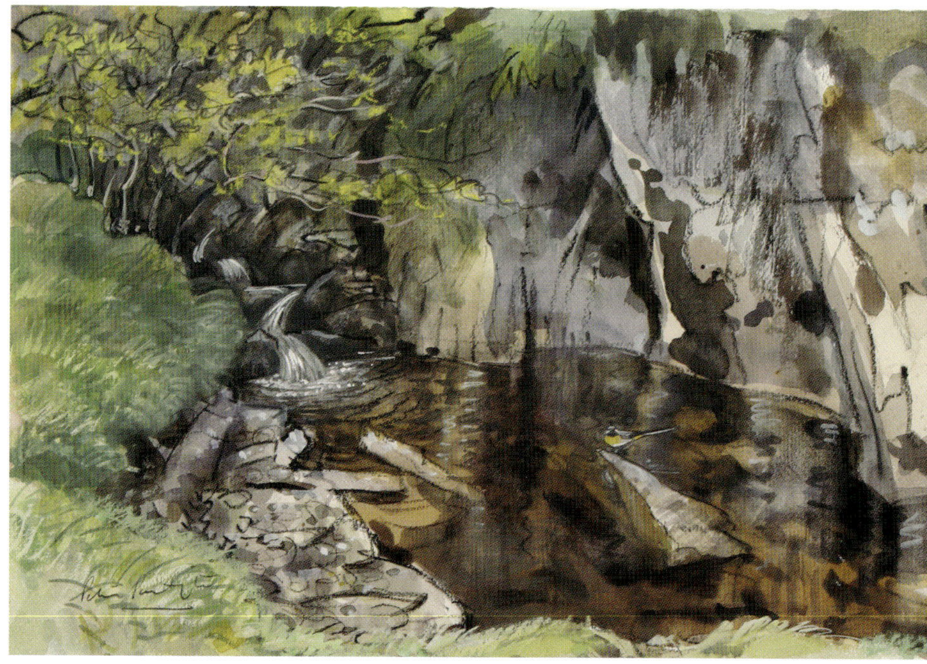

1

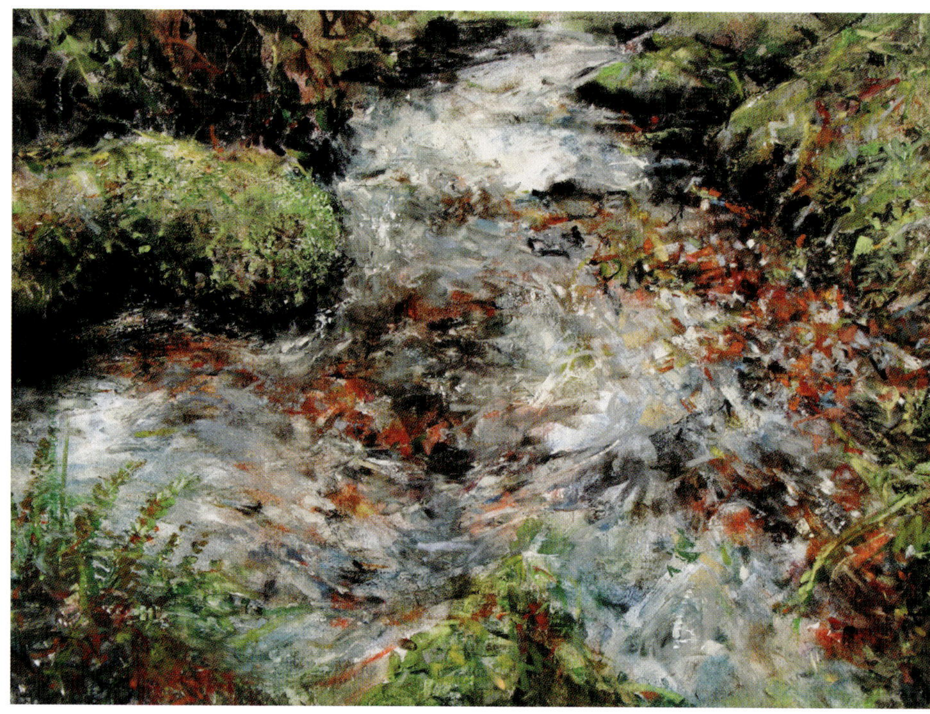

2

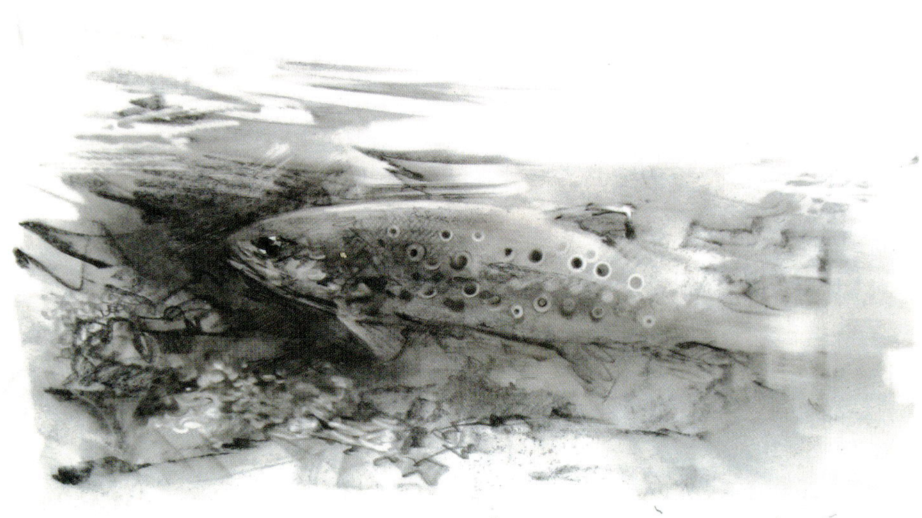

3

1. Peter Partington *The Glen Pool, Sunart*
   watercolour · 31.5 x 49 cm
2. Carl Ellis *Barnluasgan stream (field study)*
   pastel on paper · 20 x 29.5 cm

   Every bend in the stream is dressed with autumn leaves fashioned by nature... Even the trout are in this season's colours!
3. Carl Ellis *Trout*
   pencil on film · 14 x 20 cm
4. Bruce Pearson *Oakwood gorge, behind Resipole Studios, Sunart*
   mixed media · 82 x 48 cm

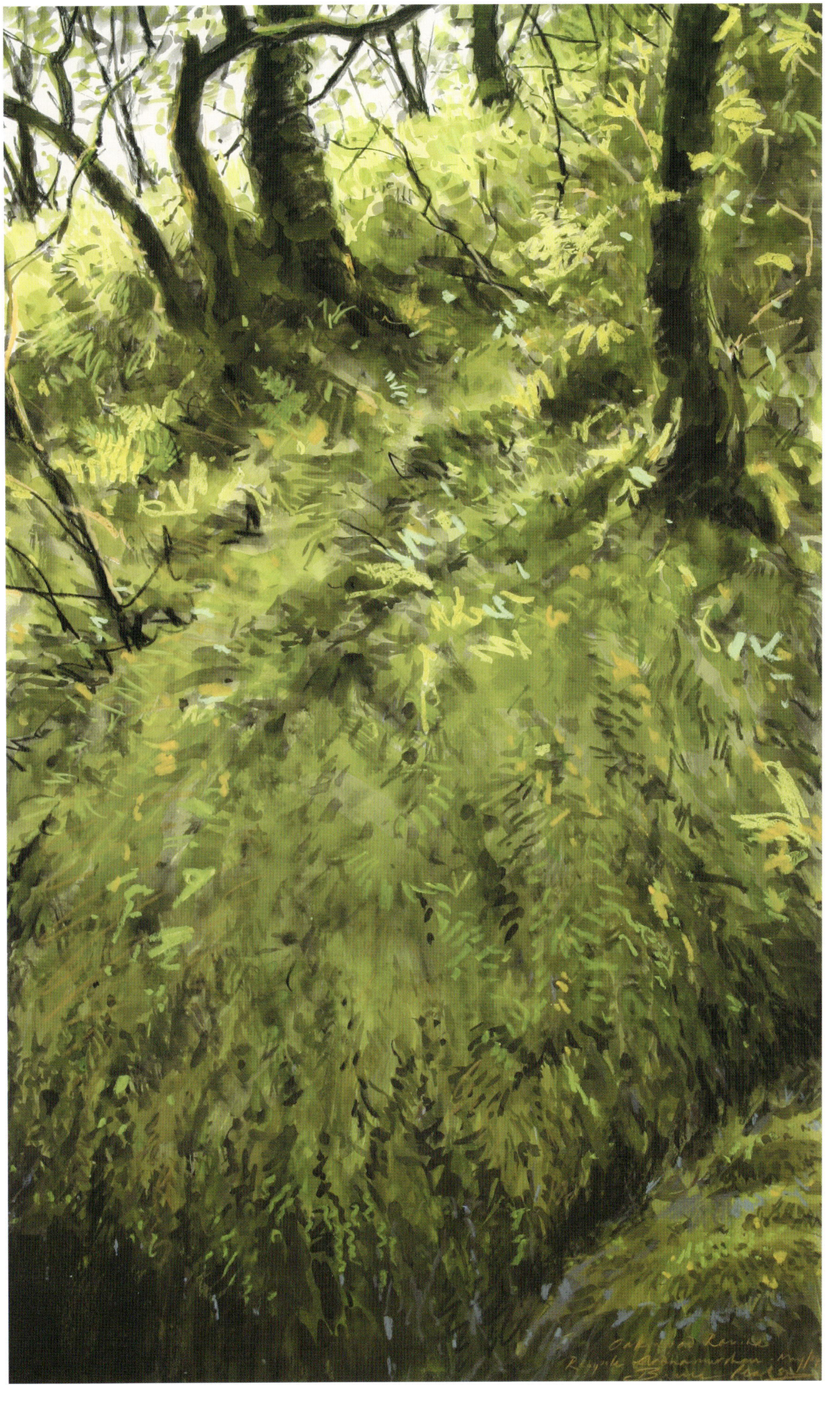

4

WOOD ANTS

Where there is plenty of sunlight, the woods swarm with wood ants. You sit down and become aware that there are ants all around you. They are running along the ground, climbing over boulders, and swarming up trees. At about 1 cm long, they are obvious once you notice them, especially when they are streaming along a trail leading to the nest. There is a two-way traffic of ants passing and repassing, heading out empty-handed and returning with prey and building materials.

Look for a gang of ants dragging a beetle, caterpillar or even a wasp to the nest. They are rather uncoordinated but each ant has an idea of which way to head and the victim moves slowly in the right direction. Some ants appear to be returning empty-handed but they probably have a stomach full of honeydew. They will have visited aphids in the tree canopy to collect the sugar-rich honeydew that the aphids secrete when concentrating and digesting the sap on which they feed.

On one hand, wood ants prey on the caterpillars of pine looper moths and other insect pests; on the other hand they protect and encourage aphids, which also cause significant damage to trees. However, it is not known whether wood ants have a significant impact on the populations of any of these pests, but they are an important link in the forest ecosystem. In their turn, they are food for squirrels, woodpeckers and other birds. They also help to disperse the seeds of common cow-wheat, violet and wood anemone.

The nest is a mound of pine needles, twigs and other bits of plant debris and, on a warm day, is a seething mass of ants. Although apparently just a 'heap', the nest has a structure. The surface is carefully tended to make a rainproof thatch and inside there are galleries where the queens (note the plural; there are several in a nest) lay their eggs and the workers tend the larvae and pupae. The interior temperature is carefully controlled by opening and closing the entrance holes. In spring, the ants behave as a living 'solar heater'. Masses of workers come out to sunbathe, and then they go back inside, where their body heat warms the galleries.

The species most likely to be found in the oakwoods is the Scottish wood ant *Formica aquilonia*, one of six British species. It is classed as 'nationally scarce' and its numbers have declined sufficiently for it to be the subject of a UK Biodiversity Action Plan (as have the other species of wood ant). It needs undisturbed, open woodland where there is plenty of sun to warm the nest, so glades and clearings are good places to find nests. Forestry practices have driven out wood ants – dense commercial forests are too shaded, and clear felling ruins their habitat – but wood ants are safe in the old oakwoods. They could be called nature's woodland managers, and Forestry Commission Scotland has issued guidelines for their protection. For instance, clumps of trees are left around nests during felling operations.

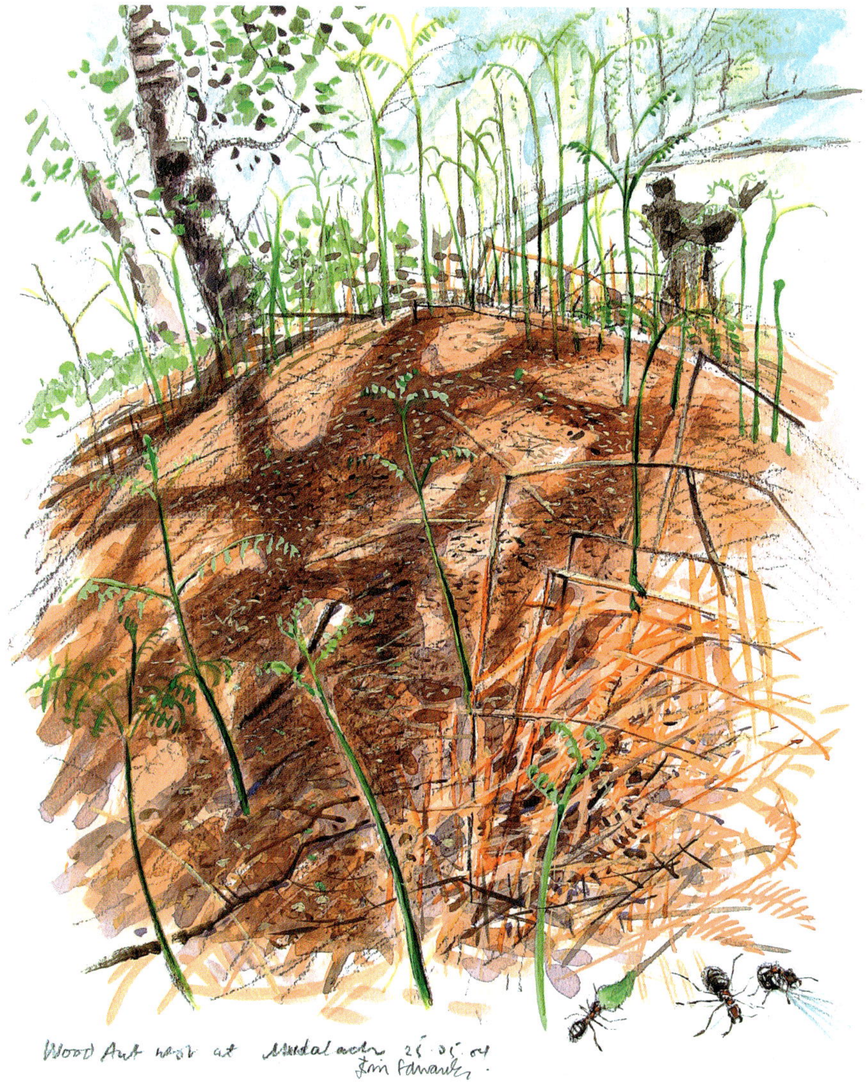

1

INSECT-EATING PLANTS

Scatterings of pretty violet-blue flowers are a common sight in glades and along the edges of tracks where the ground is wet. They could be mistaken for real violets but for the rosette of pale green, glistening leaves pressed to the ground like a many-armed starfish. They are butterwort, an insectivorous plant which flourishes in poor, acidic soil. Look closely at the leaves and you may see tiny insects stuck to the surface. Through a magnifying glass, the glistening is resolved into tiny droplets of a sticky substance. They trap small flies, ants or sometimes even a butterfly, while special glands pour out a digestive juice that pools around the insect. The proteins in its body are digested and absorbed into the plant's tissues.

Much less conspicuous, but sometimes given away by a head of tiny white flowers, is sundew, another insectivore. Its rosette of round, reddish leaves nestles among cushions of *Sphagnum* bogmosses. Each leaf is covered with a pile of sticky-tipped hairs that act as an active flypaper. As the insect attempts to pull clear of one hair, nearby hairs bend over and stick to it until its struggles are subdued. Over the next few hours the leaf curls over the insect like a grasping hand and digestion starts.

Neither butterwort nor sundew needs insects to survive but they produce more flowers and set more seed if they can catch some insects to provide nutrients that are in short supply in poor soils.

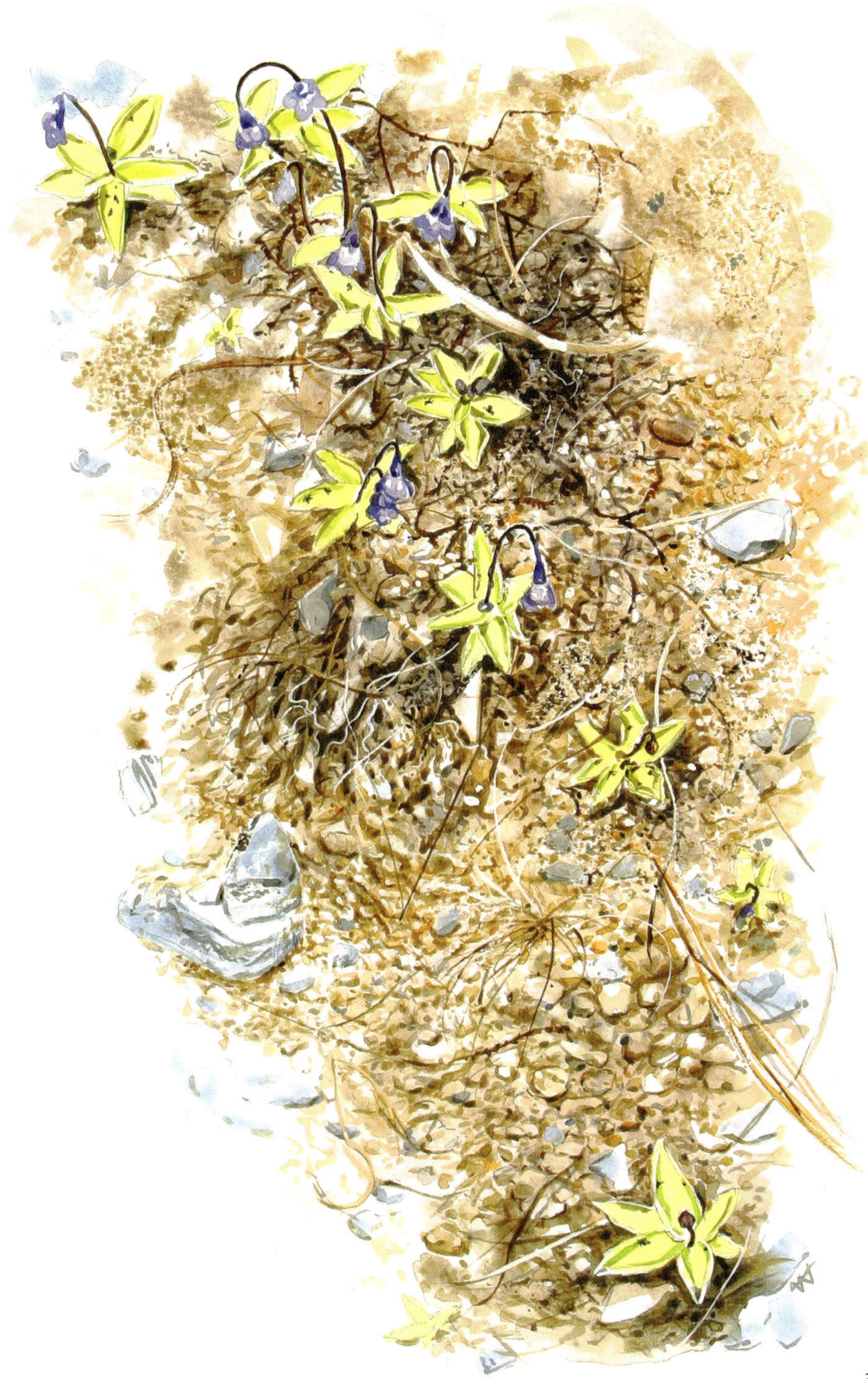

3

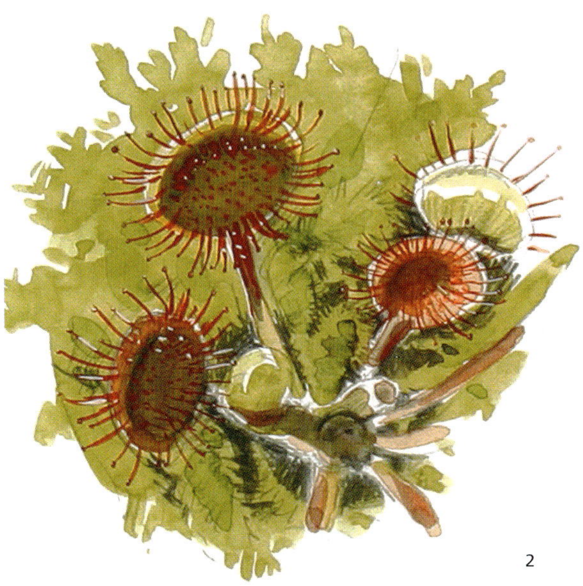

2

1. Brin Edwards *Wood ant nest at Mudalach*
   watercolour and gouache · 29 x 22 cm
2. John Cox *Sundew*
   watercolour · 8 x 8 cm
3. Brin Edwards *Butterworts*
   watercolour · 30 x 20 cm

   These small insectivorous plants grow along the wet tracks and banks at Kinloch woods. They give the impression of scattered stars against the mud and stones.

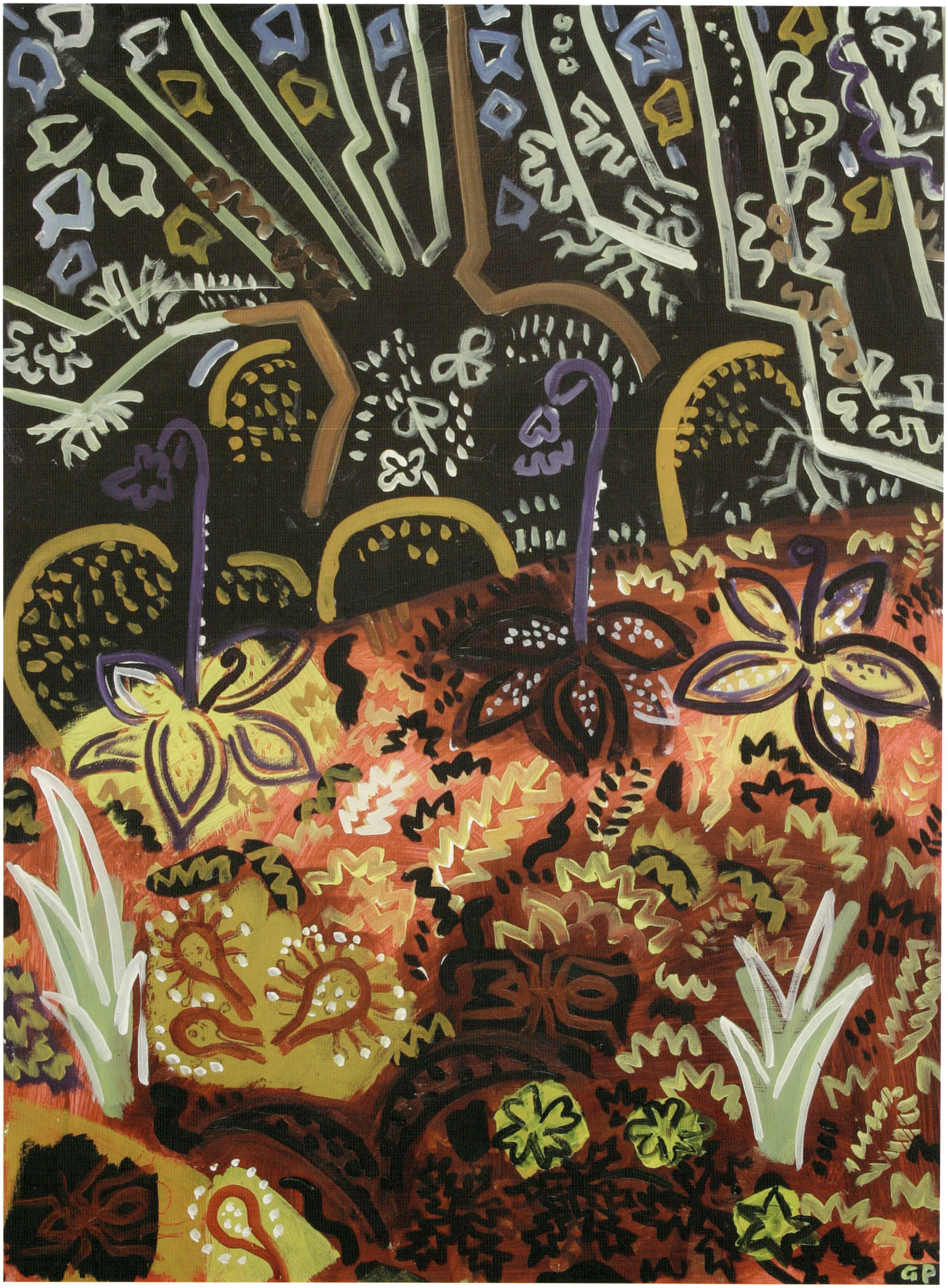

1

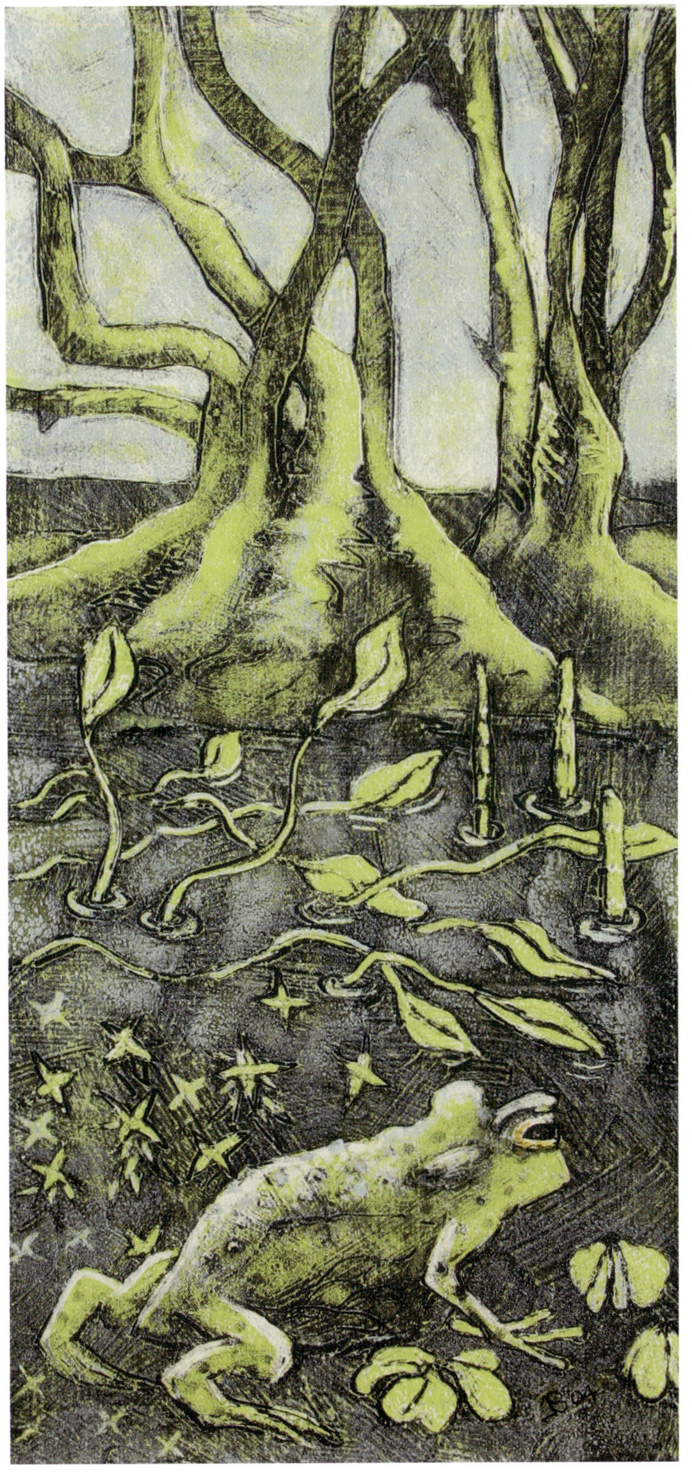

2

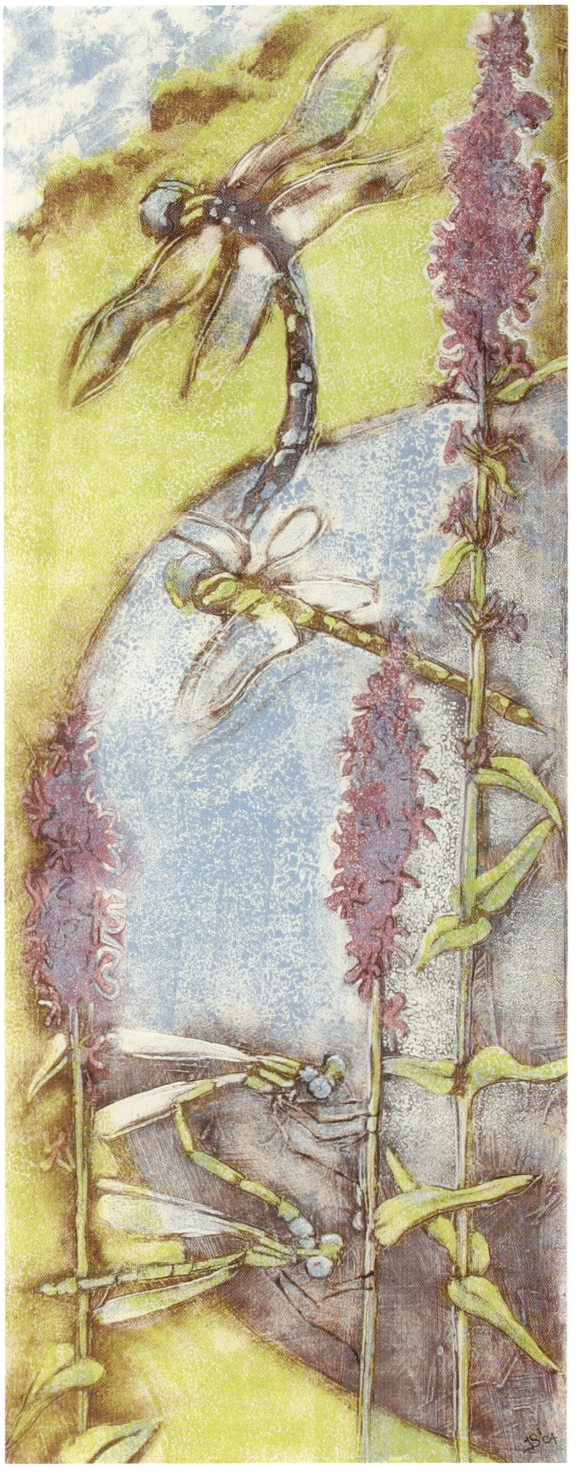

3

1. Greg Poole *Insectivorous carpet*
acrylic on paper · 75 x 55 cm

I lay out on my mac to get a close look at the plant life in one of the damp patches below the lichen-bearded hazels. Through the magnifying glass I gradually enter another world. A red ant makes its way through a forest of moss, avoiding the sticky dewdrop tentacles of the sundew. Purple butterwort flowers rise out of a whorl of their insect-trapping leaves. Dark-spotted leaves of marsh orchid and glaucous spikes of young iris. Tormentil creeps and hugs the mossy hummocks.

2. Jane Smith *First signs of spring (toad)*
monotype · 40 x 19 cm

I first sat down to draw the bog trees, with their glowing mossy coats, and after sitting still for a while, the wood resumed its life around me. I suddenly realised that a chiffchaff had been singing for a while – spring had started without me noticing. There were channels through the new, crazy-green waterweed, where an otter had been hunting. I caught a movement from the corner of my eye and realised what the otters had been after – the toads had started to emerge.

3. Jane Smith *High summer (dragonflies)*
monotype · 72 x 28 cm

I'd never tried to identify dragons and damsels before this summer, but once I'd started, it became an obsession. Looking at them closely, it's hard to imagine how something so delicate can withstand the stresses of such vigorous flight. That a larva can crawl out of the bottom of a ditch and transform itself into a highly engineered flying machine, more manoeuvrable than a helicopter and more beautiful than a jewel, is breathtaking.

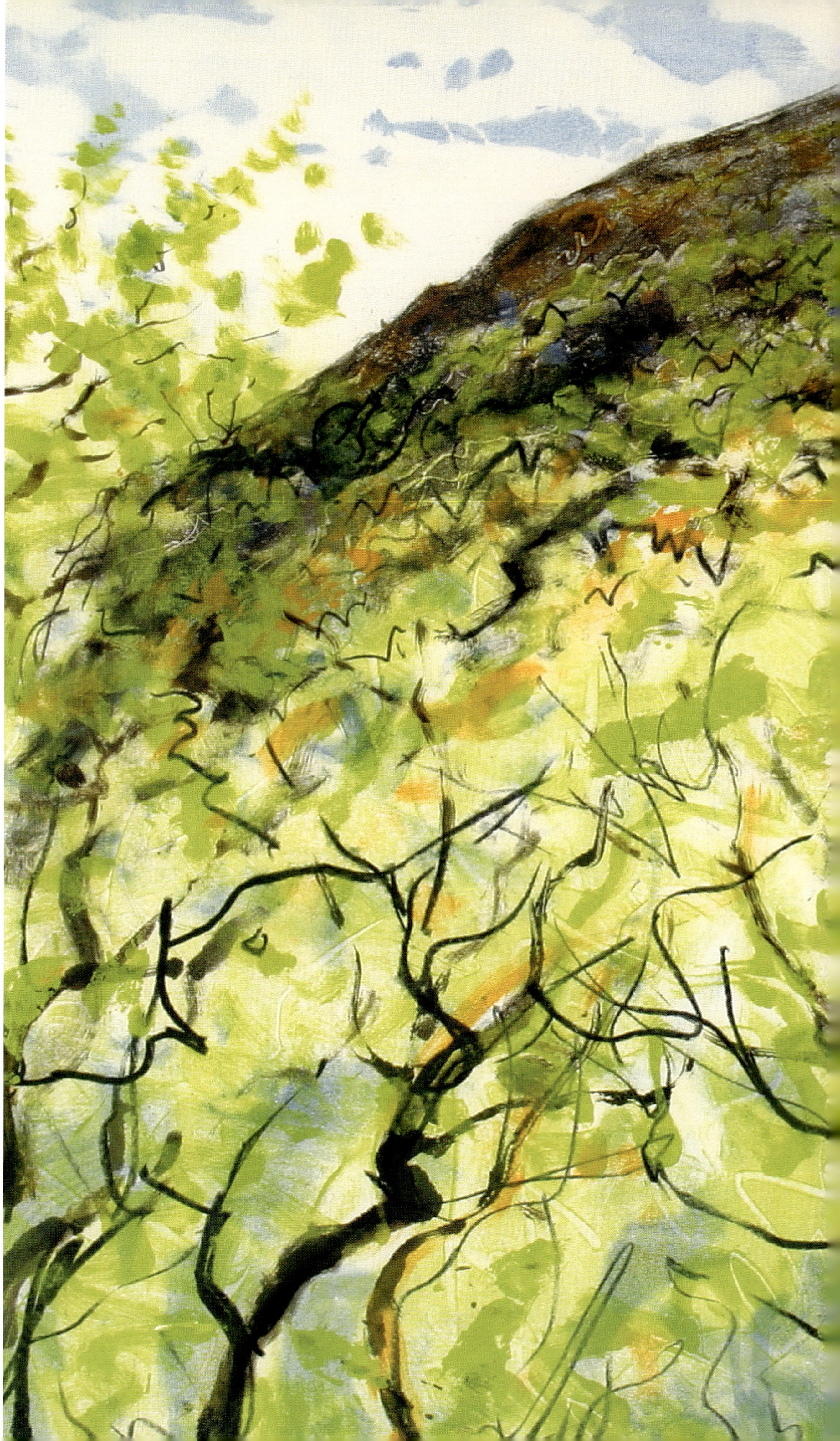

Bruce Pearson *Oakwoods, June 1st, Ardnamurchan*
monotype · 64 x 92 cm

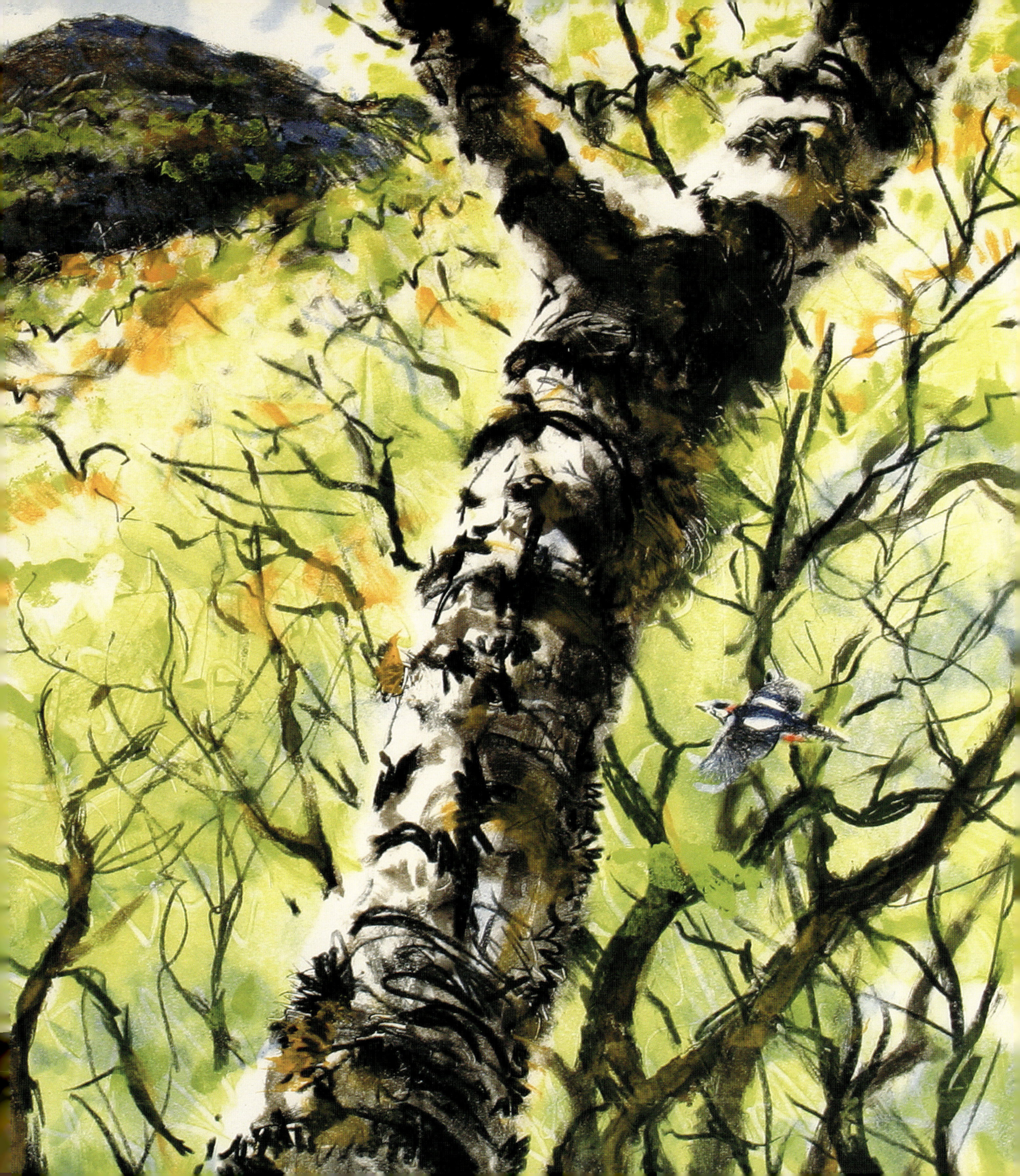

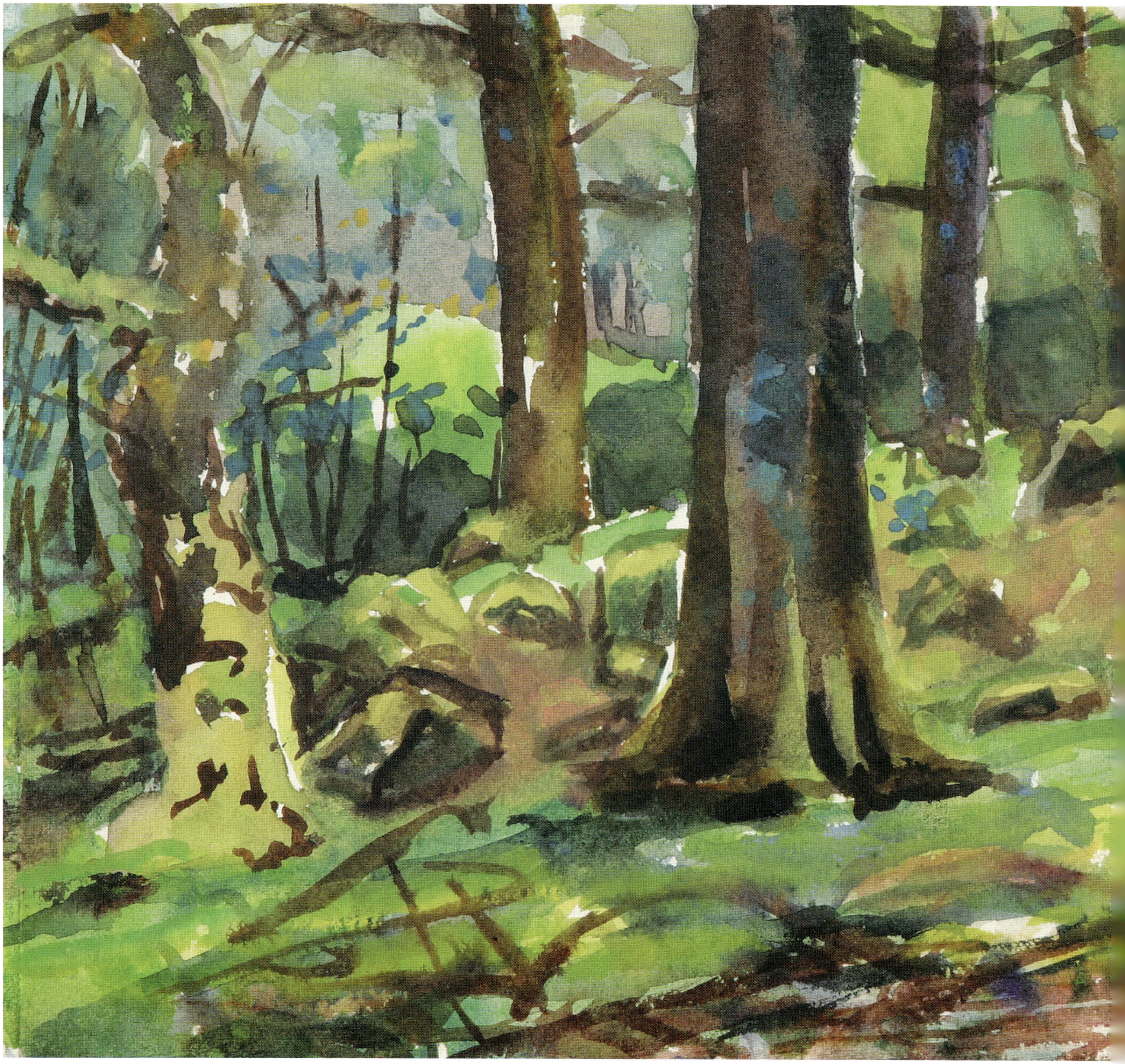

1

1. David Guy Measures *A glade in Ariundle Forest*
   watercolour · 20 x 28 cm
2. David Guy Measures *Oaks standing deep in moss*
   watercolour · 28 x 23 cm

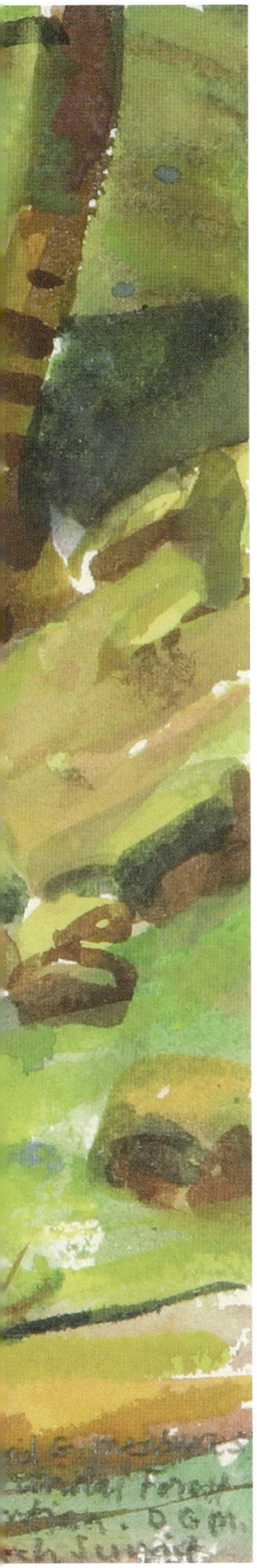

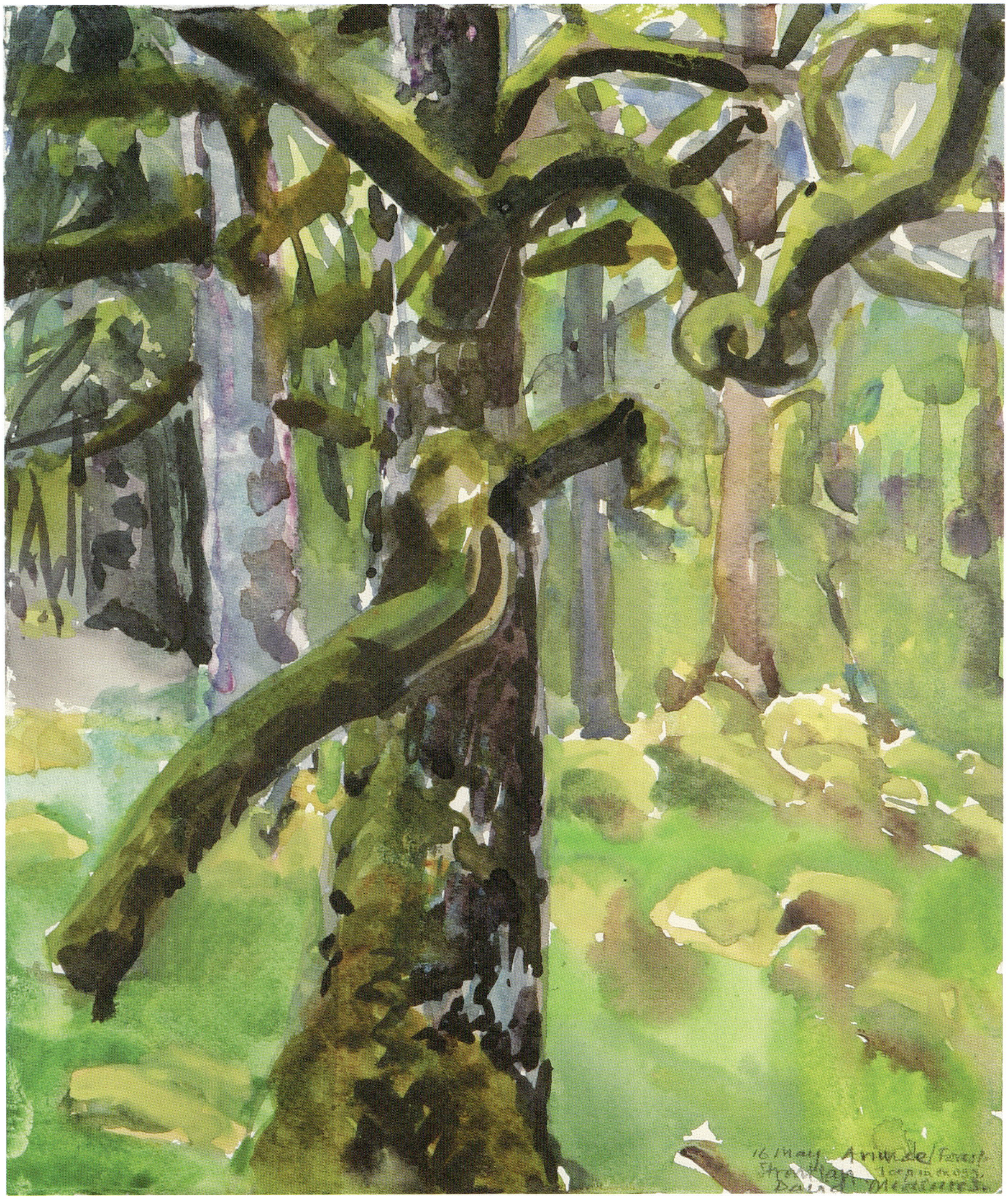

2

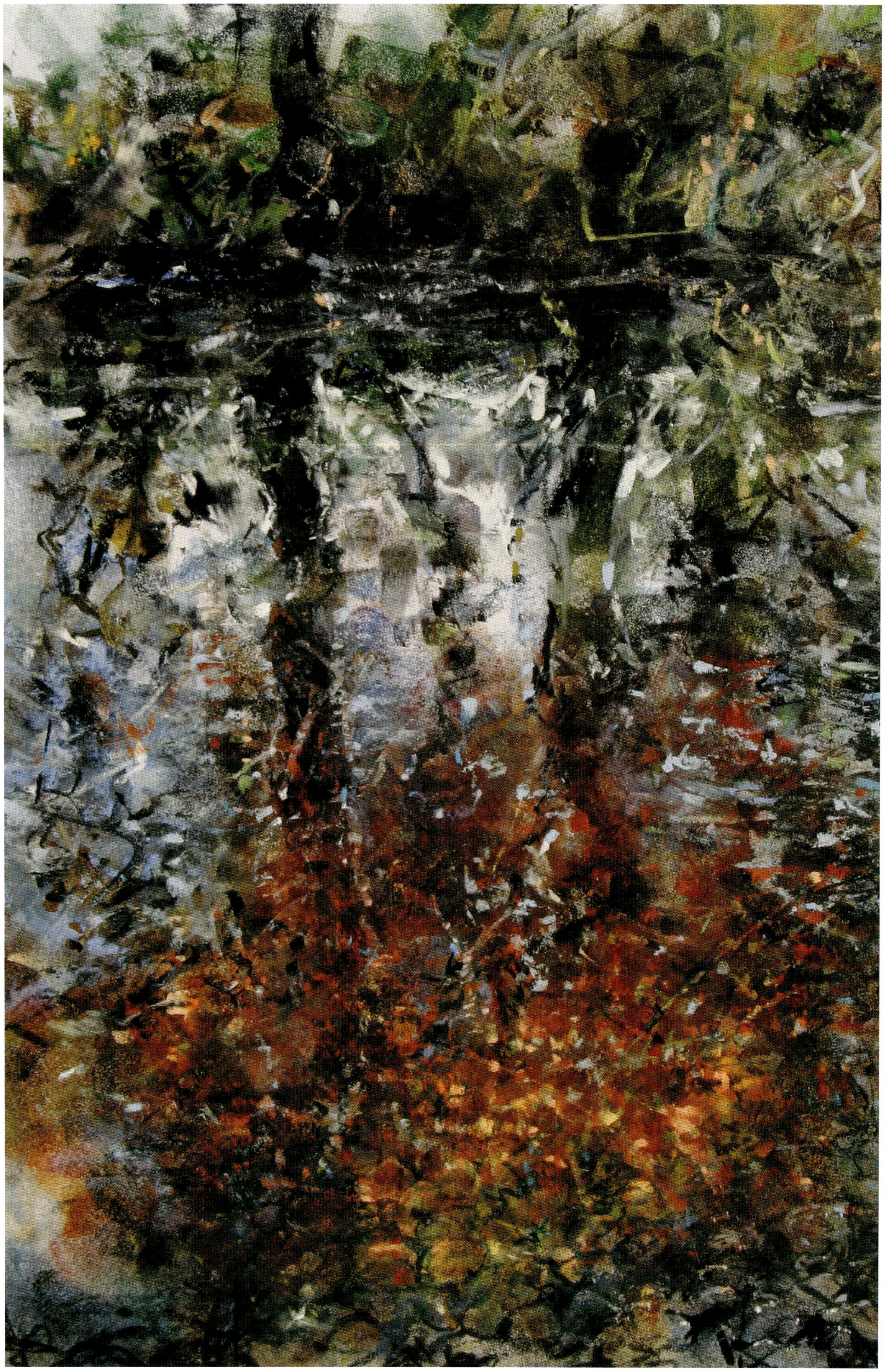

1

1. Carl Ellis *Autumn alders (field study), River Add, Knapdale*
pastel on paper · 28.5 x 18 cm

It was a chill morning – I had already been soaked up to the knees in a muddy ditch and carelessly tripped over barbed wire. As I stumbled across a shallow, pebbled stretch of the river, the thought of cleaning some of the mud off my hands seemed like a good idea. As I sat back down to drink some coffee, this unremarkable scene suddenly burst into life as the sun's first rays illuminated the river bed. Before my eyes the pebbles and stone seemed to be heated up, like molten rock!

2. Andrew Stock *Looking south across Caol Scotnish*
oil on board · 91 x 60 cm

A still, dank morning in November. Rain was threatening and I worked quickly on a watercolour sketch. There was no movement until the lone herring gull purposefully crossed my view. I painted this picture back in my studio in Dorset.

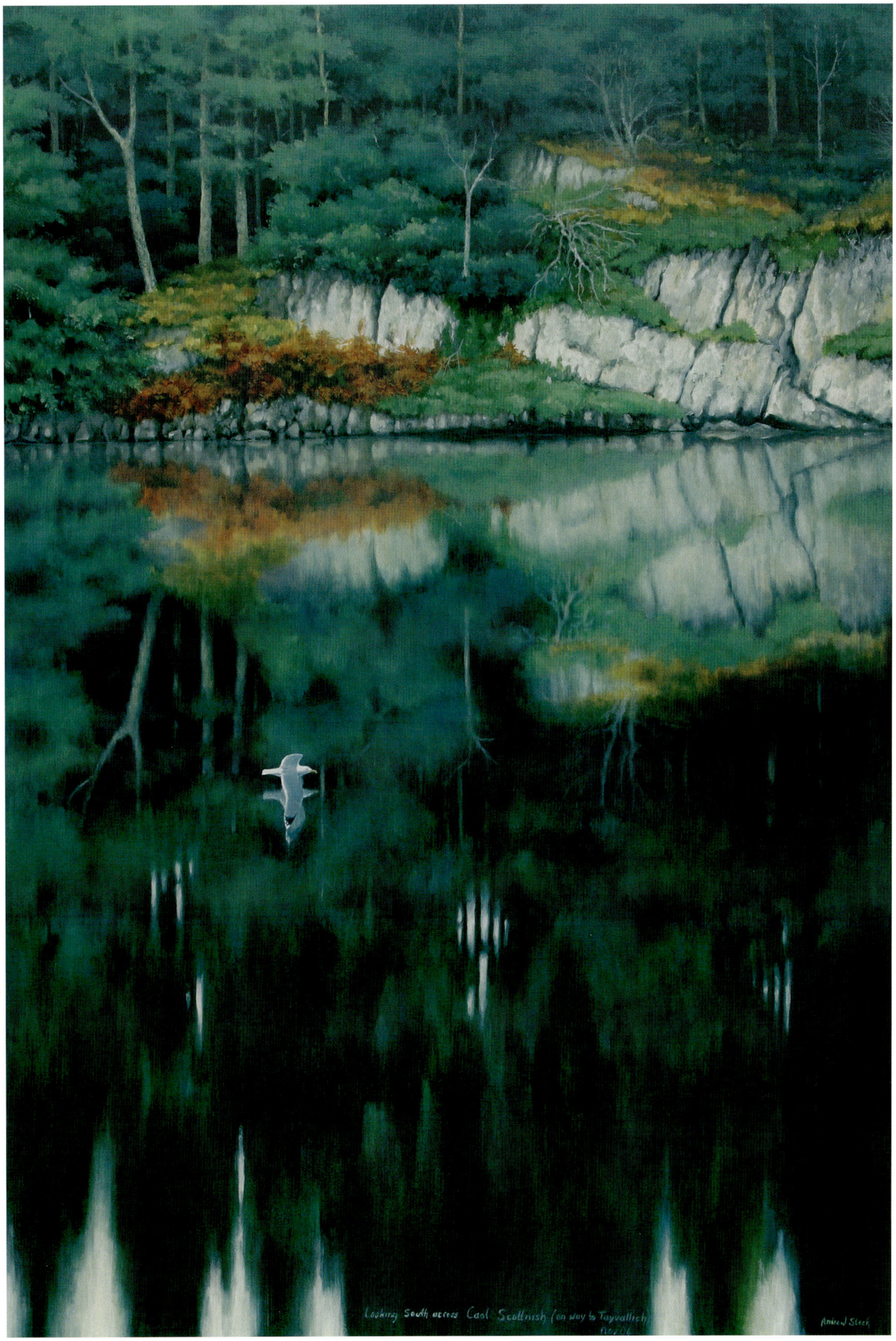
Looking South across Caol Scottnish (on way to Tayvallich)
Andrew J Stock

2

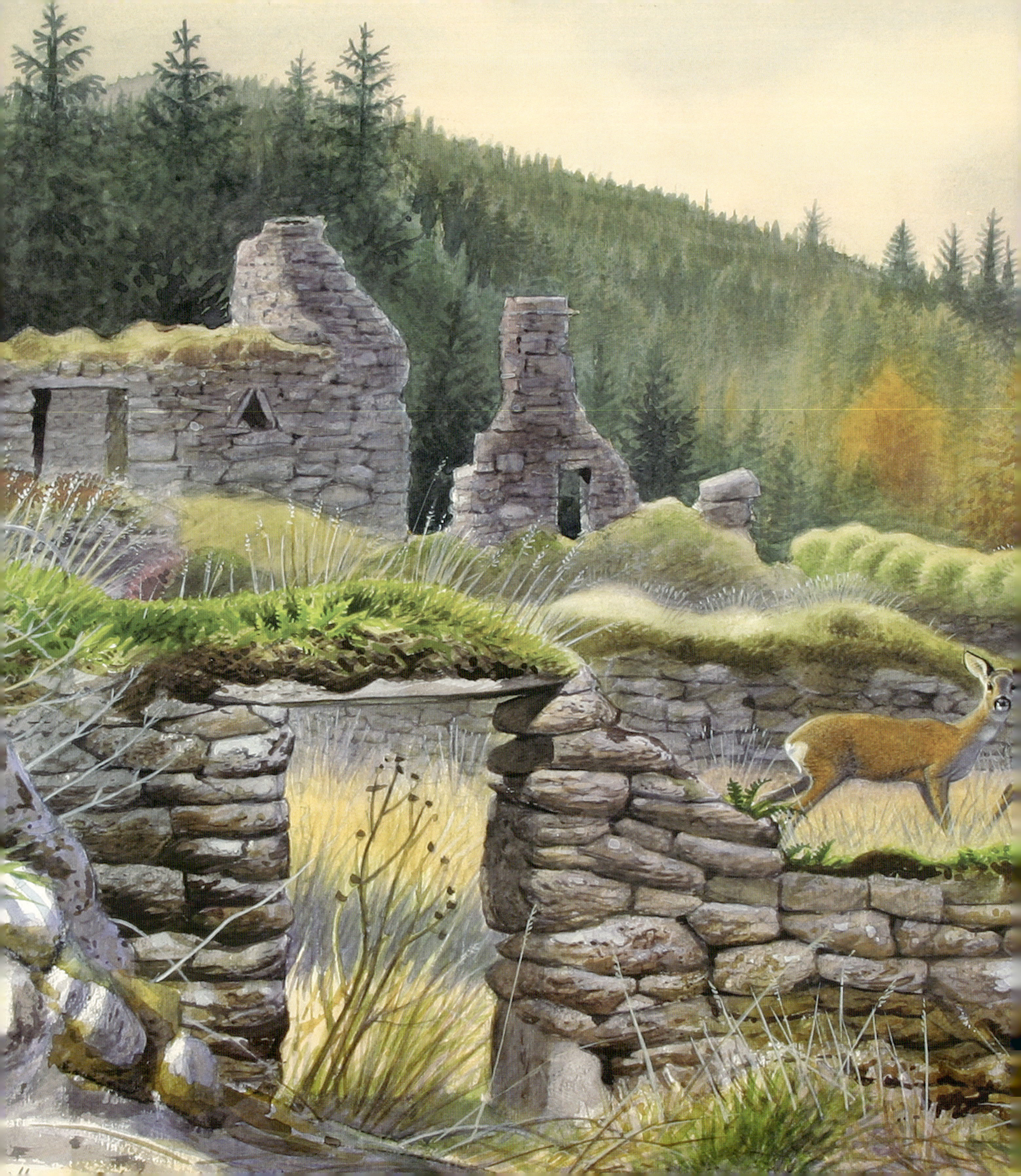

3

Living in the woods

The castles that dot the Highland landscape are part of the cultural heritage of Scotland but the woods once played as vital a role in the lives of the Highland people. Castles were the setting for the deeds of the great and powerful, as recounted in story and song; the woods were the setting of the untold, unsung, everyday lives of the common people. Both castles and woods are testaments to a vanished way of life.

Walking through these woods is like visiting one of Scotland's archaeological or historical treasures: Skara Brae or Melrose Abbey perhaps. Their ruins open a window on the past and help the imagination conjure up the continuity of past generations who lived and died there. But even with a ruin, you need a guide or guidebook to get the full meaning of what you are looking at. This is even more true of the historical significance of an oakwood, which would go unnoticed unless you are already aware that even a wood can be shaped by history.

The woods that fringe the west coast of Scotland are the remnants of a vast forest – the Wildwood or Greenwood – that once covered much of Britain. The appearance of this forest is not known but it was not a continuous mass of trees, dark under a dense canopy, as was once believed. It was more likely to have been a mosaic of open woodlands and areas of heath, moor and meadow. The open nature was maintained by large herbivorous mammals. As well as today's red and roe deer, there would have been elk, wild boar and beaver, which no longer live in Britain, and extinct tarpan (wild horse) and aurochs (wild cattle).

The composition of the woodland was dynamic, and the dominant types of trees changed as the climate got wetter or drier, colder or milder. It also depended on the soils and exposure. In the Mesolithic period, about 6,000 years ago, western Britain was, it is believed, largely an oakwood habitat, but much of the western Highlands north of Loch Linnhe was still birch and hazel. Even when the forest was at its greatest extent, about 5,000 years ago, perhaps only 85 per cent of the Highlands was covered with trees. Thereafter, the forest began to retreat. This was partly due to climate change; cool, damp summers and mild winters favoured peat bogs over woodlands.

Woods have existed on the sites of present-day woods since trees invaded the land after the last Ice Age, but no natural woodland survives and there has been none for centuries. People came spreading up from the south, hard on the heels of the trees, and their activities, barely perceptible at first, modified the structure of the woods where they dwelled. There is no truly natural woodland left in the British Isles, and ecologists refer to 'semi-natural woods', which are those that have existed, unbroken but modified by Man, since primeval times. They could be called 'cultural woods' to emphasise the importance of human influence.

Change started with the arrival of the superior Neolithic (New Stone Age) people, who brought agriculture as they spread across Europe from the Near East. A greater scale of change came with people wielding bronze implements. With the grazing of their flocks and herds and by clearing spaces for agriculture, Bronze Age people began to make a significant impact on the woods. Then,

John Davis *Roe deer in Arichonan (detail)*
watercolour · 35 x 51 cm

O CHOILLE GU BEARRADH

Coille na greine
's i éibhneach is mireagach:
a' choille ioma-ghaothach,
an leug fhaodail dhrithleannach;
coille na sgàile
's i tàmhach neo-dhribheagach:
coille a' chrònain
's oranach luinneagach.

Os cionn no coille beithe 's calltuinn,
Caoruinn agus feàrna,
'S os cionn nam bruthaichean uaine
Far a bheil an fhraineach òg
'S am fiar òg 'nam brat-làir.

WOODS OF RAASAY

The sunlit wood
joyful and sportive,
the many-winded wood,
the glittering-jewel found by chance;
the shady wood,
peaceful and unflurried,
the humming wood
of songs and ditties.

Above the wood of birch and hazel,
rowan and alder,
and above the green braes
where the young bracken
and the young grass are a carpet.

BY SORLEY MACLEAN

around 600 BC, the Celts arrived in Britain, bringing skills in working iron and ploughing heavy soil. The timing of these events, especially in the Highlands, is vague, but they left enduring evidence of their activities in the west Highlands in the form of small stone forts or duns, many of which are marked on Ordnance Survey maps. People now began restructuring the woods. As the numbers of people and their domestic animals rose, the forest and the wild mammals went into retreat.

We know tantalisingly little of the lives of the early inhabitants of these woods, the significance of trees in their imagination and beliefs, or the practical uses they made of them. Much of our knowledge of the past history of the oakwoods is a matter of conjecture. We can only infer that the inhabitants of the west coast who were descended from Irish Celts and Scandinavian Vikings would have had an attitude towards the woods similar to that of their ancestors. The Celts had an affinity for trees, which was, and still is, expressed in their poetry. A hint of the importance of trees is given by Martin Martin, who wrote one of the first accounts of western Scotland in the late 17th century. He described a small wood in the north of Skye which 'none of the natives dare venture to cut the least branch of it, for fear of some signal judgement to follow upon it'. This suggests a reverence for trees that echoes the importance of sacred groves in early Celtic society.

There is no better place to get a feel of the conti-

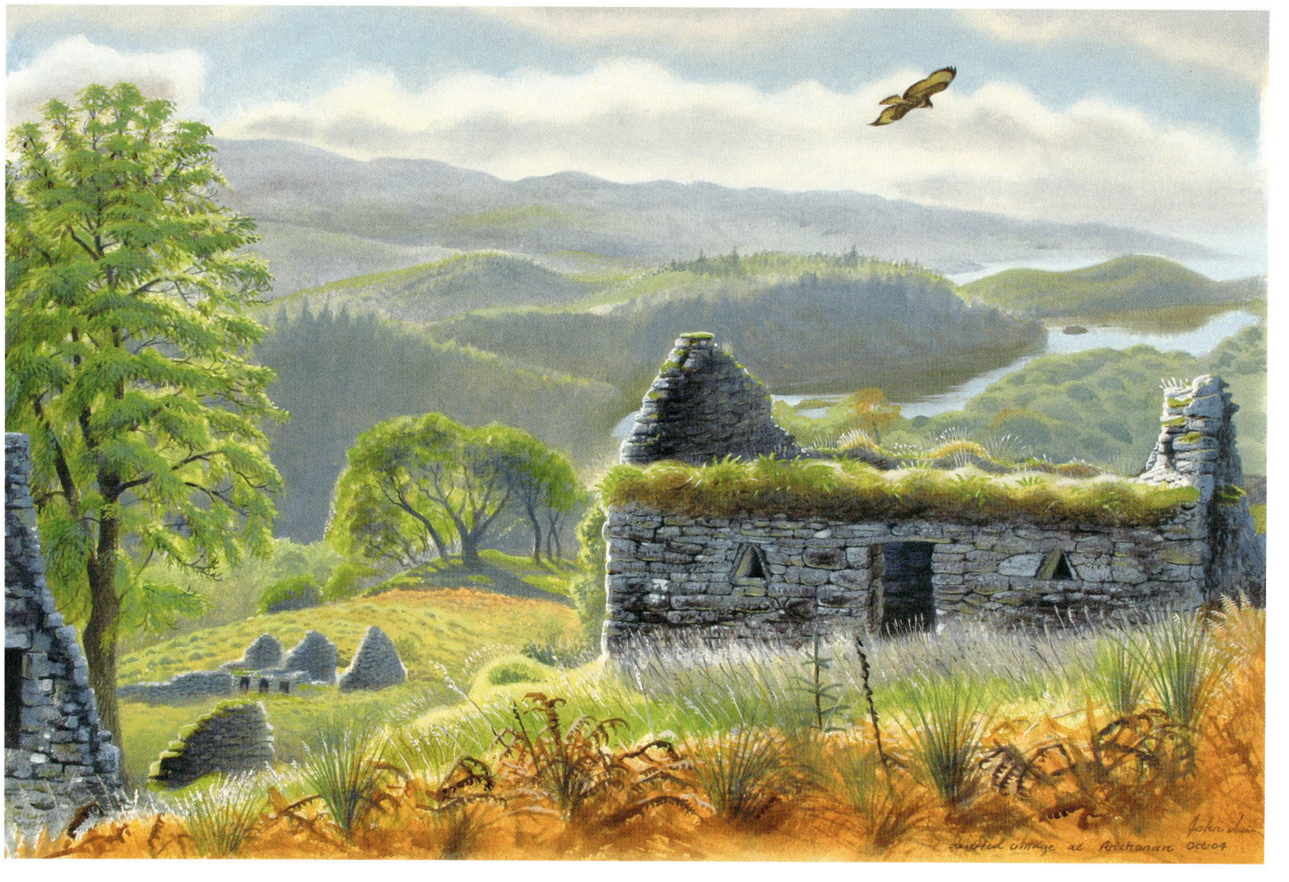

nuity of human occupation of the oakwoods than Leitir Fura, an abandoned settlement in the Kinloch Hills of Skye. (It is also easy to reach along a path from a car park.) Even the name is evocative of the past. It is believed to be derived from *Fura Mhór* – a great oak tree which had shade for forty to fifty cattle on a hot summer's day – whose fate is an indication of the importance of trees in local life. There is a tradition that the family of Iain mac Mhaol-Chaluim (Malcolm) was evicted after his children lit a fire near the tree and burned it down. The settlement was abandoned in about 1790, when the inhabitants were removed during the infamous Clearances, but its occupation predates history. In 1996, a cave was found at the foot of the low cliff just behind the shore below Leitir Fura. Remains of domestic utensils on the floor showed that it had been occupied as a dwelling in the first half of the 19th century, but excavation revealed a history of near-continuous occupation from the 2nd century BC to the 6th century AD. Throughout this long span of time, the trees of Leitir Fura would have been a resource that was essential for the survival of the inhabitants. Then, through the 18th and 19th centuries, the Macdonalds of Sleat attempted to exploit the woods commercially to prop up shaky finances.

There is very little information about the relationship between trees and people in the Highlands before the 18th century. Indeed, even then the Highlands were Terra Incognita to the Lowland Scots. As Dr Johnson wrote of his travels through the Highlands in 1773, 'To the southern inhabitants of Scotland, the state of the mountains (Highlands) and the islands is equally unknown with that of Borneo or Sumatra. Of both they have only heard a little, and guess the rest.' Guesswork is now being supported by firmer evidence from archaeology and by what we know of life in similar situations elsewhere, but conjecture still colours ideas of how this tree-orientated culture operated.

A picture emerges of small, tight-knit communities living close to nature at little more than subsistence level. People were part of the ecosystem and their survival depended on the integrity of the ecosystem, just as is the case with any animal. Marion Campbell of Kilberry wrote, 'In the Gaeltacht (Gaelic-speaking region) the land owns the people, not the other way round.'

The importance of woods in the economy of these people is difficult to imagine as we walk around empty woods where the sound of a single chainsaw is an intrusion. The Highlands had a far higher population than now. (In the Sleat Peninsula of Skye, the population in 1841 was 2,706; in 1971 it was only 452, although the downward trend has since been reversed.) At times the woods would have been as busy as a high street, with scores of local people, old and young, at work. To get an idea of life in a tree-based culture, read Thomas Hardy's book *The Woodlanders*, set in Wessex at the other end of Britain. In these days of metal and plastic, when even expensive possessions are quickly discarded, it is not easy to appreciate how people lived when almost their only source of raw materials was what grew around them. If they wanted a length of rope, they made it out of birch twigs or heather. Anything that could not be simply made from whatever materials could be found nearby was virtually an heirloom, but of practical rather than sentimental value.

There are so few written records about the use of woodland in the western Highlands before the 17th and 18th centuries that the subject is full of conjecture and controversy. No doubt there was no universal legal or customary regulation, but the few records that do exist show that woods belonged to landowners and that there was no 'right of common' to give the local population access to woods, as there was in England. There were laws to protect woods from exploitation and destruction, or to restrict and manage their use. However, in practice,

John Davis *Arichonan village*
acrylics · 46 x 66 cm

A bright day in a beautiful place. Perhaps a feeling of guilt at enjoying painting 'pretty pictures' in a spot that has seen its tenants evicted, but while they lived here it must have been a special site to them.

the niceties of law would not always have penetrated the Highlands, and supervision in these remote places would have been weak. There would have been unwritten arrangements with landowners for tenants to have privileges of wood use, and we can imagine there would have been local customs governing the privileges, much as the custom of souming governed the allocation of communal grazing. Parts of the woods were set aside for local use; landowners would reserve valuable oaks for themselves, while their tenants could use 'black wood' or 'barren timber', such as birch, alder and hazel, for their own purposes.

Yet, even without the final breaking of the clans at Culloden and its aftermath, daily life had been changing. The growing human population and a change towards a market economy were putting pressure on the woods. Although predominantly a subsistence economy, the Highlands had an income from traditional 'black' cattle. Herds were despatched annually to southern markets along a network of drove roads. In the mid-18th century William Pennant recorded that 3,000 head of cattle were sent annually from Lochaber alone. It is still possible to walk along the drove road from Kinloch to Kylerhea, where cattle had to swim the 500 metres of sea across the Kyle of Lochalsh to the mainland opposite. They were driven to markets as far away as southern England, where John Clare, the Northamptonshire poet, was struck by the outlandish appearance of:

Men so oddly clad
In petticoats of banded plaid

The accounts of the Macdonald estates in Sleat on Skye date from 1720. At this point, and presumably for many years earlier, the management of the woods was controlled by the laird and managed by his tacksmen and paid woodkeepers. No doubt practices varied from estate to estate, depending on the relationship between laird and tenants. Permission was needed to fell timber and take wood, and there are records of prosecutions for taking timber and removing bark for tanning. One man was evicted for taking timber to repair his house without permission and two women were prosecuted for collecting sticks.

Yet there are also records that show that parts of the wood were set aside for 'common country uses', as Dr Johnson put it. There still needed to be arrangements for grazing in the woods, because their shelter was vital for horses, cattle and sheep in winter, but goats, which could climb trees and eat the bark, were often banned. Around 1770, James Riddell of Ardnamurchan fined tenants the huge sum of £5 for each goat found on their land. This must have caused real hardship because goats were the mainstay of the common people's economy. Doctor Johnson found a family living by Loch Ness who were entirely dependent on their sixty goats. They were allowed to keep them in return for acting as woodkeepers. Presumably duties included controlling their own flock!

It seems that during this period a conflict was developing between the landlords, who wanted to reserve the woods to make a profit for supporting a lavish lifestyle, and the local people, who regarded taking timber for their own use as an age-old right, at least in practice. A Highland proverb stated that three things in life were free: 'A fish in the stream, a deer on the hill and a tree in the wood.' The Highland people were increasingly finding that this was not the case.

In 1763, Sir James Macdonald wanted to enclose the oakwoods in Sleat because they were 'entirely consumed by the cattle'. His object was the commercial development of the woods. However, rather than harvesting and selling wood products in an open market, landlords could make an easier profit by selling the timber or leasing the woods to entrepreneurs, who would then have the chore of extracting the raw material.

David Bennett *Ouzel and goat*
ink and watercolour · 43 x 57 cm

Hidden in the dense heather and bracken on the edge of birch and oak scrub, I noticed a small group of feral goats. My attention was initially drawn to the area by an ouzel calling, a familiar sound from my home in Yorkshire. Ouzels can be very difficult to locate once breeding has started, and judging by the beak full of succulent morsels, this male had started in earnest.

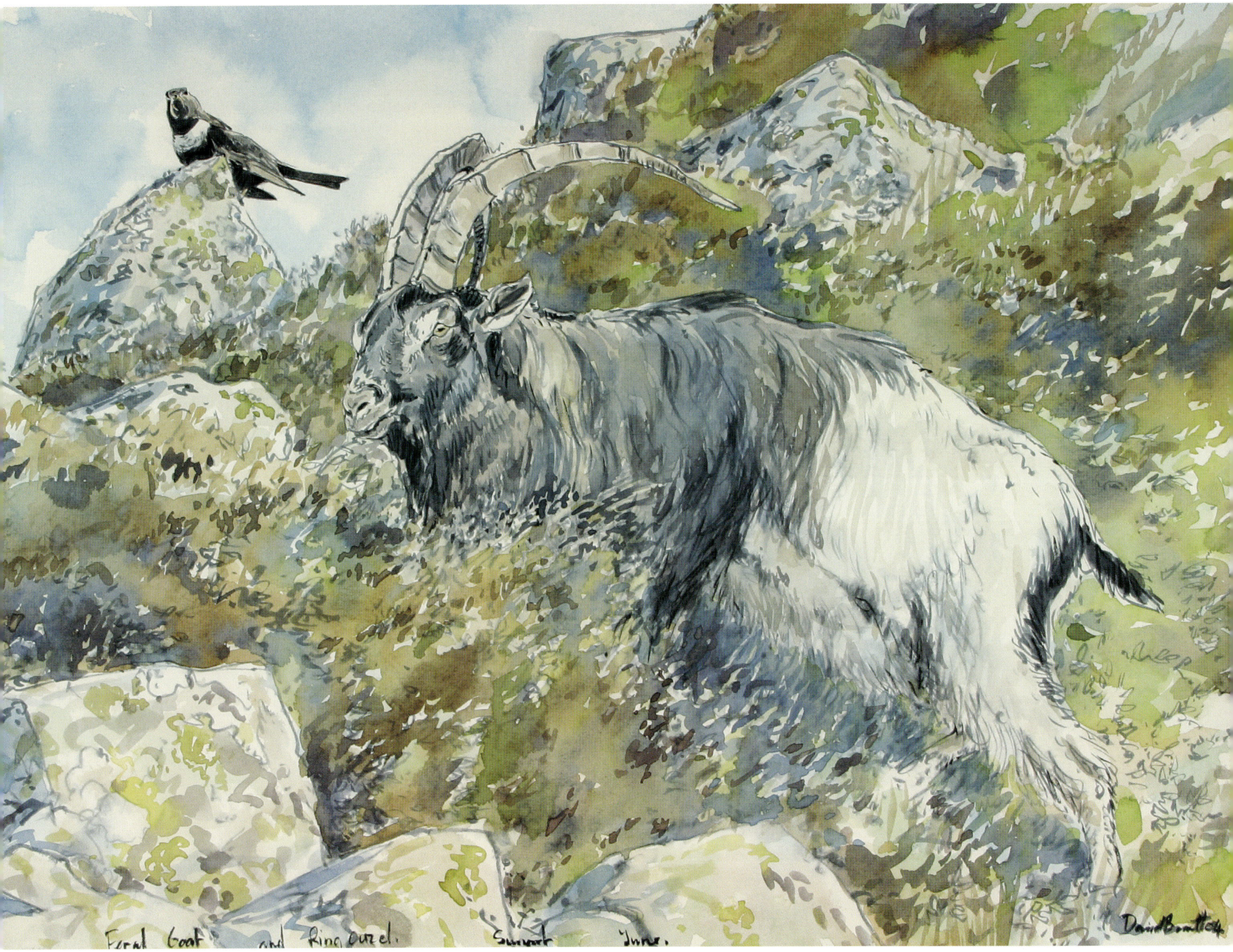
Feral Goat and Ring Ouzel.
Summit June.

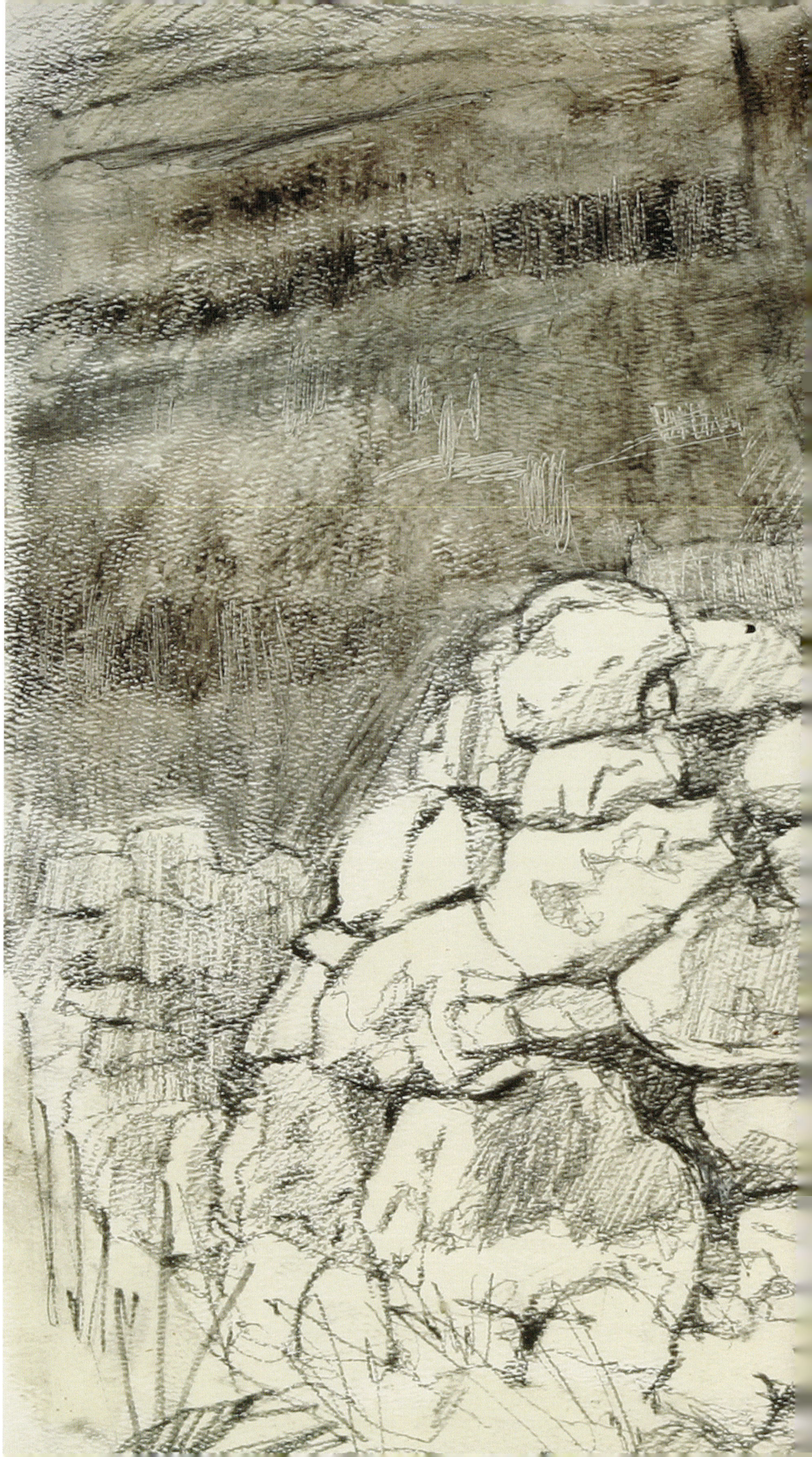

Pascale Rentsch *Ruined village of Inniemor, Morvern*
oilbar, conté and pencil · 38 x 55 cms

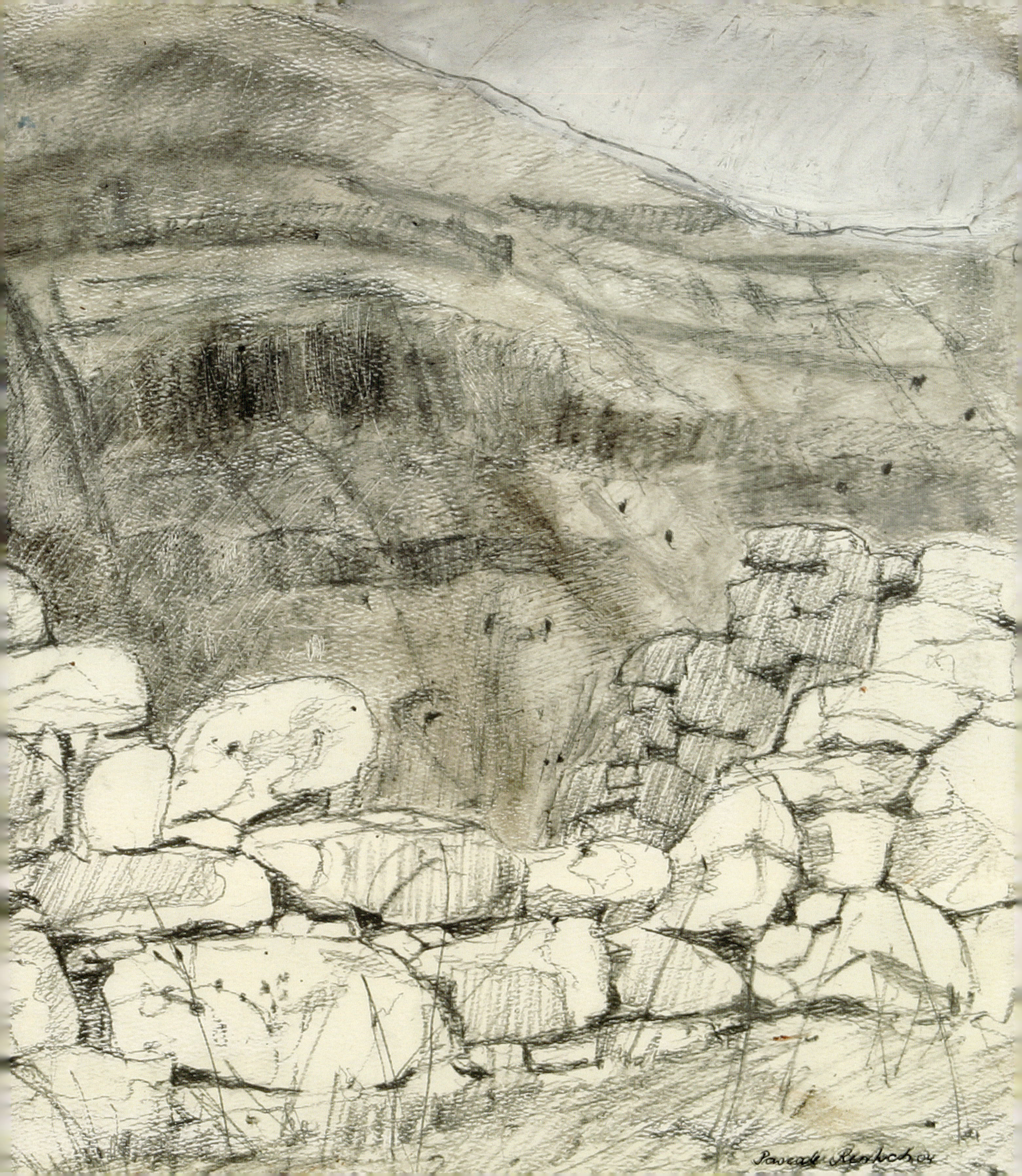

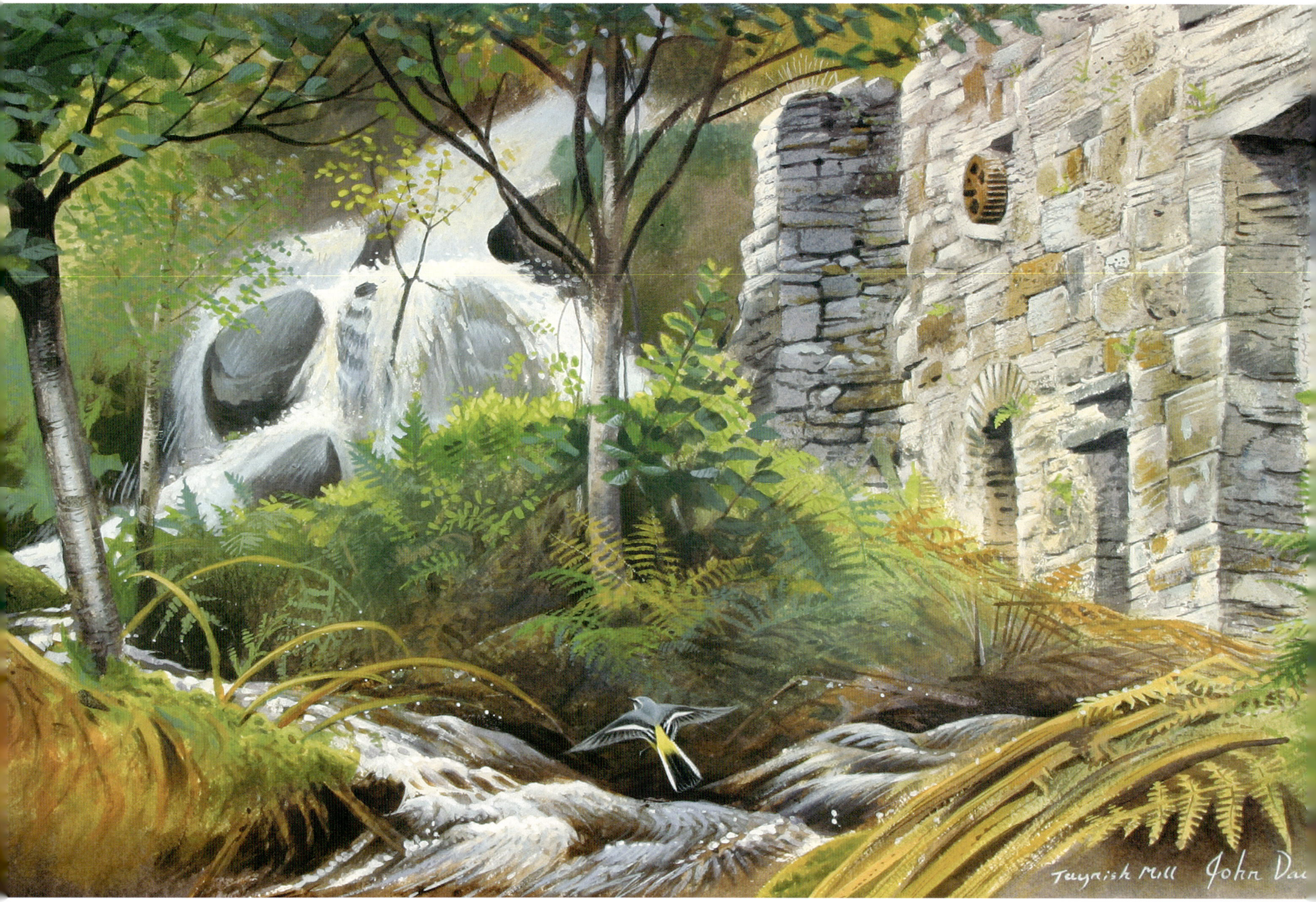

1

1. John Davis *Taynish Mill*
acrylics · 35.5 x 52 cm

A wet day, spent painting under a fishing umbrella (like several other artists!). At one point the wind blew the umbrella into the stream – causing much cursing and a bruised shin.

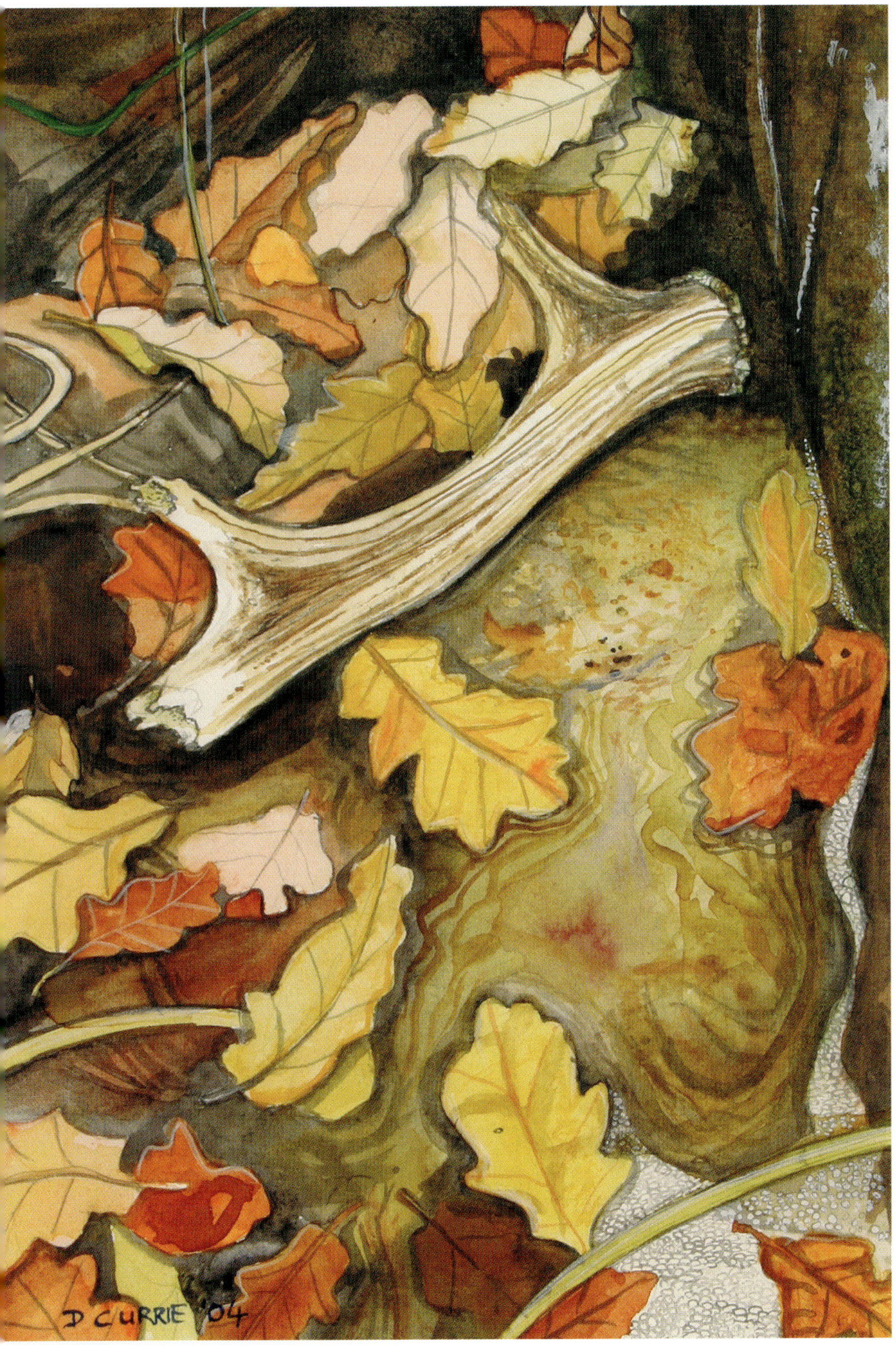

2

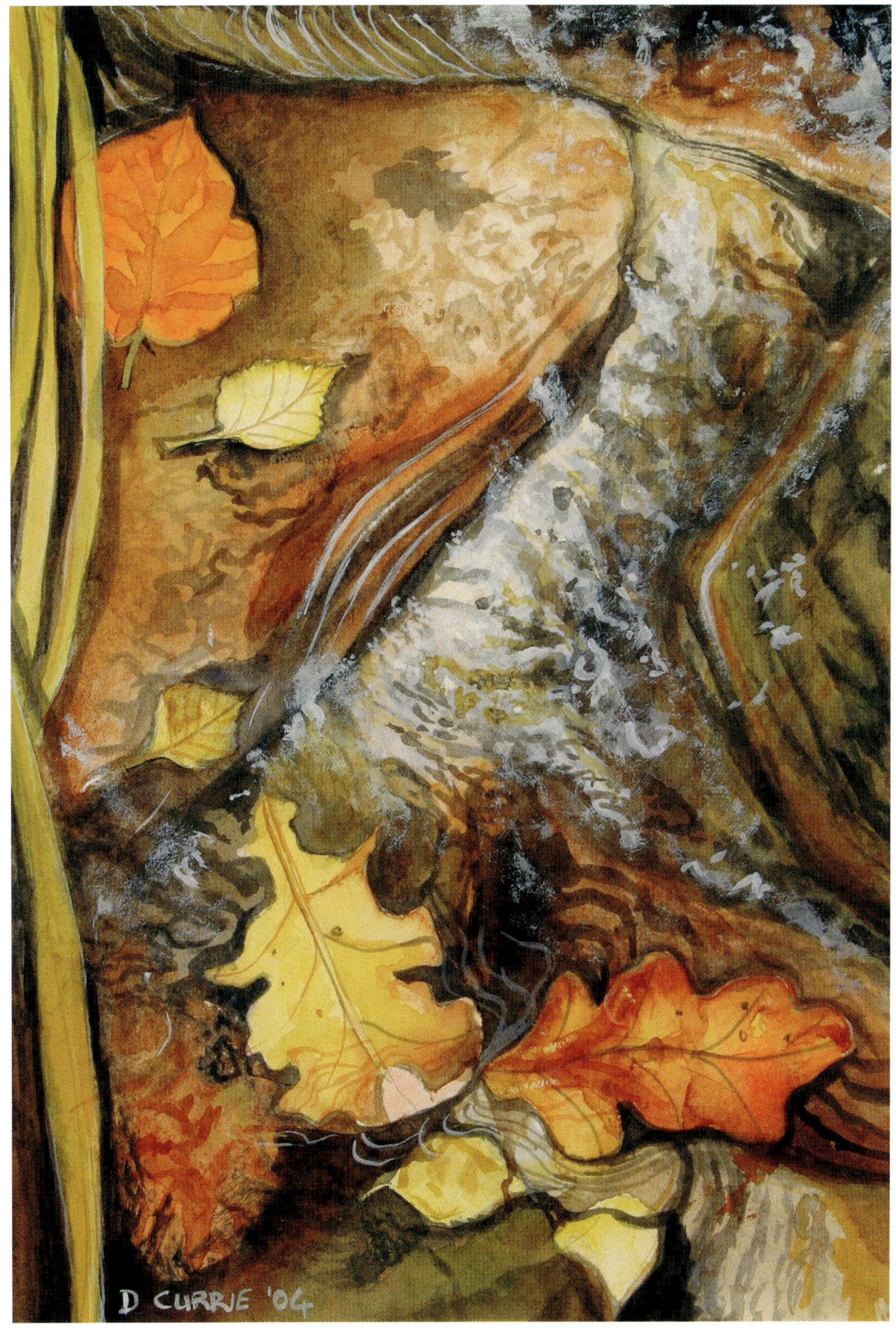

3

2. Duncan Currie *Autumn leaves, small stream, Kinloch woods I*
   watercolour (and bodycolour) · 27 x 18 cm
3. Duncan Currie *Autumn leaves, small stream, Kinloch woods II*
   watercolour (and bodycolour) · 27 x 18 cm

In a way, water is the lifeblood of the wood, so it seemed appropriate to paint the fallen leaves caught in the pools of the burn running through the wood. The leaves represent several species of trees found in the wood, thus capturing a miniature snapshot of the environment here at Kinloch.

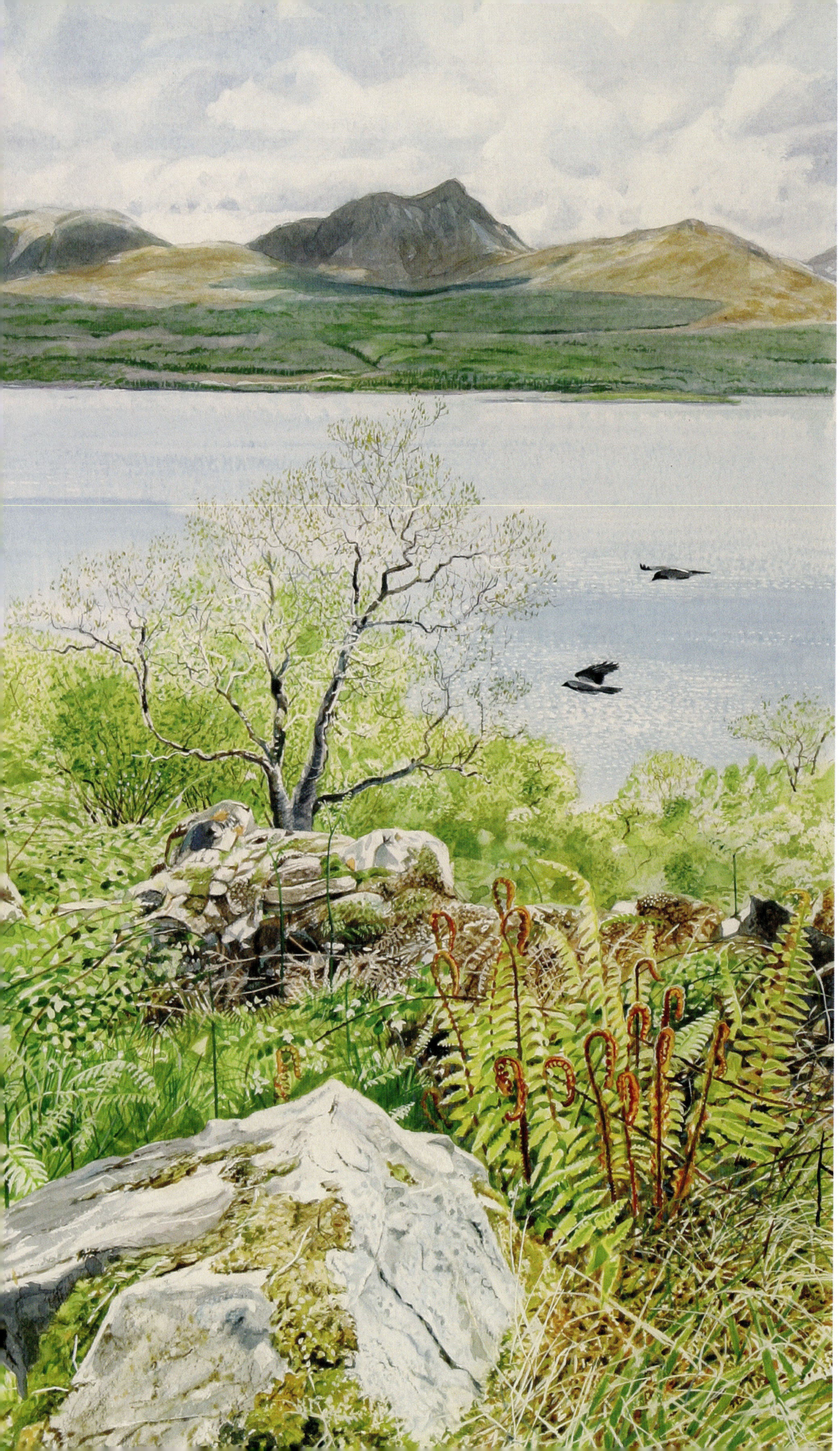

1

1. Brin Edwards *Leitir Fura*
watercolour and gouache · 47 x 27 cm

2. Greg Poole *Leitir Fura settlement*
acrylic on paper · 55 x 39 cm

The bare outlines of ancient lime-walled buildings, bare stone rectangles more like graves than habitations. Around the tops of the ruined walls, sprouting crowns of what I think was scaly male fern. Glowing copper-orange new growth, nodding shepherd's crook heads and clasping, unfurling filigree shoots.

Rocks softened by mossy hummocks, the empty compartments filled with tussocks of bleached straw molinia grass.

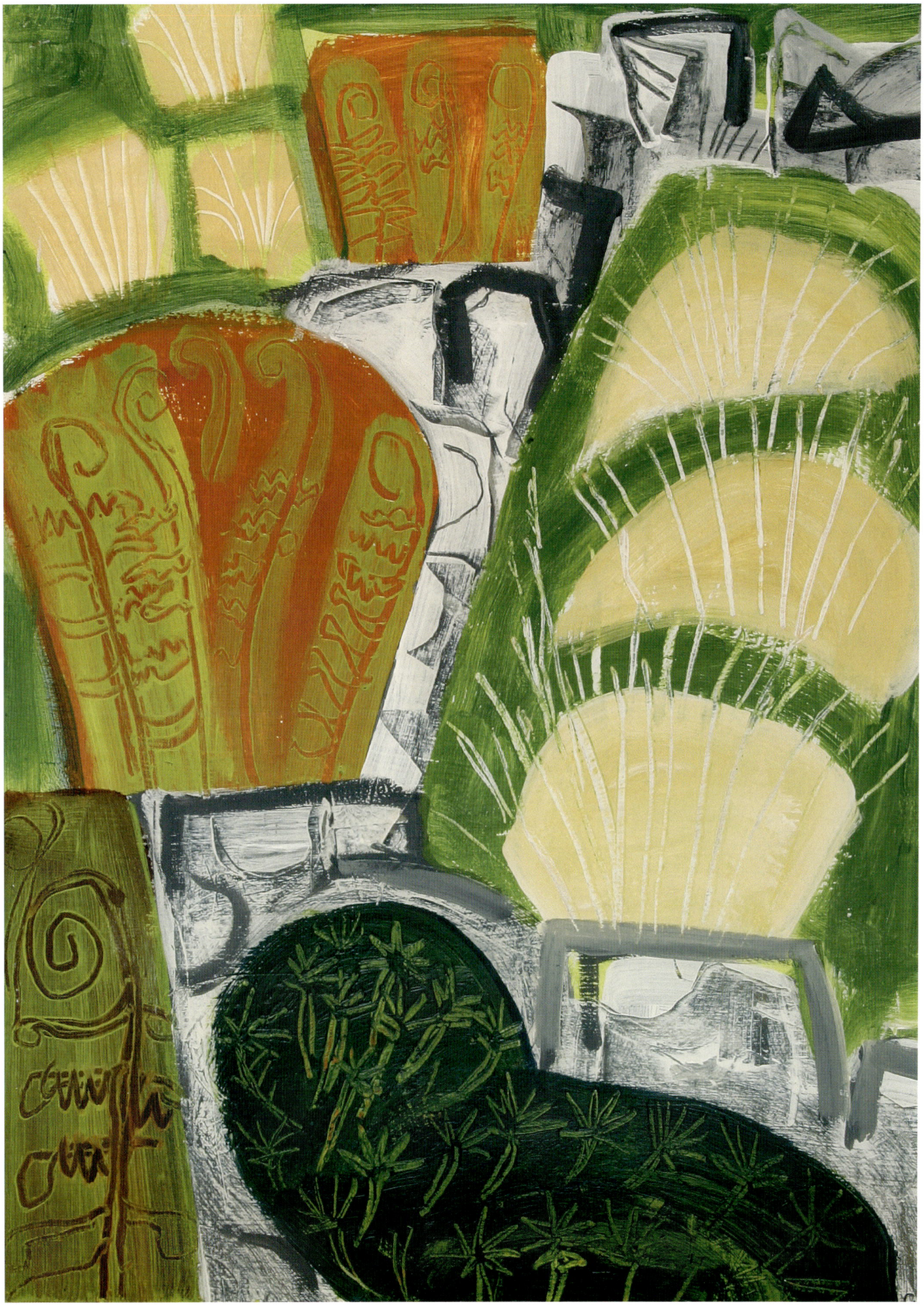

2

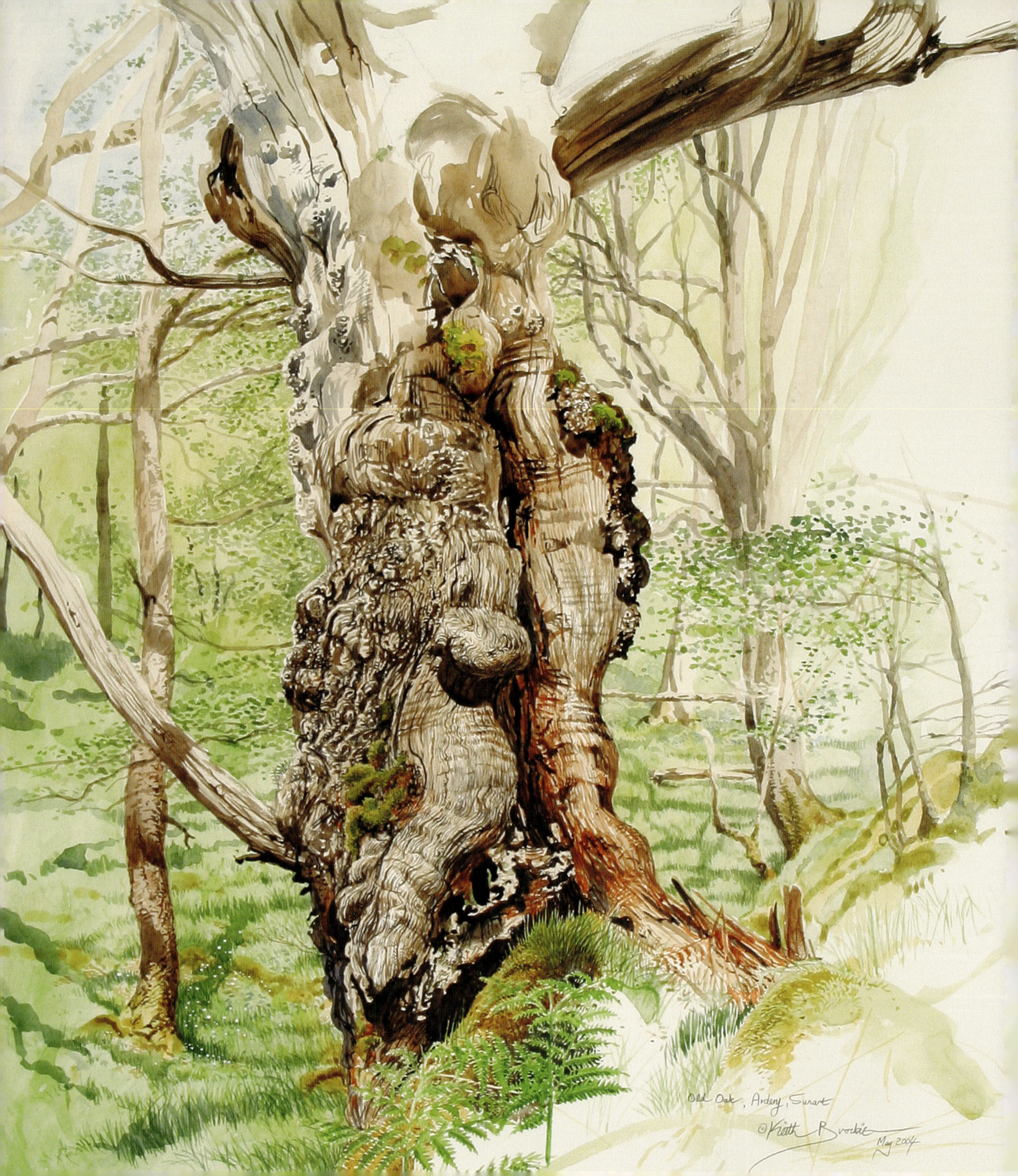
Old Oak, Ardery, Sunart
©Keith Brockie
May 2004

4

Using woods

WOOD PASTURE

At Ardery and Resipole, on the north banks of Loch Sunart, I have walked through woods that bear signs of a landscape that has almost disappeared from the rest of Britain. This is wood pasture, which provided grazing for livestock. The important part of the woodland was not the trees but the ground under them. Wood pasture is about as remote as woodland can be from the natural condition. It is more like the parks surrounding country houses in southern counties, where scattered trees are set in open grassland.

The trees in wood pasture were pollarded to protect them from browsing by animals. Pollard comes from the Norman word for 'head' (as in poll tax). The tops of the trees are cut off at head height to give a single stout trunk, 2.5–3.5 m high, from which new shoots spring. The shoots are either harvested on a rotation to provide poles for timber or lopped annually and thrown down for stock to eat. The advantage of pollarding is that the tender new growths are out of the reach of domestic animals and wild deer, so wood pasture had a dual function. The trees produced both timber and fodder, and the ground underneath provided pasture. Two further advantages are that there is no need to fence the woods to keep animals out and the trees provided cover for animals through the winter. This was important in the west Highlands, where winter storms sweep in from the Atlantic.

We can surmise that the system of wood pasture was viable only when a few cattle were reared for domestic use. Nevertheless, the woods were still important to the local economy, as is shown by the business records that still survive.

VETERAN TREES

Walking through an old wood pasture, there is a sense of history. The oldest pollards – some dead, some barely alive – are centuries old and, not without reason, are known as veterans. Because their hearts have rotted away, ageing by tree rings is impossible, but Peter Quelch, the Forestry Commission Scotland Biodiversity Advisor, has estimated that they are at least 300 years old and perhaps double that, and so date from medieval times. The veterans are awe-inspiring structures to behold. With the broad girth of the trunk, the contorted branches and a covering of mosses and lichens, the veterans are the wildwood monsters of children's stories. Francis Kilvert described veterans in his diary for 1876 as 'misshapen oak men that stand waiting and watching century after century. They look as if they had been at the beginning and making of the world, and they will probably see its end.'

Hollow trees may look as if they are near the end of their lives and about to fall over. They are often felled as hazards to human life but this is in ignorance of the trees' biology. The living part of any tree is just under the bark. The bulk of wood in the trunk and branches is dead. In young trees, wood provides structural support, but as the tree grows, it becomes an increasing burden. Losing the surplus through the activities of fungi and woodboring insects is a positive advantage. A hollow tube is much stronger than a solid bar of the same weight: think of scaffolding or the structure of the Forth rail bridge. When a hurricane hit south-east England in 1987, 100-year-old trees with solid trunks were felled but hollow veterans survived.

For naturalists and conservationists the value of veterans lies in the wealth of wildlife they support. Woodpeckers, owls, treecreepers, tits, redstarts and bats breed and roost in holes. Hordes of insects and other invertebrates live in the rotting timber, which also supports flowers and small trees. Even the veteran feeds on its own dead tissues. It sends out

Keith Brockie *Old oak, Ardery*
watercolour · 53 x 39.5 cm

TAGHADH FIODH

Tagh seileach nan allt,
tagh calltain nan creag
Tagh fearna nan lòn,
tagh beithe nan eas
Tagh uinnseann na dubhair,
tagh iubhar na leuma
Tagh leamhan na brùthaich,
tagh duire na grèine.

CHOICE OF TIMBER

Choose the willow of the streams,
choose the hazel of the rocks
Choose the alder of the marshes,
choose the birch of the waterfalls
Choose the ash of the shade,
choose the yew of resilience
Choose the elm of the brae
choose the oak of the sun.

A. CARMICHAEL, CARMINA GADELICA

roots from the base of its branches to feed on the compost forming in the rotting trunk.

Eventually the veteran tumbles and comes to rest on the woodland floor. With the passage of many more years, it crumbles into dust and returns to the soil. Throughout this process it is home to a succession of species. The amount of dead wood in a wood is an indicator of its naturalness. Traditionally it was cleared for timber and firewood or because it was a reservoir for pests and diseases that could infect the living trees. Leaving dead wood is a simple way of increasing the wildlife value of a wood, and the Forestry Commission now manages its woods to increase the amount of dead wood.

COPPICED WOODS

'Travellers are delighted in passing through any district in which regular attention is paid to the forests, even when reared for the purpose of charcoal... No one can traverse the lands without a feeling of this kind; when the former waste state of that large tract is also contemplated, and contrasted with the marks of industry which appear, and the beautiful appearance of the regularly preserved and rising trees.'

W. SINGERS 1829

Between 100 and 200 years ago, the oakwoods of Argyll went through a period of intensive management by coppicing to produce charcoal for iron smelting. The effects of this industry are still to be seen in the form of solid archaeological remains of enclosure walls, charcoal-burning hearths and packhorse roads, but especially by the structure of the woods. The 'regularly preserved and rising trees' noted by W. Singers are still there, and these coppice woods do not have the tangle of understorey, brambles and fallen logs that can make it so difficult to walk through more natural woods. They are more like plantations, with regular stands, almost monocultures, of even-age trees, cathedral-like with their soaring trunks, arched tracery of foliage and a clear floor underfoot.

Coppicing is a very ancient form of woodland management that dates back thousands of years and which is based on the ability of a tree to grow new stems from its base. It is used to produce thick poles, which could be used for tools and houses, and slender rods, which were needed for domestic uses such as wattles for fences, fishing creels and so on. Hazel, oak, ash and birch were managed in this way. Hazel coppices so well naturally that it is rare to find one with only a single stem. As the stems get taller, they lean out and leave space for new ones to grow up between them.

In its simplest form, suitable rods would have been cut as required. Then, at some point in prehistory, the observation that the stumps of felled trees sprouted new growth was put to good effect for increasing the yield. Trees were felled and new stems

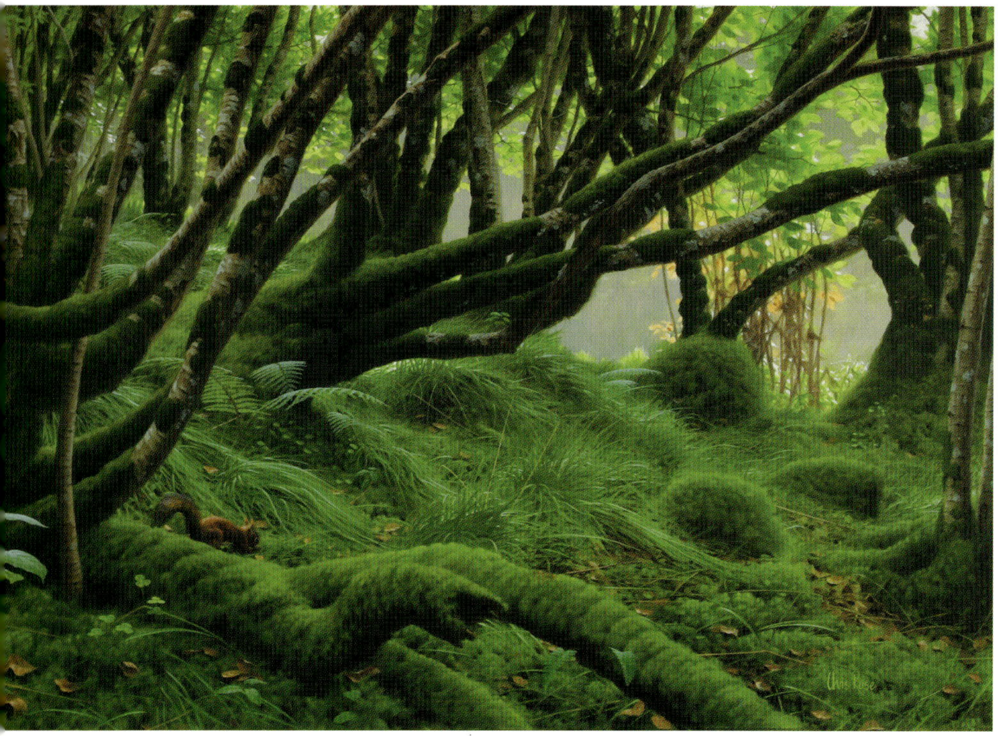

1

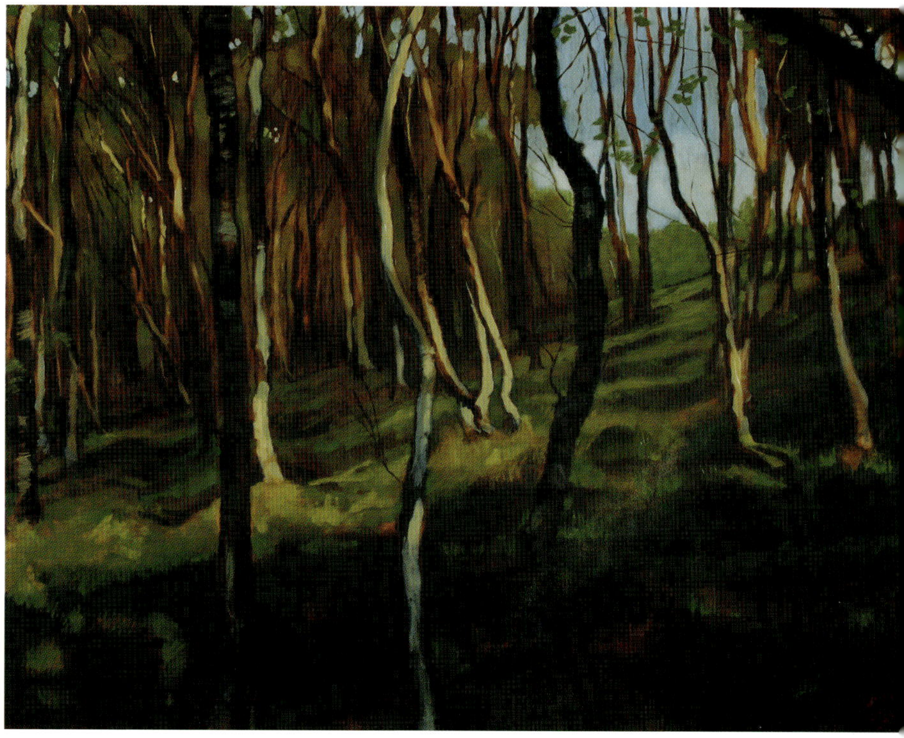

2

allowed to sprout from the stump or stool. With a root system already well established, growth is rapid. It is believed that only a few stems would have been taken from a coppiced tree in a year. This had several advantages. There was less stress on the tree; the new growths were protected from browsing animals by the existing stems; and, for hazel, the trees continued to produce a valuable harvest of nuts.

The lack of tools made handling large timbers difficult, and even houses were built of slender poles. These were wattle and daub creel, or basket, houses, which were no more than simple huts. A report to the Duke of Gordon in 1767 describes the construction of houses as they must have been built for centuries:

'First they place upright standarts about nine inches distant one from the other & about eight feet tall all round of the straightest young wood. Then with smaller wood they work up like a basket the height they design the side Walls and Gavells for Couples they use some old wood But the roof is finisht with wood like the standarts of the side walls. Those houses are annually repaird & often renewed from the foundation.'

The annual repair and renewal would have recycled as much wood as possible, if only for the convenience of the builders, but there was a continual whittling away of the nearby woods as houses were built and rebuilt, and broken tools and utensils replaced. A simple creel house, like that described above, required an estimated 2,000 poles.

TANBARK AND CHARCOAL

As Highland woods moved from providing local needs to generating a cash income, the harvesting of trees became more intensive and a major source of employment. Tree products could be exported in bulk to distant industries thanks to the proximity of the sea, which by-passed the problem of transport across the difficult Highland terrain. Oak was the main raw material.

The use of oak bark for tanning leather is an extremely old process. Leather was used locally for making brogues and domestic utensils, while boatmen preserved their sails and cordage by boiling them in an infusion of bark. Early in the 17th century, tanbark began to be exported from the western Highlands to Ireland, where a large leather industry became very profitable when the wars with France generated an enormous demand.

Oak provided the best bark because it had the highest tannin content. It was harvested in spring, from early May to early July, when the sap is rising and the bark is loose and easy to remove. Whole communities were involved. Larger trees were stripped where they stood, but smaller poles, down to 3 cm in diameter, were cut down and carried to a suitable place, where they were

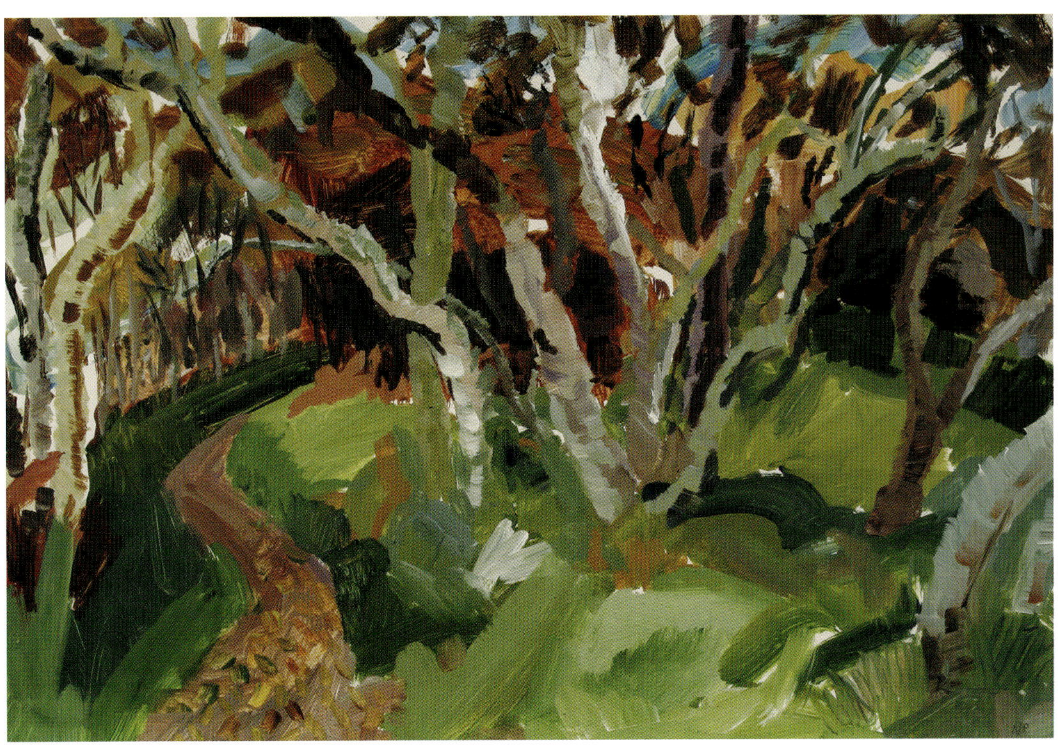

3

1. Chris Rose *Hazel coppice*
acrylic on paper · 47 x 66 cm
As I sat painting amongst the trees of this hazel coppice at Barnluasgan, a red squirrel approached, running expertly along familiar pathways up in the trees, leaping sure-footedly from branch to branch. It descended to the ground and foraged amongst the grasses, mosses and leaf litter, picking up hazel nuts and burying them for its winter larder.
2. Andrew Sinclair *Birch woodland*
oil on board · 80 x 100 cm
3. Nik Pollard *Path through silver birch, Taynish*
acrylic on paper · 42 x 59 cm

stripped by the women and children. The bark was first loosened by beating with a mallet and then removed with a wedge or a special 'barking iron'. It was then dried and packed for transport.

The second half of the 18th century saw heavy industry come to the western Highlands. English ironmasters came north to seek ways of increasing their output. They found it was worth shipping their ore from Furness in Cumbria for processing because of the abundant and regular supplies of charcoal available from the local woods. Charcoal made up 60–70 per cent of the cost of smelting. It was cheap in Argyll because it could be transported by sea. It was a happy coincidence for the ironmasters and the landowners with trees to sell that oakwoods thrived on the coast, and packhorses were needed only to carry bags of charcoal to loading points on the shore.

Only two blast furnaces operated for any length of time in Argyll. Furnace, as Inverleachann was renamed, on Loch Fyne worked from 1755 to 1812 and The Lorn Furnace Company's ironworks, whose well-preserved ruins may still be visited at Bonawe, was on Loch Etive. Bonawe started operation in 1763 and continued until 1876. It produced up to 700 tons of iron and consumed charcoal from 700 acres of woodland every year.

Both ironworks relied on charcoal from scattered tracts of woodland to take advantage of the local labour force. The ironmasters brought in a system of coppicing that was widely used in England. Parcels of oakwood, called haggs, from a Norse word for 'hew', were cut on a rotation of about 25 years. The trees were felled and a mass of new shoots was allowed to sprout from the stump. It was not simply a matter of hacking off the poles. An early regulation stated that the cuts were to be 'raised and smoothed as to prevent the diminishing thereof by water'. In other words, the stool was shaped so that rainwater was shed and rotting prevented. At intervals of four, seven and 12 years, the new stems were thinned to allow room for the remaining half-dozen to grow. Not all the trees were coppiced; a scattering was left to mature into 'maidens' or ' standards' to provide large timbers.

Over the course of coppicing, other trees were 'weeded' out of the woods, and gaps were planted with more oak. Larch and other conifers were sometimes planted as 'nurses' to give shelter to the young oaks and were felled to yield an extra crop to help the cash flow as the oaks grew. Acorns often had to be imported from farther afield, because good crops of acorns are fickle in the Highlands and, at best, occur only at five- to seven-year intervals. Chris Marsh, the forester at Kinloch, told me how, with six companions, he spent a day collecting acorns at Aslaig. They returned with thirty-six! This was bad luck; in other years acorns carpet the floor and woodpigeons grow

1. Duncan Currie *Changing light, changing colour, shifting season*
mixed media · 23.5 x 51.5 cm

I wanted to catch the leaves as they began to change into their autumn colours – just on the cusp between summer and autumn. It turned out to be fortunate, because when I returned later, gales had taken all the leaves. On this particular day I was very lucky, as there was a strong, low sun, which gave a lovely glowing light through the trees and accentuated the lovely yellows, oranges and greens of the changing leaves.

2. Peter Partington *Redstart display – the oakwoods*
watercolour · 27 x 36.5 cm

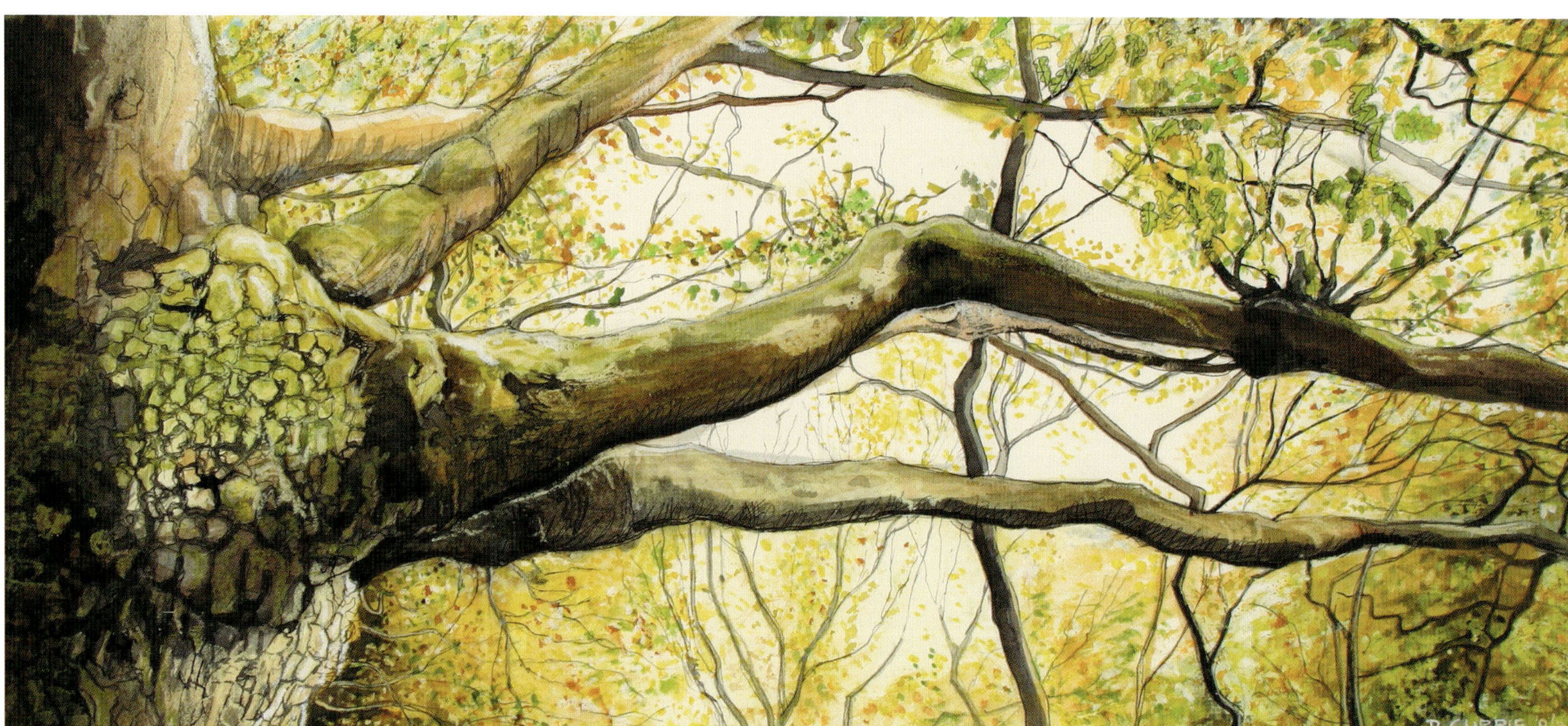

1

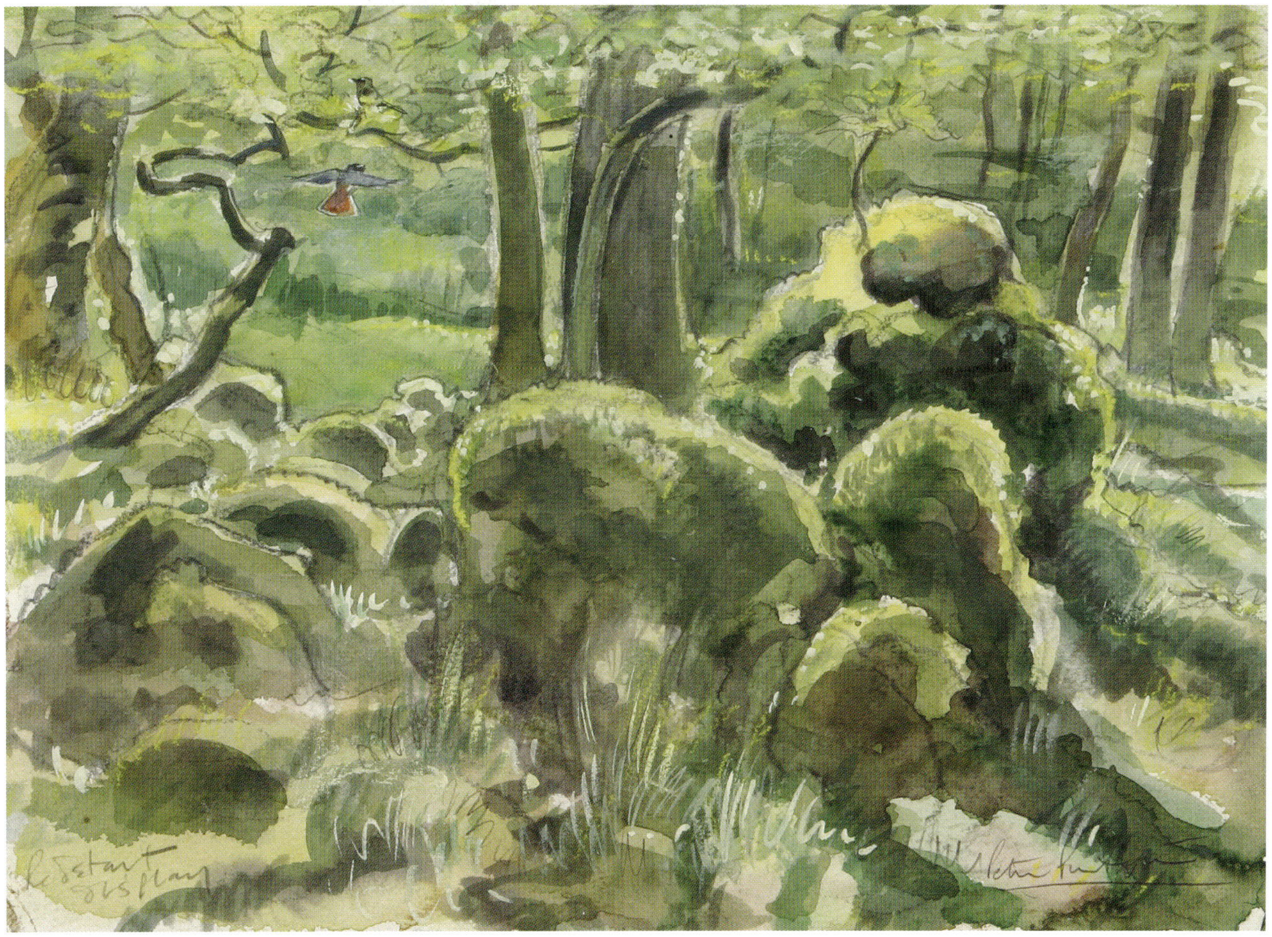

2

fat. Nurseries, such as the one at Strontian, provided saplings for planting out when two or three years old. The resulting woods became monocultures of even-age oaks, whose remnants can still be seen. Some of the woods at Kinloch were planted by 18th-century Macdonalds, and recent DNA analysis of the trees suggests that the acorns came from Germany – an interesting provenance given the clan's antipathy to the House of Hanover!

ENCLOSURES

After a round of cutting, the new shoots had to be protected from grazing by enclosure within stone or turf dykes or fences for six or so years, after which livestock was allowed back in. Many dykes are still to be seen in the woods, and they can be picked out on Ordnance Survey maps. In their present state they do not look as if they could have kept out goats, sheep or even agile cattle, but there is a record of tenants being required to build 'a dyke and ditch seven feet high and seven feet wide'. Low stone dykes were raised with layers of turf, into which branches could be stuck. Alternatively, less permanent enclosures were made from woven wattles. A third system involved reinforcing natural barriers by making a 'pareing brae', in which a steep slope was cut away to make a vertical wall, which might be reinforced with stones. Later in the 19th century the effective height of dykes was raised by the addition of strands of steel wire, whose rusting supports can still be seen. The effectiveness of the barriers was reinforced by the herders, usually the younger members of the family, who kept a watchful eye on their charges.

CHARCOAL BURNING

The oakwoods of Argyll are studded with hundreds of charcoal burners' hearths. They are not conspicuous until you learn to look for flat circles, 6–12 metres across, set in the hillside. Here, again, I needed guidance from Jamie McIntyre, the Sunart Community Forester, who did much to impress on me the link between woods and people, both then and now. He showed me not only the hearths at Ardery but also the tracks, complete with bridges over burns, that were used by the packhorses. The

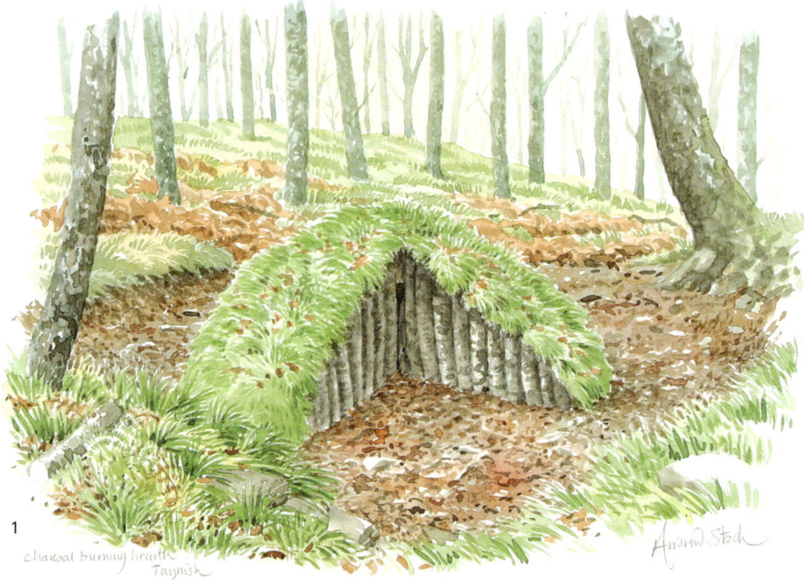

1

hearths were made by cutting into the slope and throwing the spoil out to build up a level platform behind a retaining wall of stones. Recent excavations have revealed that they may be of great antiquity and were originally bases for dwellings. It is likely, however, that they were reused by charcoal burners, but they are now called 'recessed platforms', a term that describes the structure without commenting on its function.

Making charcoal was a skilled business and was directed by a professional coaler. The cut and dried timber was stacked carefully around a central stake and covered with turf. The stake was then removed and a fire started in the 'flue' that it left. The coaler and his team had to maintain a continuous watch and stop any leaks that would let too much air into the stack. Otherwise the wood would burn into ash. The slow combustion converted the wood into charcoal over a period of several days, after which it had to cool before it was put into sacks ready for transport.

As well as providing the best bark for tanning, oak produced hard charcoal, which is best for smelting. It was stripped of its valuable bark in spring, but converted into charcoal later in summer. Other trees, such as ash and birch, were known as 'winter wood' because they were cut at the end of winter to prolong the coaling season and provide the furnaces with a steadier supply of charcoal.

At one time it was believed that commercial charcoaling had been a major cause of the deforestation of the Atlantic oakwoods. On the contrary, it is

1. Andrew Stock *Charcoal-burning hearth, Taynish*
   watercolour · 18 x 25.5 cm

2. Chris Rose *Boggy tree (detail)*
   acrylic on board · 75 x 94 cm

   This is a wet place – wet overhead, wet underfoot and wet in the middle – but I was captivated by it just the same. The trees literally drip with mosses and lichens, the moisture saturating the colours into vivid greens and oranges. I liked the way that the trees reflected darkly in the peaty water of this mire in the Taynish woods; and even when it wasn't raining, water dripped from the rain-soaked trees, spreading circular ripples on the water.

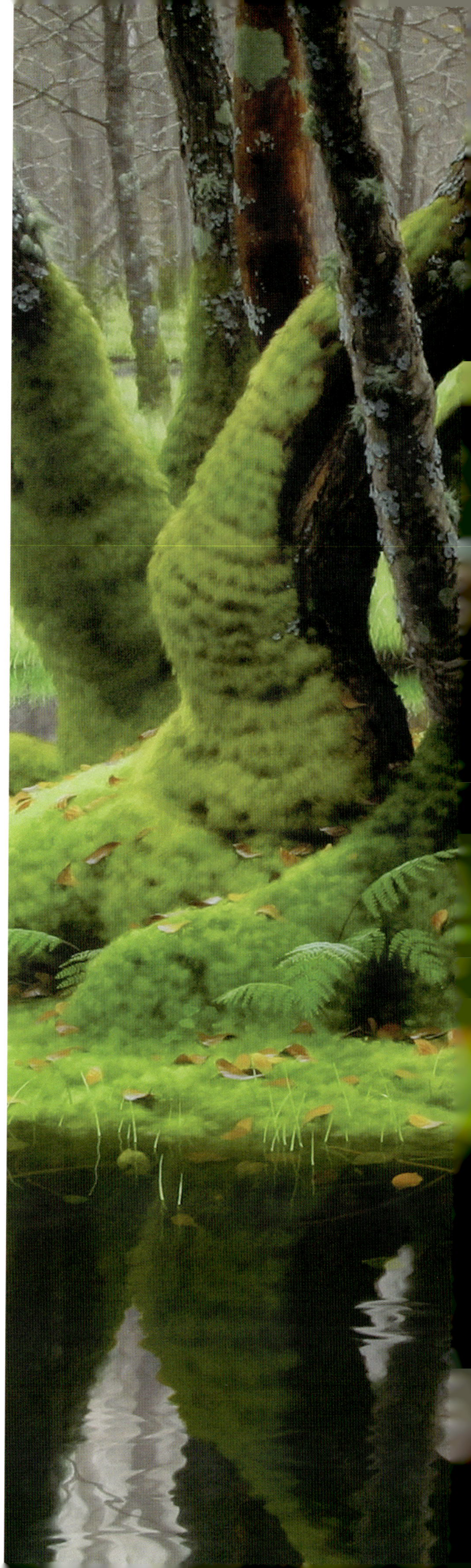

2

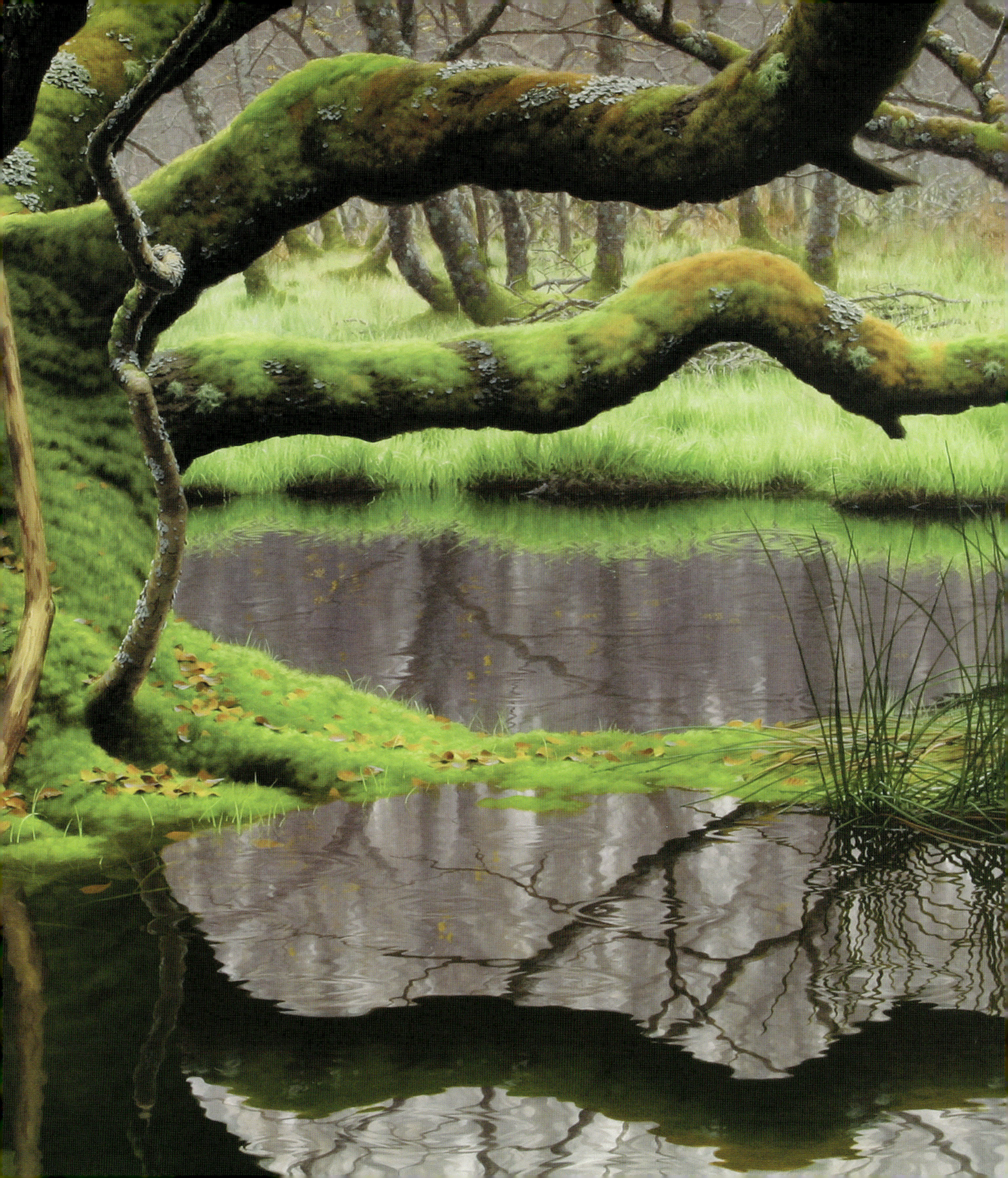

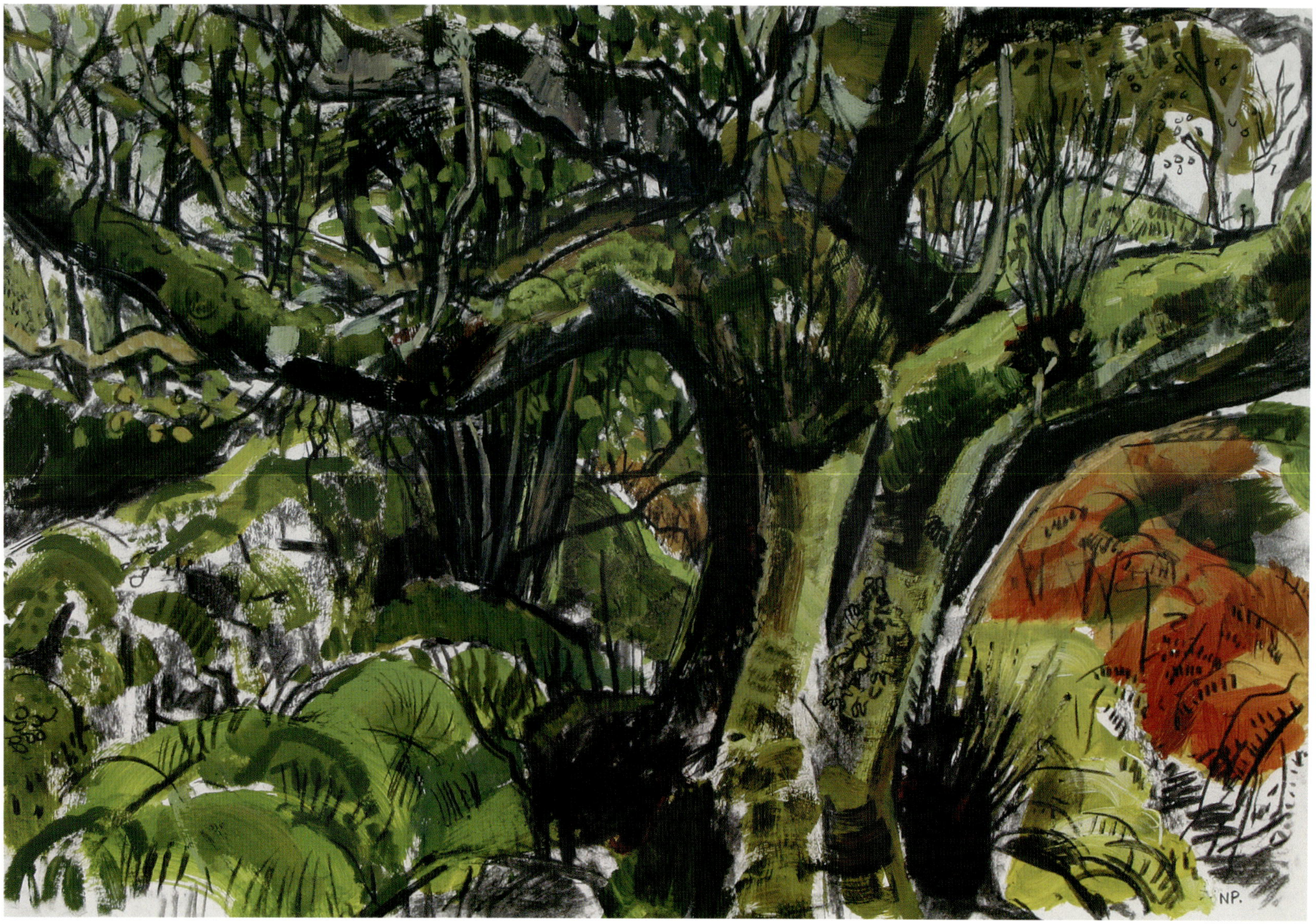

1

clear now that the ironmasters are more likely to have preserved the woods and even extended them. It was in their interest to conserve trees as a renewable resource for their charcoal. What is true is that their demand for charcoal altered the nature of the woods, both in structure, by coppicing, and in nature, by the selective planting of oak and its attendant nurse trees.

Eventually coke replaced charcoal as the source of carbon in iron smelting but charcoal continued to be needed for other purposes. Coppice timber was used for barrels and wheel spokes. The iron-works at Furnace was converted into a gunpowder mill, in which soft charcoal from alder, aspen and willow was a main ingredient. The lead mine at Strontian also required charcoal, and there was a 'pyroligneous acid' works at Crinan. Acid making was the same process as charcoal burning but the vapours driven off the charring wood were condensed to yield acetic acid for the printing and dyeing industries.

When the market for charcoal collapsed, coppicing went into decline. Some trees were then singled – one stem only left to grow – to produce larger timber for shipbuilding. There were a few other outlets. The bobbin mill at Salen needed 1,400 tons of wood each year from the Sunart region for making bobbins or pirns for the weaving industry. But, in general, the woods became neglected and the enclosures fell into disrepair. Even the local use of woodland products gradually dwindled and by the end of the 19th century had almost ceased to exist. One of the last exports from the woods was sprigs of holly sent to Glasgow markets at Christmas.

1. Nik Pollard *Untitled*
   acrylic on paper · 42 x 59 cm
2. Matt Underwood *Rite of spring*
   gouache · 84 x 29 cm

   I like the force of everything at this time, the upward feeling and battle for light and place. Looking into the wood it was so dark.
3. Matt Underwood *Unfurling*
   mixed media · 84 x 33 cm

   From a tight coil, through to violin forms, to an unfurling fern. This attracted me, as did the colours against the colours of the rocks – the orange. Warmer colours against the green are a sense of danger – the adder.

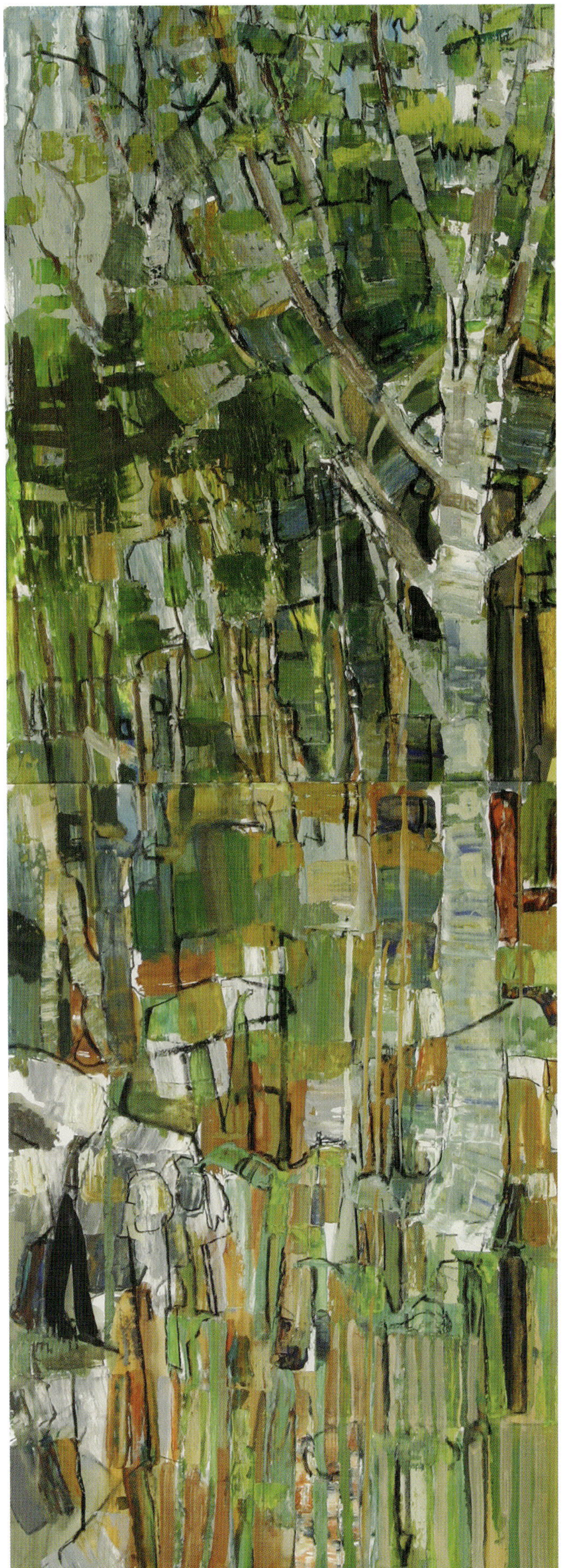

2

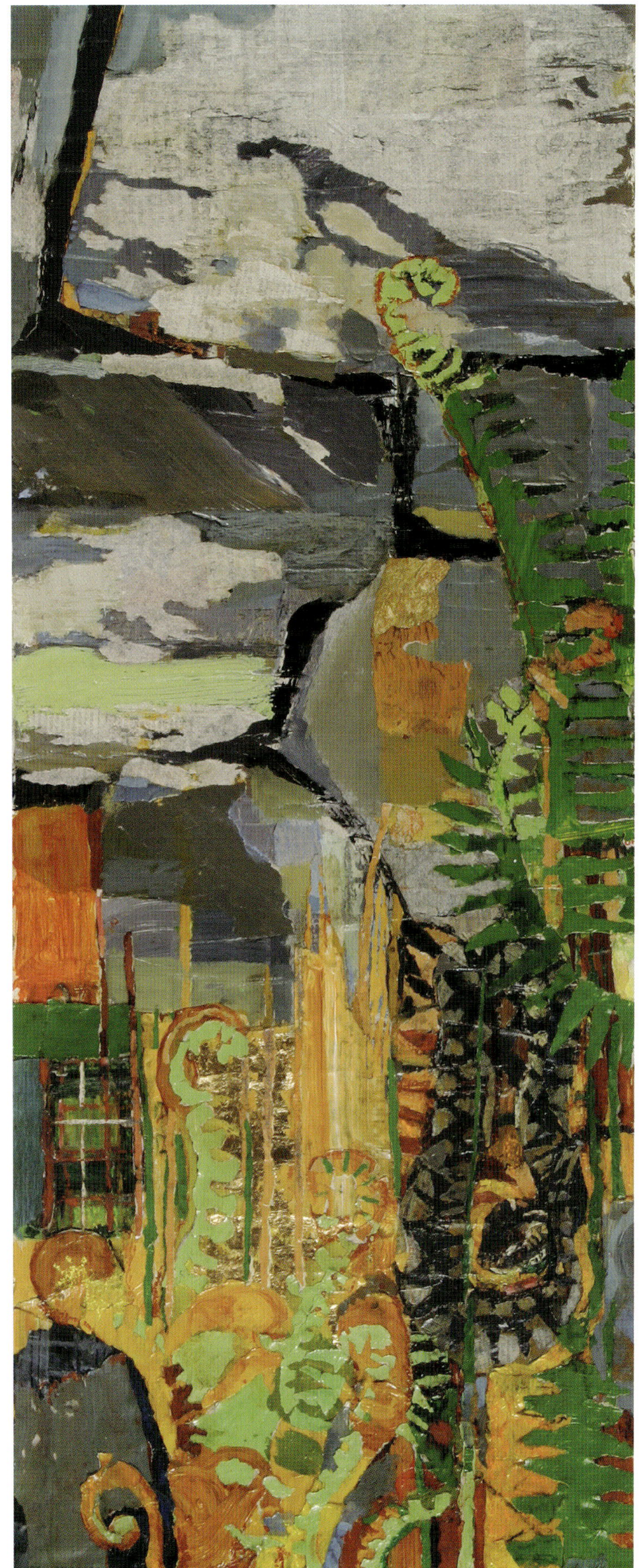

3

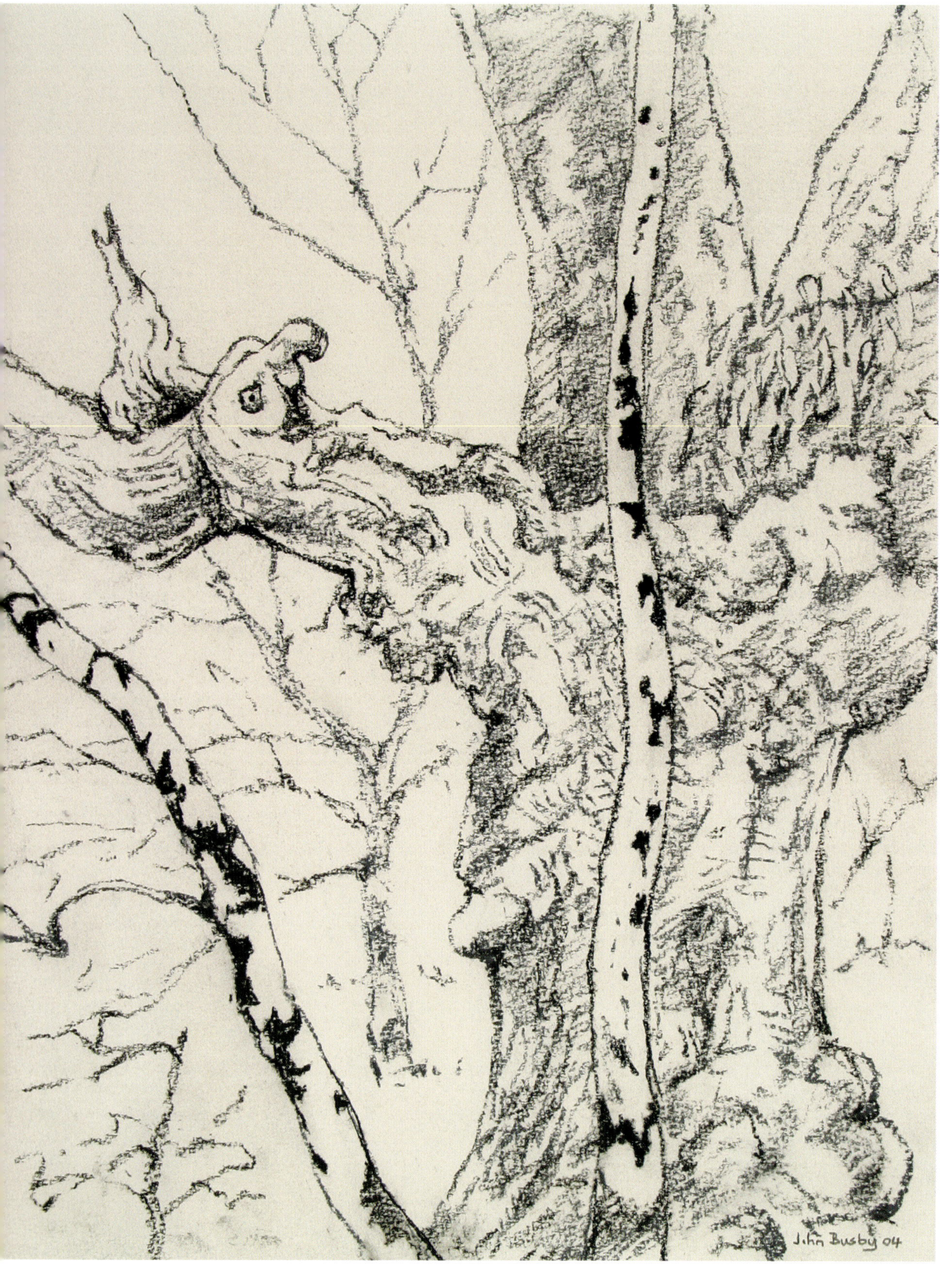

1

1. John Busby *Venerable oak and young birches, Ardery*
   charcoal drawing · 32 x 24 cm
2. David Guy Measures *The pollarded oak*
   watercolour · 28.5 x 25 cm

   Up the track on the hillside behind the caravans on the shore of Loch Sunart was the only pollarded oak that we found during the week. This was painted rapidly, in a haze of biting mosquitoes, on our last day.

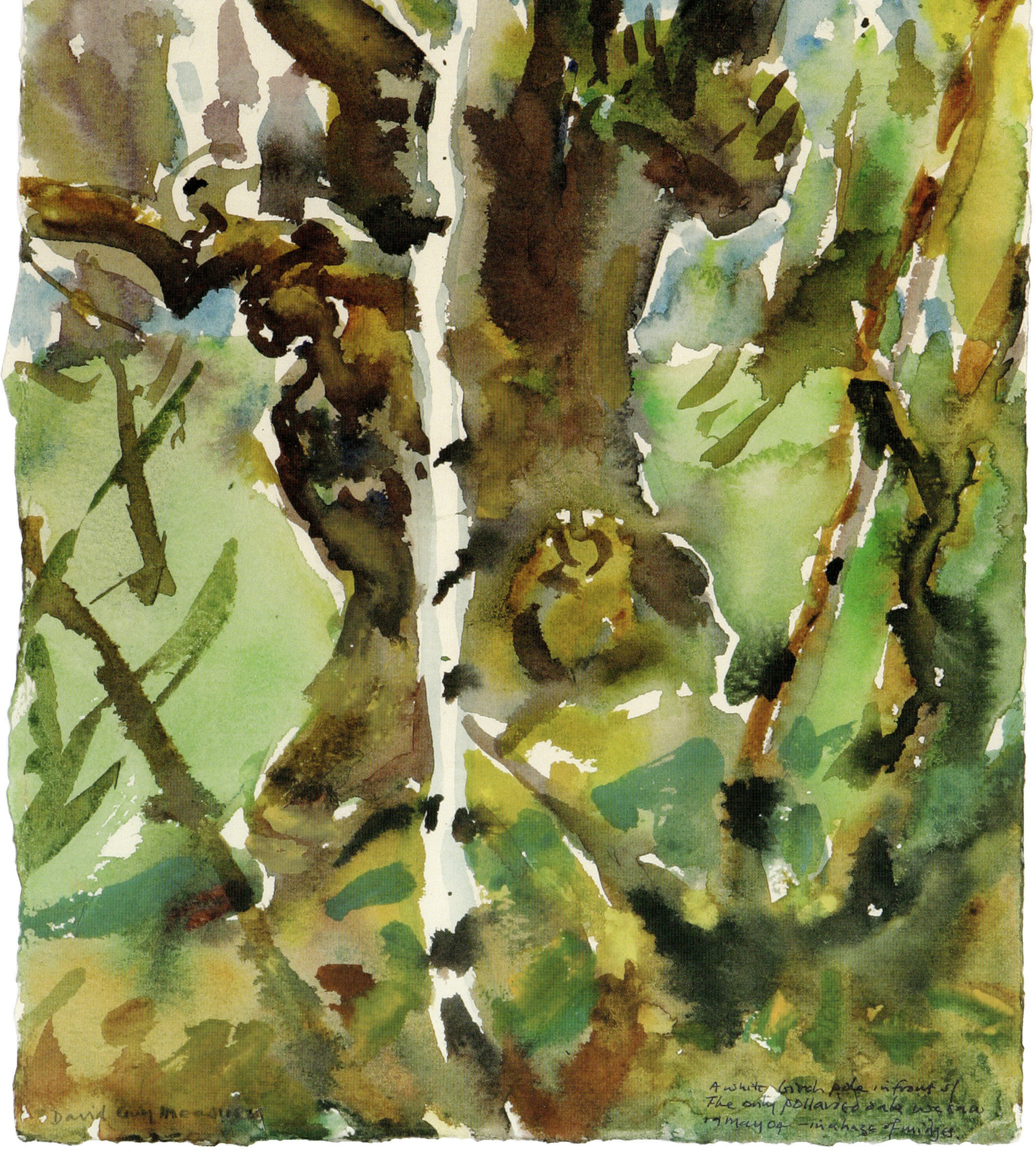
A white birch pole in front of
The only pollarded oak we saw
19 May 04 – in a haze of midges.

2

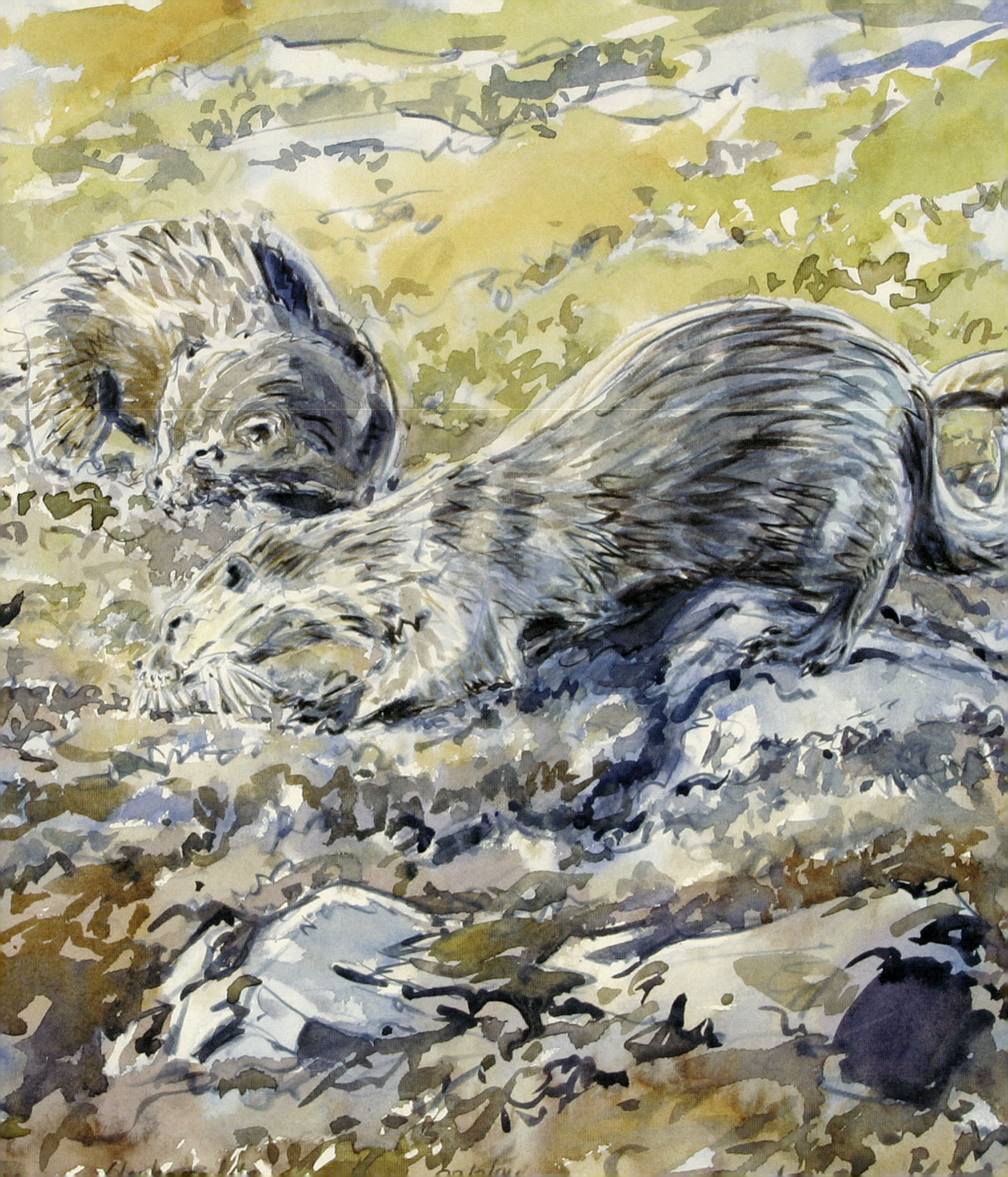

5

Woodland refuges

David Bennett *Otter family (detail)*
pencil and watercolour · 36 x 57 cm

This family party appeared out of a golden, undulating carpet of weed. The cubs seemed a little giddy, and chased around before making their way back to mum, who was doing her scenting duties on a nearby rock. The cubs were very vocal, chittering loudly, a sound which could be heard from a considerable distance.

The Atlantic oakwoods are important for conservation because of their great variety of wildlife. They form a marvellous refuge in the western Highlands for a rich, often unusual and sometimes unique, assemblage of animals and plants. They have survived partly through their remoteness and the poverty of the environment, which have discouraged the widespread industrialisation, urbanisation and intensive agriculture that swamped most of the country. Consequently, there is still enough space for preserving viable populations and communities of wildlife. This does not mean that nature can be left to her own devices. Space is not unlimited; many of the woods are small and human activity always poses a danger. Intervention is frequently necessary, even if it is no more intrusive than monitoring to check that all is well with key species of animals and plants.

It was only when Scotland's Atlantic oakwoods caught the attention of modern naturalists that their great diversity came to be appreciated. In the 1970s, when Brian Coppins began to study lichens on hazel trees, he found species that were new to Britain and even new to science. The white script lichen *Graphis alboscripta* is a species that has never been found outside the west coast of Scotland. Far from being 'scrub' of no particular interest, hazel woods have proved to have a unique collection of lichens, which are of great conservation value. This has been recognised possibly just in time. They were threatened by the revival of coppicing hazel, partly to provide wood products but also as a conservation tool. Many of these lichens only grow on old wood, so widespread coppicing would wipe them out.

It has been said that conserving diversity requires a 'diversity of conservationists'. Each one draws attention to their own speciality and prevents the management plan for somebody else's favourite species harming their own. So thinning a wood to allow more light for the benefit of flowers and the butterflies that feed on them could be detrimental to mosses and other shade-loving plants.

Preservation and restoration of the oakwoods is increasing the amount of habitat for rare species. Some may spread naturally to take advantage of these new opportunities but others may need help by reintroduction. This has been suggested for bringing back black grouse to the Kinloch Hills, but, more controversially, plans have been put forward for establishing the beaver on a trial basis in Knapdale, after an absence from Scotland of four centuries. Although this would be the return of a native, the ecosystem has changed in the intervening years, not least through Man's dominant role. The beaver's engineering would encourage wetland habitats and diversify woodlands, and so encourage a variety of species. However, there are those who regard a large tree-felling rodent as a serious threat to agricultural crops, trees and the fish that breed in the streams. The beaver's supporters point out the benefits to tourism and, if the new population became a problem, that it would be easy to contain such a conspicuous, slow-breeding animal.

BLACK GROUSE

The black grouse is one of the most fascinating birds to be found in the west coast woods, although unfortunately one of the rarest. It is one of only three British birds with the extravagant mating displays

ORAN AN T-SAMHRAIDH

Bi gach doire dluth, uaiguidh
'S trusgan uain' uim' a' fhs;
Bi an snodhach a' direadh
As gach freumaich is isle,
Troimh na cuisleanan sniòmhain
Gu meudachadh blath
Cuach is smeòrach 's an fheasgar
Seinn an leadain 'nam bàrr.

THE SONG OF SUMMER

O'er groves close and secret
A green mantle grows;
The juices ascending
From roots lowest bending,
Through arteries winding
To distribute the bloom;
On their tops thrush and cuckoo
Their sweet litanies hum.

BY ALEXANDER MACDONALD

known as lekking. For most of the year, males – blackcock – gather every morning at traditional lekking grounds, perhaps in a grassy glade, on a forest track or in a rough pasture. There they defend small territories and, during April and May, compete for the attention of the females – greyhens. The males circle with tails spread to show off the white undertail-coverts, wings half-spread and red combs inflated. All the while, they utter a bubbling sound that can be heard a mile away in still conditions. It is worth getting up before dawn to get to a lek. The birds are very wary and easily driven off. A parked car makes a good hide but I once crawled behind a stone dyke to get a view.

At one time 30–40 blackcock made a good lek, but leks have been getting smaller and the last I saw had a lone male displaying by himself. Black grouse have been in decline throughout Europe over the last century, and during the 1990s the British population dropped by about 10 per cent per year. Black grouse now only occur in pockets through the country, and the species is a UK Biodiversity Action Plan Priority Species.

The natural habitat of black grouse is woodland clearings and edges, where there is a mix of trees, heather and blaeberry, and wet patches with plenty of insects for the young chicks. As the woodlands fragmented and disappeared, the grouse adapted to moorland fringes, and they thrived in young conifer forests. As grazing and forestry have intensified, the preferred mosaics of habitat have been replaced by monocultures. The grouse disappeared from the conifer woods when the canopy started to close. The hope is that by restructuring the woods through planned clearfelling, black grouse will be able to use the edges. Although not strictly birds of the oakwood, black grouse use them for feeding. They survive in birch woods and the edges of conifer forests, and they benefit from the fencing out of deer and sheep that is allowing the oakwoods to regenerate. There is, however, a real danger of collision with deer fences, but the Forestry Commission and other landowners have been removing redundant fences and making the remainder conspicuous to flying birds.

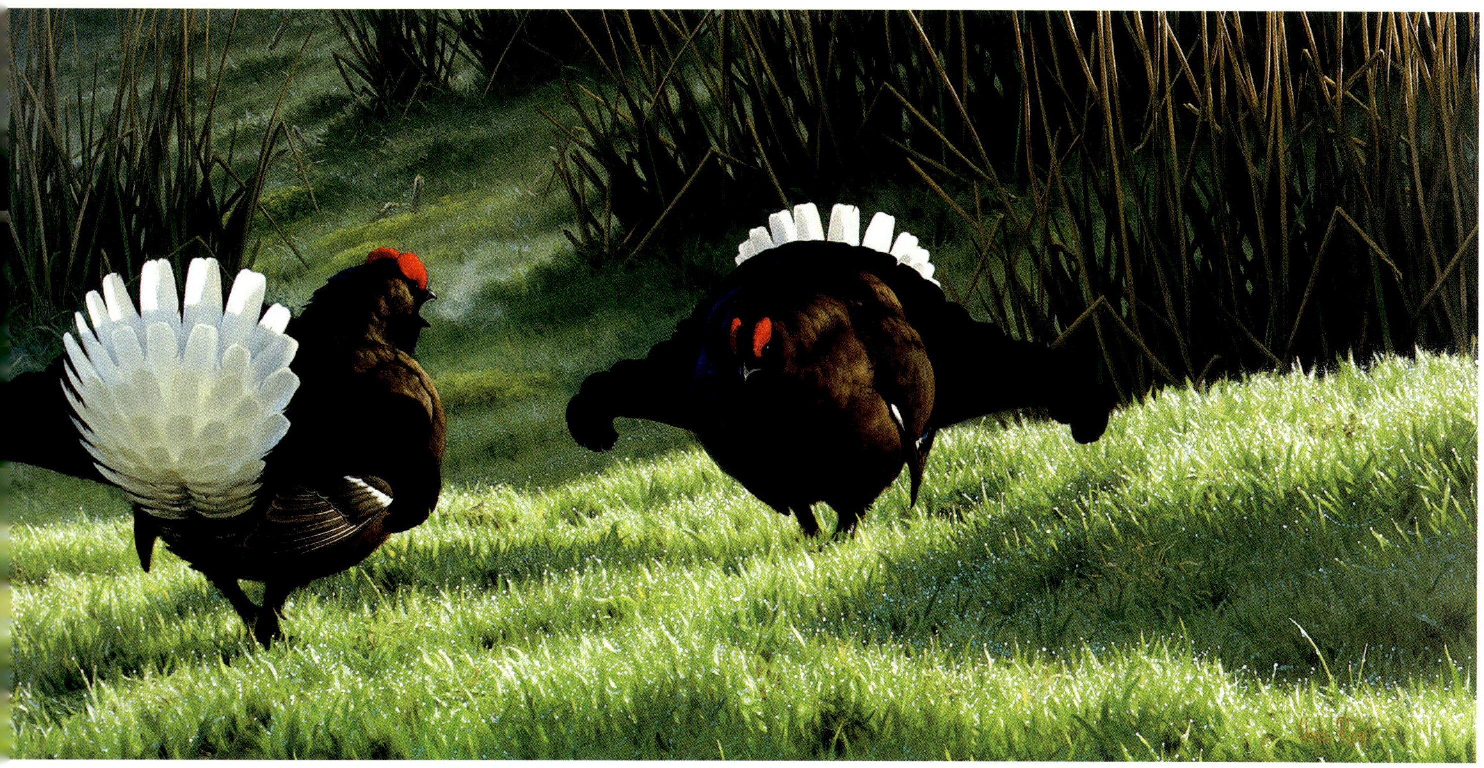

1

1. Chris Rose *Duel at dawn*
oil on board · 43 x 84 cm

Early morning is the best time to witness blackcock lekking. The newly risen sun cast a dramtic light over this scene and made the dewdrops on the grass sparkle like jewels.

Although painted in Scotland, this picture was produced outside the project but serves to illustrate the species.

2,3 John Busby *Sleeping pine marten*
pencil and watercolour sketches

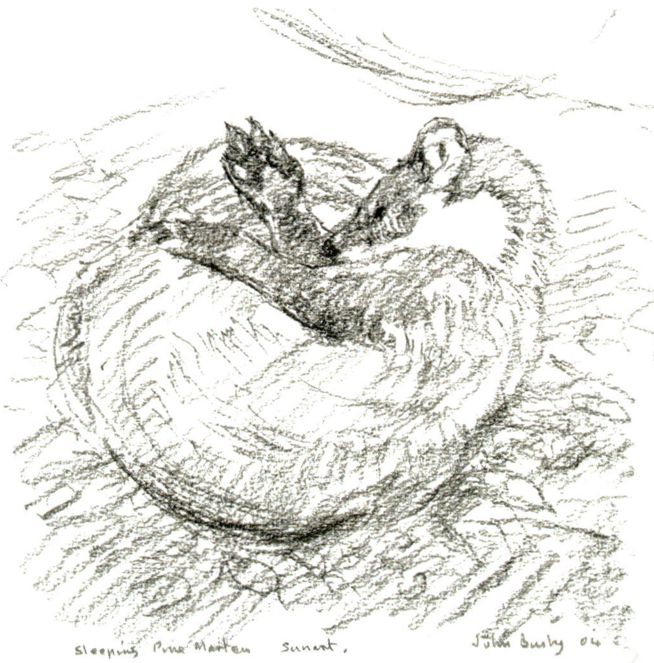

2

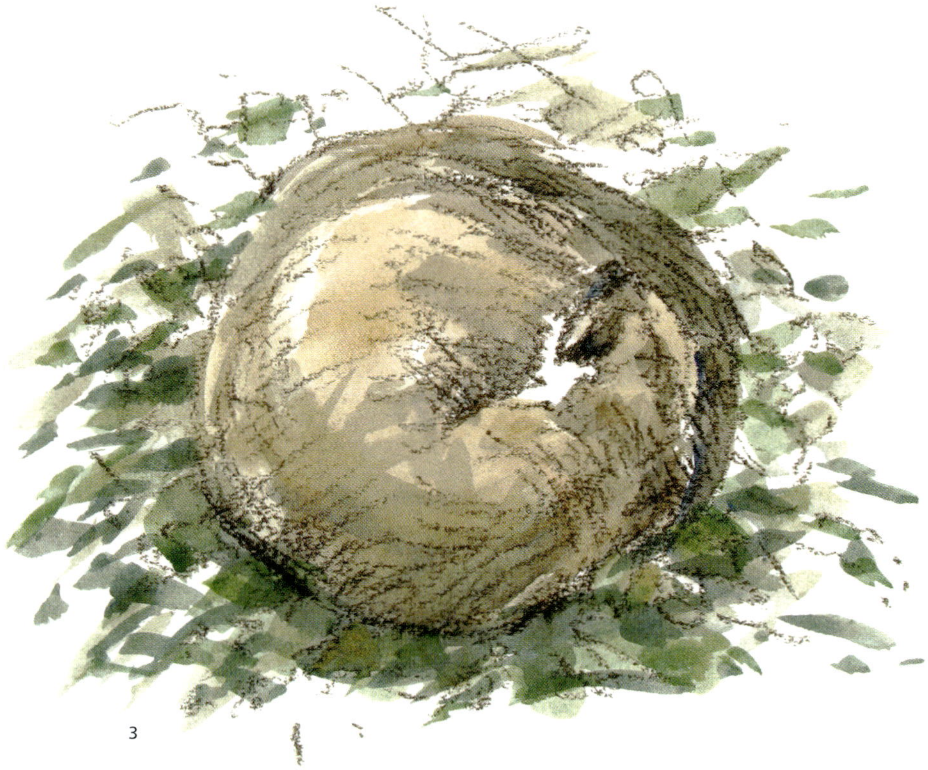

3

PINE MARTENS AND RED SQUIRRELS

These are two tree-dwelling mammals which were once found throughout the country but subsequently struggled for survival. The pine marten is staging a recovery but the red squirrel seems to be going into free-fall.

Despite its name, the pine marten is found in both coniferous and broadleaved woods and even on open hills and moors. Persecution as a robber of game and poultry was so severe that by the 1920s it was confined to a small area of upland forest and rocky moor in north-west Scotland. However, by the 1960s, there were signs of a revival, and martens spread south and west into Argyll. They have continued to spread and increase, and they colonised Skye after they had been seen running across the Skye Road Bridge.

Pine martens hunt mainly on the ground, although they are excellent climbers. Their main prey is voles, with squirrels forming only a small part of their diet in Scotland. Birds, beetles, carrion and fungi are also eaten and berries are important in autumn. A good sign of their presence is droppings and small piles of half-digested rowan berries deposited on woodland paths. However, martens are now becoming known as visitors to bird tables, and people put out food to attract them into their gardens.

In the 18th and 19th centuries the red squirrel fared worse than the pine marten. It almost became extinct in Scotland but hung on in the Highlands, where the population was boosted by introductions from England and the Continent. Numbers recovered but there was another decline in the 20th century. The reasons are unclear, but habitat fragmentation and disease are believed to have played a part. Subsequently, the spread of the grey squirrel has driven out its smaller relative and once again the western Highlands have become one of the red squirrel's last refuges in Britain.

The red squirrel's home on the west coast is mature conifer woods with a mixture of pine, larch and Norway spruce, which gives a broad harvest of cones, but the squirrels also spread into adjoining hazel and oak. Places like the Sunart oakwoods and

Knapdale are refuges, which the grey squirrel has not yet reached. It is ironic that linking the fragments of woods improves the red squirrels' habitat but will also make it easier for the greys to spread.

OTTERS

Thirty years ago there was alarm about the status of the otter in Britain. From inhabiting every stretch of water, it had vanished from most of lowland Britain. Its last stronghold was the Highlands and Islands of Scotland. The reappearance of the otter in some of the worst-hit regions over the last decade has been a conservation success story, but western Scotland is still the place where you have the best chance to see an otter.

If you are going to Skye, visit the Forestry Commission's Otter Haven at Kylerhea. The hide looks down on a stretch of shore favoured by otters and is equipped with CCTV for improving the chance of a sighting. Another good spot is the hide at Ard Airigh on the northern shore of Loch Sunart. However, there is just as good a chance of spotting an otter anywhere along the coast. According to a recent survey, there are more signs of activity on stretches with less human activity, which on the west coast leaves plenty of places where a quiet watch may be rewarding. The pleasure of watching an otter eating its prey at the surface is surpassed only by watching a mother with her cubs.

At one time, otters seen along the Scottish coast were confusingly called 'sea otters' as if they were different from 'river otters'. The same animals work both fresh and salt water. The focus of activity is the shore and shallow water, and the otters' main prey is fish, crabs and sea urchins. Most of the holts and couches are within 50 metres of the coast. However, signs such as spraints (droppings deposited in conspicuous places and surprisingly sweet-smelling) are commonly found on burns flowing down through the woods. Otters travel upstream to hill lochans 500 metres or so above sea level, especially when frogs and toads are gathering to spawn, and they enter the woods to make homes under boulders and uprooted trees. Access to fresh water is also vital for washing salt from their fur.

Despite being expert swimmers, otters are not so well adapted for an aquatic life in some respects. Time spent in the water is limited mostly to bouts of feeding, and otters suffer, as we do, from getting cold by spending too long in the water. A study at Taynish by Alan McCluskie of Glasgow University has shown how otters' feeding habits are influenced by sea temperature. In summer, when the water is warm, they dive in deeper water for edible crabs. When it is cold, long dives use up too much energy and more time has to be spent on land recovering after feeding. So it is more economical to hunt in shallow water, even though this means subsisting on poor food like sticklebacks and doing without their favourite edible crabs.

Another finding from otter studies shows why the best time to look for them is in the early morning. Apart from the lack of disturbance by people, they tend to feed at this time of day because their main prey, such as fish, are inactive and easier to catch.

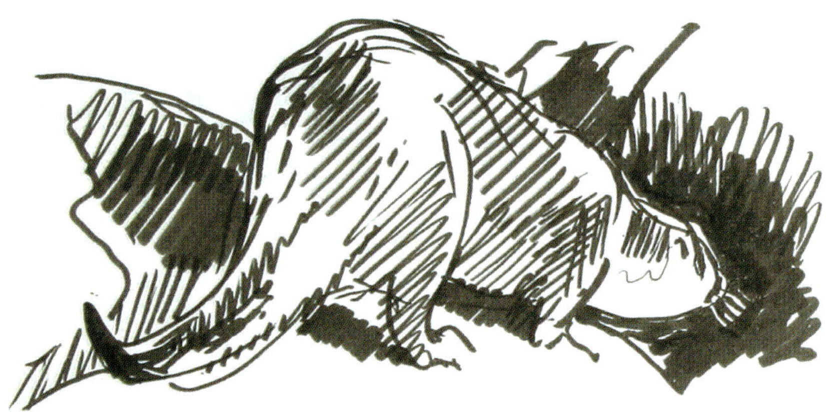

1

1. William Neill *Otter*
felt pen · 9 x 16 cm

2,3 Keith Brockie *Otter, Sunart*
pencil · 19 x 23 cm

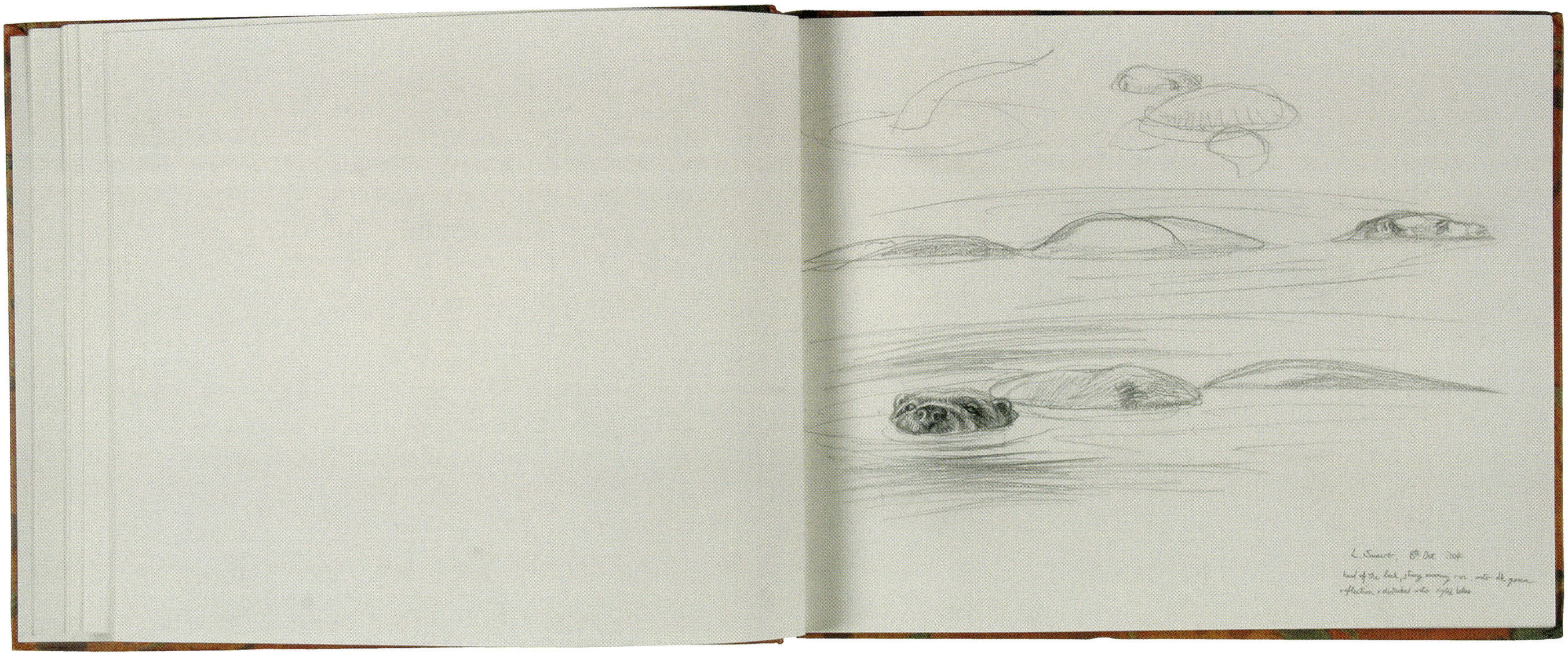

2

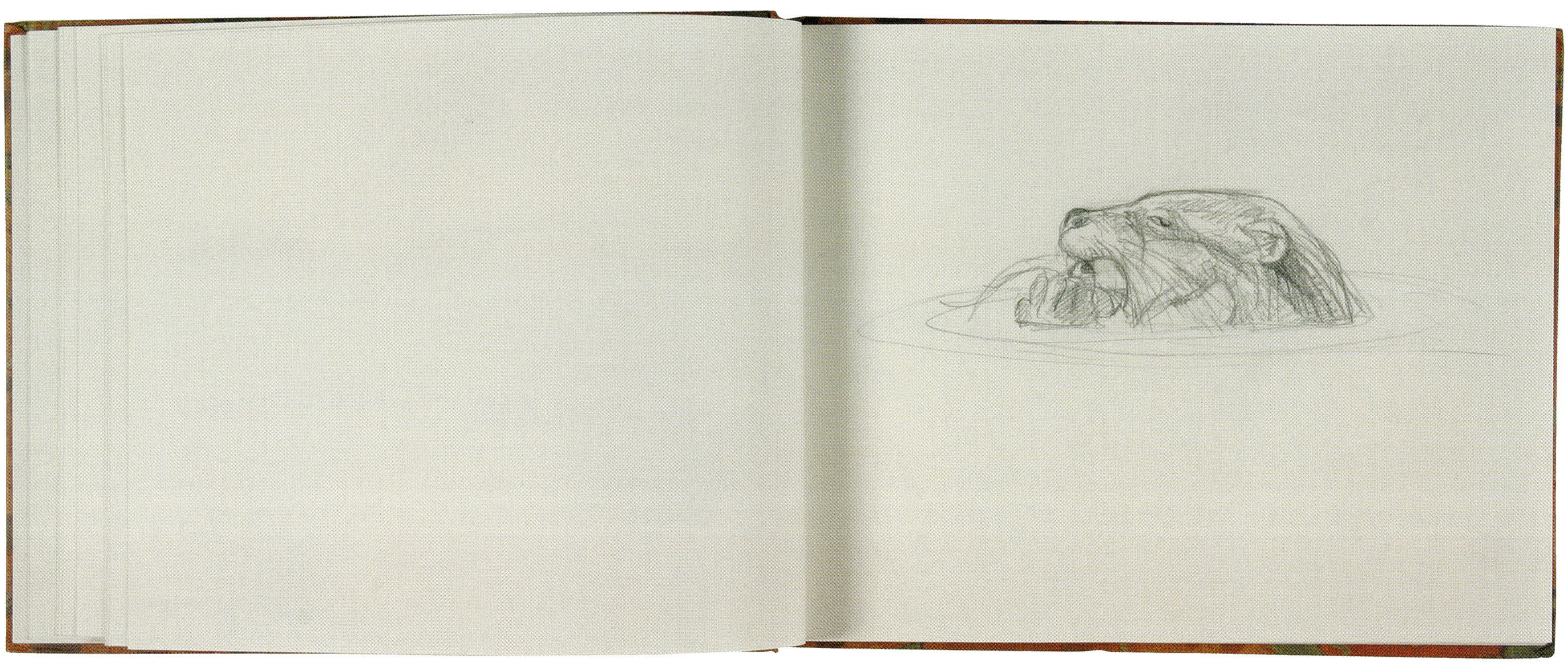

3

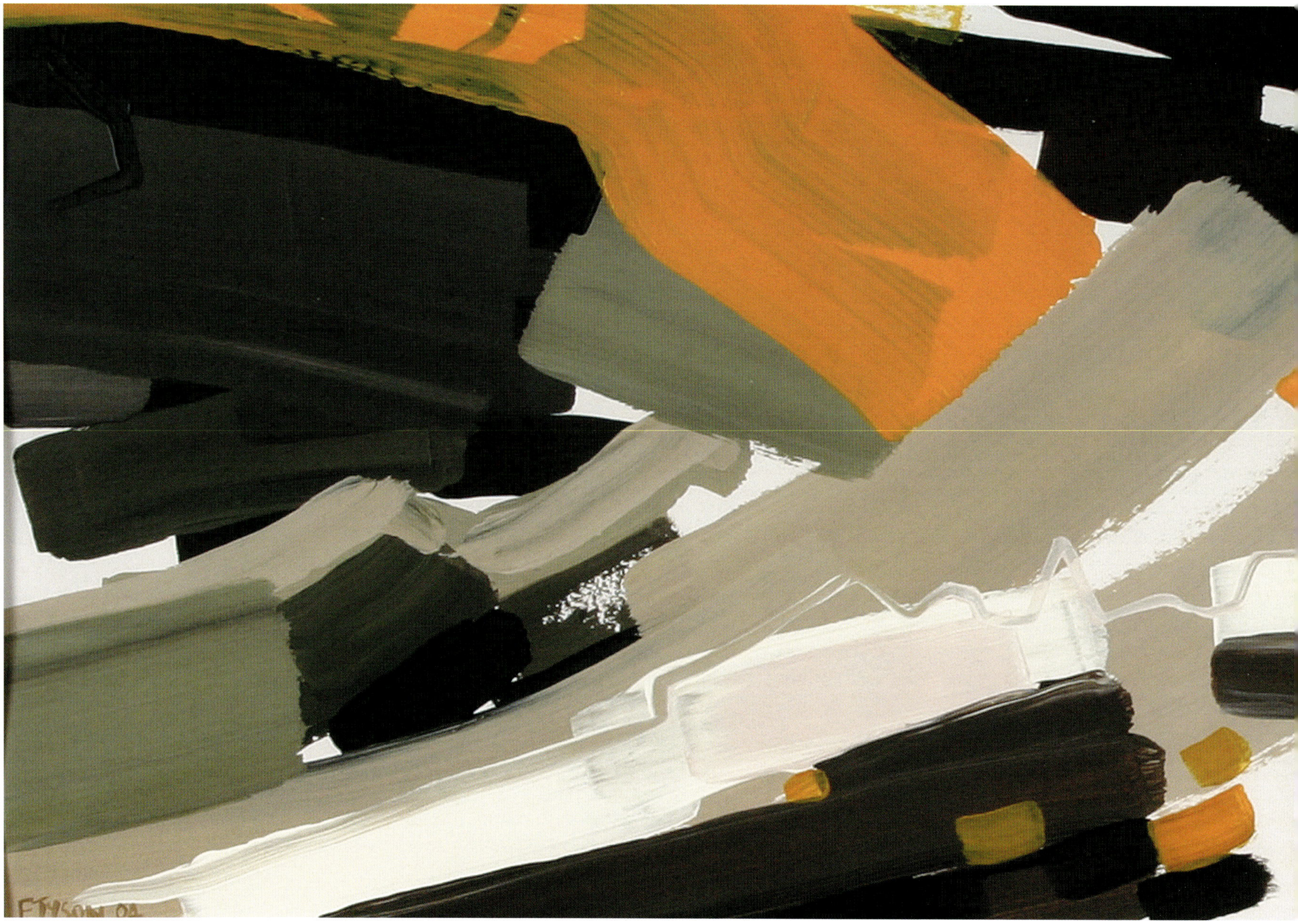

1

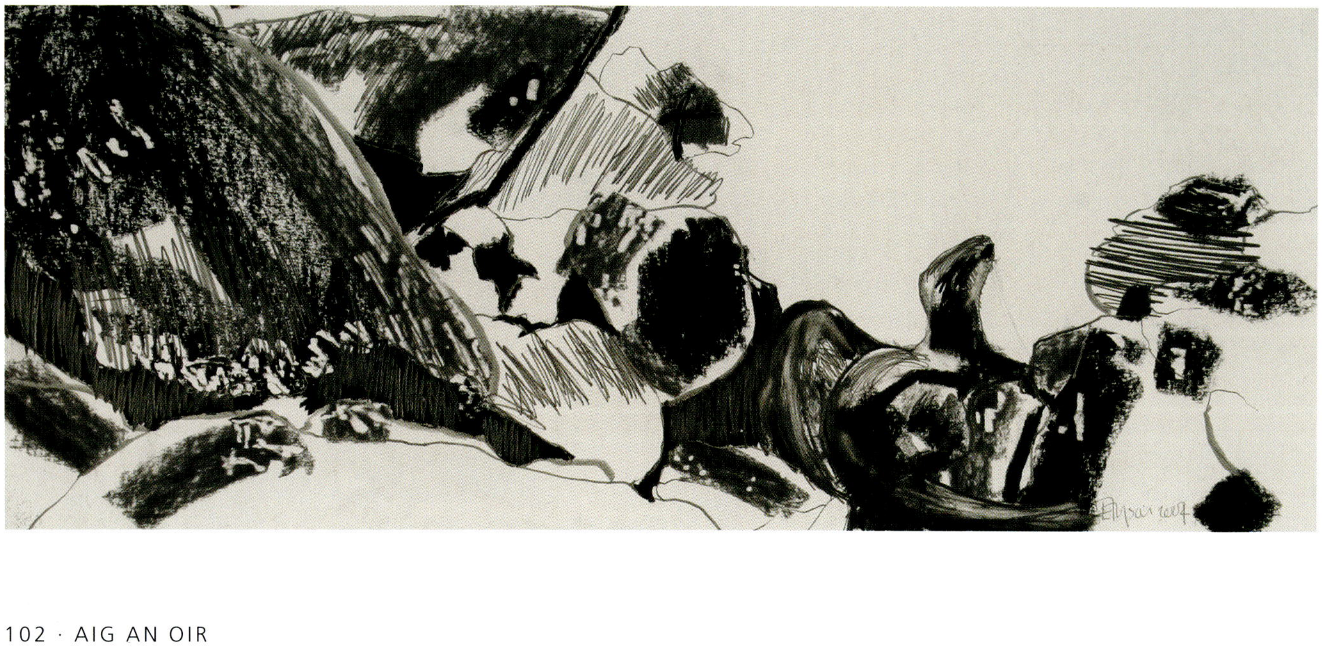

2

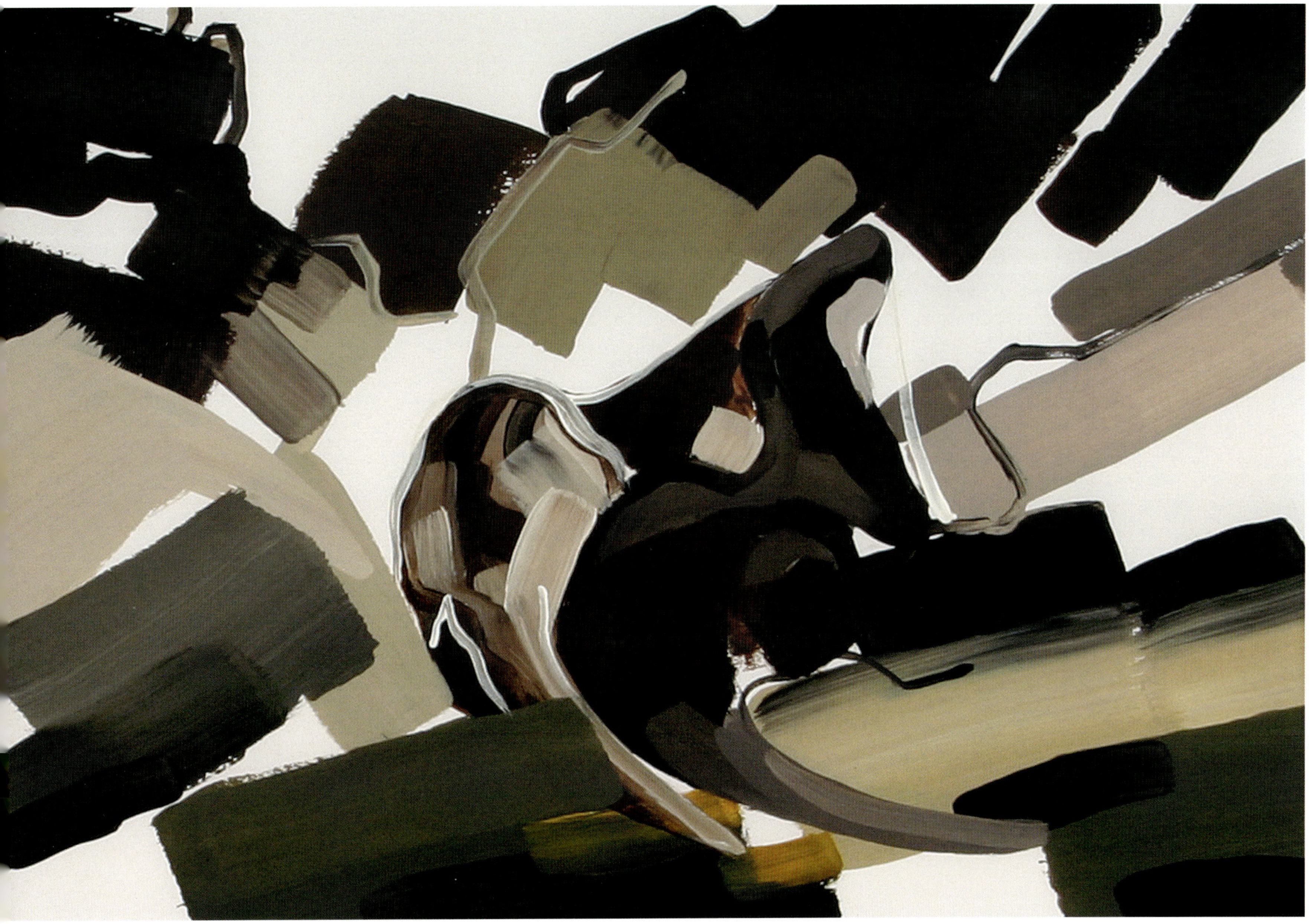

1. Esther Tyson *Otter and cub feeding, on the edge of Kinloch woods*
   acrylic on paper · 27 x 78 cm

   Early evening. I have been painting for a couple of hours. The breeze has kept the midges away till now. I scan the point. Movement. Otter! Two. Three. A head above water. Gone. Closer. Head back, chewing something small. Gone. Head above water. Larger catch. Crunching. Crab claws either side of her mouth. Playing cubs clambering on her, trying to get food. Gone. Closer again. Female now has what looks like a white sack with long tentacles. She stretches them from the body, one by one. Cubs continually at her side.

2. Esther Tyson *Otter and cub*
   charcoal and pencil on paper · 24 x 59.7 cm

Two days ago we came across an otter's holt, some way into the woodland. I picked up a trail about 200 yards away, not wanting to get too close. The ground is very boggy; I should have worn my wellies! There is a definite trail leading toward the shore. Heading downward, I follow a small stream in a shallow ravine. The trail crosses to the far bank. Soft ground but no tracks other than roe deer. I have found roe droppings regularly along the way, and I am beginning to wonder if that is all I will find. Steep climb around boulders and rocks. Up to higher ground. The trail is running parallel to the shoreline. I sit for a while under an old oak. Bones. A skull. The lower jaw is missing but already I am interested. I find a stick and poke around in the leaves. First right, then left, lower jaw. One tooth. Another. The midges are in my face as I disturb the leaf litter. An almost complete otter skull. The midges are too much! I move on. The trail is close to the edge. Narrow in places. Boulders and rocky outcrops. Jump down. Another boulder. Crab remains! An otter has been here! I follow at a faster pace. The ground is well trodden. Signs of activity every place I look. Trails leading through gaps between boulders. Many secret places for an otter to hole up. Spraint! Fresh on a predominant rock. Exciting. I move on. Another small stream winding its way to the open water. Soft ground. Otter track! One single, clear paw print...

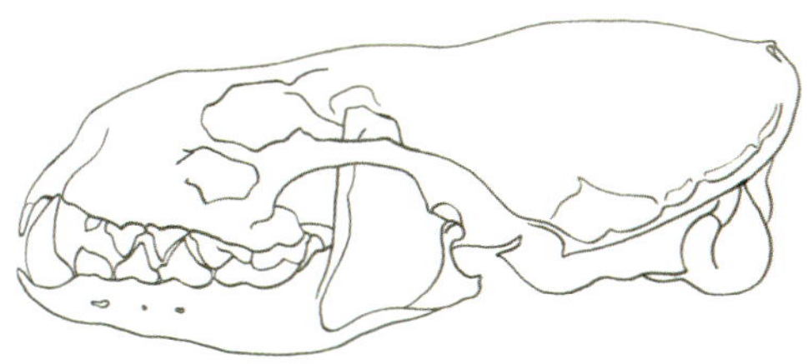

LICHENS

You cannot look closely at the oakwood trees without noticing that they are smothered with a variety of lesser plant life – ferns, mosses, liverworts and lichens – growing on the bark. These are epiphytes, which means that they are simply growing on the tree and are not behaving as parasites by deriving sustenance from it, like mistletoe.

Epiphytes are an important part of the diversity of species that makes the Atlantic oakwoods a priority for conservation. Their profusion is a result of the high rainfall, which regularly soaks the bark and maintains a damp atmosphere, together with the long, uninterrupted existence of the woods, which allows their slow-developing communities to become established. Mosses and liverworts, collectively called bryophytes, are simple plants that grow in moist, sheltered conditions. In woods, lush growths are found in sheltered north-facing sites, at the bases of trees and in ravines. Lichens like more light and grow on sunny slopes in open woods, and along the edges of glades.

Early writers described lichens as 'scurf' or 'mould', and it is easy to dismiss them as no more than discoloration or perhaps a deformity of the bark. But lichens are one of the glories of the Atlantic oakwoods. The 10 hectares of Barnluasgan Wood in Knapdale, for instance, are known to support 300 kinds of lichens, most of which live on trees, and some of which are rare or scarce.

Whether rare or not, lichens are worth our attention because they are a unique life form. Not plants, they consist of a fungus and a green alga (in some cases a blue-green alga or cyanobacterium) living in a close relationship for mutual benefit, known as symbiosis. The alga manufactures carbohydrates by photosynthesis and shares them with the fungus. The fungus, in turn, gives the alga support and shelter. In particular, it protects the alga from the damaging rays of ultra-violet light and from desiccation in dry weather. So close is the relationship that neither alga nor fungus can live on its own.

A closer look at these lichens, preferably through a magnifying glass, reveals an exquisite variety of form and colour. The problem is that most lichens are difficult to identify. I was lucky to be shown around a small hazel wood in Knapdale, called Barrandaimh, and introduced to its lichens by Peter Quelch. As he put it, 'Some lichens are definitely not for amateurs', but he held my attention by pointing out interesting facts about the species we encountered. The scientific names were lost on me unless he pointed out some clear and interesting feature of the lichen by which I could remember them. *Usnea*,

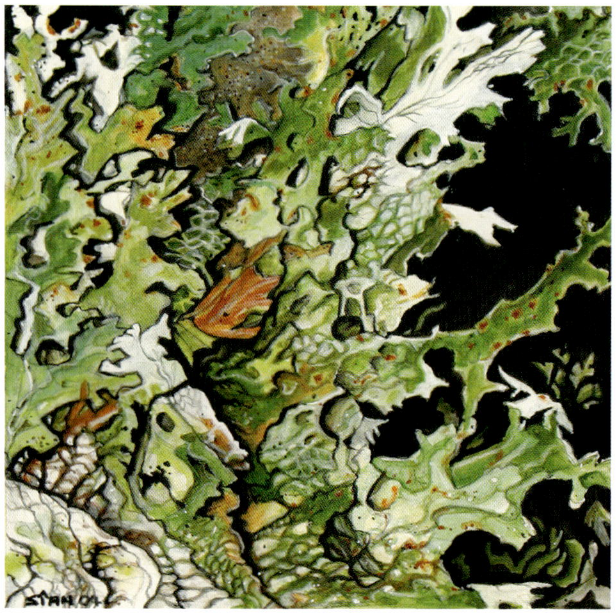
1

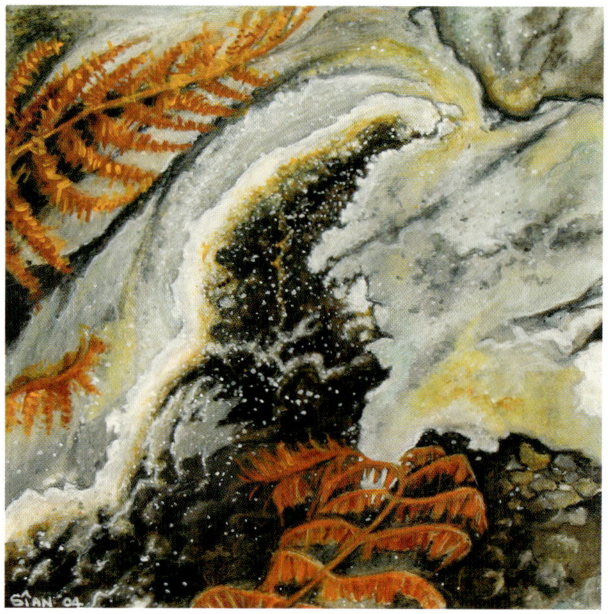
2

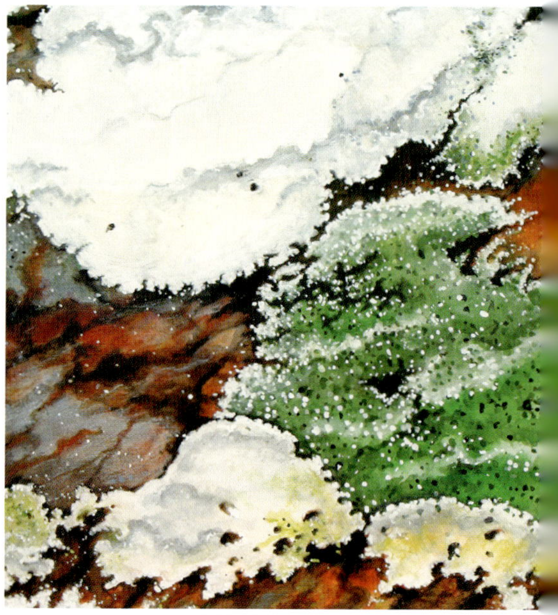
3

or old man's beard, hangs in hairy festoons; *Platismatia glauca* looks like lettuce; and *Sphaerophorus globosus* has a remarkable resemblance to coral.

Lichens live in characteristic communities, with different collections of species on different trees. The types of lichen growing on a tree are partly a measure of the acidity of its bark. Birch, alder and oak are more acidic than hazel, willow and ash. The roughness of the bark also plays a part. Smooth bark is colonised by crusting lichens, which form a closely fitting mosaic on hazels and young oaks. One of these is grey, warty cudbear *Ochrolechia tartaria*, from which the Highlanders used to make a crimson dye by steeping it in rancid urine.

Our walk took us from birch and into hazel, and Peter pointed out how the characteristic lichens changed. When we moved among the hazel trees, there was *Parmelellia triptophylla,* which smells strongly of iodine. Much more striking were the four species of *Lobaria* lungworts. They are so named because the underside of the flat 'leaves' looks like lung tissue. On the strength of this resemblance they were once used for treating lung ailments. Peter also showed me how some common lichens were good colonisers and took up residence on twigs and saplings that were only two or three years old. As the tree grows, they are replaced by

6

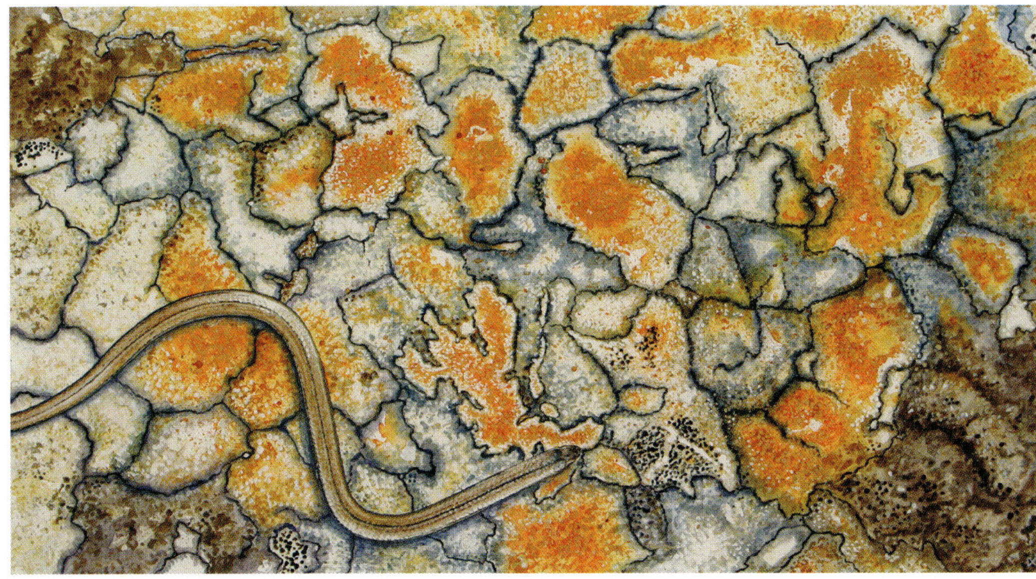

1. Sîan Armstrong *Layered lichens*
   gouache, watercolour and ink · 17.5 x 17.5 cm
2. Sîan Armstrong *Recurring form, bracken and lichen*
   gouache and ink · 17.5 x 17.5 cm
3. Sîan Armstrong *Like a wave breaking*
   gouache, watercolour and ink · 17 x 17 cm
4. John Paige *Birch woodland, Taynish Mill*
   watercolour · 28 x 38 cm
5. Jane Leycester Paige *Colony of lichens on oak branch*
   watercolour and ink · 31 x 24 cm
6. Brin Edwards *Slow-worm with map-like lichens*
   watercolour and gouache · 20 x 36.5 cm

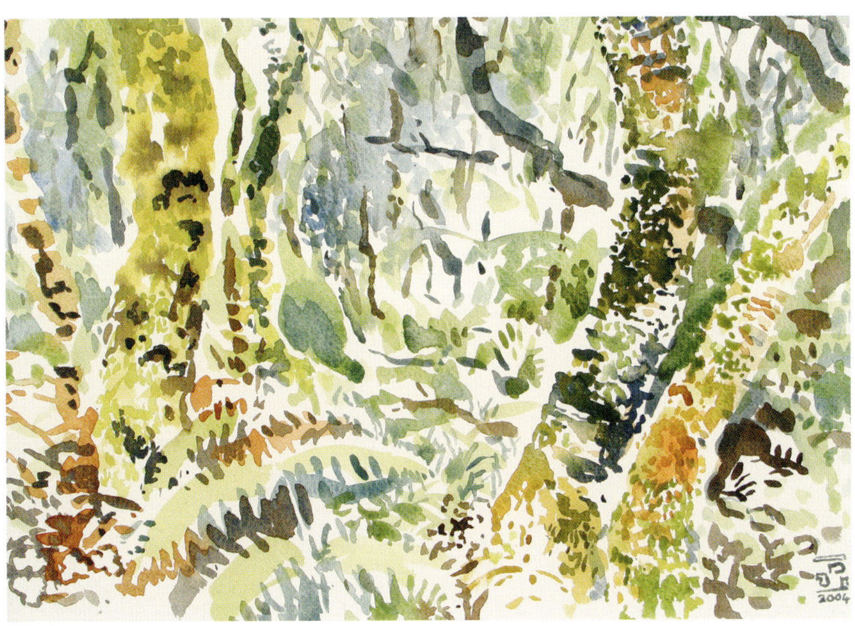

4

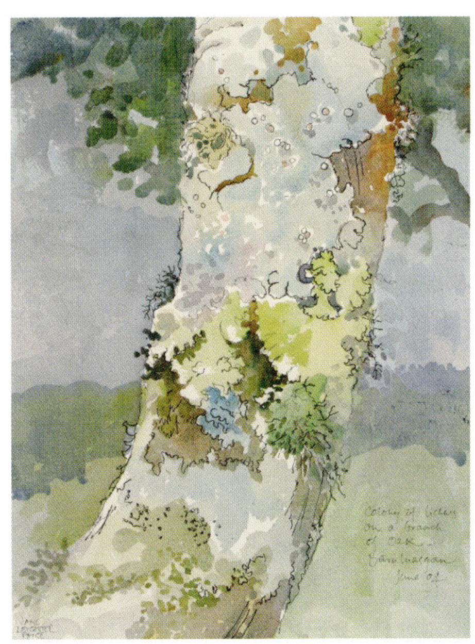

5

Brin Edwards *Slow-worm with map-like lichens*

I was fascinated by the map-like lichens covering the rocks along the woodland paths. The slow-worm completed the picture, like a sinuous river.

Sîan Armstrong *Layered lichens*

At first I was overwhelmed by the variety of potential subjects and approaches, and I wandered around for ages – so much to see and take in. Eventually I decided to focus on 'pattern' – itself a huge, varied subject! I really liked the way these lichens 'arranged themselves' in rhythmic layers against the dark background of a tree trunk.

species that need many years to become established. The rare ones need a century of tree growth to become established.

A walk through a wood of oaks would have revealed yet another community, although many species would have been the same, including tree lungwort growing to the size of dinner plates and sometimes falling off the tree under its own weight. There are several reasons why the Atlantic oakwoods are so well endowed with lichens. They thrive in the damp, mild air and they also like its purity. Lichens disappeared from industrial areas because they are so susceptible to acid rain. The remote west coast of Scotland is a sanctuary for rare species, and there are rich communities because the air has never been polluted. Linked with the absence of industrialisation there is the continuity of the woodlands, which enables slow-growing and slow-colonising species to maintain a presence. Despite the history of management by coppicing and pollarding, there has been continuous tree cover as a habitat for lichens.

There is more to the lichen community than lichens. The carpet of growth covering the trees is the foundation for a unique ecosystem of animals that feed on lichens, which hugely increases the diversity, and hence conservation value, of the lichens. It is not obvious because many of the animals are nocturnal and are, in any case, small and obscure. Earwigs and woodlice scavenge on dead tissues, while slugs and snails scrape the lichen with their rough tongues. If they are not visible, their presence is given away by the zig-zags trails where they have exposed the pale deeper tissues of the lichen. Moths that eat and rest on lichens, as either caterpillars or adults, are hard to spot because they are exquisitely camouflaged. These herbivorous animals are the prey of the ecosystem's carnivores, which include spiders, beetles, lacewing larvae, harvestmen and predatory flies.

1. John Paige *Lichen on rocks by the shore, Taynish*
watercolour · 24 x 34 cm
2. Jane Leycester Paige *Dog lichen study*
watercolour · 18 x 26 cm
3. Anna Kirk-Smith *Sea edge*
mixed media · 68 x 50 cm

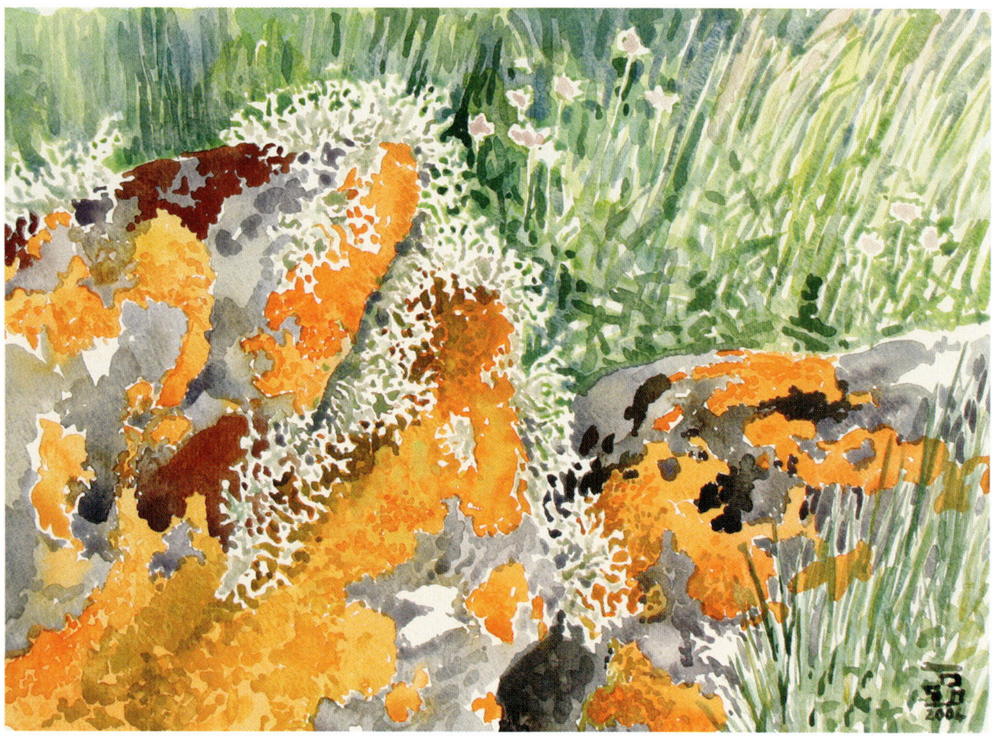

1

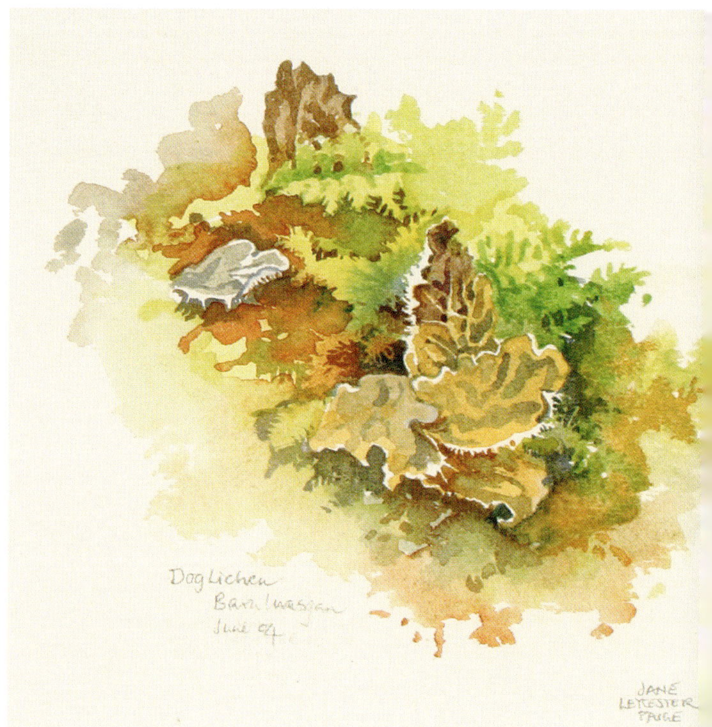

2

3

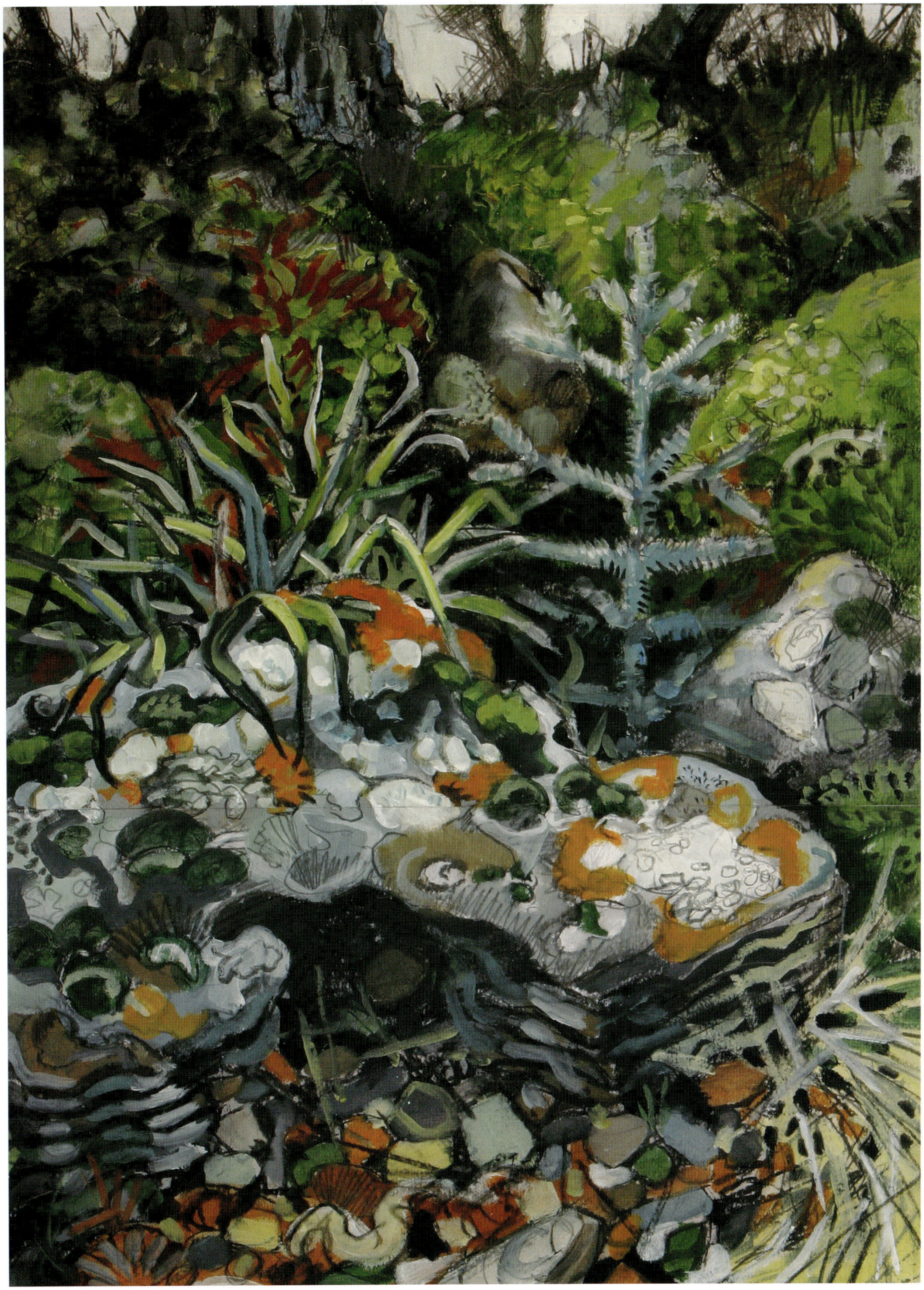

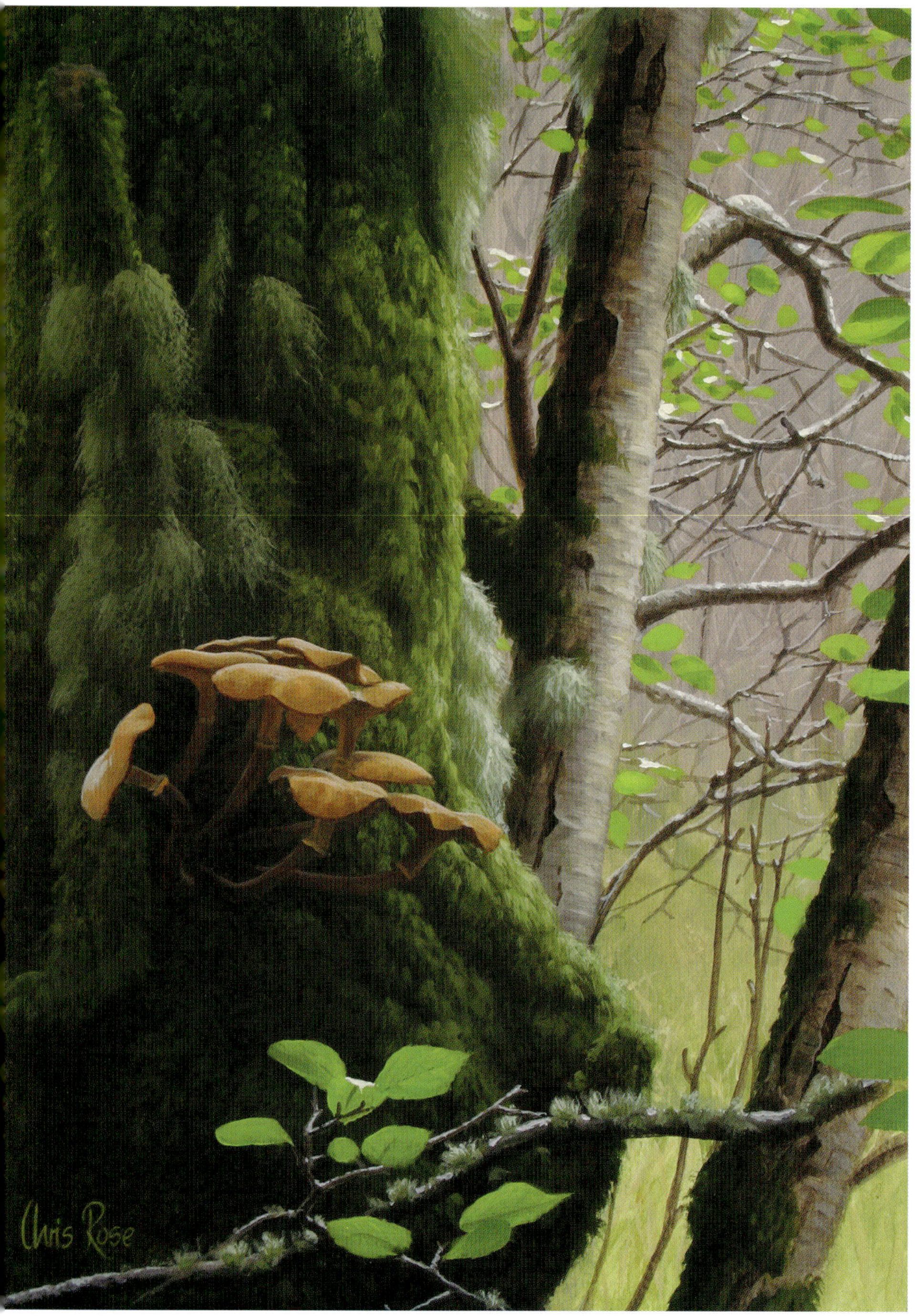

1

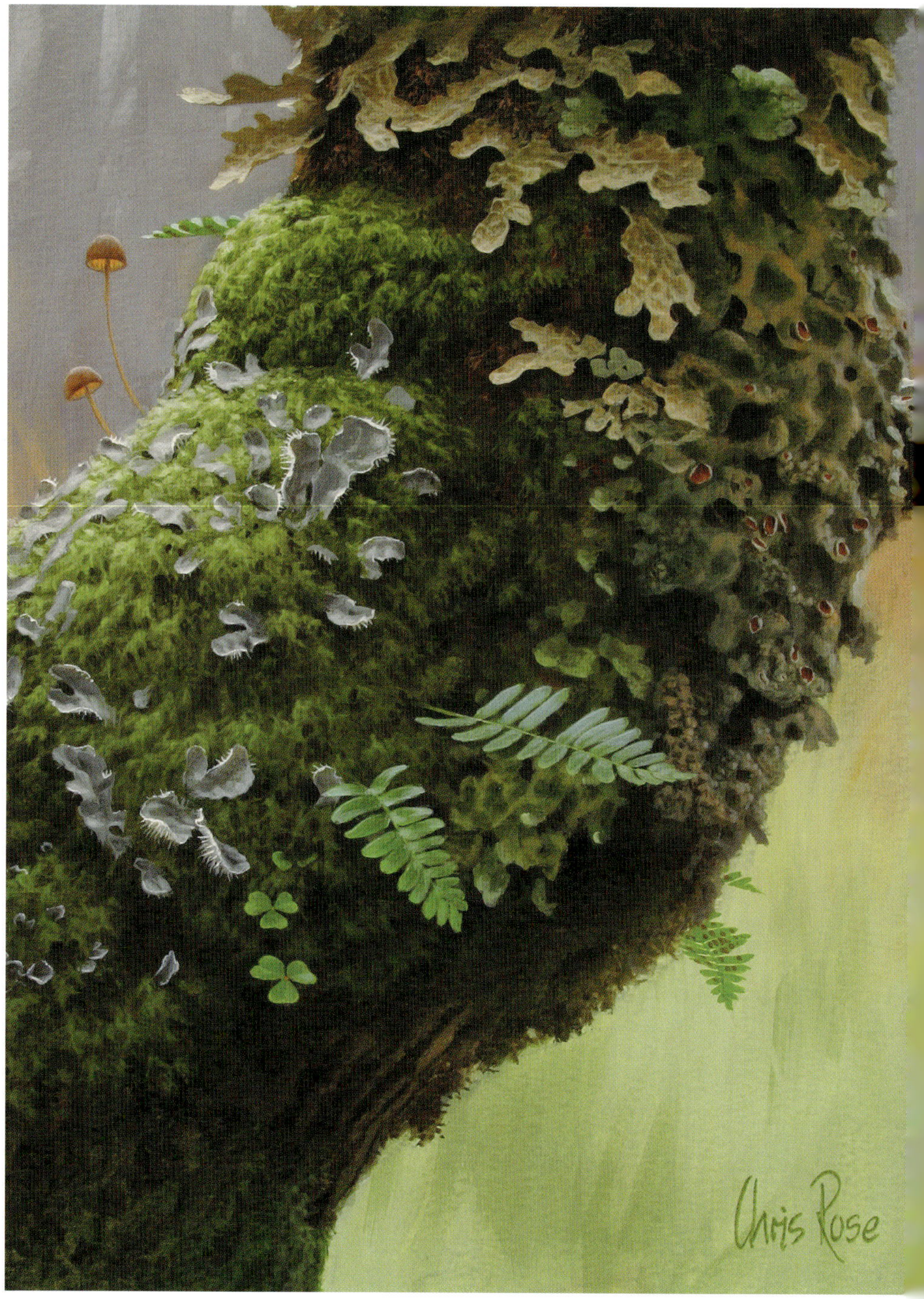

2

1. Chris Rose *Fungi*
   acrylic on paper · 39 x 30 cm
2. Chris Rose *The living cloak*
   acrylic on paper · 30 x 22 cm

   Everywhere you look in the oakwoods, there is evidence of the profusion of plant life. Every tree, log, stone and branch is covered in a bewildering array of lichens, mosses, ferns and fungi. This stem of a coppiced oak in the Taynish woods at Knapdale was typical.
3. Barry W. Van Dusen *Oak forest epiphytes, Ardery Reserve*
   watercolour · 27 x 34.5 cm
4. Richard Tratt *The silver ground carpet*
   oil on canvas · 30.5 x 40 cm

   Painted outdoors amidst a cloud of midges, this is an ancient lichen-covered oak at Ceol na Mara woods. I couldn't resist painting in a moth – the silver ground carpet.

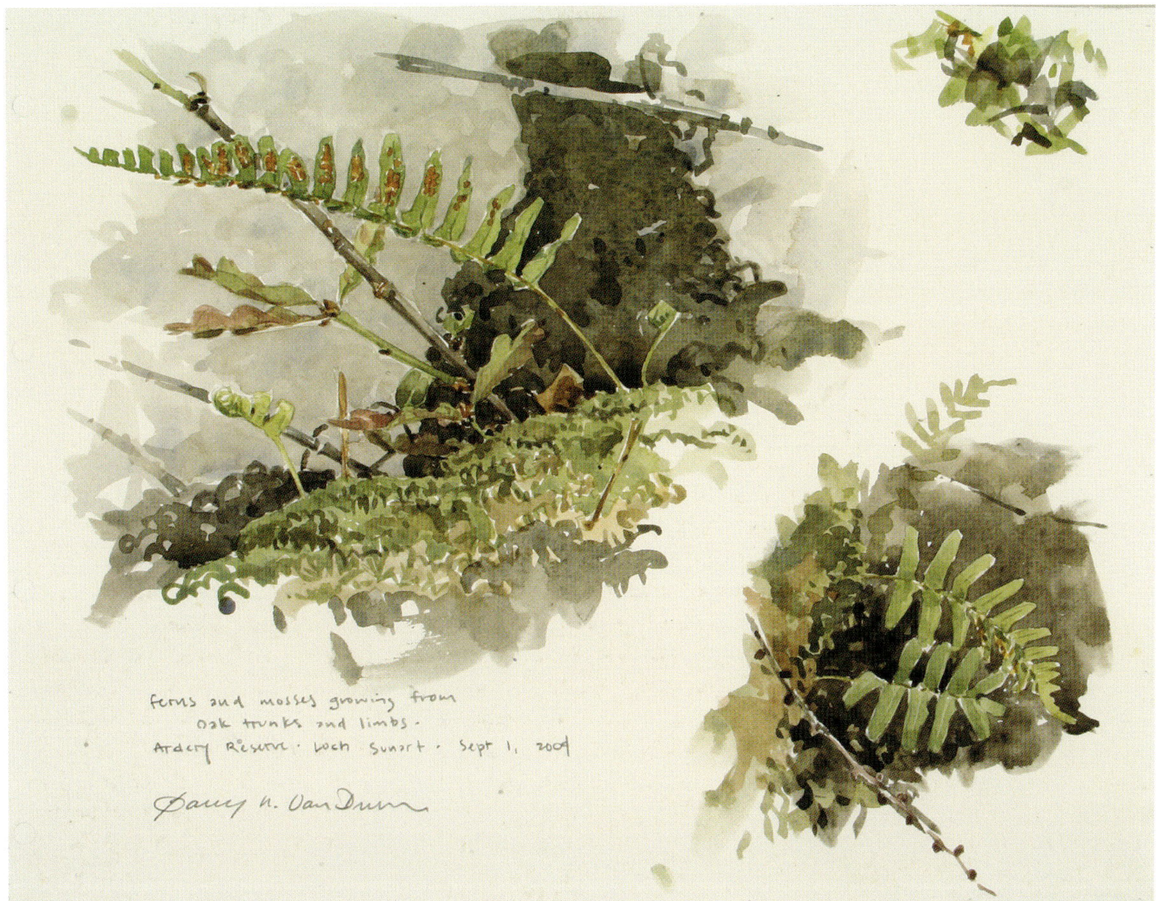

3

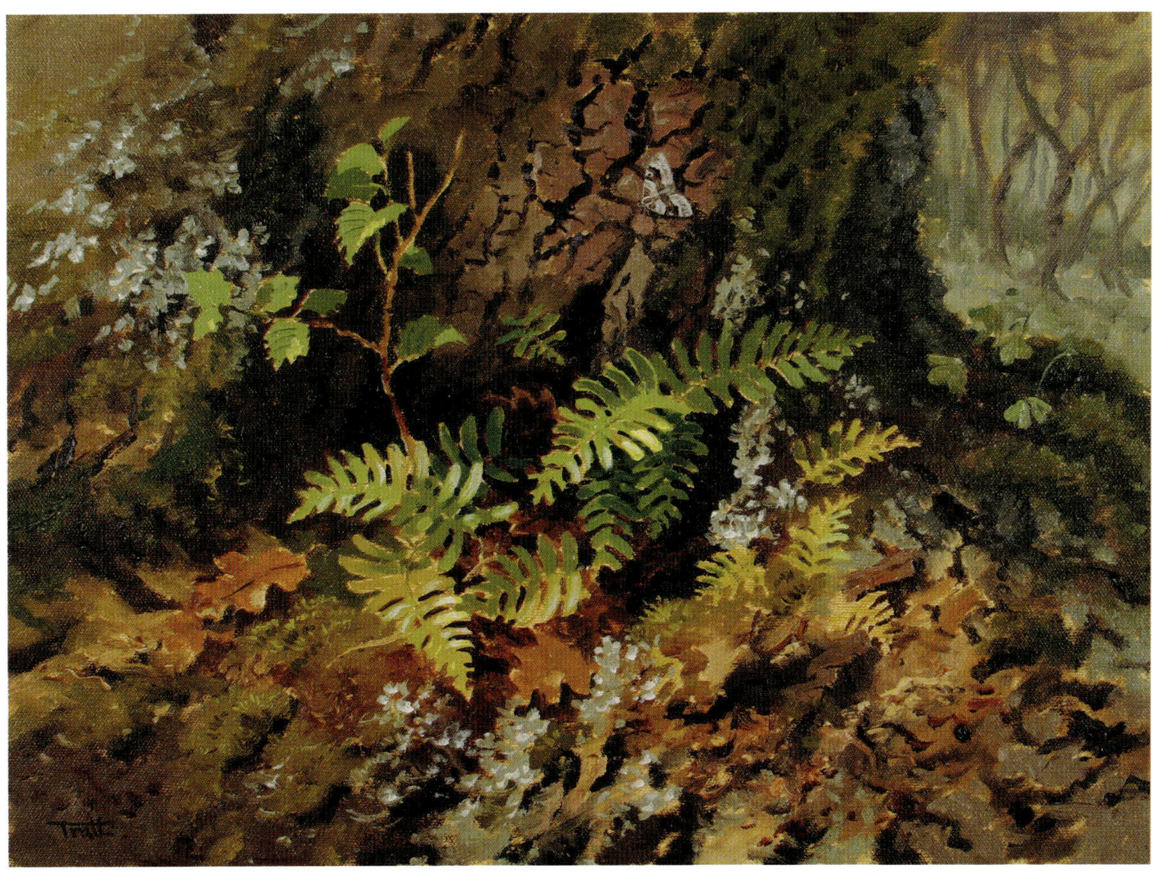

4

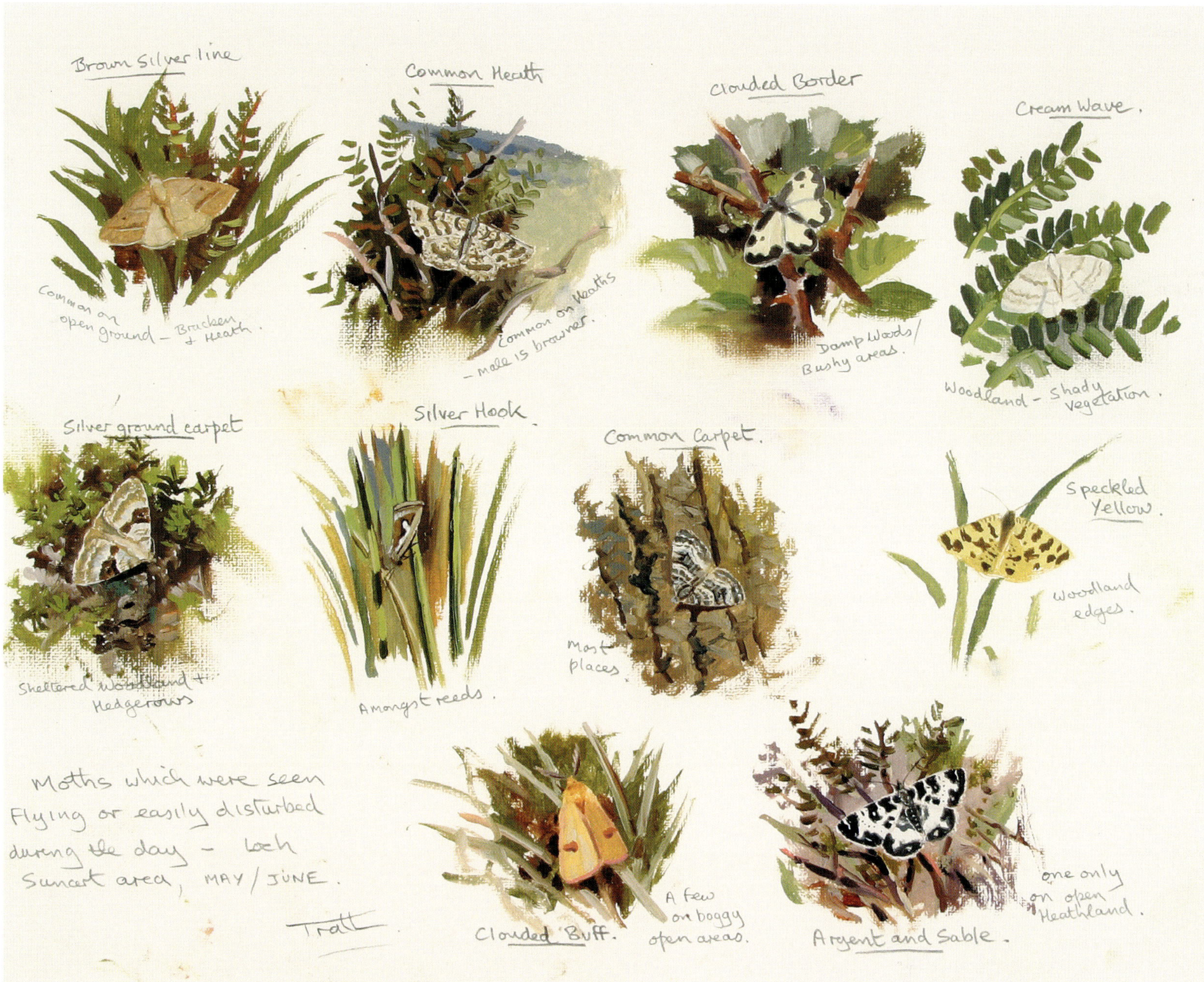

1

1. Richard Tratt *Day moths – Loch Sunart area*
oil on paper · 23 x 30.5 cm

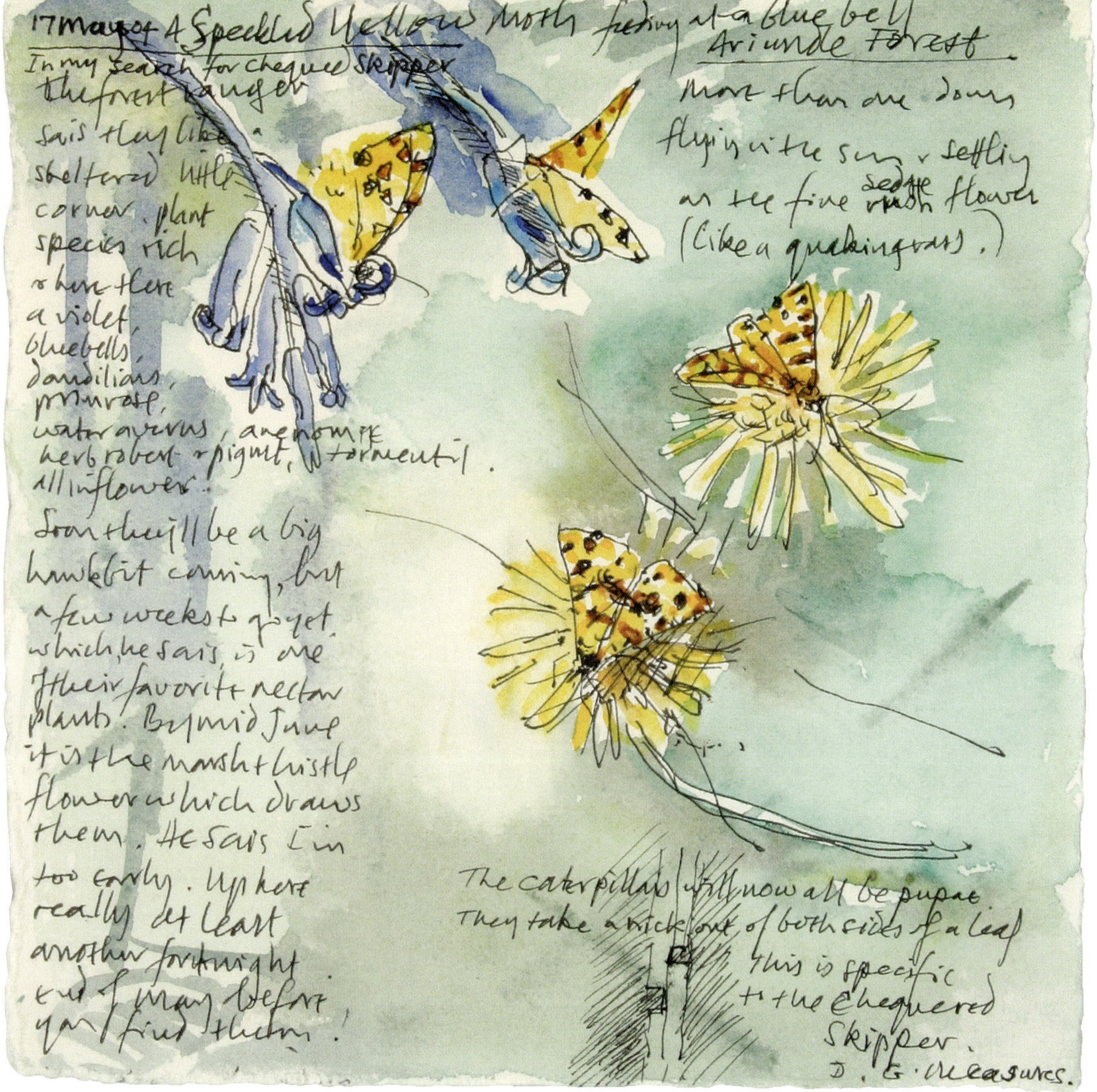

2

2. David Guy Measures *Speckled yellow moth*
pen and watercolour · 16 x 15 cm

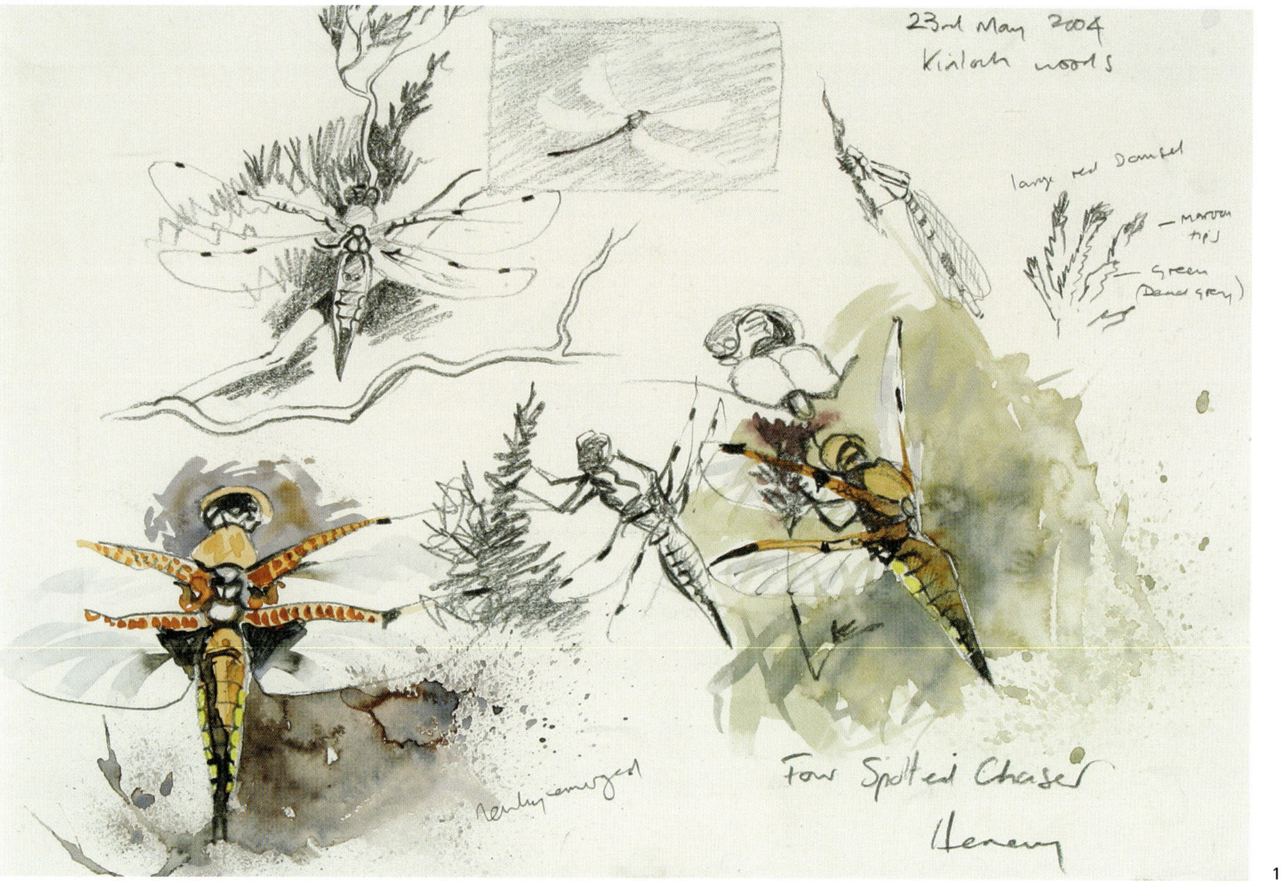
23rd May 2004
Kinloch woods
Four Spotted Chaser

1

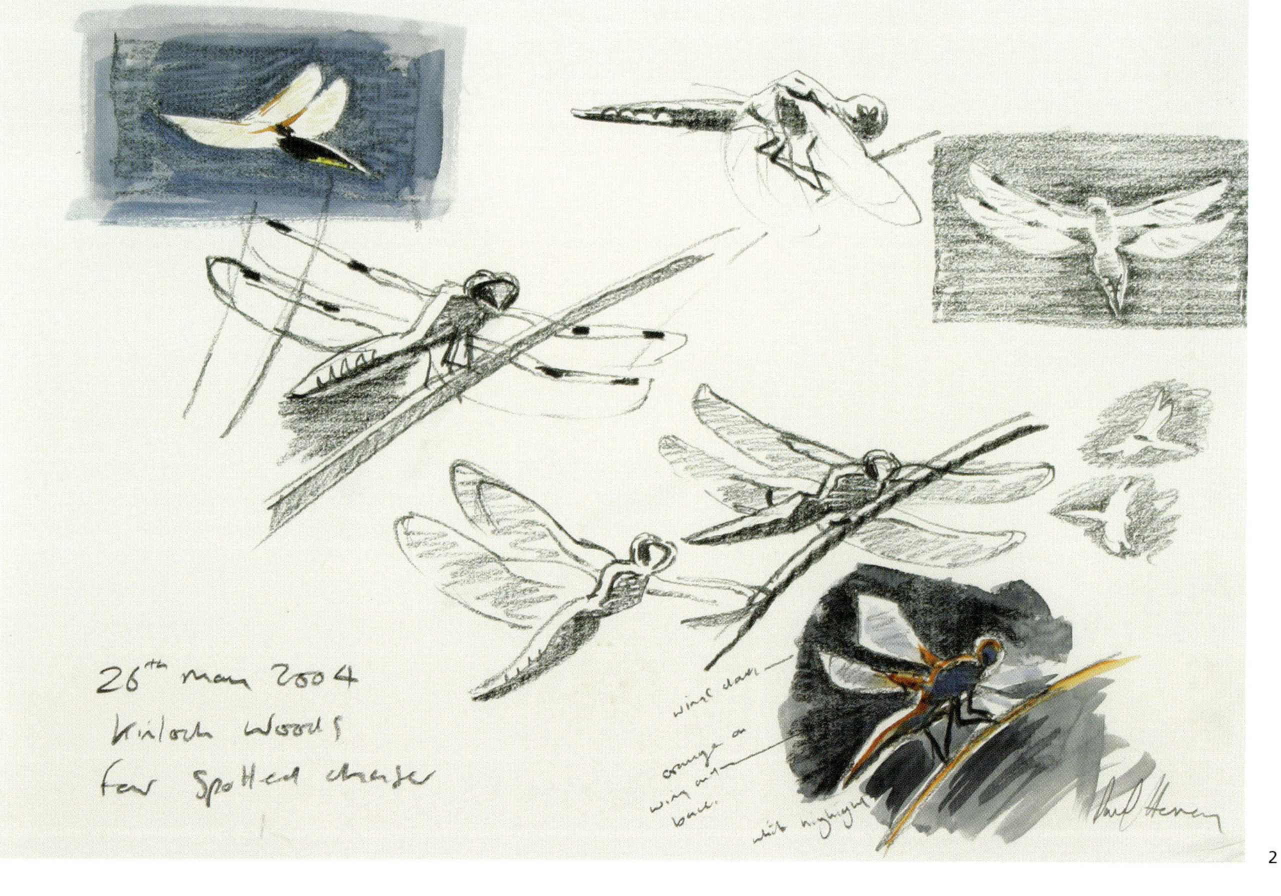
26th May 2004
Kinloch Woods
four Spotted chaser

2

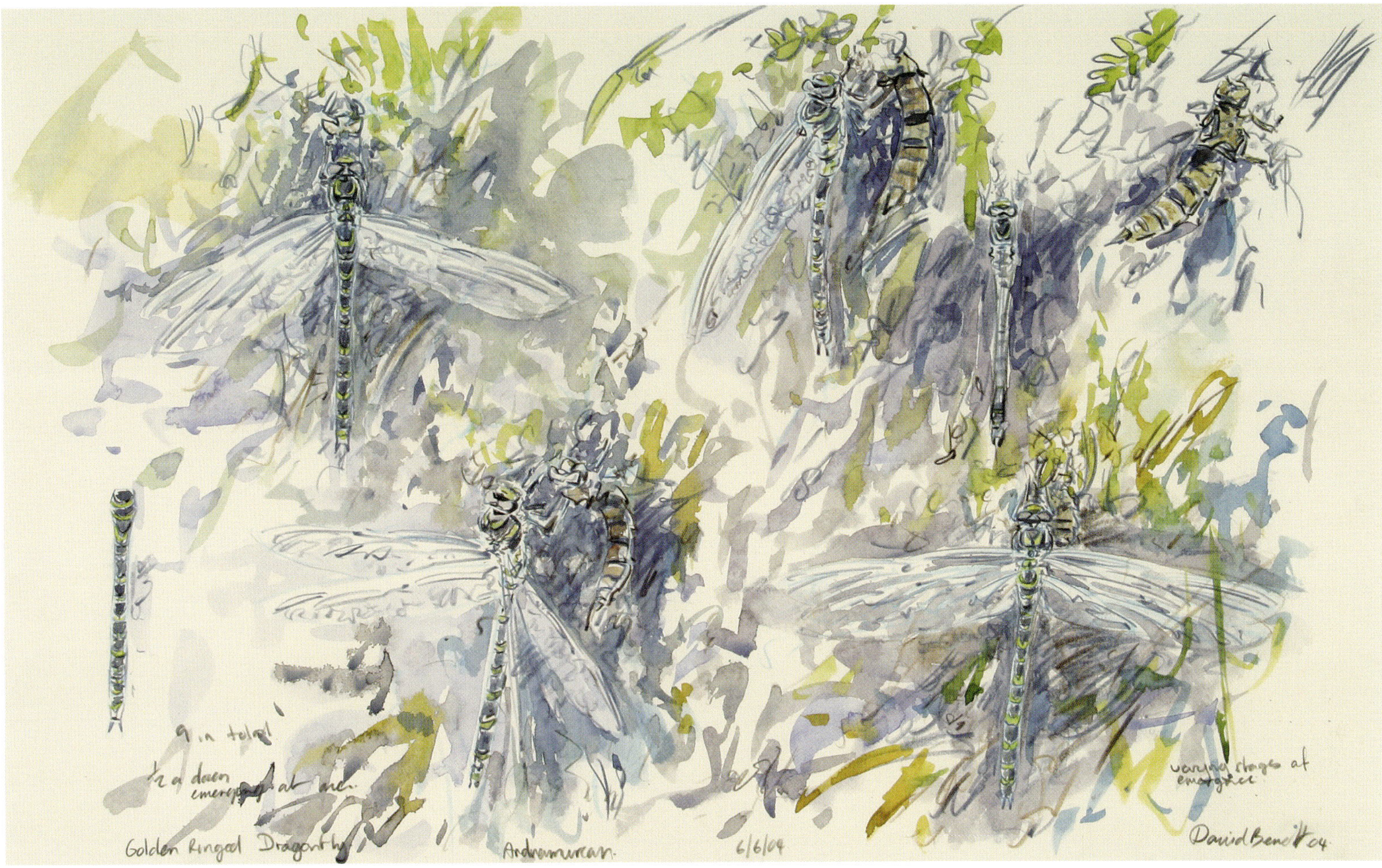

3

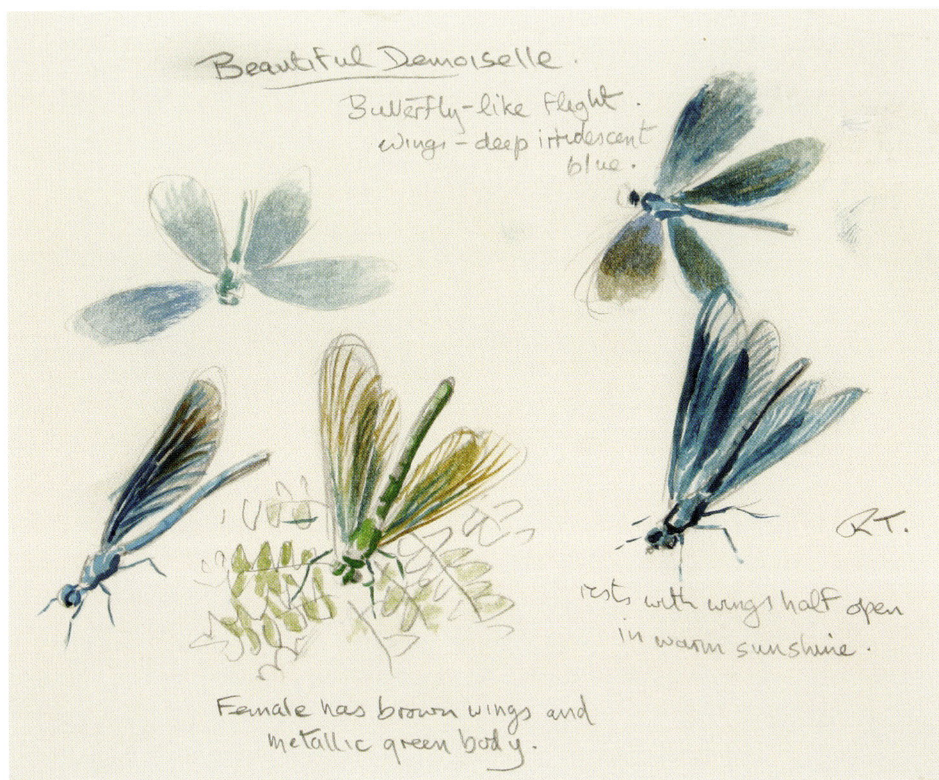

4

1,2 Paul Henery *Four-spotted chaser studies*
conté and pencil · 27 x 38 cm

3. David Bennett *Golden-ringed dragonflies emerging studies*
pastel and watercolour · 36 x 57cm

A mere trickle of a stream was the setting for this mass emergence. Nine dragonflies were in various stages of unfolding. Their little bodies vibrating as fluid pumped around them. Truly a wild wonder.

4. Richard Tratt *Beautiful demoiselles – sketchbook*
oil and pencil on paper · 15 x 20 cm

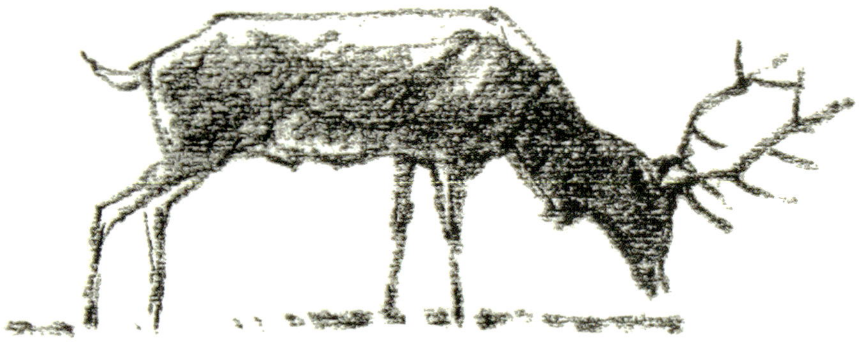

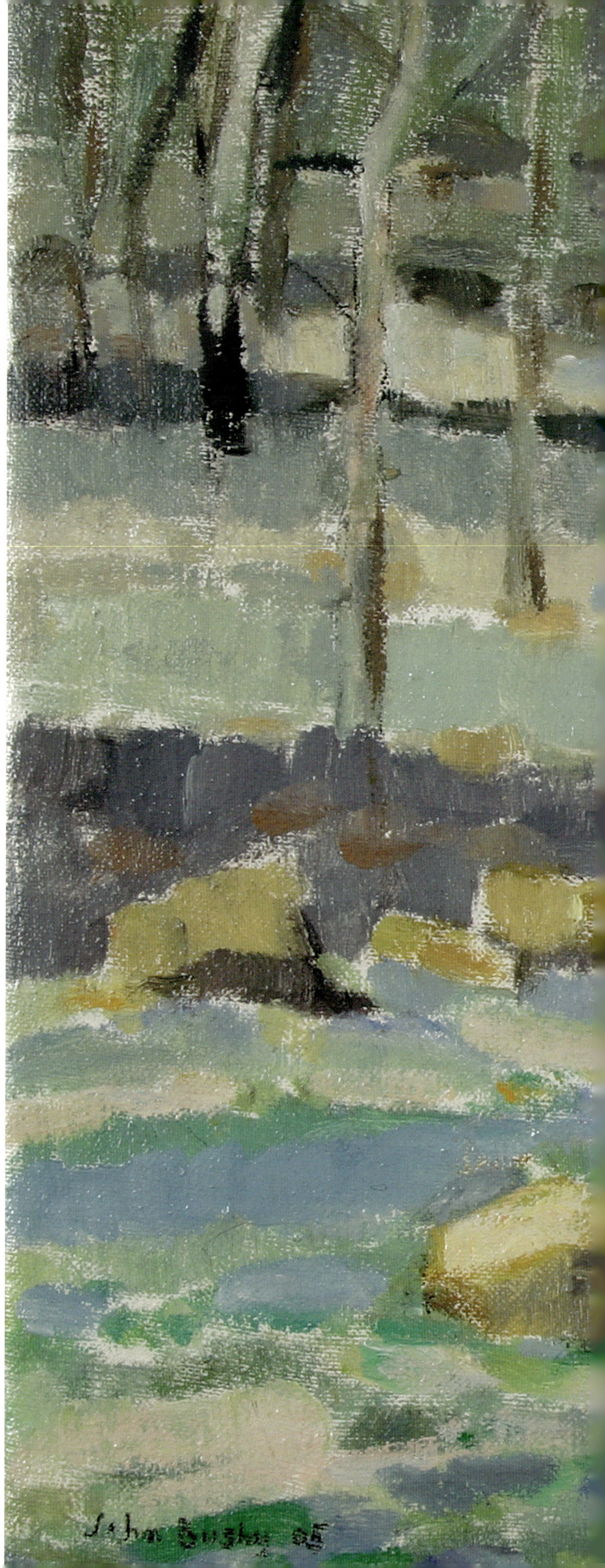

John Busby *Oaks, deer and bluebells, Ariundle*
oil on canvas · 27.5 x 35 cm

The oak woods in early May. Trees in bud with few leaves out. Bluebells on the ground. All the many boulders covered with lichen, forming soft, golden-yellow, rounded shapes.

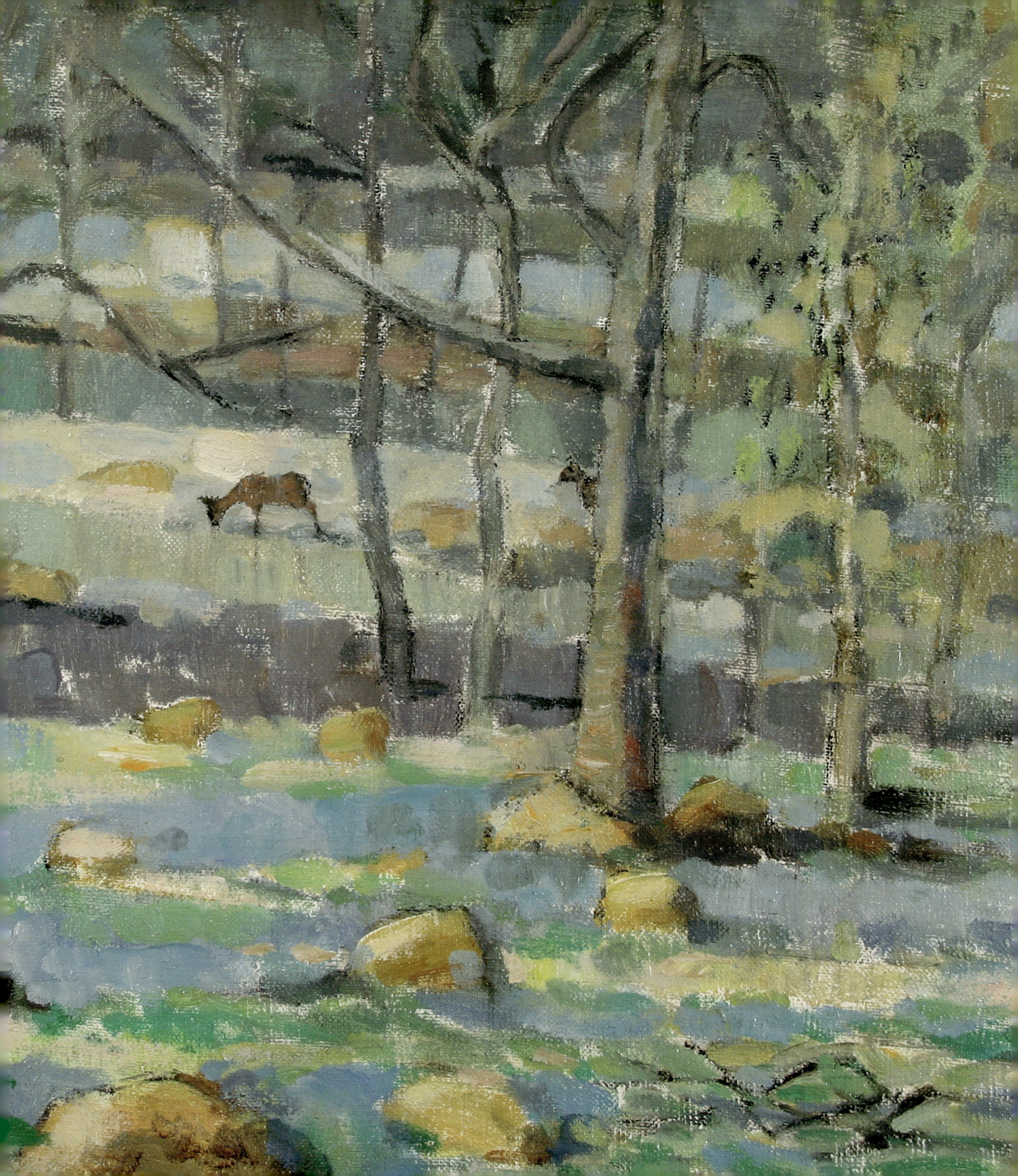

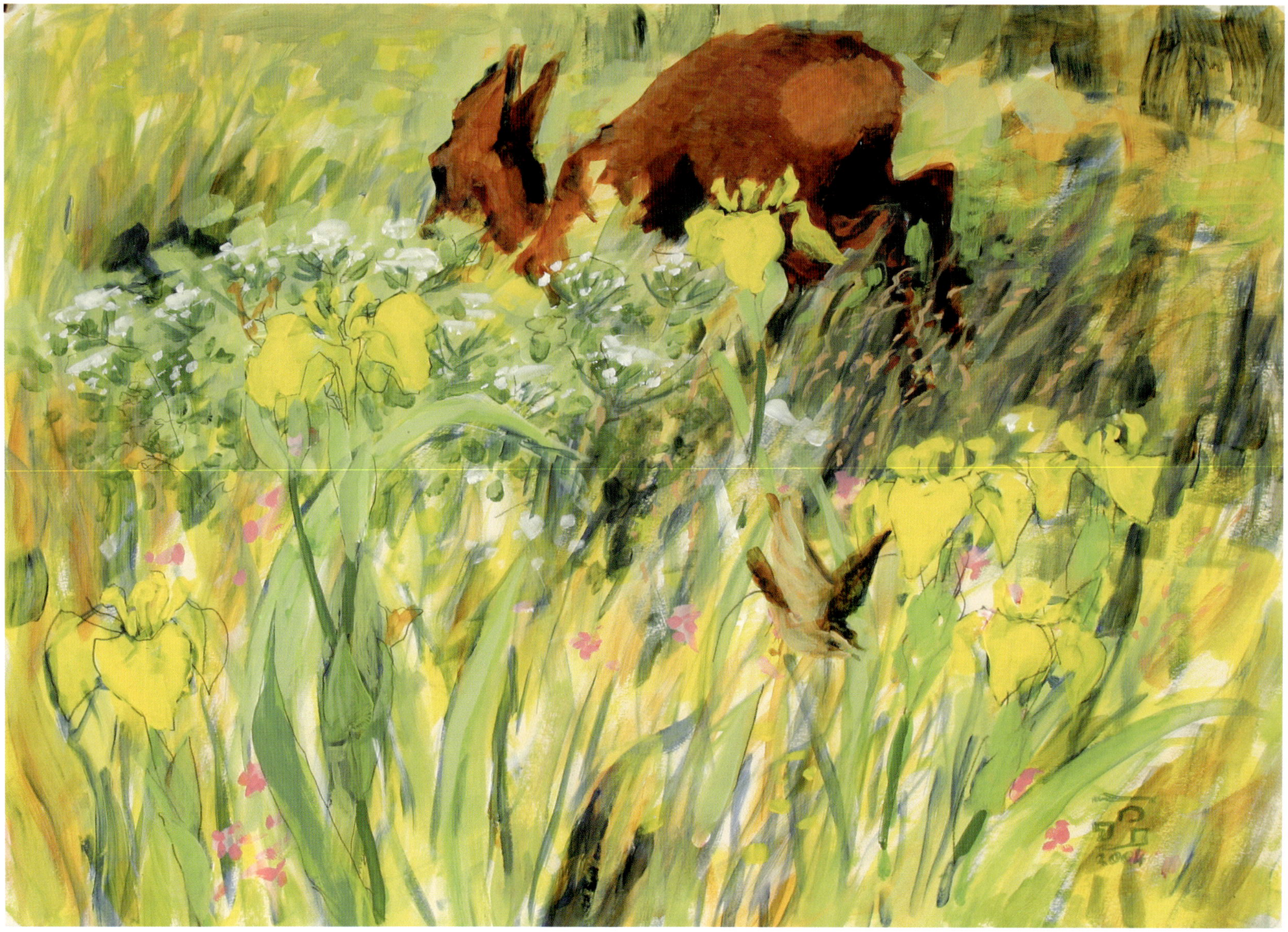

1

1. John Paige *Yellow flag water meadow, Tayvallich*
acrylic · 56 x 76 cm

We could see this water meadow from our cottage window. Full of yellow flag, ragged robin and hemlock water dropwort. A sedge warbler had his territory on our side and made frequent display flights, with slow, butterfly wing action. One morning a female roe deer jumped through the meadow.

2. Keith Brockie *Stags in velvet*
watercolour on coloured paper · 35 x 32 cm

There were stags in the woodland at Ardery but it was much easier to get to grips with them out on the open moorland. These were sitting in the sun amidst the nodding white heads of cotton grass. Their winter coats were worn and faded prior to moulting into a rich red summer pelage. The antlers were almost half grown and covered in 'velvet', which they would scrape off in the coming months, when the antlers had fully developed. The strong sunlight helped to highlight the strong sculptural facial form, and the play of shadows added more interest to the composition.

2

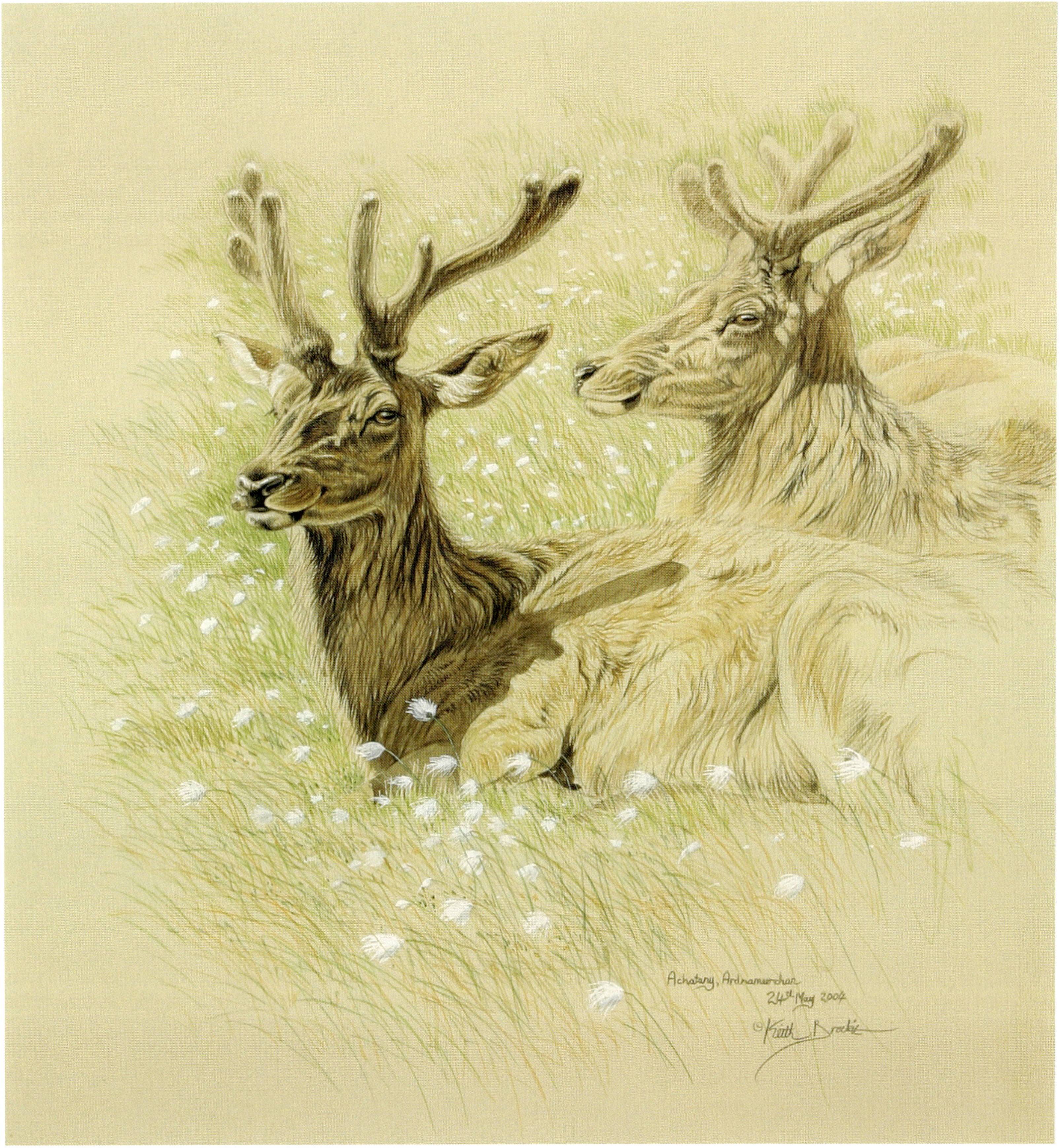

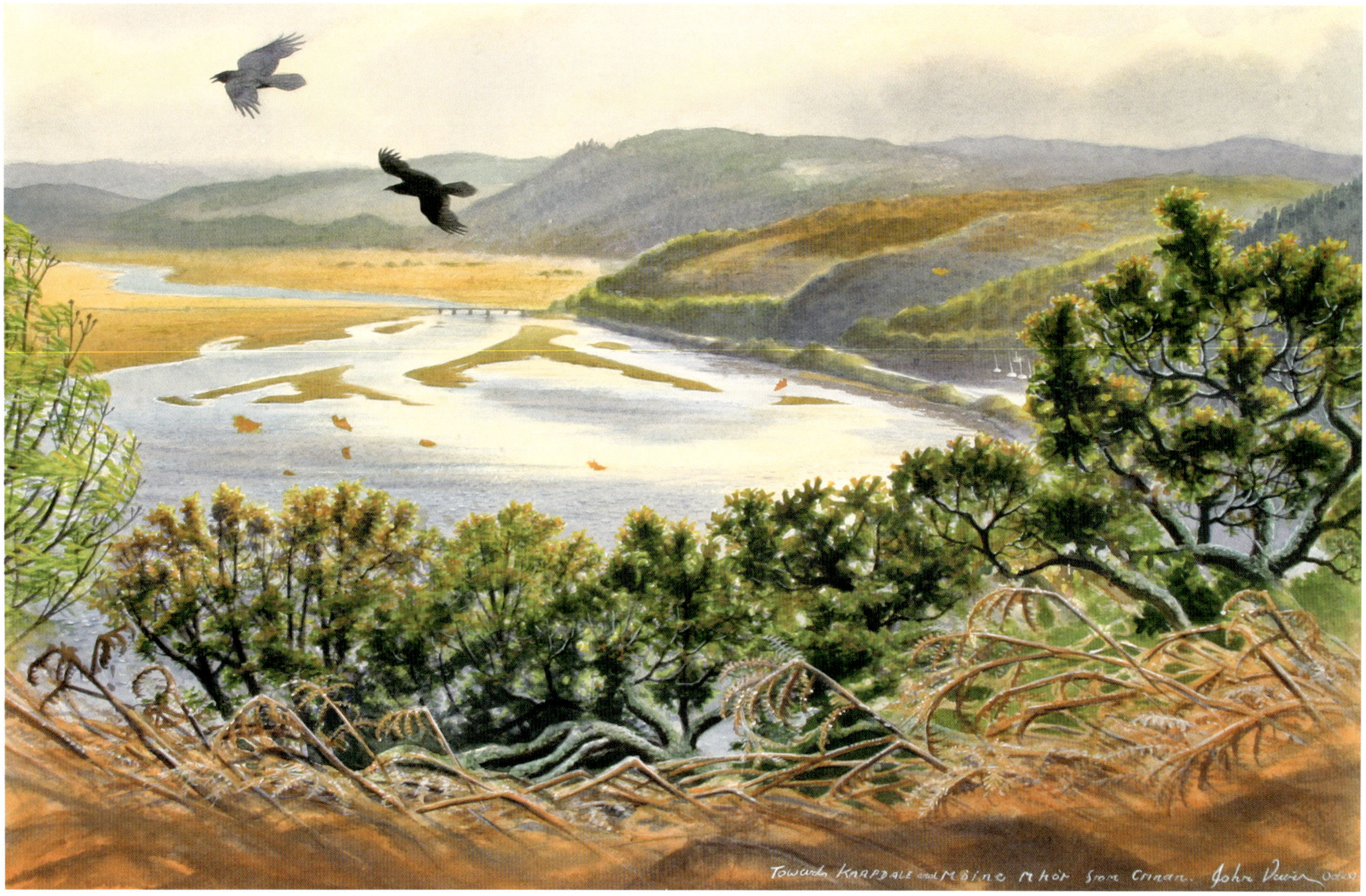

1

1. John Davis *Towards Knapdale and Móine Mhôr*
watercolour · 42 x 61 cm

A blustery, rainy day with occasional glimpses of the sun. The ochre expanse of Mòine Mhór, the steep hills of Knapdale and the Crinan Canal can all be seen. Ravens occasionally croaked as they enjoyed the buffeting winds.

2. Keith Brockie *Raven brood*
watercolour on paper · 35 x 49 cm

A brood of raven chicks sitting in a cliff nest overlooking a riverine gully in an oakwood above Glen More. I sat on the opposite bank and sketched and painted them via a telescope. One chick was panting in the strong sunlight, exposing a startling red gape.

3. Keith Brockie *Raven sketch*
pencil on paper · 24 x 33.5 cm

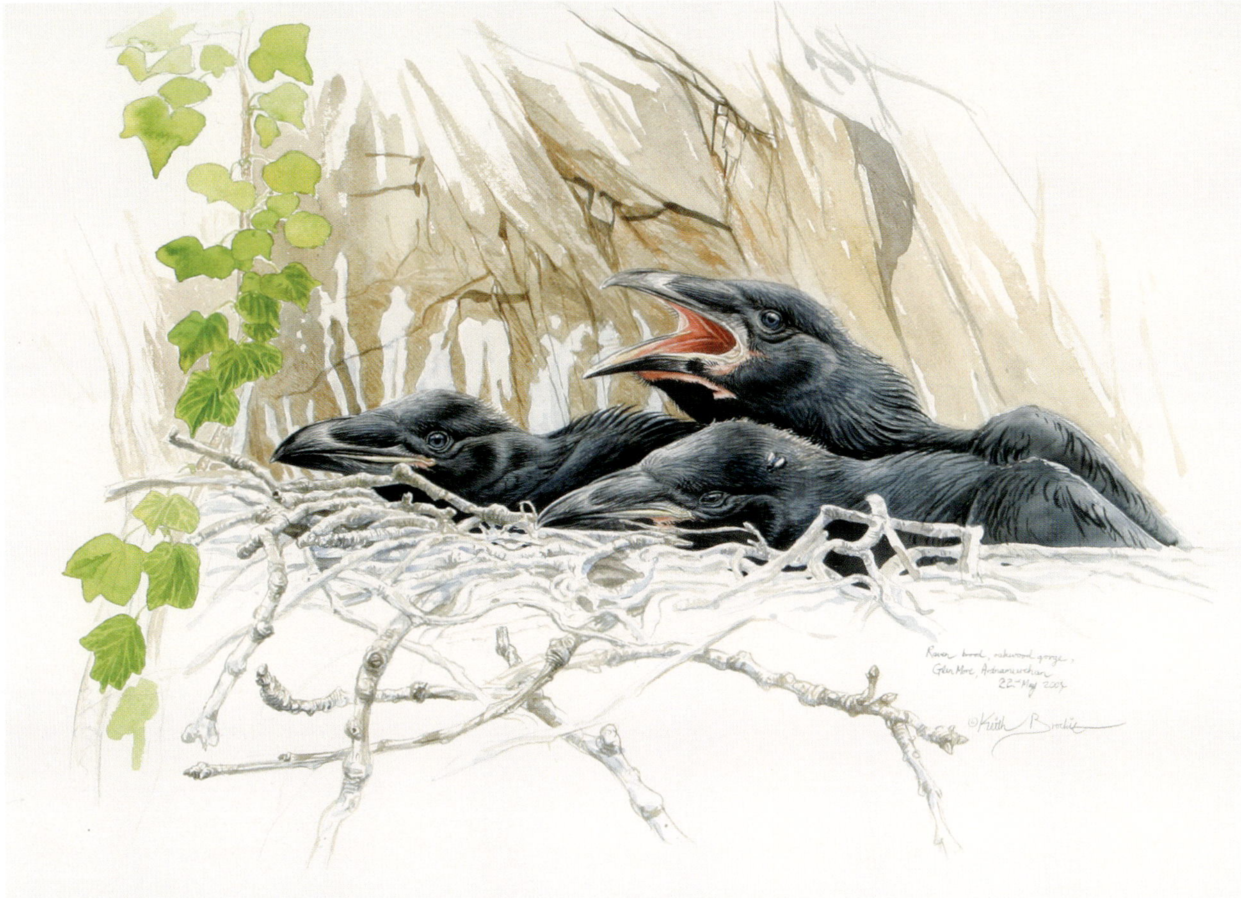
Raven brood, oakwood gorge,
Glen More, Ardnamurchan
22nd May 2004

2

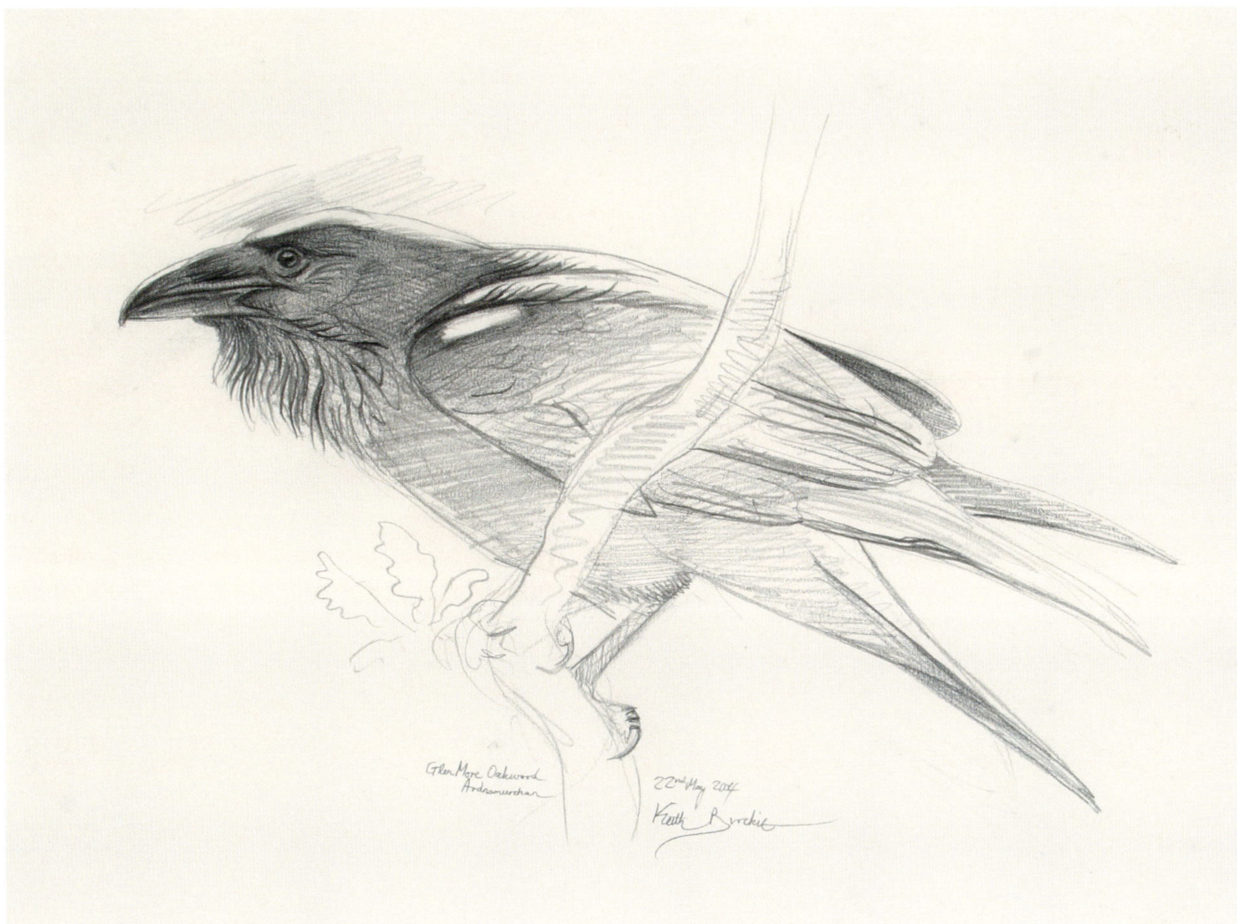
Glen More Oakwood
Ardnamurchan
22nd May 2004

3

Katrina Cook

Fore Druim to the island of Danna: as the raven flies.
Part I Looking south-west past Barnluasgan
Part II The Faery Isles, facing north-east
Part III Taynish and south-west out to sea

A triptych in graphite · each panel 121 x 152 cm

I wanted to produce a single piece of work accentuating the elongated ridges and lochs running NE–SW, which characterise the Knapdale region. I explored a number of options and travelled extensively during the residency, clocking up an astounding 600 miles during my stay. I drew each landmark from several directions, often being seen working from my car 'safari style', standing through the sunroof. I did become rather obsessed with getting the geography 'right' and was constantly buried in my map. From the beginning I knew an aerial view was necessary; Margaret and Mags were enormously helpful in providing me with aerial photographs taken previously, but I needed to get up there myself in order to really understand. I made a desperate plea to Mags to help me here, and on a memorable day this indeed came about. Many thanks to Mags for organising this, to Margaret for coming to find me and, of course, to Duncan McNair for the microlight flight and many subsequent photographs. I'll never forget that day. This work is dedicated to Duncan and Mags.

The next problem was physically producing the work, as I no longer have a studio of any sort. I tried renting a shared space for Part I, but this did not work out; so I had to move all the furniture in my bedroom out of the way and use the wall in there. I'll really miss being involved in these pictures, but it will be good to have my bedroom back!

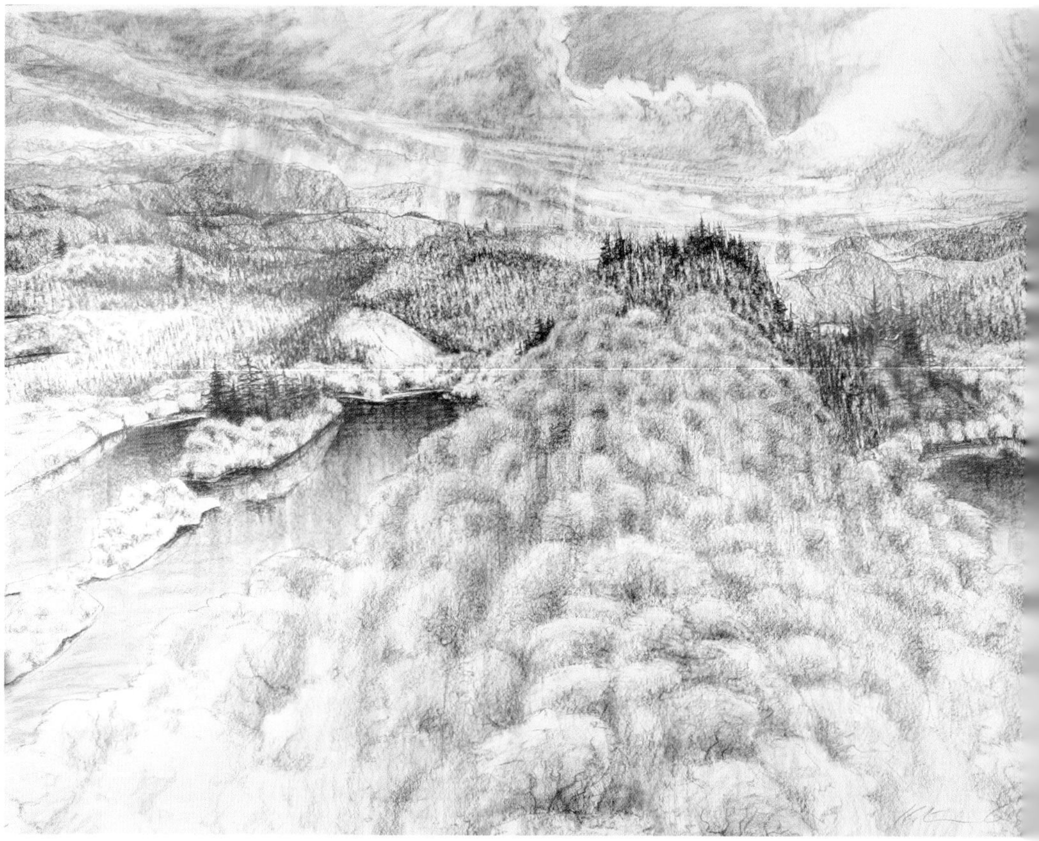

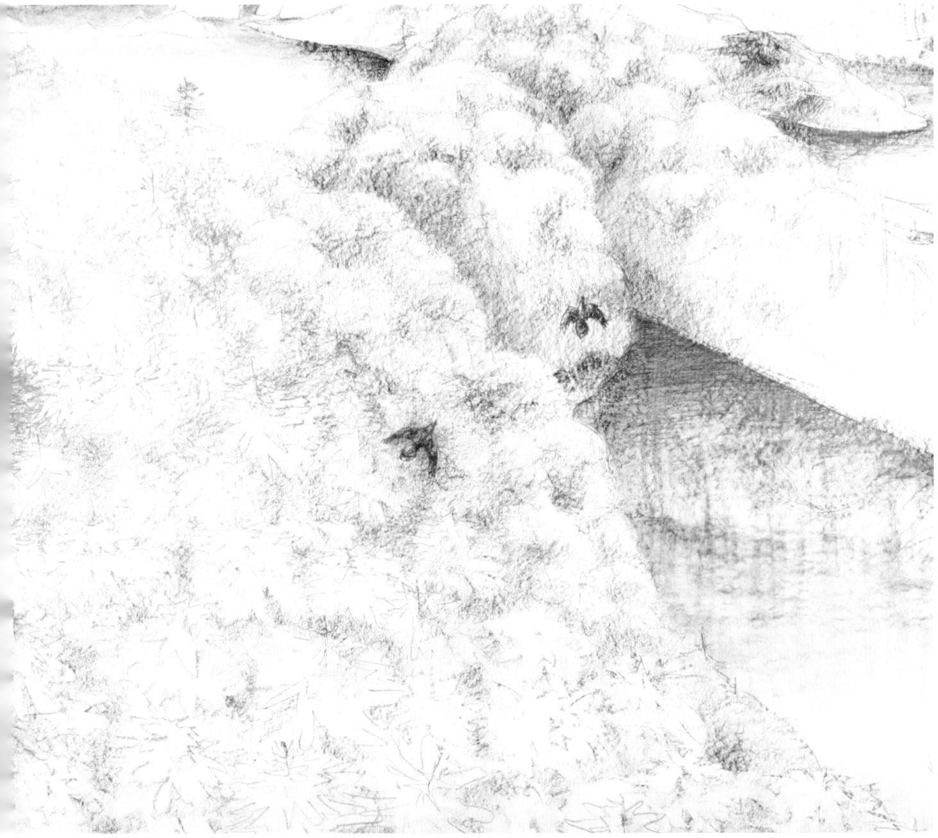

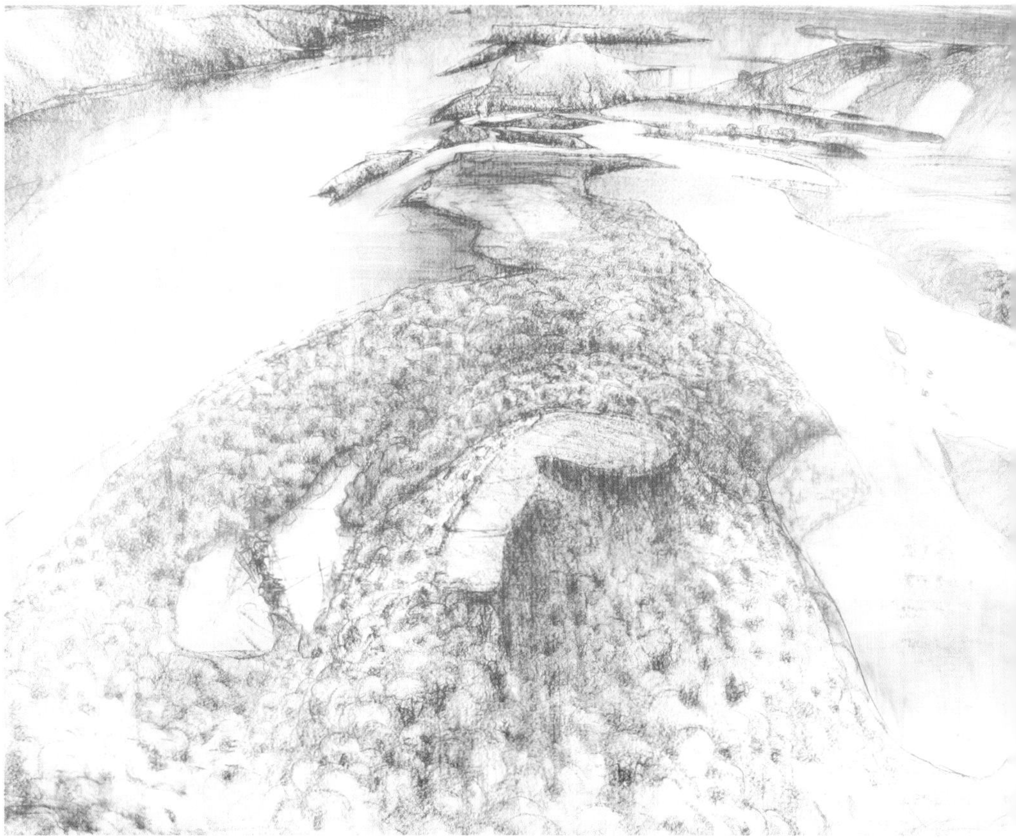

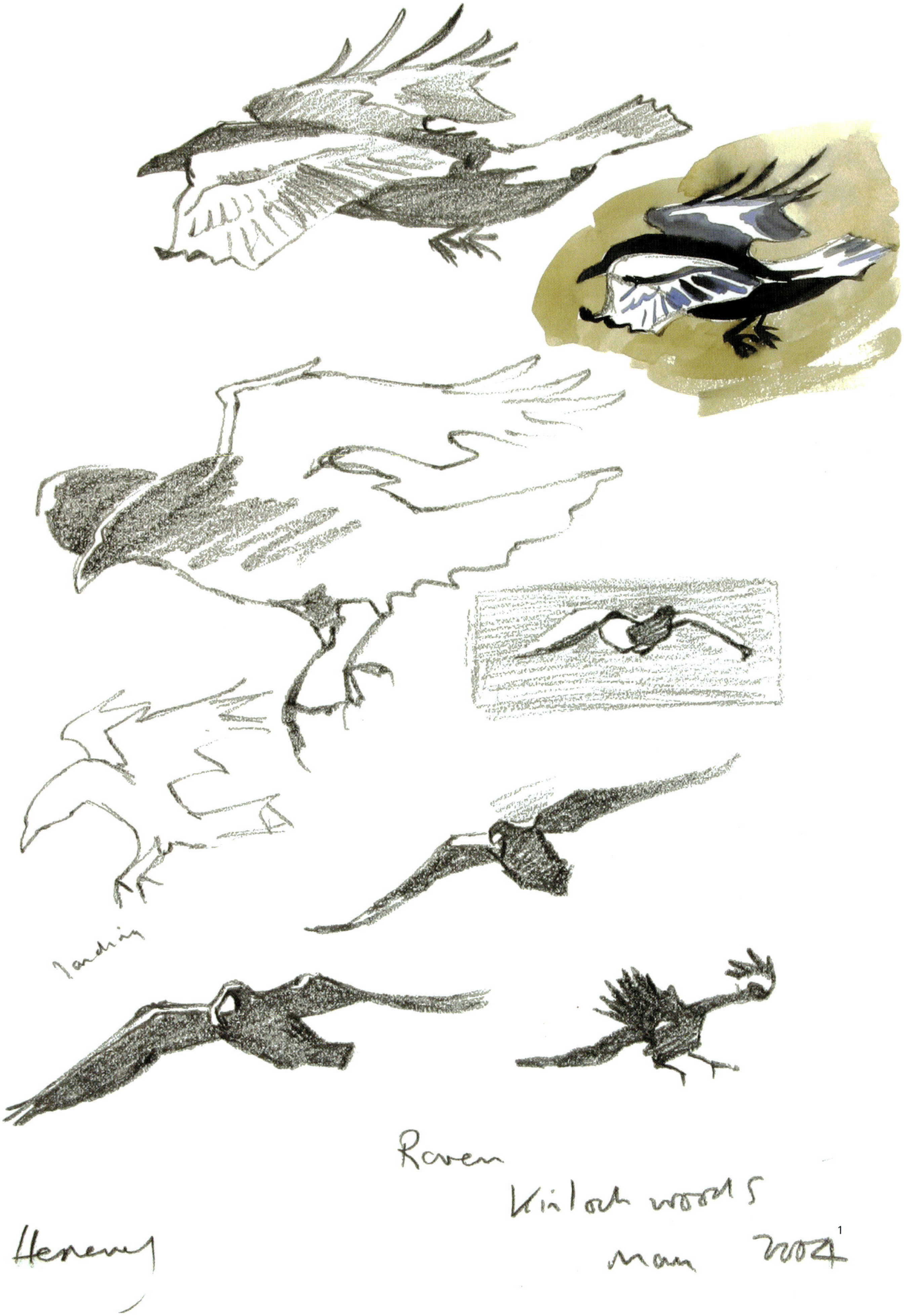
landing
Raven
Kinloch woods

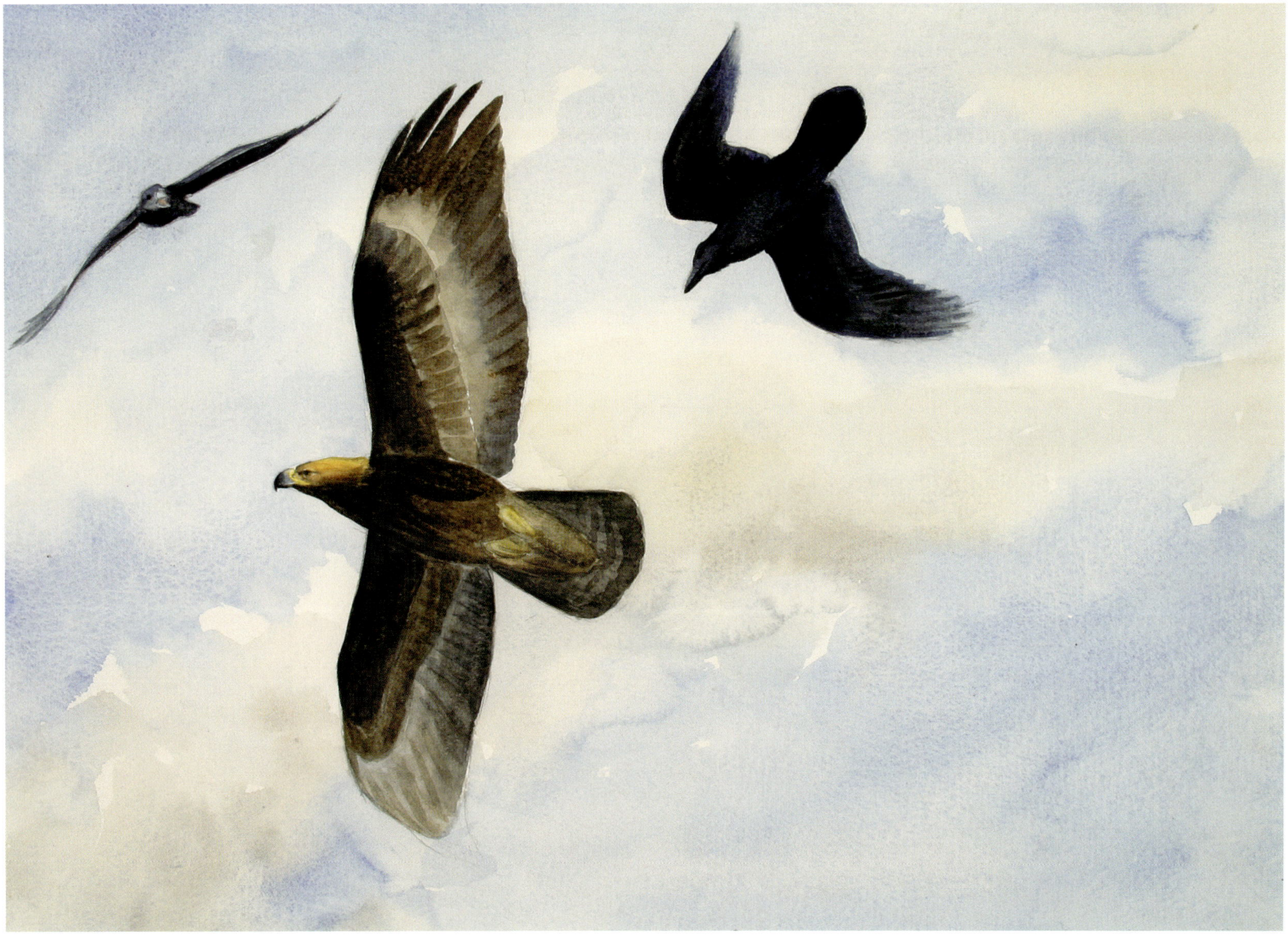

2

1. Paul Henery *Raven studies*
pencil and watercolour · 29 x 21 cm

2. Alastair Proud *Golden eagle mobbed by ravens*
watercolour · 30 x 39 cm

It was a wonderful, sunny morning. I had gone up the forestry track towards Ben Aslak with the hope of seeing eagles. I was not disappointed as I was treated to a pair of eagles, one of them sunning itself for half an hour. Some ravens were also about, mobbing the eagles from time to time.

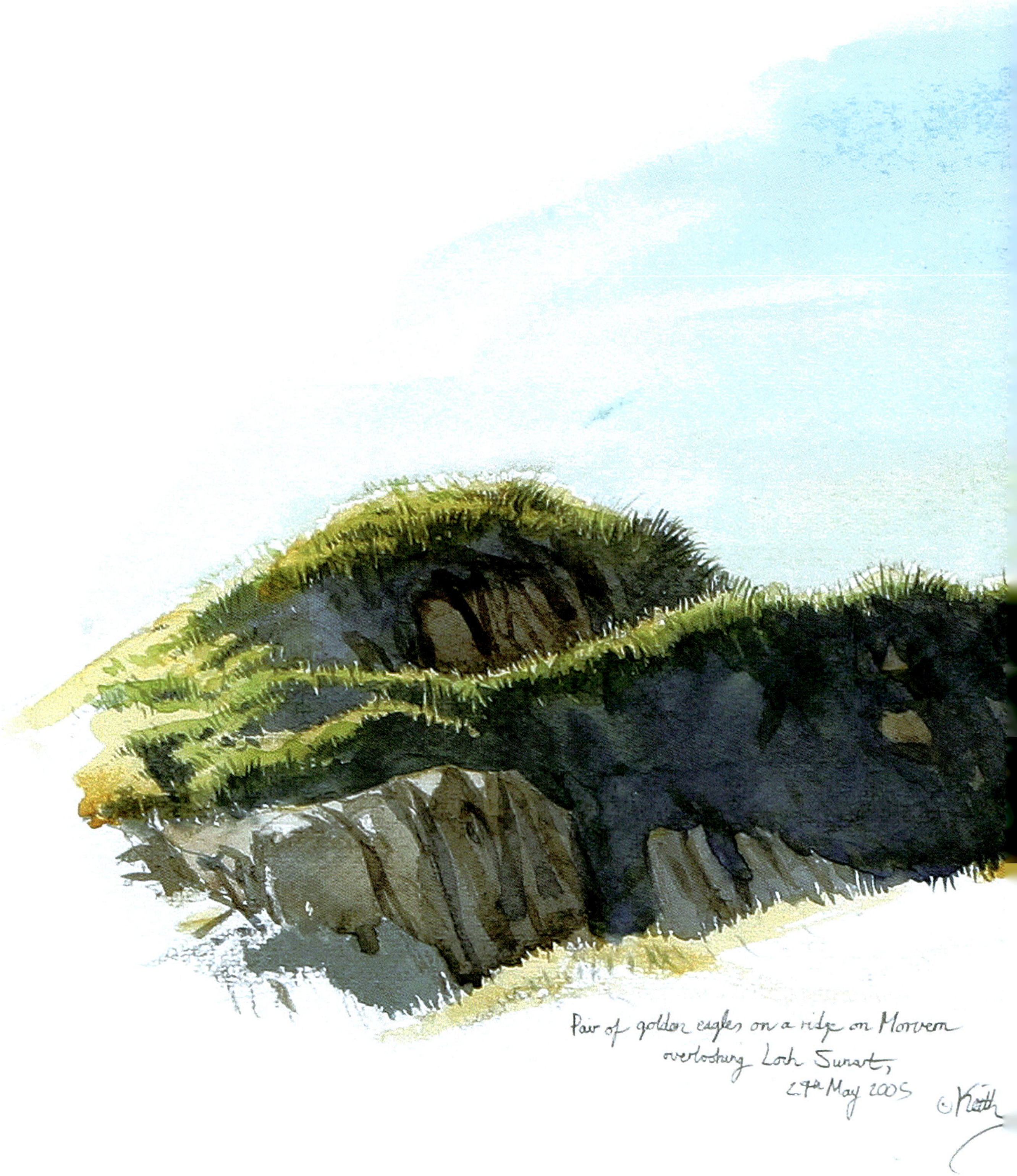

Keith Brockie *Golden eagle pair on a ridge*
watercolour on paper · 24 x 42 cm

A pair of golden eagles sitting on a ridge on cliffs high above the shores of Loch Sunart, sketched via a very powerful telescope from the road below.

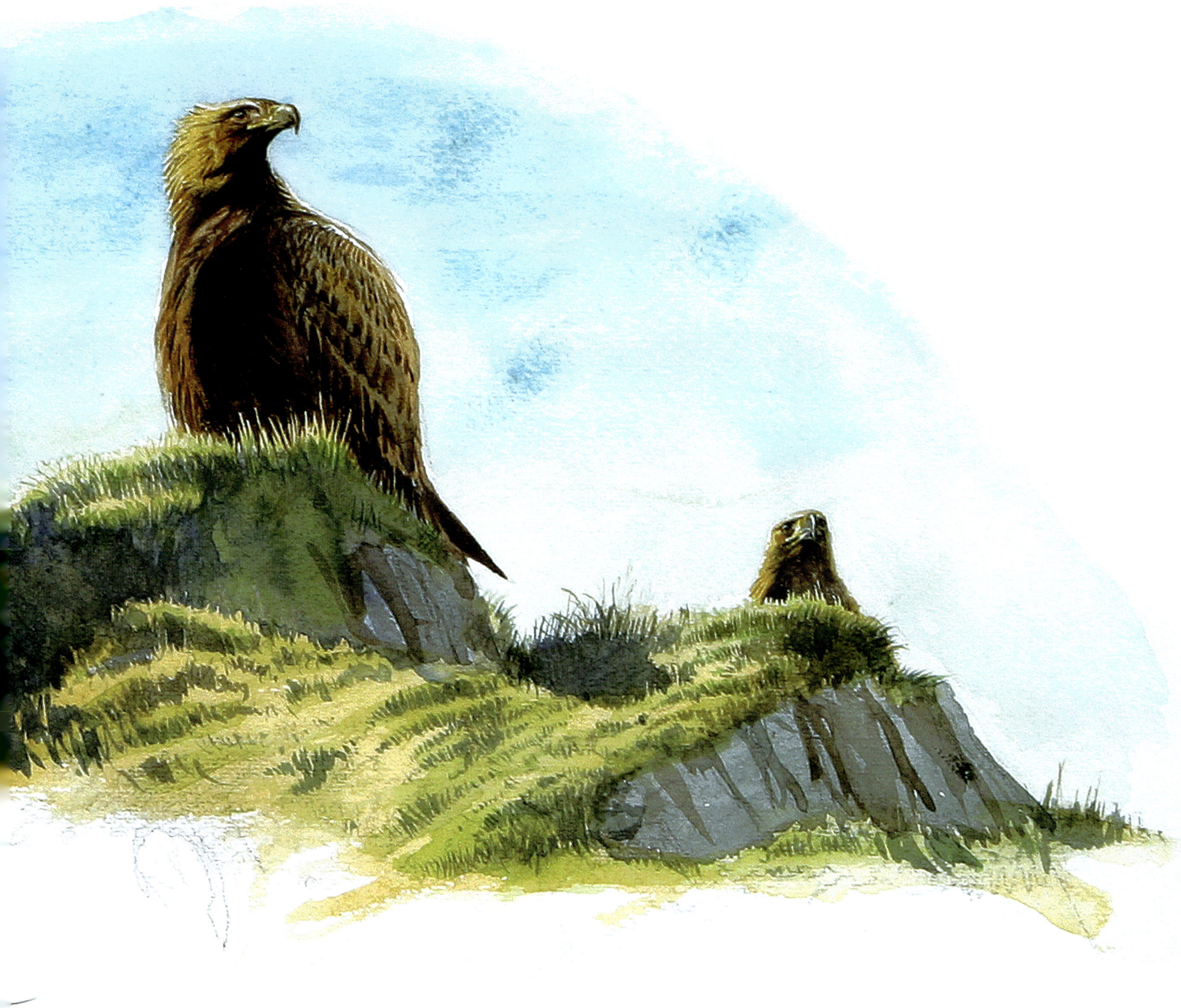

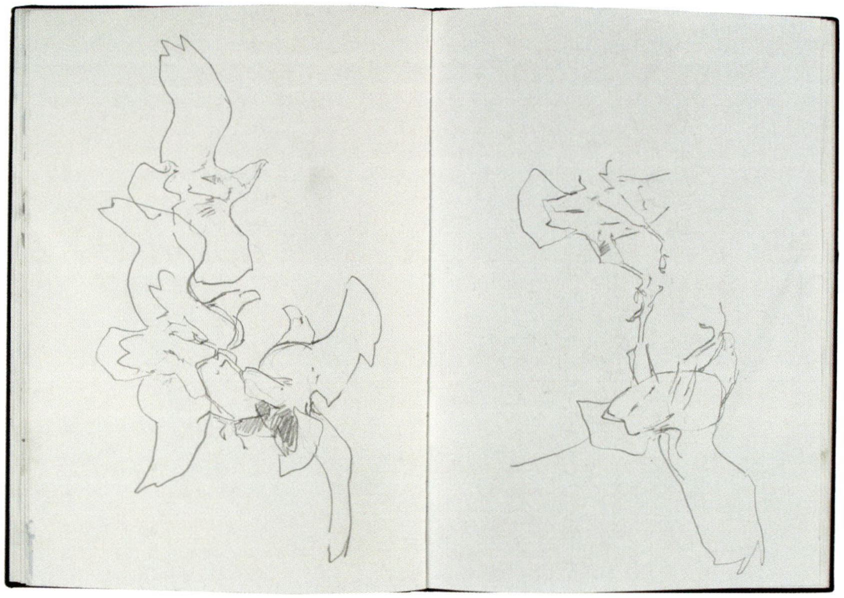

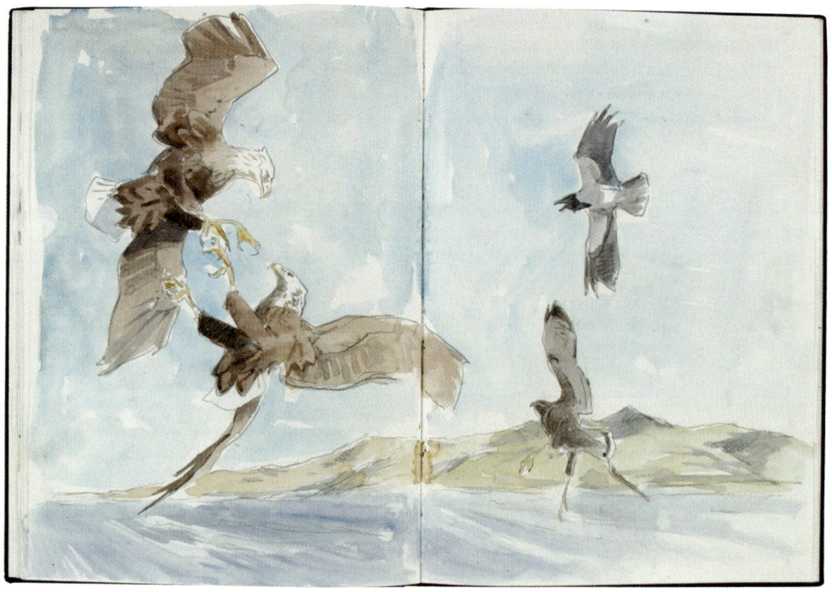

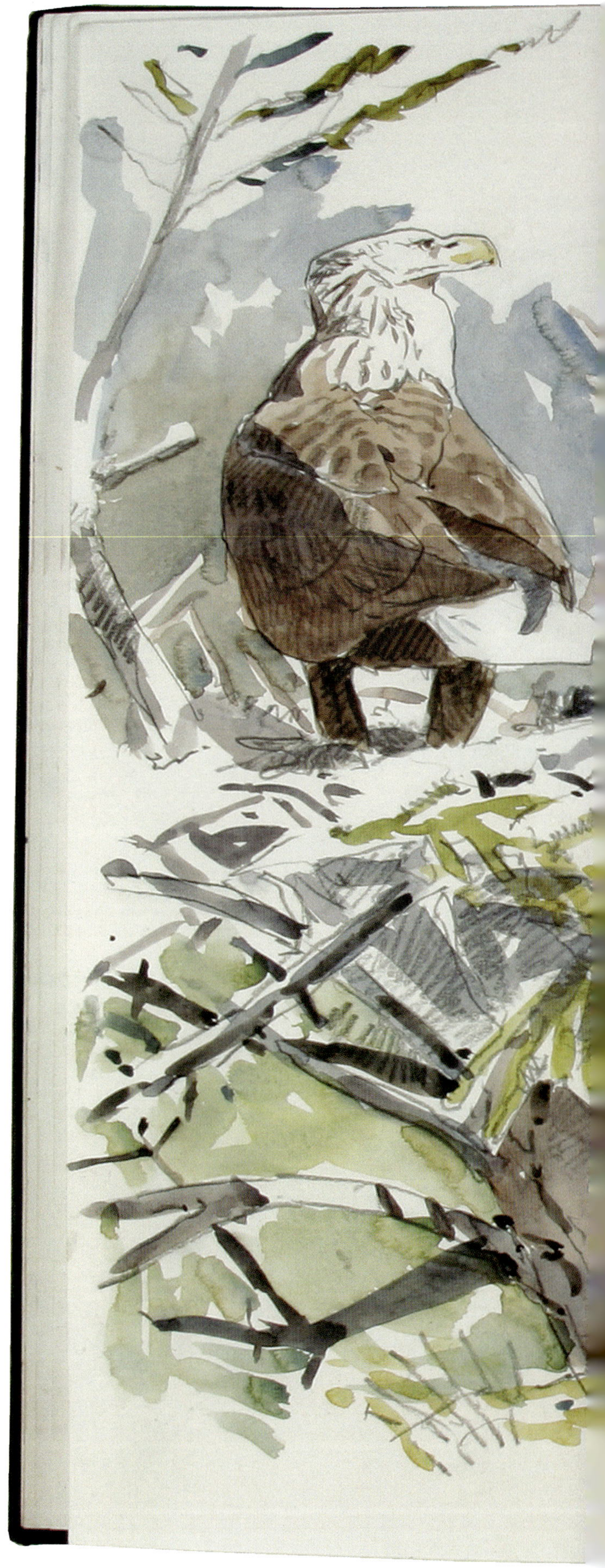

Darren Woodhead *White-tailed eagle sketchbook pages*
watercolour and pencil · 42 x 60 cm

Both adults spent much time around the nest, watching the world below and manicuring feathers from their lofty precipice. Whenever they left the area, they were greeted by raucous attention from neighbouring buzzards, ravens and hooded crows. This would often be a physical clash, the eagle rising steadily with neck outstretched before flipping to one side and presenting talons. On one occasion whilst the male was engaged in combat, the female joined the crowd. This culminated in the male and female eagle talon grappling, where the adults clash in mid air, momentarily grasping each other's talons, to confirm their pairing and territory. The manoeuvre left me speechless and full of silent rapturous applause.

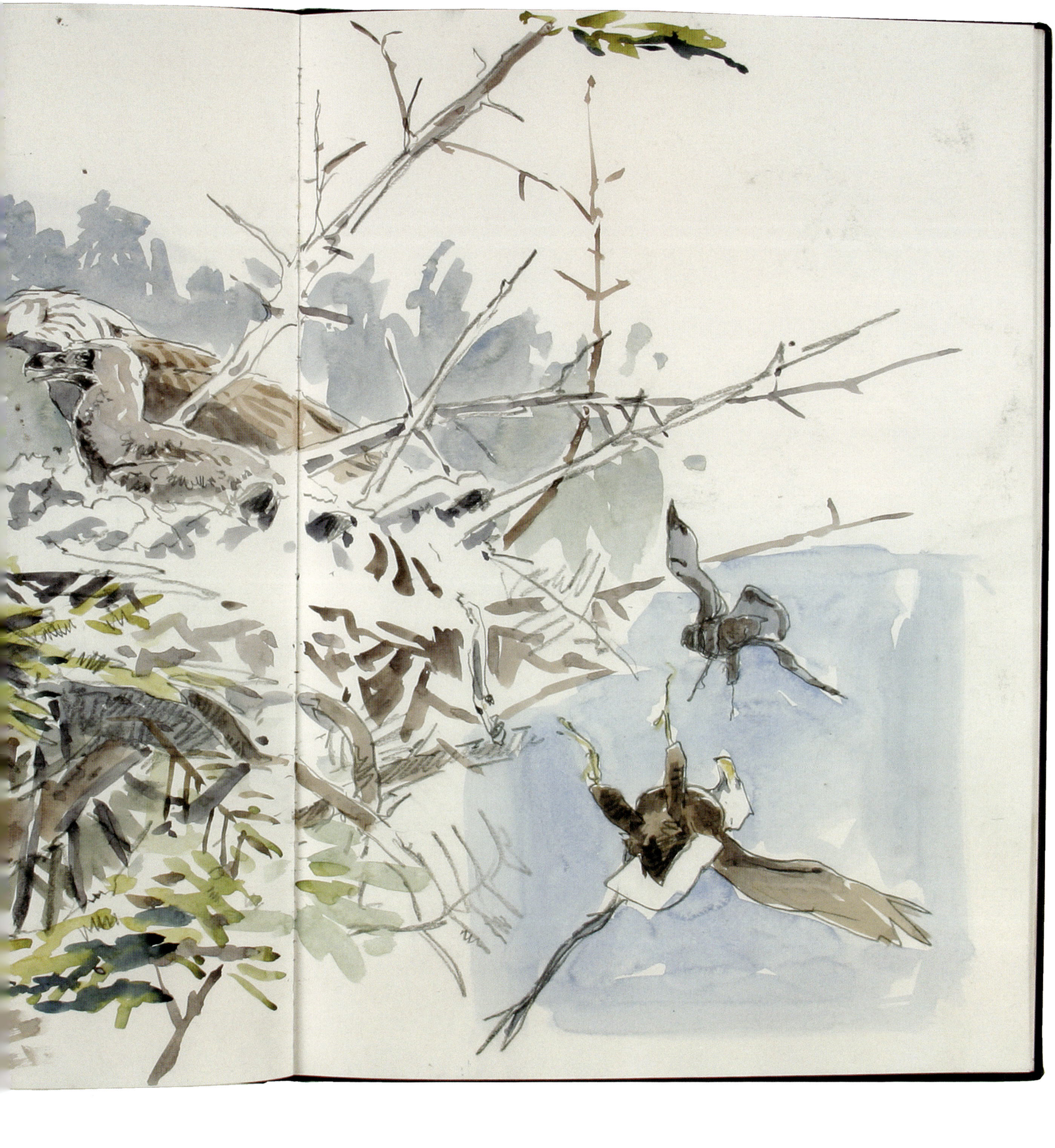

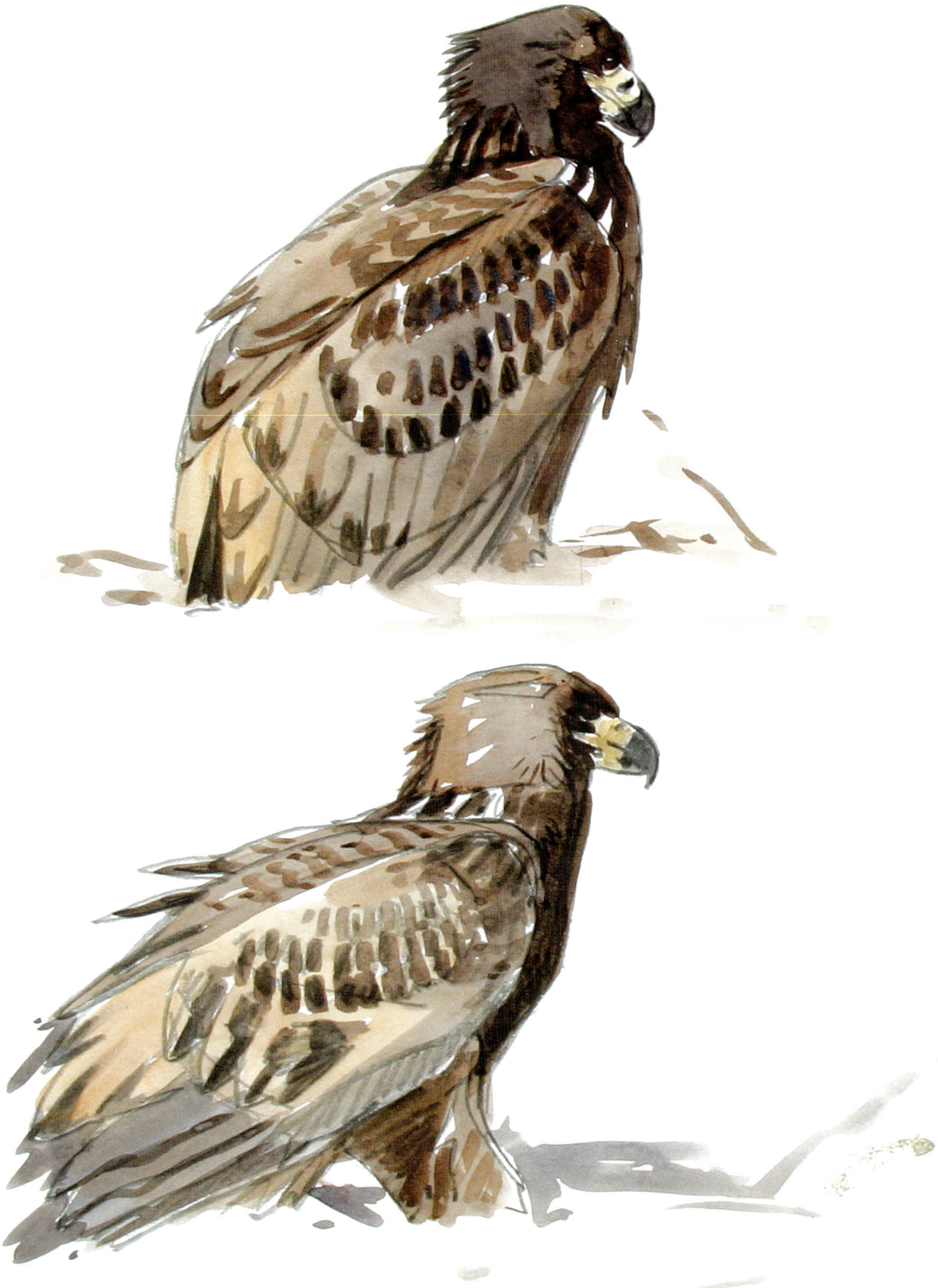

Darren Woodhead *White-tailed eagle studies*
watercolour and pencil

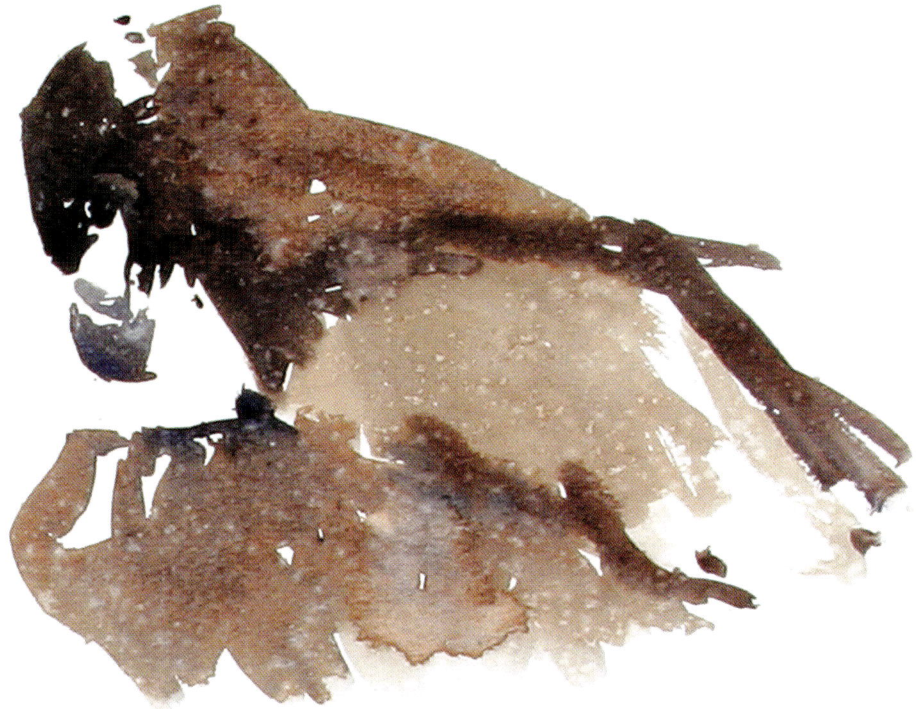

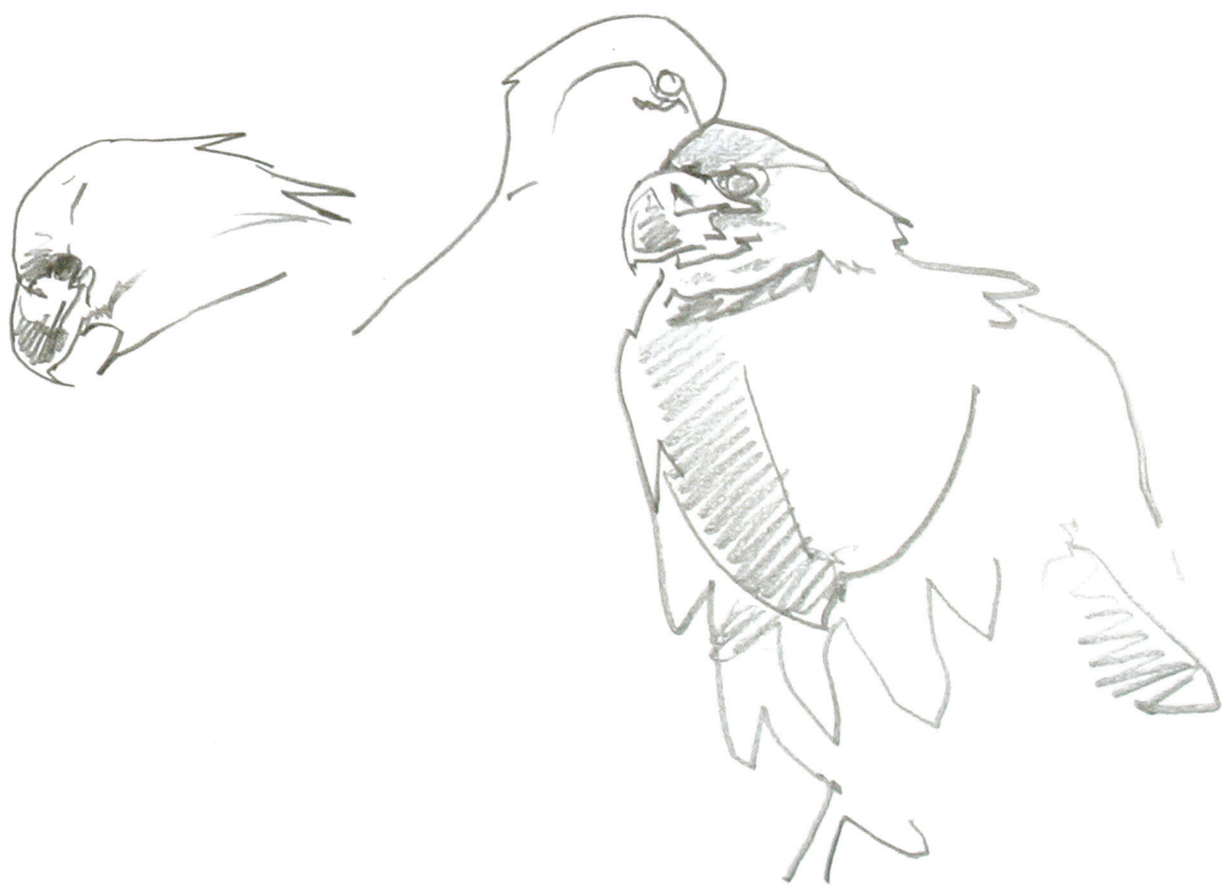

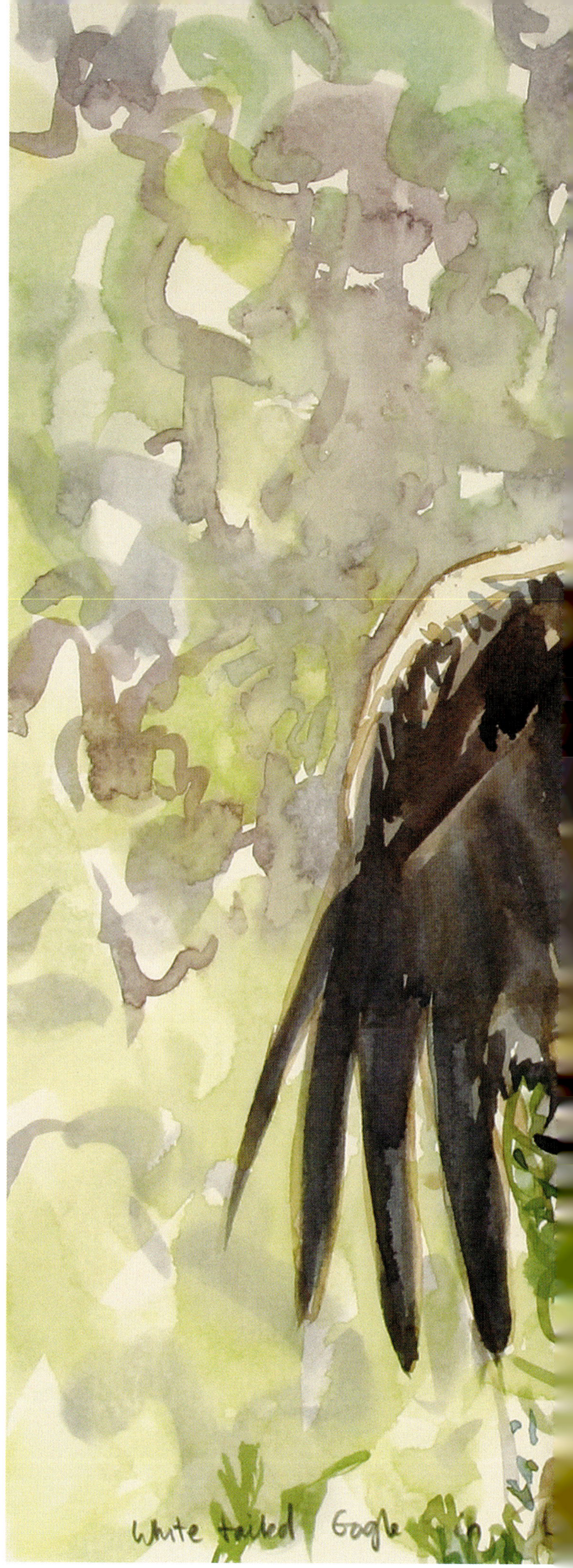

David Bennett *White-tailed eagle*
watercolour · 41 x 57 cm

I had seen the adult eagles visiting the nest, where a solitary juvenile sat looking quite pathetic in the persisting rain. On my return journey, I spotted an adult eagle landing nearby on a larch. It chose the very top of a spindly larch, like the star on a Christmas tree, the twigs bowing under its weight. Stretching out its wings to gain balance, it bounced, bungey style, for a short while, until a hooded crow flew in and mobbed it.

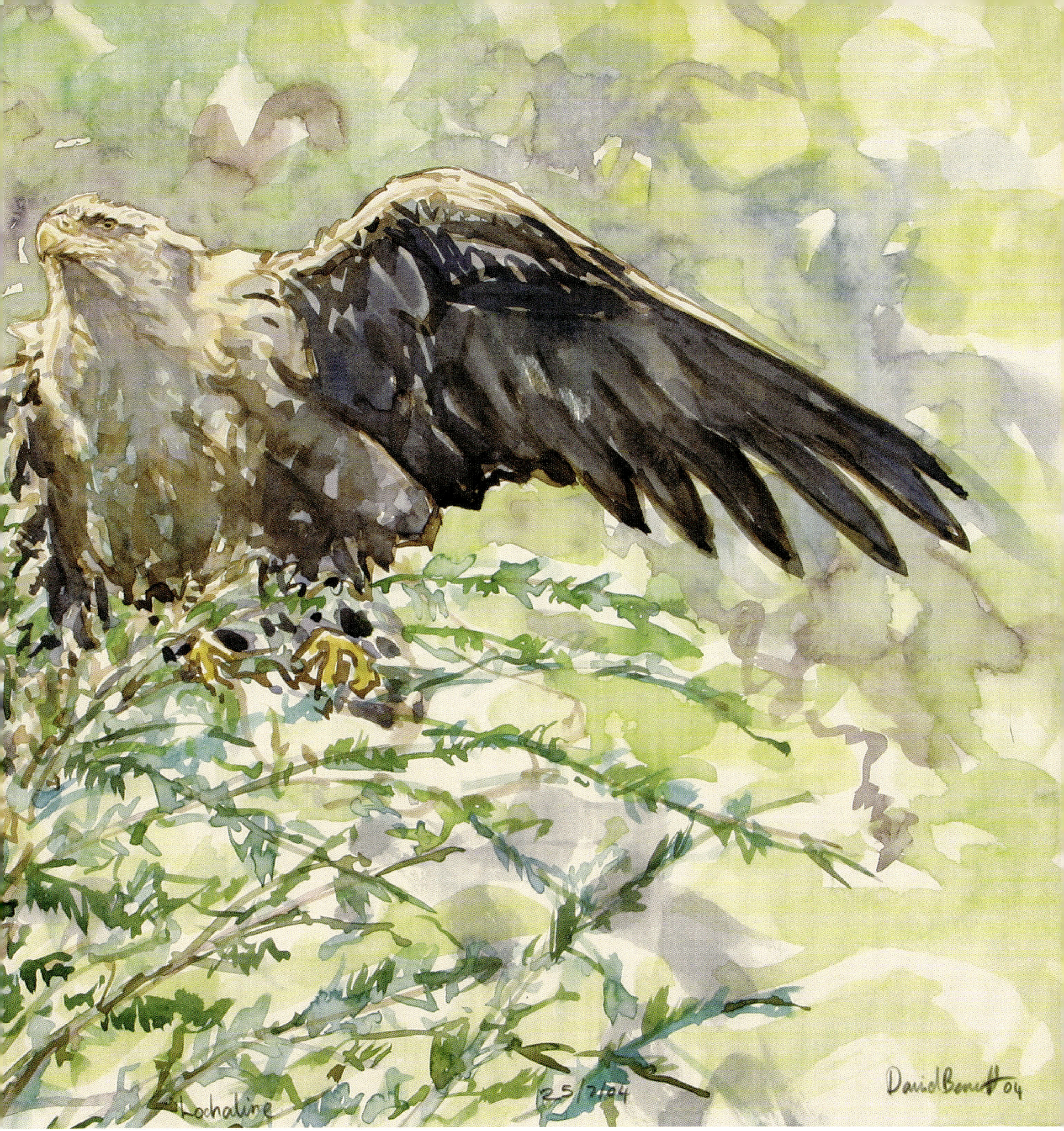
Lochaline
25/7/04
David Bennett 04

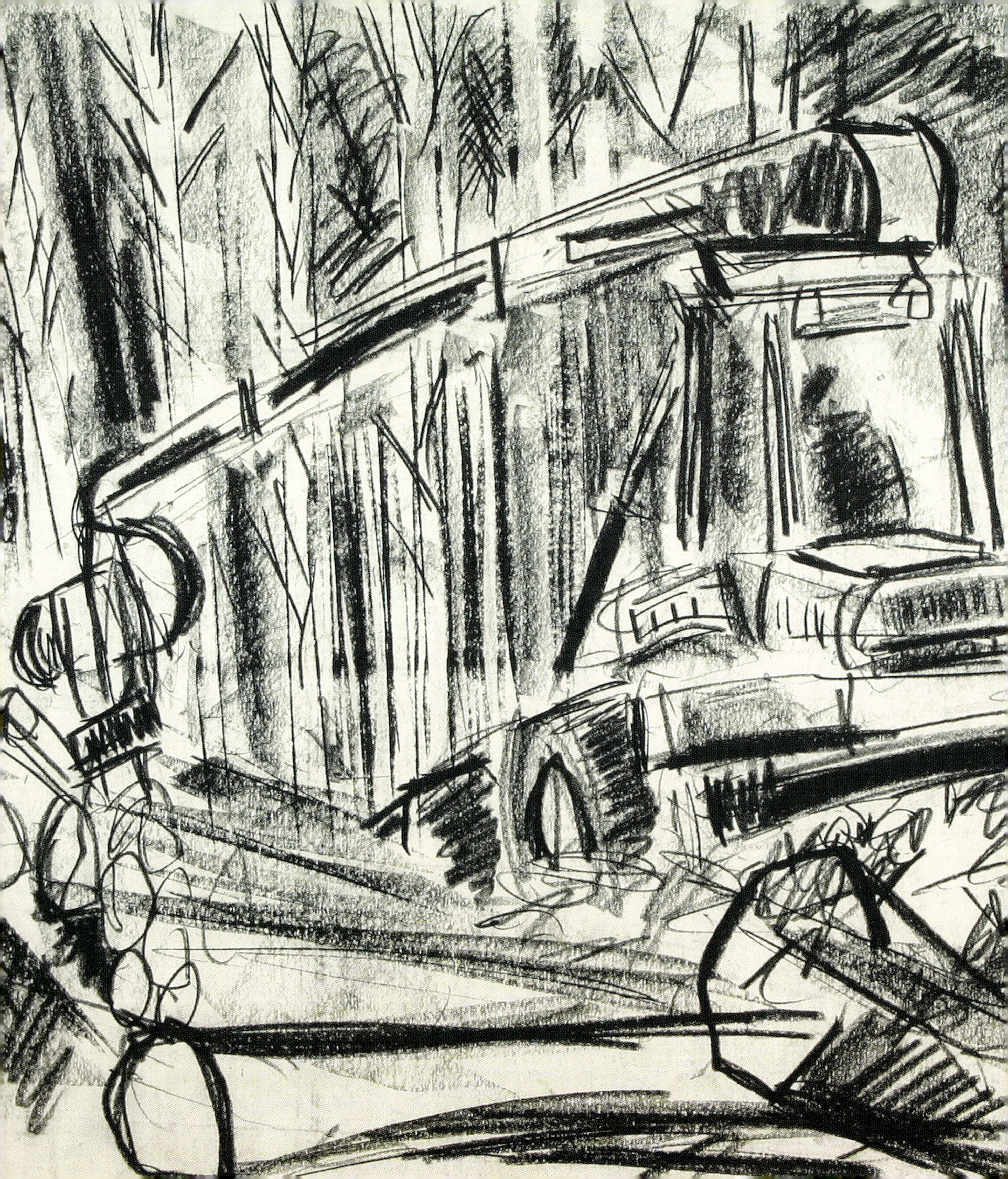

6 Saved in time

The oakwoods survived into the 20th century as hundreds of scattered fragments, ignored, left to sheep and deer, and at the very edge of survival. Many continued to exist because they were on land that was too poor or too steep for any profitable use or else they were too remote to exploit. Only a few continued to be managed for timber. The woods in Sleat were reprieved twice. In the 1880s and again in World War I, clearfelling was contemplated but found not to be commercially worthwhile. Survival of these remnant, neglected woods finally depended on the longevity of trees. When I drove past stands of oakwoods around my home in Argyll back in the 1970s, I noticed that the trees were uniform in size. They were all around 120 years old and were survivors from the age of coppicing. I was concerned that when they eventually died, there would be nothing left but open grassland.

At this time, the Forestry Commission was determinedly planting every available patch of their land in Argyll with Sitka spruce. This included planting under the trees in native woodland. The oaks and other trees would act as nurses, protecting the young conifers from frost, but they would die, or be killed by ringbarking, when the spruces grew up through them. Apart from 'amenity' strips planted beside roads, broadleaved trees were being treated as worthless 'scrub'. I was sorry to see this because I could see older forests that had reached the 'thicket stage', in which the evergreen foliage was so dense that nothing grew in the mat of dead, brown needles that accumulated under the trees. Interestingly, as I have recently learned, the older conifer forests contain some of the rarer species of shade-requiring plants, especially if they are growing on or adjoining sites that were once ancient woodland.

I did not know it then but attitudes were beginning to change. The older generation of foresters had been brought up to produce the maximum volume of timber on their land, but a new generation was being allowed to have a regard for ecology and natural processes. This led to an appreciation that land could be used for purposes other than timber production, and now there are foresters who see woodland restoration as one of their most important duties.

At Dalavich, on the north bank of Loch Awe, there is an old coppice which once supplied charcoal to the Bonawe ironworks. When planted by the Forestry Commission in 1958, almost all the oaks had been ringbarked. The remaining 22 hectares were left as amenity for the village. In 1983 they were notified as a Site of Special Scientific Interest (SSSI) and a management plan was prepared. Forestry Commission staff also started to clear conifers from the rest of the site. Although there was little money for this type of pioneering work, it helped demonstrate what could be achieved. Much of the initiative for this woodland restoration work came from forest manager Alan Stevenson, who had seen how the old coppices were being restored at Grizedale in Cumbria. Appropriately, by a nice twist of fate, these woods had been exploited by the same ironmasters who had established the coppices in Argyll to feed their furnace at Bonawe.

Then, in 1984, came the European Year of the Environment. The Forestry Commission decided to back some conservation projects and expanded the

Nik Pollard *Harvesting (detail)*
conté on paper · 41 x 57 cm

restoration work at Dalavich. This was followed a year later by the Government's Broadleaf Policy Review, and the idea of preserving and restoring semi-natural woods took hold as a worthy aim for foresters. In 1992 the Earth Summit at Rio de Janeiro committed the British Government to sustainable forestry, which included better woodland management and the wider conservation of natural resources in the form of species, air, soil and water. Another consequence of the Earth Summit was a European Union Directive that led to the creation of the Natura Sites and Special Areas of Conservation. These include our three Aig an Oir sites. In 1994 David Bellamy helped the Forestry Commission launch an ambitious initiative to restore and expand the Atlantic oakwoods, and that year the Commission was awarded the Ford Conservation Project for its contribution to the conservation of the Atlantic oakwoods.

The Government's policy is being put into effect with a series of species and habitat action plans. The oakwoods in the Aig an Oir project fall into the *Habitat Action Plan for Upland Oakwoods*. Its target for the 15 years following 1998 is to maintain the existing areas of oakwood and extend them by planting new areas and restoring areas that had been converted to non-native forests. The woods are the home of species which need conserving, and these species have been given their own Action Plans. The species range from obscure lichens and fungi to the familiar red squirrel, song thrush and pearl-bordered fritillary butterfly. Each of these species plans states an objective – to restore the population to a certain level – and a method, which is usually a suitable form of habitat management. All these plans have a bearing on how the oakwood habitat will be managed.

Restoration of the oakwood habitat is being carried out in several ways, each of which can have a profound effect on the ecology of woodlands. The usual first step is to erect fences to exclude deer and sheep, or at least control their numbers. Deer are

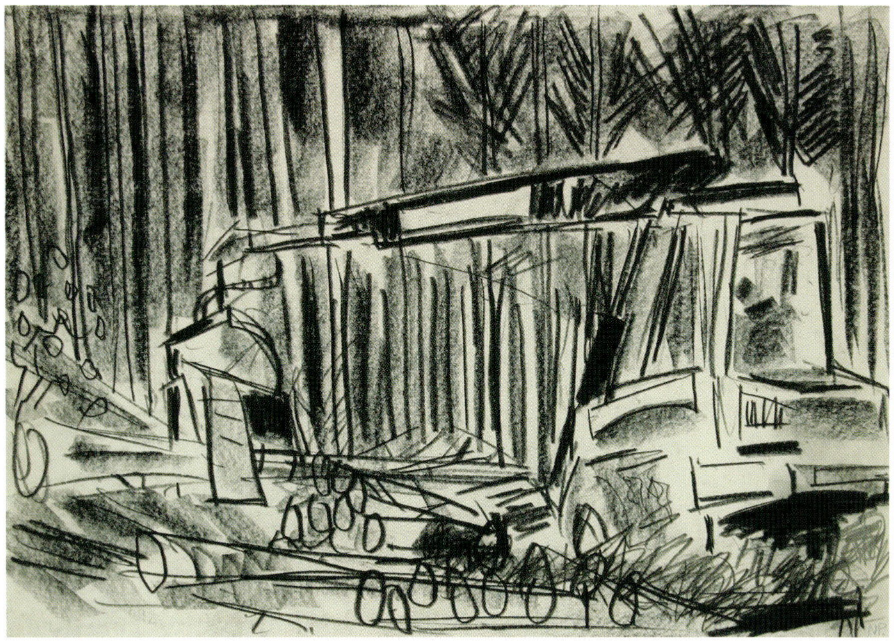

1

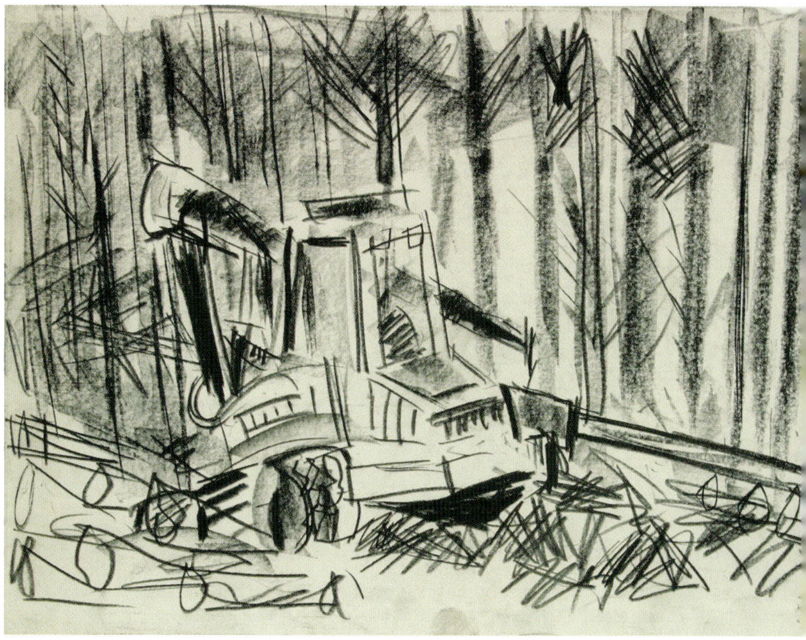

2

4. John Davis *Rhododendron removal*
watercolour · 15 x 22 cm

not completely eliminated but in some areas populations have been reduced from 10–15 animals per square kilometre, or even more, to less than half that number. Lowering the pressure of grazing and browsing enables trees to start regenerating, but the presence of a small number of deer is acceptable because they prefer grass to seedling trees. An experiment on the island of Rum has shown that without a certain amount of grazing by deer, coarse grasses take over and the tree seedlings are crowded out. The woodland floor soon develops a characteristic flora with a scattering of tiny oak, birch and other seedlings, which now have the chance to grow into trees and shrubs.

Another major challenge has been to remove the rhododendrons that smother large areas of woodland on the west coast and prevent anything from growing under their thick, dark green canopy. Over 300 hectares have been removed in what has proved to be an expensive and often difficult process. Workers have had to dangle from ropes as they wield chainsaws to attack bushes growing out of rock faces. The cutting is backed up with chemical sprays to prevent regeneration from the stumps and the growth of seedlings. As with the fencing, the effects on tree regeneration have been dramatic.

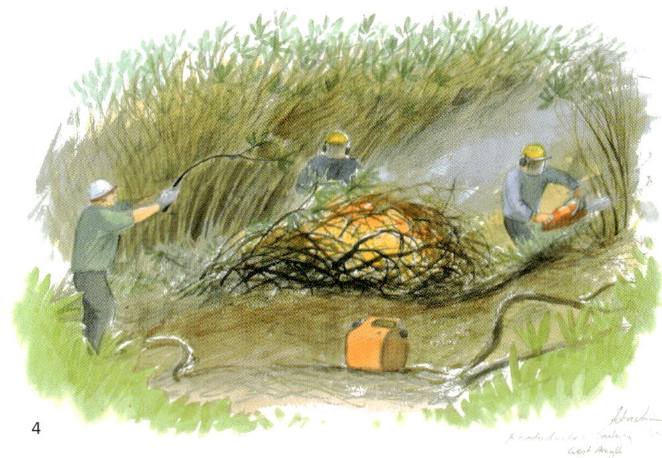

4

The greatest visual impact has been the removal of large areas of conifer forests planted from the 1920s onwards. Sitka spruces that I had seen being planted in the early 1970s and that had grown into 'Christmas trees' have been felled to let the native trees take back the ground. Sometimes the conifer timber has been removed and sold to help finance the operation. Elsewhere it has been left to rot. It looks unsightly but the process is called 'fell to recycle', and the dead trees will eventually provide nutrients for further growth. In the meantime the piles of dead brush provide shelter for young trees and other plants. Chris Marsh showed me a site in the Kinloch Hills where over 100 hectares of conifers had been felled in a project supported by lottery funding via the Millenium Forest for Scotland Trust. When I visited in 2004, regeneration was proceeding apace. The stark cut ends of the trunks and the stumps were covered by bright green mosses, while birch and rowan saplings were growing up through the shelter provided by brash –

1,2,3 Nik Pollard *Harvesting*
conté on paper · 41 x 57 cm

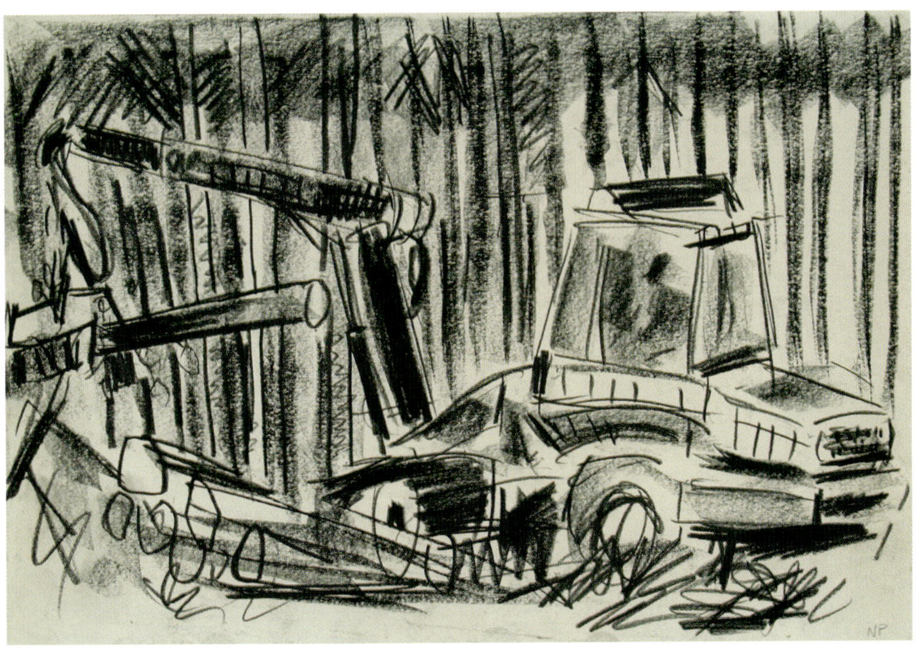

3

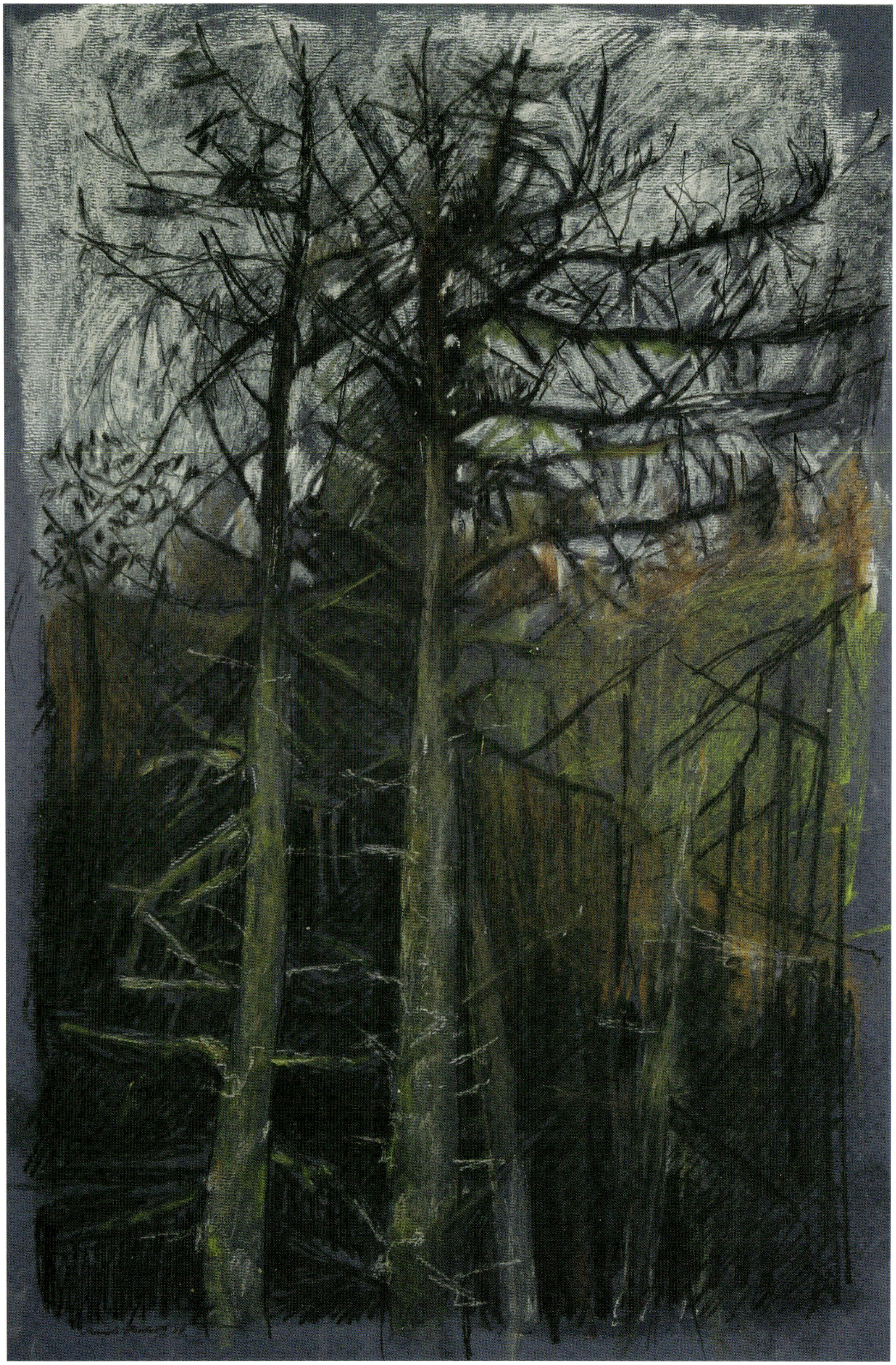

1

1. Pascale Rentsch *Morvern Forest*
   mixed media · 67 x 51 cm
2. Katrina Cook *Stacked logs*
   pen · 15 x 42 cm

the piles of dead conifer branches. There were also good growths of brambles.

Natural ecological processes will slowly become re-established and the semi-natural habitat will be restored to something like it was before the 19th-century grazing and 20th-century planting all but destroyed it. Signs of felling, drainage channels and even-age stands of trees will slowly recede as a testament to the 20th-century planting, but the bottom line of the restoration process is the improvement in the diversity of native species and thus the conservation of threatened species in this habitat. This will be achieved either by natural colonisation of the restored habitat or by planned introductions.

The Kinloch Hills, for instance, were once the home of the only black grouse in Skye but they died out a few years ago. Black grouse were once an important part of the ecosystem as food for golden eagles, as well as being interesting and spectacular birds in their own right. As the restoration of the woods progresses, the hope is that either the grouse will return on their own or a re-introduction programme will establish a viable population.

The programme of restoring old woods is being bolstered by planting native trees using local seed. This will not produce instant woodland habitat, but if the newly planted forests connect with old woods, species will have the chance to move in. Birds, mammals and some insects may move in quite quickly as trees mature and food and shelter become available, but specialists such as snails, beetles, lichens and fungi may take many years to become established. Not only do they spread very slowly but they also need a mature habitat to move into. Some will have to wait until the first trees have died.

Foresters have realised recently that there are more fragments of native woodland scattered around the Highlands than had been thought. There are several plants whose presence is an indication that a wood is ancient and has never been cleared. These include bluebell, dog's mercury, wood anemone, wood sorrel and wild strawberry, and small colonies of the decorative beech fern and false brome-grass are found on chalk or lime. Conversely, if these plants are found on open ground, they are an indication that the site was originally woodland.

It is a well-established fact in conservation that small fragments of habitat hold fewer species than large tracts and that small, isolated populations face a greater risk of extinction. Linking up these frag-

TAOBH LOCH SEILE

A' sealltainn gach àit' suas air dà thaobh Loch Seile
Còisir cheòlmhor nan craobh 's iad cho aobhach 's na meangain
'S a' ghrian thar na sgurr, 'togail smùid às an talamh.
Tha na bruthaichean cian, torach fiarach gu mullach
Tha gach lagan 's cùil dosrach, flùranach, lurach
Tha na craobhan 'sa choill 's iad a' boillsgeadh gu cladach
Agus cuid dhiu le loinn ag ath-shoillse sa chamas.

BESIDE LOCH SHIEL

On a warm, balmy day, I'm in the forest shade
Looking up and all around both sides of Loch Shiel
The musical choir of the trees so cheerful in the branches
And the sun above the crag creating a ground mist
The vast fertile banks inclining to the summit
Each little hollow and lovely, leafy, blossoming nook
The trees in the forest glitter to the shore
And some are elegantly reflected in the bay.

DONALD MACCOLL

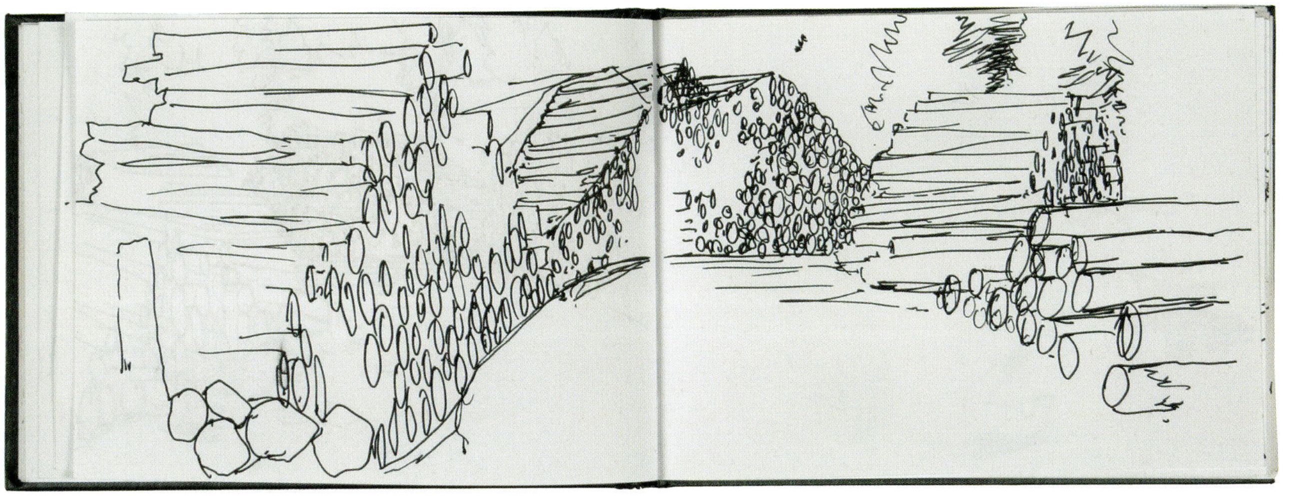

2

ments with the larger blocks of semi-natural woodland will raise the conservation status of the whole beyond the sum of the many parts. Part of the programme for preserving the oakwood habitat is to form cooperative links with private owners in order to join fragments and to prevent loss of woods that would isolate species into small, non-viable populations. This can be seen in Ardnamurchan, where the members of the North Sunart Woodland Group, which include the Forestry Commission, large landowners and crofters, work together to conserve a continuous swathe of 1,300 hectares of land, most of which is woodland.

RESTORE TO WHAT?

Any habitat-restoration programme needs a decision about what to restore to. What precisely does restoring an oakwood mean? Should the aim be to try to turn a wood into primeval Mesolithic Wildwood or to revive a 19th-century coppice with its artificial preponderance of oak trees? The Sunart oakwoods are good examples of artificial woods. They are ancient woods, in that they have survived unbroken since the Wildwood, but they have been greatly modified by coppicing, pollarding and planting. Rather ironically, it is precisely their artificial nature that makes them so important from a conservation point of view. The coppices and pollards provide the right conditions for the rare assemblages of lichens and lower plants which are such a conservation feature of the Atlantic oakwoods.

Current restoration programmes are aiming to produce a more natural type of woodland, as opposed to commercial conifer planting. They will be maintained mostly by natural ecological processes. However, some of the new-look woodlands will be less suitable for the lichens and lower plants but they will have other valuable ecological features. It can be a delicate balancing act to reconcile the objectives of conserving a variety of wildlife forms with their different needs, as well as producing some timber for economic purposes. The preferred management option for any wood depends on both conservation and economic values, but the former is the prime consideration in the Atlantic oakwoods. George Peterken and Rick Worrell have advocated five options for sustainable management of the Sunart Oakwoods. *Natural reserves* are left to nature, although rhododendrons and other exotic plants would be removed and there would be no timber extraction. The other options involve some timber extraction, although this will not be commercially viable in such a remote and difficult terrain. *Ancient oak forest* is rather like natural reserves, with mature, old and rotting trees and a well-developed understorey. In *Native timber stands*, there is a long rotation of thinning trees and some felling of small areas at maturity. *Coppice* and *Wood pasture* recreate old economic management. *Coppices* are expensive to manage, while *Wood pasture* involves more or less constant grazing.

The option most likely to produce usable timber is the *Native timber stand* rotation. Stands can be produced by thinning of the old coppices, which are now made up of uniformly aged trees of about 130 years old. Thinning allows the crowns of the

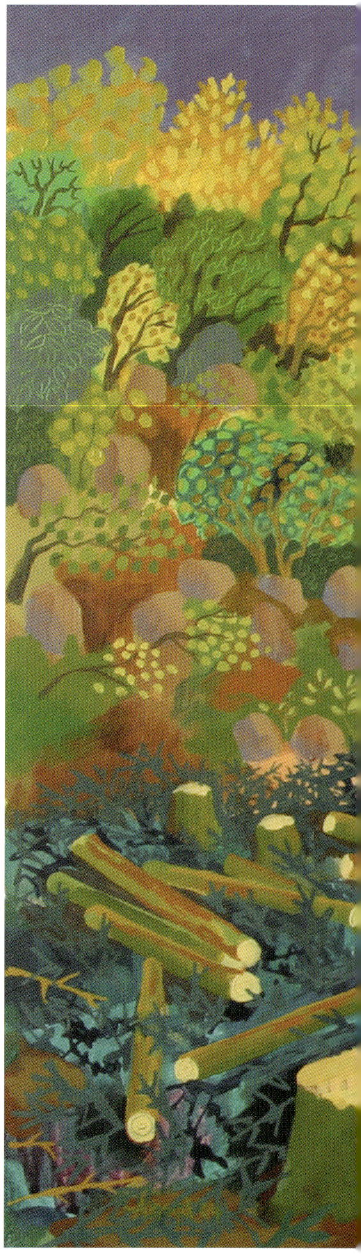

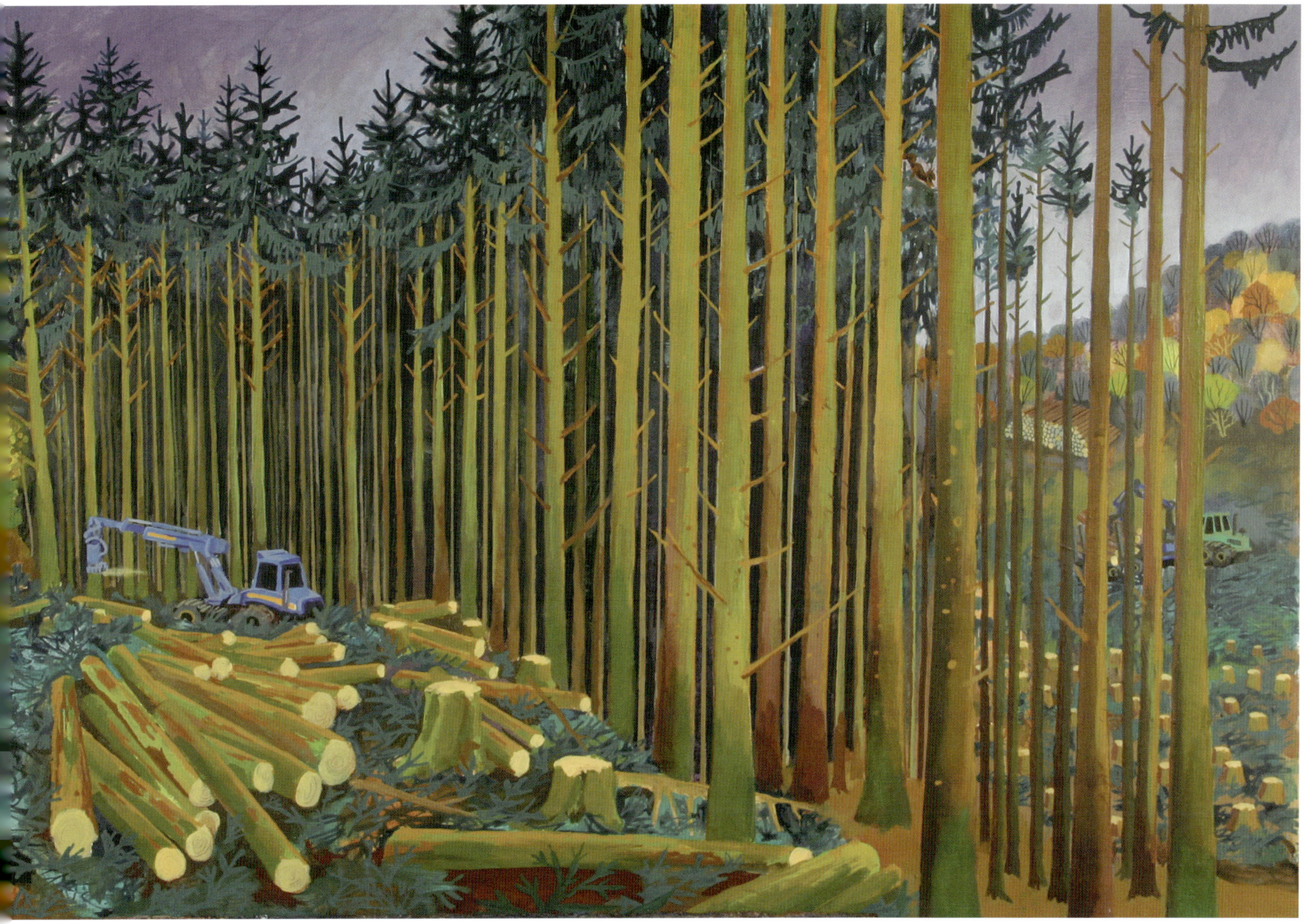

Carry Akroyd *Tree harvesting, Knapdale*
acrylic on board · 55 x 98 cm

As the efficient tree-harvesting machine steadily eats its way into the dark forest, small birds and red squirrels are disturbed. On a steep ridgeside, native deciduous trees hang on tenaciously. In the distance, the computer-graded logs are stacked by the forwarder, and slope cleared in previous years has flourishing birch and oak saplings.

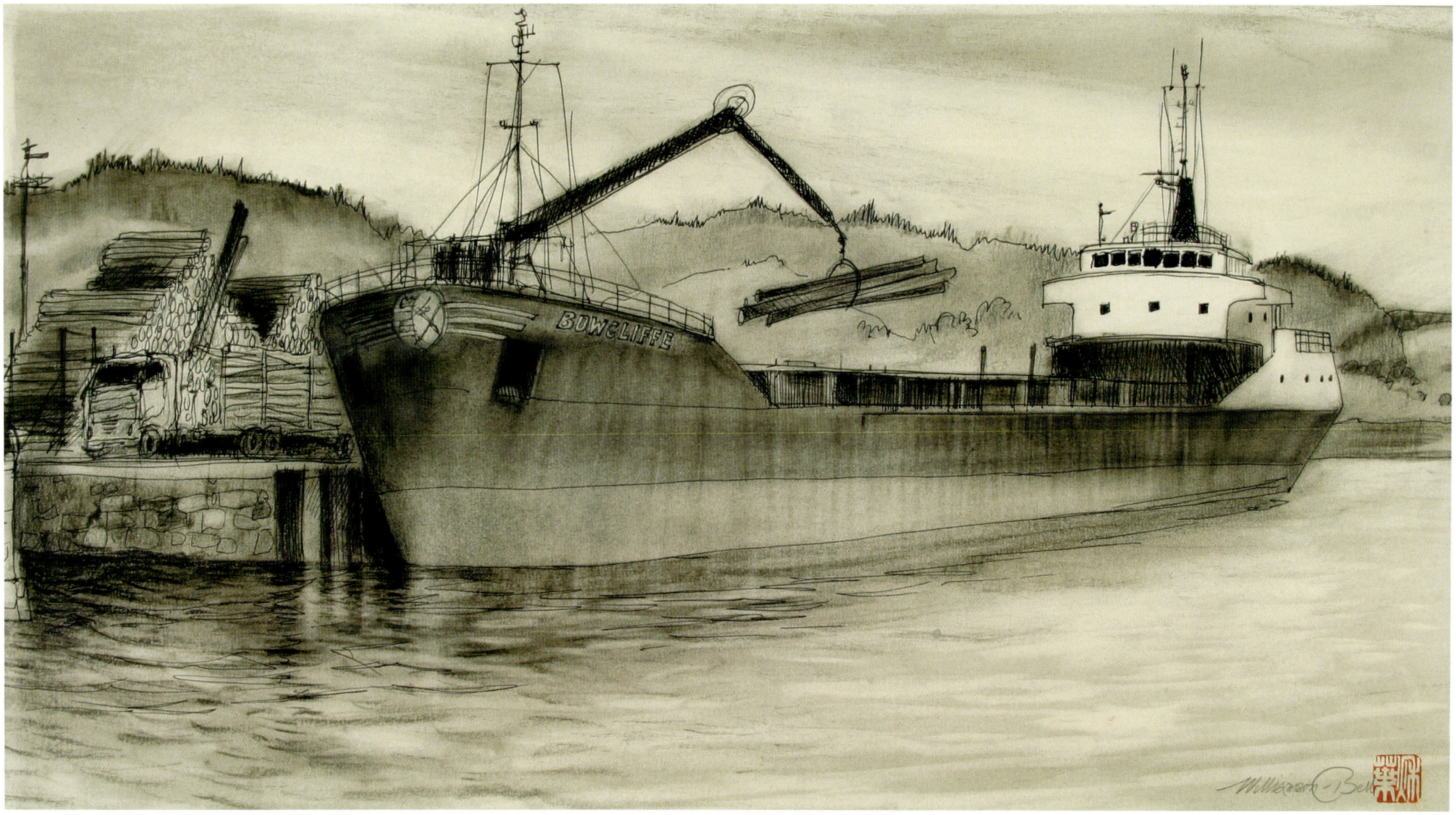

1

remaining trees to spread and bear more acorns, and the increased light penetrating to the ground favours sprouting seedlings. However, it is important that trees are individually selected for felling if the conservation interest of the wood is to be maintained. Trees with plenty of lichens, mosses and other epiphytes are candidates to be allowed to grow into the gnarled, hollow veterans of the future. Neighbouring trees can then be removed to reduce competition, but aspiring veterans must not be given too much space or they will lose the damp microclimate needed for their epiphytes. The moss *Plagiochila atlantica* is associated with ancient woodland and requires a balance of high humidity with warmth and light. This is achieved by neighbouring trees shading it from the afternoon sun when it is hot and the morning dew has evaporated. Removing the wrong tree could kill off a colony.

THE WOODLAND COMMUNITY

The Atlantic oakwoods survived because they were valued by their inhabitants. They are now being conserved for their own sake, but the vision of the Forestry Commission and its partners is not that restored woodland becomes a nature reserve in which Man is no more than a warden or sightseer. The hope is that the woods will make a contribution to revitalising rural societies and economies.

Public money has been pumped into the

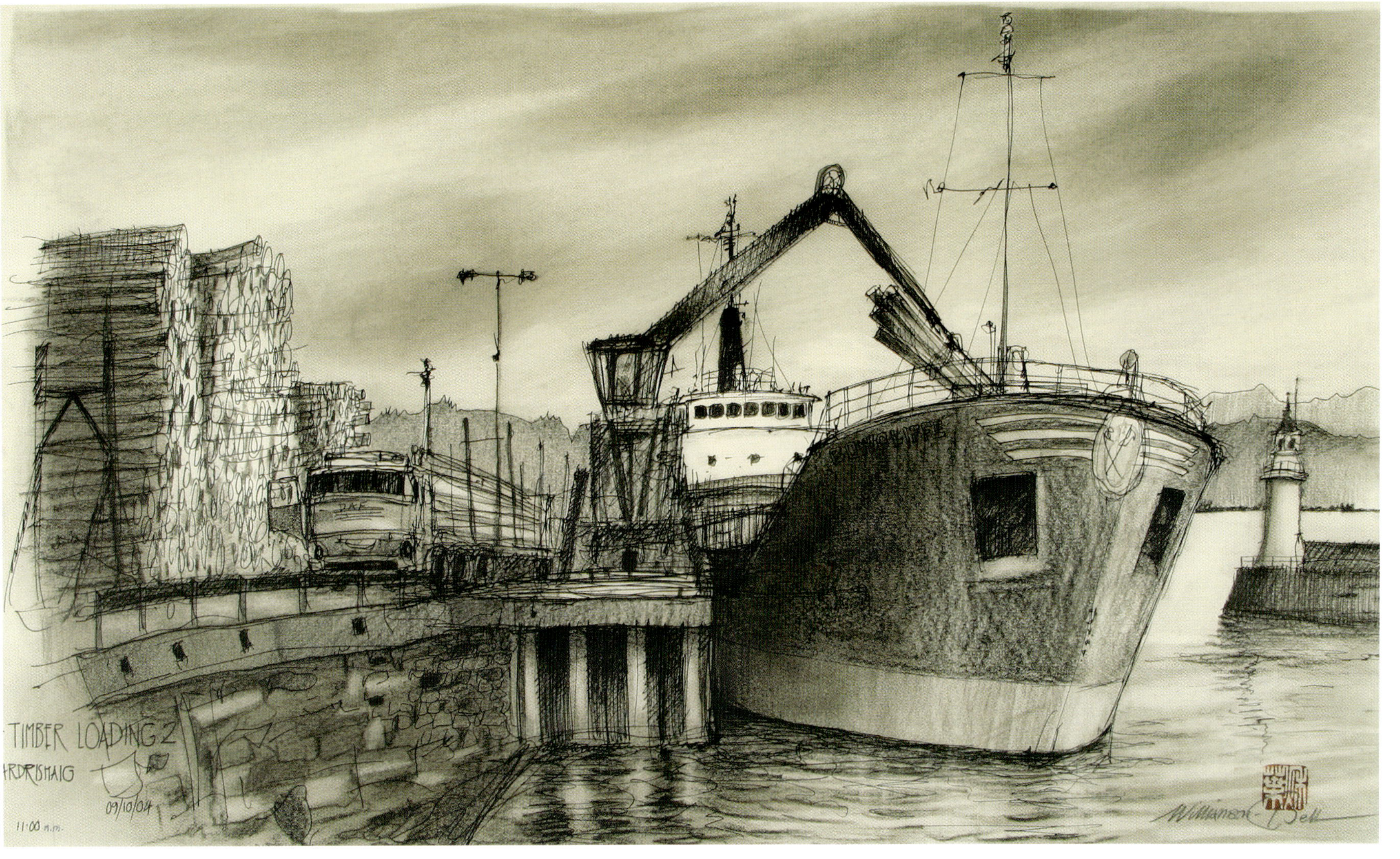

2

oakwoods to prevent their disappearance. The major threats – overgrazing and competition with exotic conifers and rhododendrons – have been removed. The woods are now much healthier and some are regenerating nicely. The question is now what the community – at the local and the national level – wants from these woods. They can be left to nature, which could lead to some rarities dying out, or they can be managed as described above to improve their conservation status, amenity value for local people and visitors, and maybe provide some timber.

Forestry used to provide a significant amount of employment from the 1950s to 1970s, when gangs of men were needed to plant the new conifer forests. New villages were built to house their families, but the workforce has since shrunk and people have often departed to find work elsewhere. Now employment is being created along different lines. There are some jobs in forestry, but with the provision of footpaths, signs and observation hides, the woods are being added to local tourist attractions (with tourists being housed in the former forestry villages!).

I find a more genuine link between woods and communities in the possibility of selling timber from the restored woods. The difficulties of extraction make commercial use unattractive, but there is a small niche market for veneer, which requires no more than a few high-quality, very valuable trees.

1. James Williamson-Bell *Timber loading I, Ardrishaig*
   pen and ink charcoal · 29 x 47 cm
2. James Williamson-Bell *Timber loading II, Ardrishaig*
   pen and ink charcoal · 28 x 47 cm

I had decided not to produce 'wildlife subjects', as I felt that these would be well covered by the majority of artists. Instead I chose industrial aspects. The docks and the Crinan Canal were ideal. These drawings carried me back to the days when I was a shipbuilding draughtsman on the River Tyne.

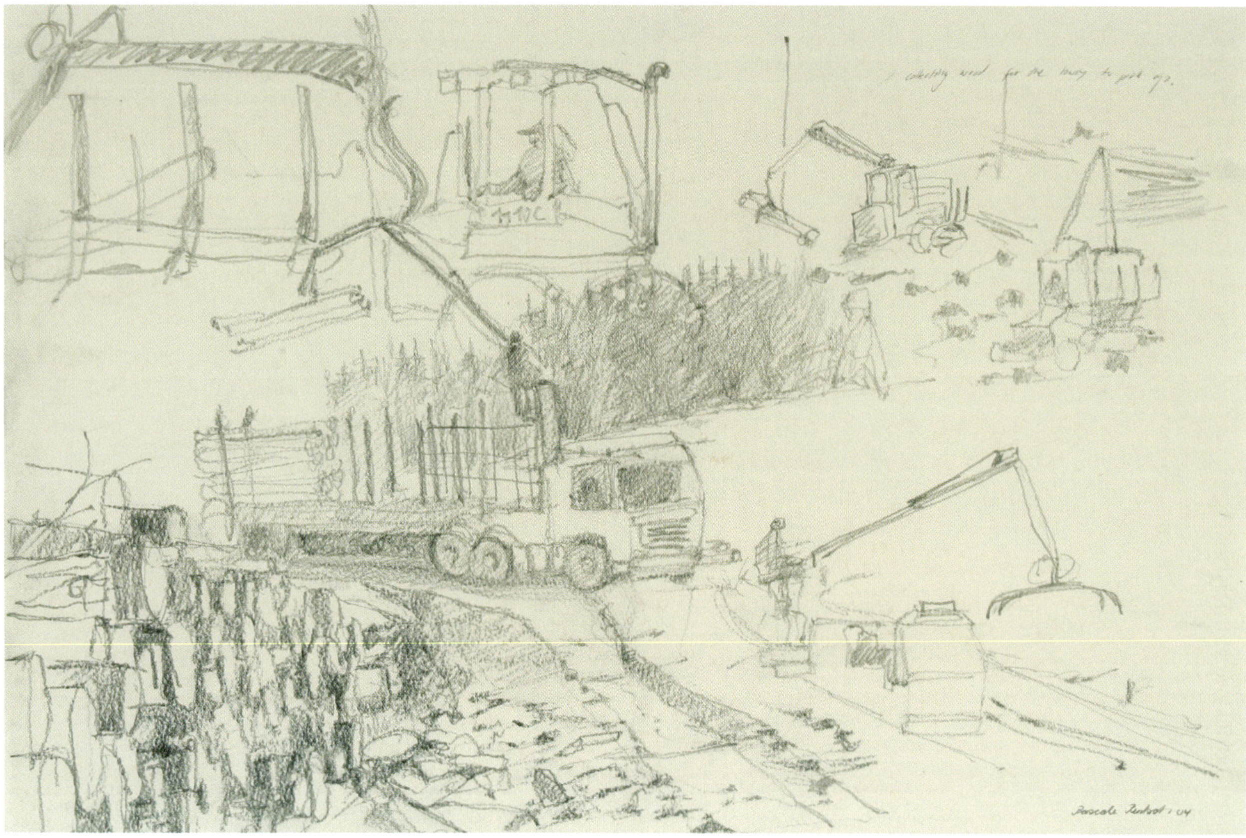

1

Dugie Cameron of Arivegaig, Lochaber, turns timber from 130-year-old oaks into high-quality bagpipes. At the other end of the market, local craftsmen use knotty timber for ornamental flooring and tables.

Although the numbers of jobs created by the woodlands would be so small as to be negligible in an urban setting, they can be significant in remote areas, where each job allows a family to stay in the community. They will help to keep shops, schools and transport services viable, so maintaining a community that is more than a dormitory for commuters and the retired and a landscape that is more than a theme park for visitors.

In almost every corner of the world, tourism is seen as a way of generating jobs and sustaining failing communities. It is also a cliché that tourism runs the danger of destroying what visitors come to see. The farming community forms the foundation of the Highland identity in terms of both the social fabric and the maintenance of the natural heritage of scenery and wildlife habitats. As the economics of small farming become more difficult, diversification is seen as the answer. Tourism can be the means of preserving what the visitors come to see. In the remote but scenic Highlands, tourism has become vital to the economy, and three-quarters of visitors say that they come for the wildlife and landscape. Restoring the oakwoods can only improve the quality of their visits and attract more visitors.

It has been said that Man preserves what he values but neglects or destroys what he does not. In the history of the Highlands, the Atlantic oakwoods were cared for when they were valued for sheltered pasture, timber, firewood, tanbark or charcoal. Thereafter there was a period of neglect, followed by woods being replaced by conifer forests. We have now entered a new era, in which native woods are valued for reasons divorced from human survival and profit. These are their aesthetic and recreational possibilities, which benefit people, and the richness of their animal and plant life, which is seen as a worthy end in itself. The future of the Atlantic oakwoods and their inhabitants is now assured.

1. Pascale Rentsch *Forest machinery, Barr, Morvern* pencil · 38 x 58 cm
2. Darren Woodhead *Forest machinery, Barr* watercolour · 47.5 x 71 cm
3. Pascale Rentsch *Processing timber, Lochaline* watercolour · 38 x 58 cm

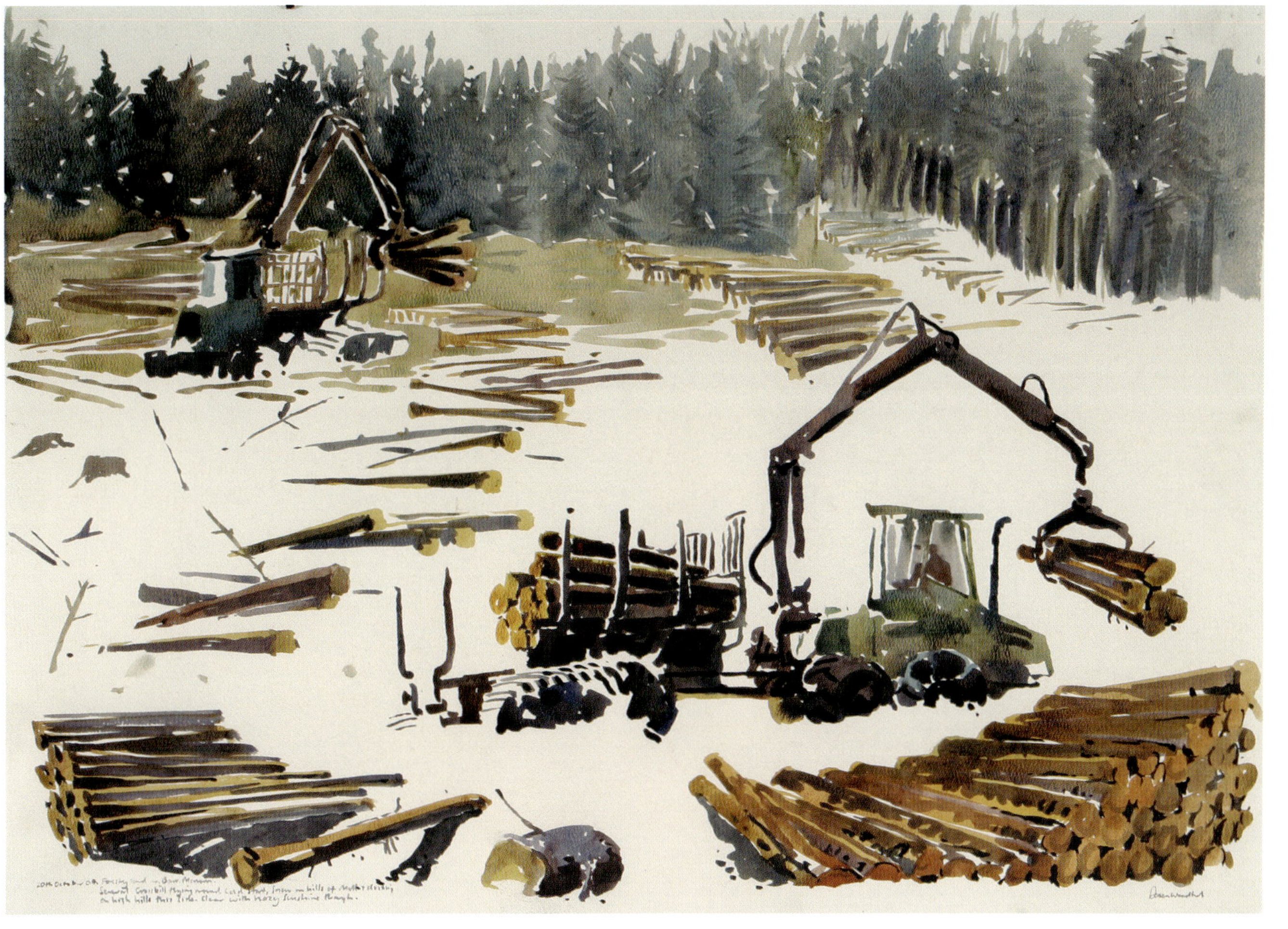
2

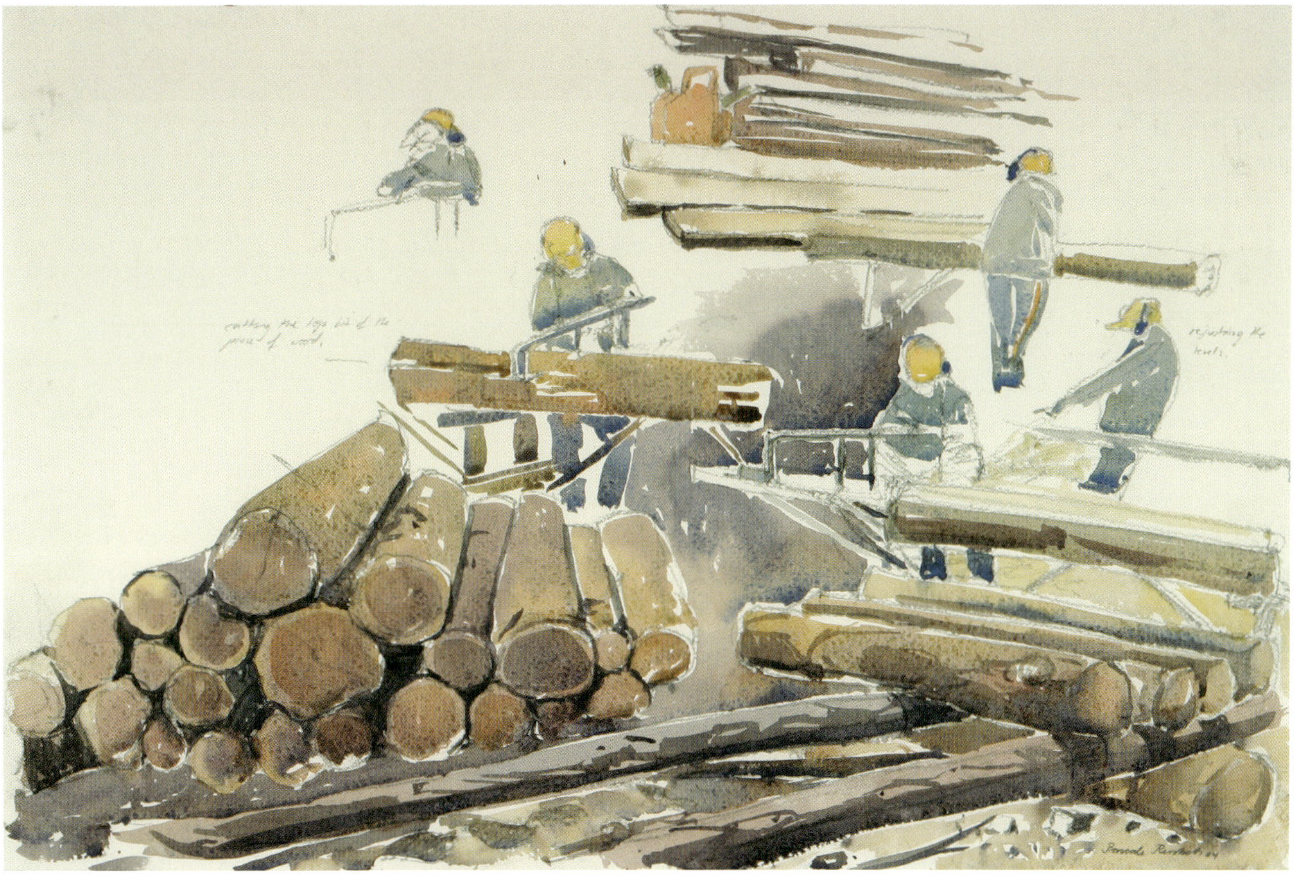
3

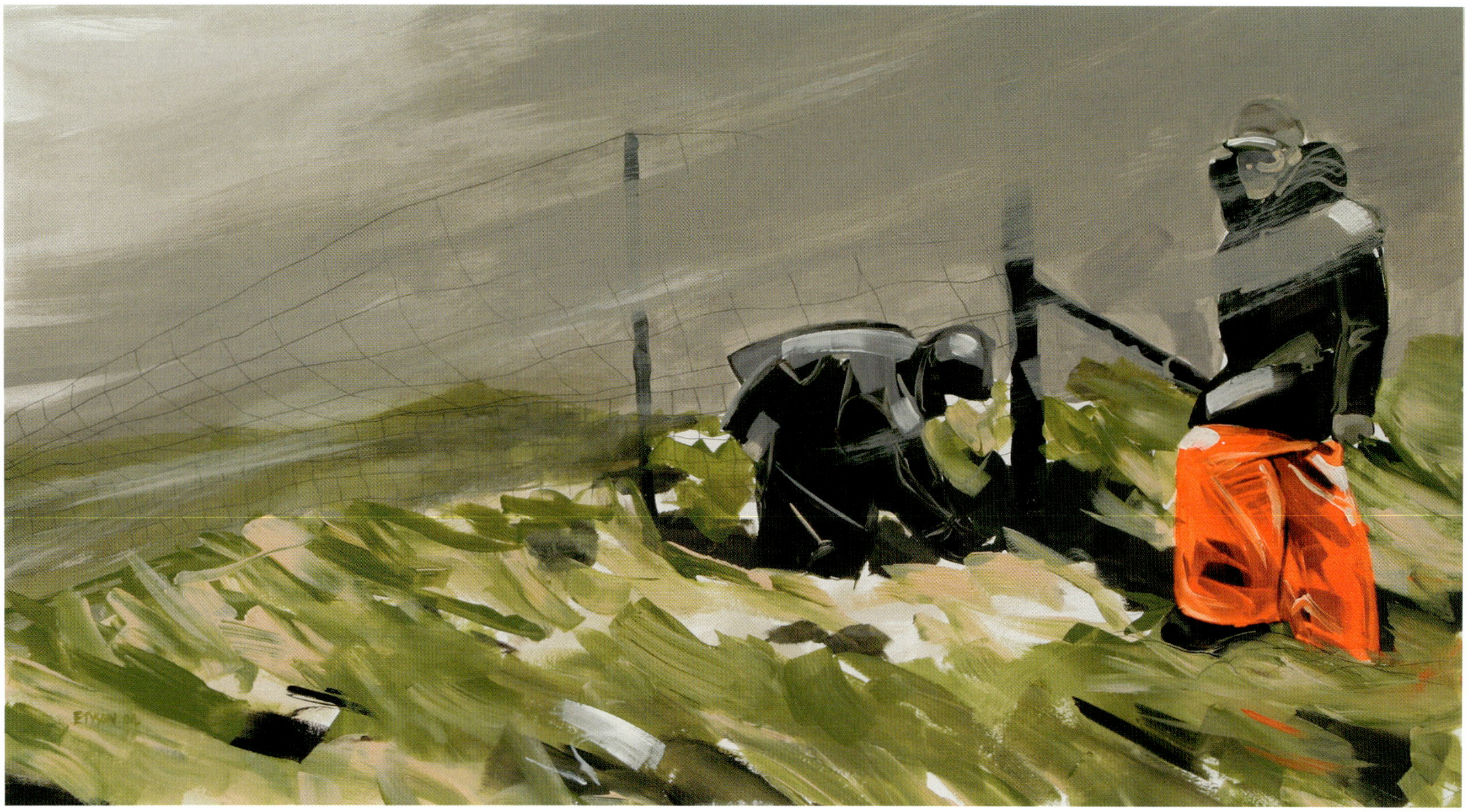

1

1 Esther Tyson *Fencing*
acrylic on paper · 44 x 80 cm

2. Chris Rose *Tree harvesting*
acrylic on paper · 30 x 39 cm

In an area of Knapdale being set aside for regeneration of the oakwoods, the final crop of Sitka spruce is being clear-felled. Three of us, intrepid artists, climbed, slipped and scrambled our way over steep terrain and treacherous fallen logs to this remote site to witness the operation. This modern, state-of-the-art tree-felling machine was an impressive and terrifying piece of hardware. We stood in awe as it gripped an 80-foot tree, cut it at the base, lifted it clear, ran its entire length through the cutting head, stripping all the branches off, and then cut it in to predetermined lengths, all in the space of a single minute. One man operated it, and alone he could fell and log 600 tons of timber in a week.

When we arrived, scrambling up the hill, this was the first view we saw. I was immediately struck by the symbolism of the darkly brooding and sterile spruce plantation contrasting with the bright optimism of the sunlit regenerated oakwoods, glimpsed at the left of the scene. In the midst of this, the machine, with its smooth, clean lines, marched unstoppably through the dark woods, cutting them down with clinical efficiency. While this operation was for the good, I was reminded of man's terrifying ability to destroy.

Painted on the spot, this picture was 'tidied up' later, in the studio.

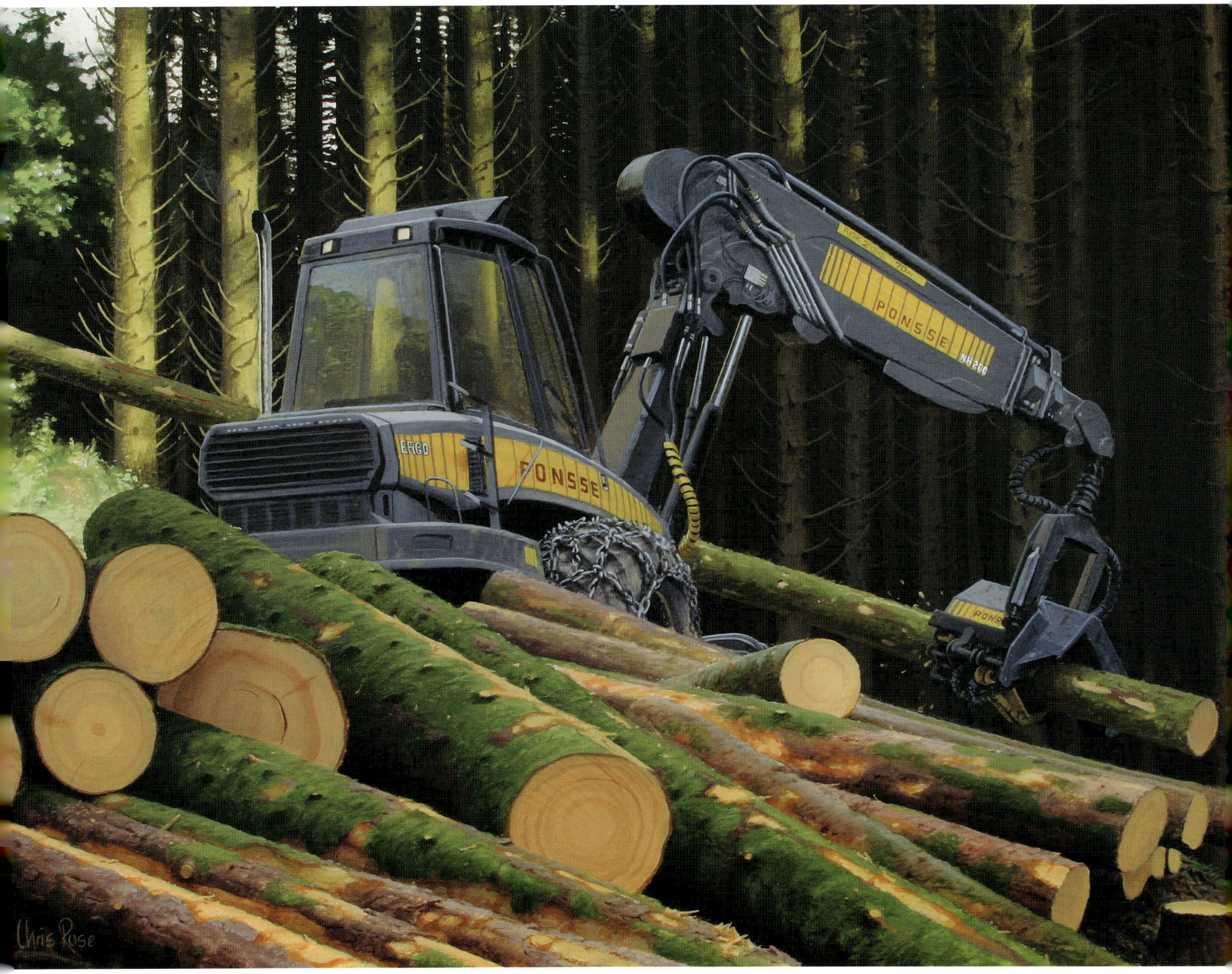

2

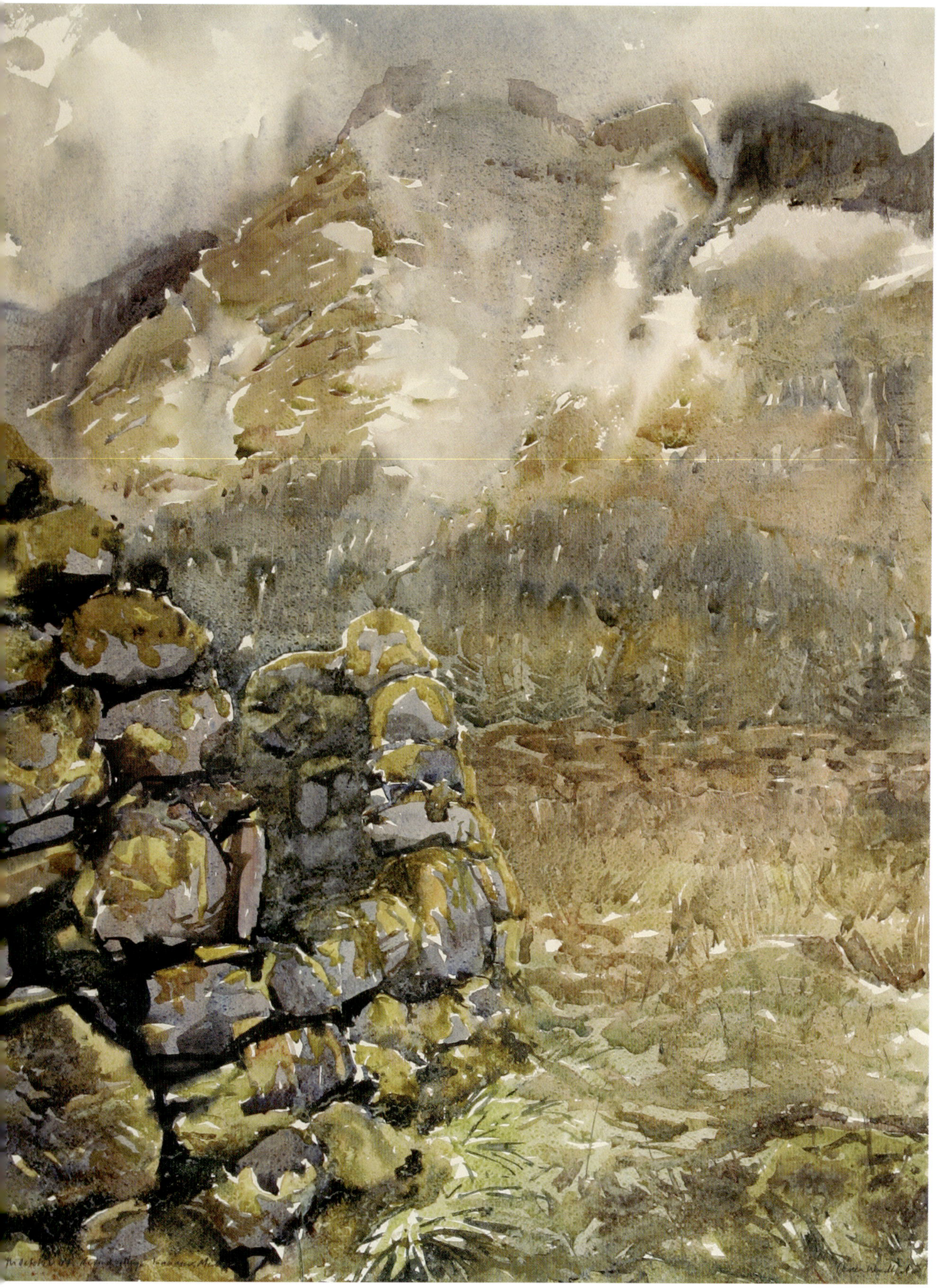

1

1. Darren Woodhead *Ruined village of Inniemore, Morvern*
   watercolour · 76 x 38 cm
2. Darren Woodhead *Fossil track, Morvern*
   watercolour · 76 x 38 cm

Our first evening in Morvern , a memorable visit to a special area of woodland, with glorious ochre larches illuminating lichen-covered boughs. A flock of redwing cascade in to roost as a pair of raven croak overhead, sharply adjusting their course upon noticing the visitors below.

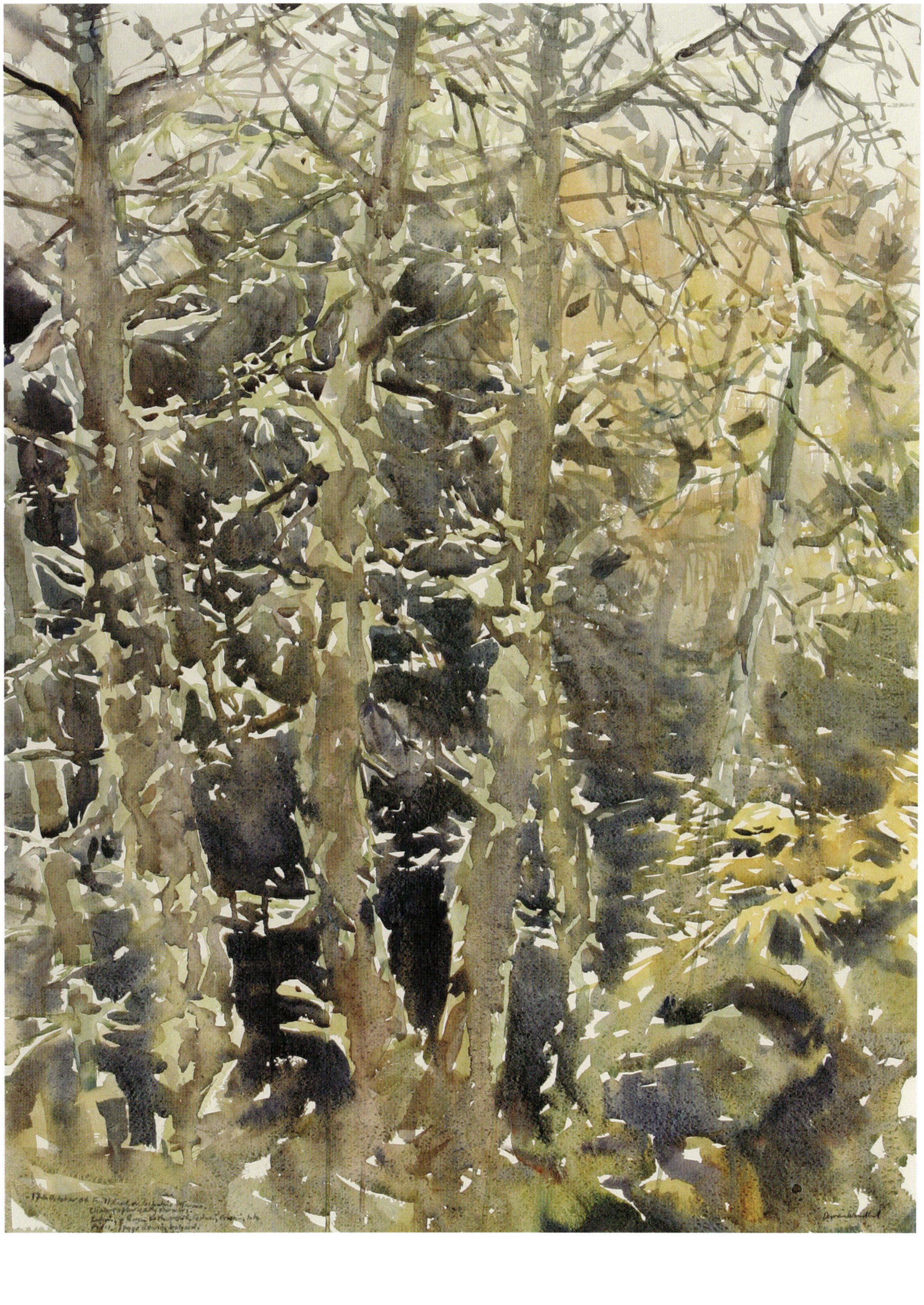

2

Pascale Rentsch *Jake's workshop and chickens*
watercolour · 42 x 60 cm

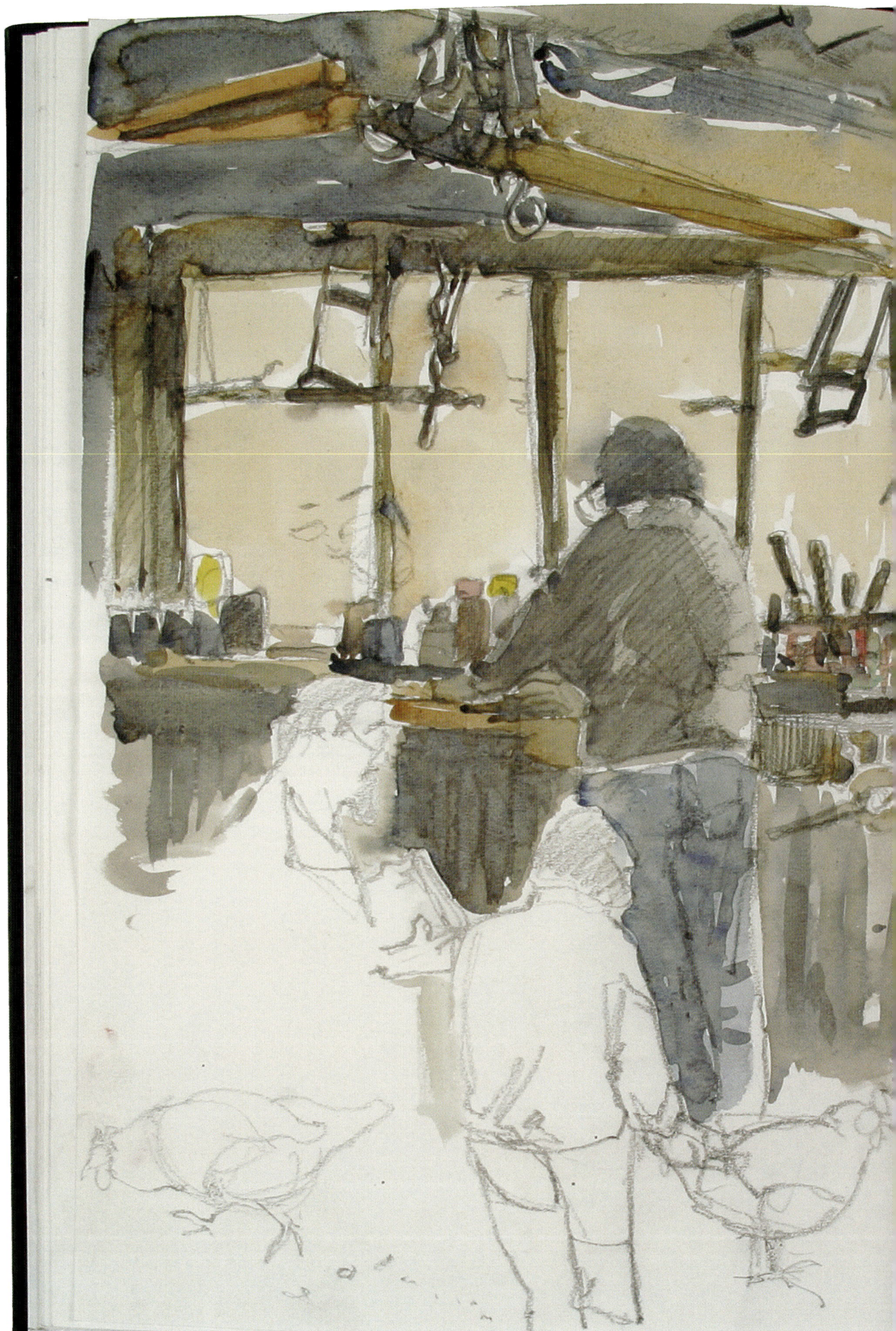

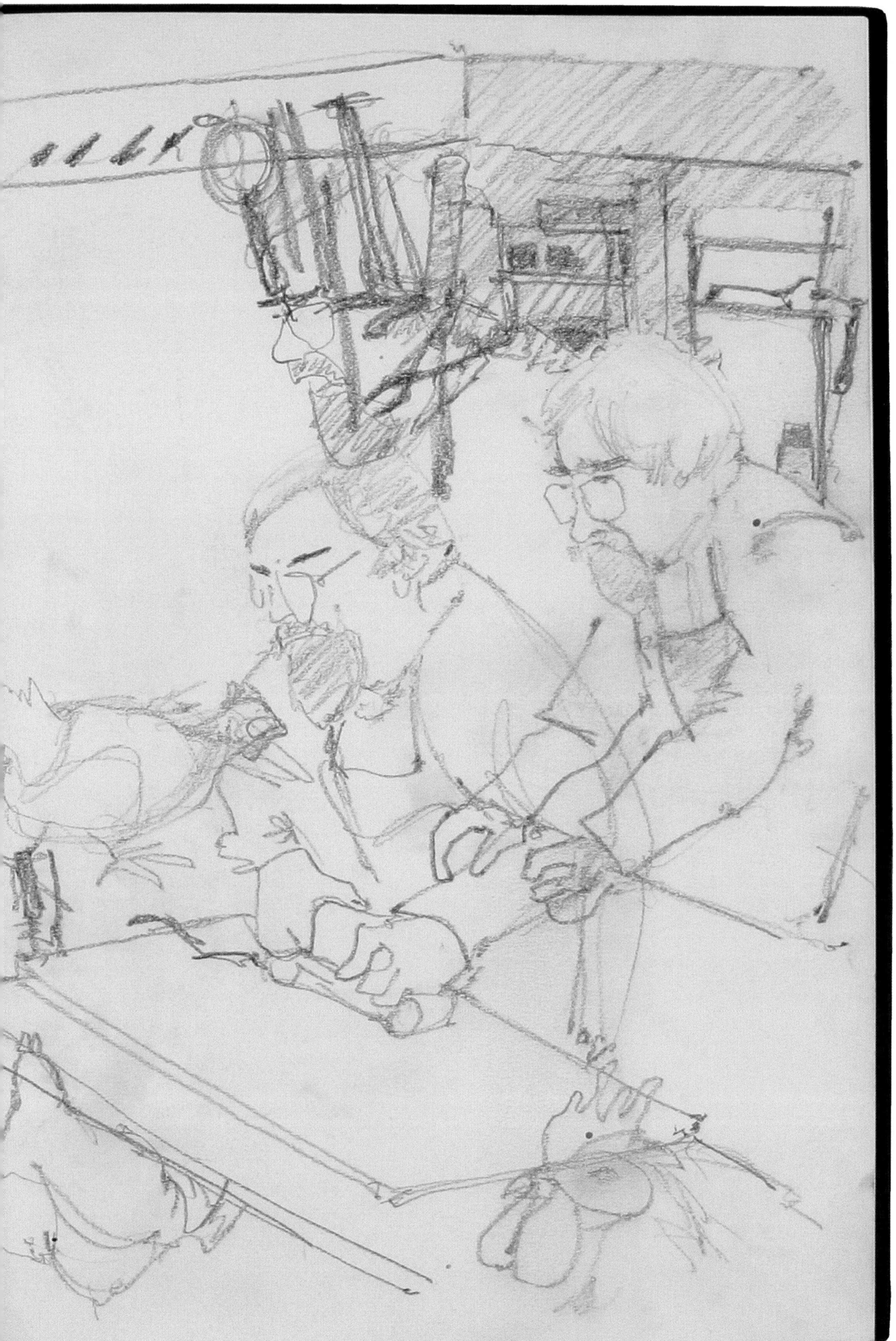

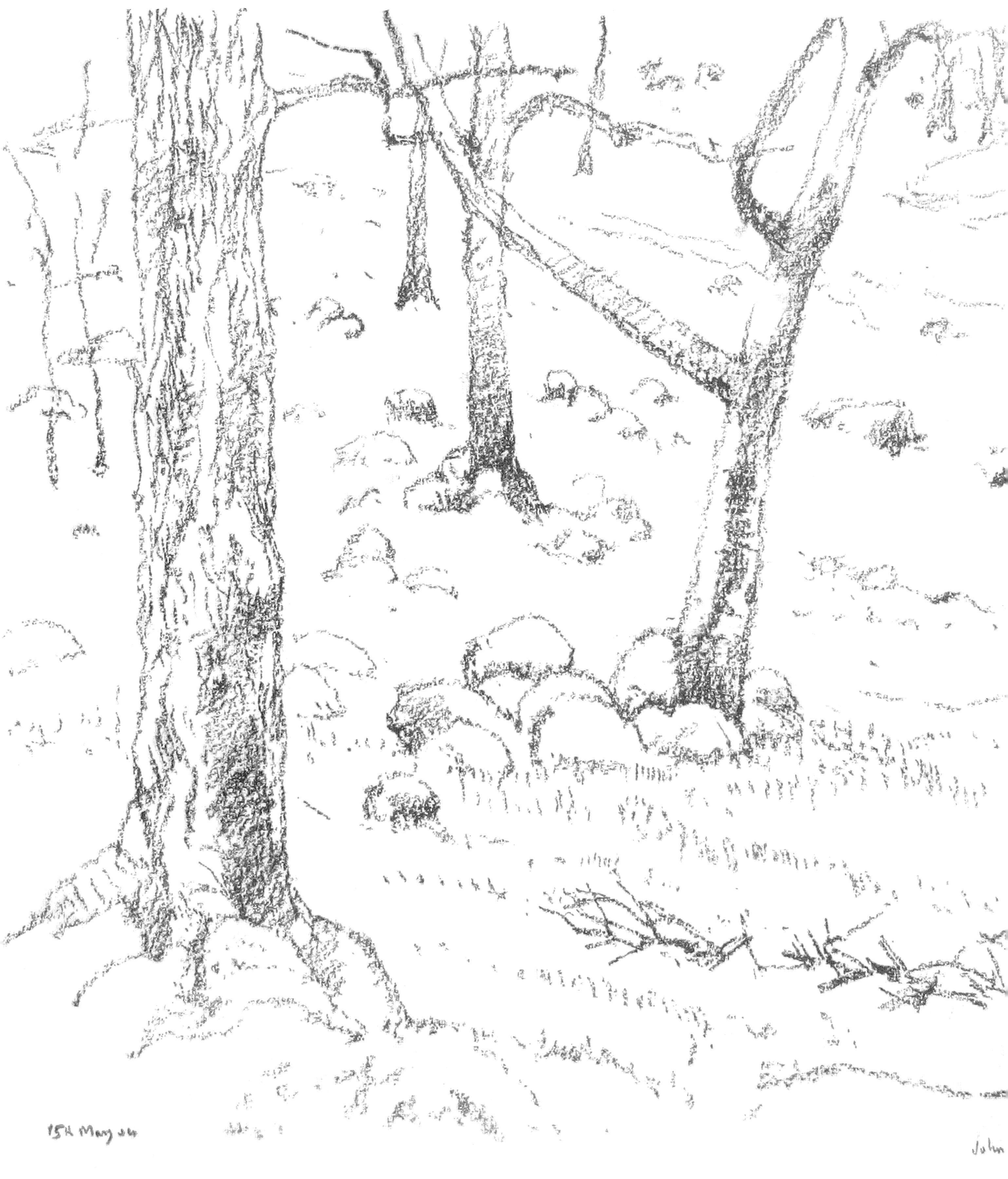
15th May 04
John

Appendices

John Busby *Oak woods, Ariundle, Loch Sunart*
conte crayon · 30 x 30 cm

Study areas

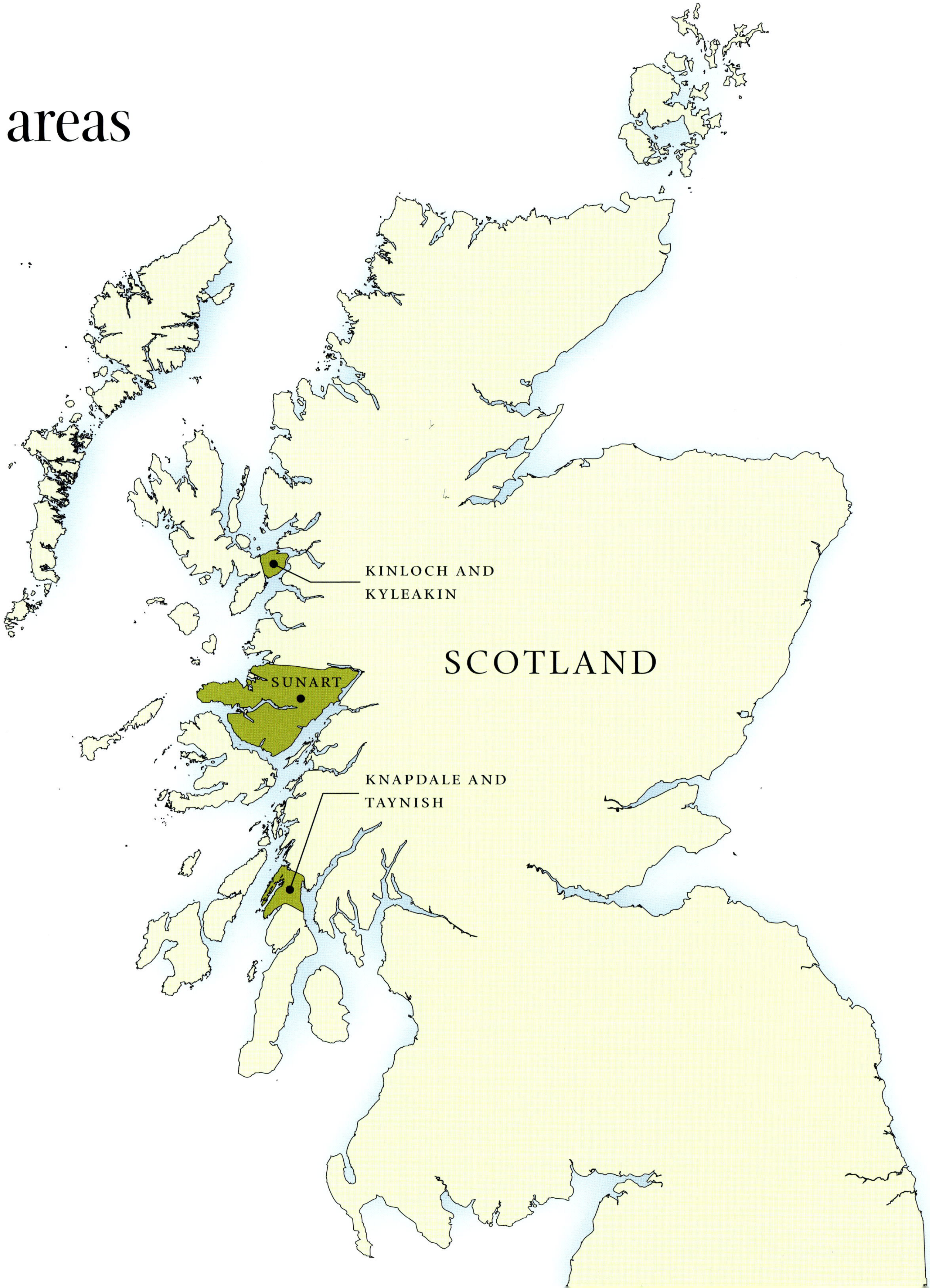
KINLOCH AND
KYLEAKIN
SCOTLAND
SUNART
KNAPDALE AND
TAYNISH

KINLOCH AND KYLEAKIN

The attraction of the Isle of Skye for many visitors is the bare grandeur of the Cuillin Hills and the heritage of clan history. The scenic and historical associations of the island's native woods are all too easily overlooked. Many woods are remote from public roads and can be reached only by a determined walk along a forestry road or footpath. Woodland types are varied, most being birch with hazel, sometimes replaced by oak, ash, rowan or sallow. They are concentrated in the south end of the island, in Kyleakin and Sleat, where they are protected from the worst of the westerly Atlantic storms. Most are also on steep hillsides, where drainage has prevented the formation of bog and where past attempts at clearance have been difficult.

Forestry Commission Scotland owns the 7,400-hectare Kinloch and Kyleakin Estate in the south-east corner of Skye. Nearly one-third was planted with lodgepole pine and Sitka spruce over the last quarter-century, but significant areas of semi-natural woodland remain along the coastal fringes, mainly on steep, rocky slopes and along ravines. The largest of these are at Mudalach and Aslaig, both accessible only by rough walking or by boat, and the Kinloch Woods, which have access by a Forestry Commission road to a car park, from where the woods can be explored on footpaths. The woods at Kinloch are dominated by birch and oak, with abundant old hazel coppice, whereas those at Aslaig are almost pure oak of an even age, where grazing has prevented regeneration. It is likely that other kinds of trees have been 'weeded' to allow more space for oak. Mudalach has a totally different character; its woods are almost pure birch.

In partnership with the Scottish Forest Alliance (SFA) and with funding from BP, Forestry Commission Scotland has started to restore 700 hectares of woodland to oakwood habitat by allowing natural regeneration through reducing deer numbers and by planting with locally collected seed. This will effectively double the area of native woodland. An interesting feature of the new woodland is that it will range from the coastal fringe of existing semi-natural woodland to the treeline halfway up the hills.

The restoration project started with stands of conifer plantation being felled to recycle as a Millenium Forest for Scotland Trust project and natural regeneration being allowed to take place in the cleared ground. Then, in the summer of 2004, planting of oak and hazel seedlings started with three-dozen children from local primary schools planting three seedlings each in a plot outside Kyleakin. From this small start, around half a million tree seedlings will be planted over a five-year period. The schools are growing their own seedlings under the guidance of trained adults but the bulk will be grown in five nurseries, three of which have been set up on crofts which are diversifying from sheep farming with the aid of SFA funding.

As well as restoring the oakwood habitat, the Kinloch Hills Project plans the reintroduction of some vanished species. Black grouse no longer live on Skye, the last ones being seen in the Kinloch Hills. Regeneration of birch in the cleared areas will provide suitable grouse habitat where reintroduction may be possible. An artificial sea eagle nest has been placed in the canopy of an oak tree, which will hopefully attract eagles from the growing population that was introduced on Forestry Commission land on north Skye.

Access to the Forestry Commission's Kinloch and Kyleakin estate is very difficult at the moment, except for the paths leading to the abandoned settlement at Leiter Fura and an old drove road that continues on to the ferry at Kylerhea. Plans are under way for more footpaths and mountain-biking trails, and an otter hide has already been established at Kylerhea.

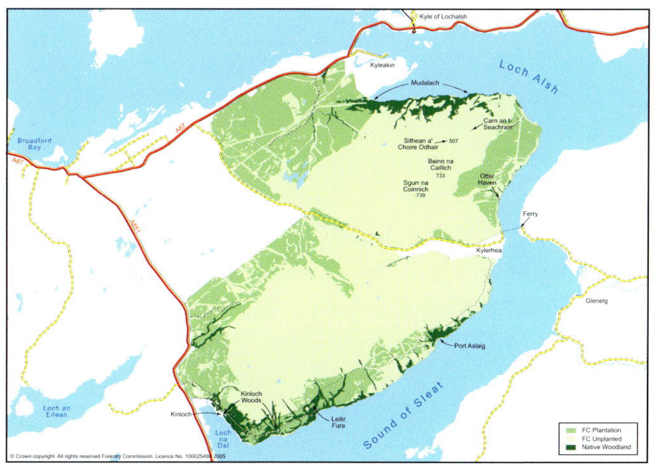

THE SUNART WOODS

The area around Loch Sunart – Ardnamurchan to the north and Morvern to the south – contains some of the largest, and richest in terms of species, tracts of Atlantic oakwood in Scotland. It is also one of Britain's largest areas of ancient semi-natural woodland. Unusually there is often an unbroken transition from the seashore, through oakwood to birch wood and open hillside.

Unlike the other two areas visited by the Society of Wildlife Artists, Forestry Commission Scotland is only one of several landowners in the Sunart area; the others include national agencies, large private estates and small farmers and crofters. The area includes Ariundle National Nature Reserve north of Strontian and Scottish Natural Heritage's Glencripesdale National Nature Reserve on the south side of Loch Sunart. Several blocks of Forestry Commission land were planted with exotic conifers in the 1950s and 1960s and the oakwoods were often underplanted or felled.

There was a change in direction in 1994 when plans began to be formulated for restoring some plantations to native woodland, especially where they would link with remaining oakwood. At the same time many of the existing oakwoods required attention in order to control grazing by deer and livestock and to remove rhododendrons. The ecological and conservation values of the oakwoods are also being enhanced with new plantings to extend them into areas recently cleared of conifers or to link with neighbouring stands.

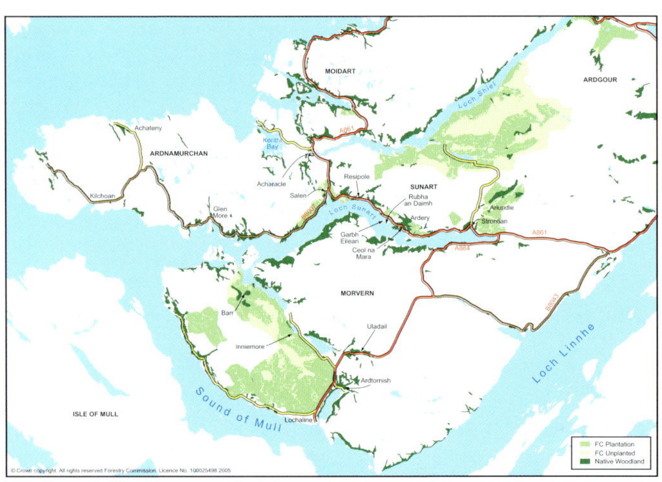

Part of the Forestry Commission's vision is that the restored woodland will make a significant contribution to the revitalisation of the rural economy. This hope is being tested in the Sunart area by a programme in which the local communities become involved with the sustainable management of the woods. This is the Sunart Oakwoods Initiative, which includes the agencies Forestry Commission Scotland, Scottish Natural Heritage, Lochaber Enterprise and the Highland Council as well as the communities. In 2003 the Initiative was extended into Morvern through the Morvern Woodland Project. As well as funding woodland restoration, the Initiative improves public access to the woods and develops community involvement through training, employment and events.

In 2001, private woodland owners on the north side of Loch Sunart joined forces with Forestry Commission Scotland in setting up the North Sunart Woodland Group, which controls a contiguous belt of 1,300 hectares of land, most of which is woodland. The Group had been set up informally in 1998 to share deer control and fence maintenance. Building a single deer fence around the entire belt was more economical and less intrusive than separate fences around each property. Subsequently the Group's objectives have been enlarged 'to optimise the combined conservation, recreation and economic value of the woodlands through sustainable management techniques'.

Sunart Oakwoods Initiative projects are aimed at linking local communities with the woods and providing employment. They include local utilisation of the conifer plantations with outlets in housing and boat building, and education in the value of the woods to conservation, local economy and culture. Schoolchildren, for instance, tend nurseries of native trees, and a Forest School (*Sgoil na Coille*) has been built at Salen, where both children and adults can gather in an oakwood to learn about the woodland habitat, its management and the use of its products. In the long term, there is the possibility of sustainable use of the restored oakwoods. This could include firewood as well as timber. Although no more than 20–70 tonnes of good timber might be produced from a 100-hectare oakwood per year, this would be sufficient for specialist uses and so would be significant at a local level. Producing high-class timber will require long-term management to produce straight-stemmed trees. Such an aim can sometimes lead to a clash between economics and conservation; for instance when felling one tree affects the lichens and mosses on its neighbour. Nevertheless, some careful felling is needed to maintain and improve the conservation interest of the woods. Some farmers are already attempting controlled grazing within the woods, and deer stalking is another option for generating income from woodland.

Knapdale and Taynish are at the north end of the Kintyre peninsula, just south of the Crinan Canal. They have a unique landscape of parallel, rocky, wooded ridges and grassy bottoms, which give Knapdale its name, from the Gaelic *cnap* (hill) and *dall* (field). The 'fields' have been drained and planted with conifers.

From a viewpoint on one of the footpaths climbing over a knap, all stages of tree growth can be seen: from native woods to small stands of the original and now-maturing conifer planting and back to regenerating native woods. The woods are varied, with oak, ash, hazel and elm growing on the more fertile, drier and sunnier west-facing slopes of knaps, and birch and alder in damp hollows. Open spaces in the wet parts of the woods on the north-facing rocky slopes of knaps and around the lochs increase the local habitats for more species. The woods had once been coppiced for charcoal and there are also the remains of wood pasture. They include the important hazel wood at Barrandaimph. Knapdale was extensively planted with Sitka and Norway spruce, starting in 1933, but Taynish was planted with non-native hardwoods – beech, sycamore, lime and chestnut – in the early 19th century.

The richness of the area is shown by the tally of 336 species of lichens and 232 mosses and liverworts in Taynish. Knapdale is well known for the variety of bats, which include pipistrelle, Natterer's, Daubenton's and grey long-eared. Management of the woods has to take into account the use of the trees as bat roosts. There are also 10 species of dragonflies to be seen on the lochs, including the scarce hairy dragonfly, and rides have been cut through the woods so that dragonflies can easily find a way from one to another.

The Forestry Commission owns 6,000 hectares of Knapdale. Just to the north is Crinan Wood, which is owned by the Woodland Trust, while to the south lies Taynish Woods, a 350-hectare National Nature Reserve belonging to Scottish Natural Heritage.

Knapdale has 600 hectares of oakwood habitat, and 700 hectares of plantation on what was oakwood habitat are now being restored by felling to recycle of the conifers. Other plantations are being restructured to make corridors for wildlife to spread. With minimal intervention, a mix of thickets of young growth, mature trees and open spaces will develop, with old decaying veterans and fallen logs slowly returning to the soil. This sort of situation can already be seen on the knaps where there was very little disturbance in the past because the steep rocky ground was too difficult to manage profitably. I was told that these places are as good a natural Atlantic oakwood habitat as we are likely to get. So we do not have to wait for the restoration projects to mature before we can see how this part of Scotland looked before Man took charge.

The conifer plantations have their own conservation value. Small stands are being left for wood ants and black grouse, and around heronries. Pine martens have recently spread back into the area and prefer conifer woods, while black grouse have declined seriously and need habitat management to aid their survival.

Taynish Woods became a National Nature Reserve in 1977 and is now one of eight UNESCO Man and Biosphere reserves in Britain. The woods were grazed after coppicing stopped and they are now managed by 'limited intervention'. A core area is left untouched except for removing birch from small areas of bog. The surrounding management zone is used to demonstrate restoration techniques, which include coppicing, planting native trees in felled areas, excluding deer, and managed grazing by cattle.

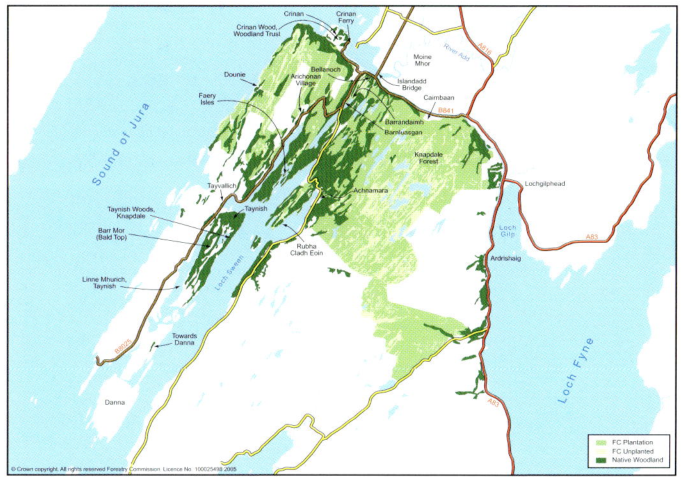

Both Knapdale and Taynish have a significant amenity value, with a network of footpaths and interpretive material for the public and schools. The Argyll Green Woodworkers Association has leased buildings at Barrandaimph, where they give demonstrations of the uses of hardwoods for furniture and building materials.

The Artists

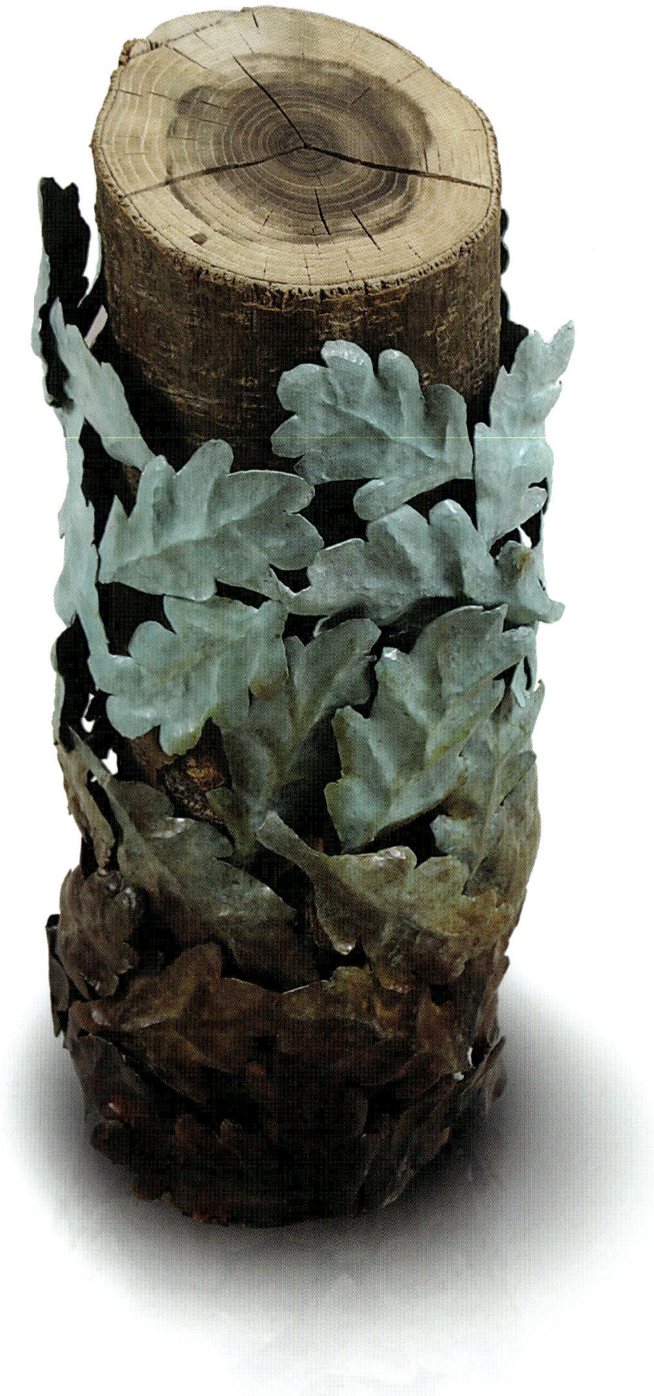

Ger Clancy *Cycle*
patinated copper and wood
height 46 cm · diameter 17 cm

CARRY AKROYD

Carry has lived almost all her life in rural Northamptonshire, an unspectacular and unlabelled countryside, where wildlife struggles to survive alongside agribusiness. This arable landscape, and that of the nearby fens, has been the main source of her imagery, punctuated by forays to wilder regions. She spends a lot of time walking around with a notebook, trying to understand the landscape, to see what is going on in it – the history and geology, the botany and birds.

Carry likes to work in different media. Each process, she finds, provides stimulation for the others. Her paintings and prints are slowly distilled in the studio to try to find the right flavour. There is a lot of mapping and planning between the first sketches and the finished state.

Carry regularly shows work in a few small galleries around the country, and was elected as a member of the Society of Wildlife Artists in 2002.

SÎAN ARMSTRONG

I have lived on Skye for the last 12 years but only resumed painting seriously approximately seven years ago, after a break of about 20 years. During that time I was involved in other things, e.g. hill farming, forestry, academic work and work with people who suffer from dementia.

Now, as an emerging artist, I have found that my approach to painting is developing, with both my increasing perception of the landscape and my – hopefully improving – technical abilities. The varying activities in which I have been involved in the landscape over the years tend to shape the subjects, compositions and the treatment of the paintings. I especially like the complexity and intricacy of details such as foliage, found objects and fur, placed in the wider context of hills, sea and light. More recently I have been exploring the movement and refraction of light on water.

DAVID BENNETT

David specialises in producing, in his unique style, distinctive studies of wildlife in its natural habitat. David's paintings are an exciting blend of observation and painting, with an impressive use of colour and light. With strong drawing and painting, mainly produced in the field, David's work is a delight to see.

He travels widely and has been involved in major expeditions to Extremadura in Spain, County Wexford in Ireland and the Copper River Delta in Alaska.

Born in 1969 in Doncaster, he studied art at Doncaster College and Leeds Polytechnic, before obtaining a Masters degree in Natural History Illustration at the Royal College of Art in London.

A member of the Society of Wildlife Artists, he has had a number of successful one-man exhibitions and is the winner of several prestigious awards, including first prize for the RSPB *Birds* magazine painting competition in 2001, first prize for the *BBC Wildlife* Magazine Art Awards in 1998, and Winner of the Colour Section of the *Birdwatch* Harper Collins Artist of the Year in 1997.

KEITH BROCKIE

Keith Brockie graduated from Duncan of Jordanstone College of Art, Dundee, in 1978, and after a short period working as an illustrator with Dundee Museums and Art Galleries he became a freelance artist specialising in wildlife.

Since then he has had six books published featuring his own work. In addition he has part or wholly illustrated many more books; the latest *Rural Portraits*, 2003, features the native farm animals of Scotland and the characters involved with them. A film, *One Man's Island*, featuring his work on the Isle of May was shown on the BBC 2 *World About Us* series in 1984.

In the course of his work he has travelled widely in countries as disparate as Scandinavia, North Yemen, Tanzania and North America. Also he has participated in expeditions to Greenland in 1982, 1988 and 1991, and Svalbard in 1993 as assistant leader with the British Schools Exploring Society, teaching about the wildlife and field sketching. Working with groups of artists, he has participated in environmental awareness projects in Schiermonikoog, Netherlands, 1990; Biezbra Valley, Poland, 1992; Copper River Delta, Alaska, 1995 and the Briere Marshes, Loire, France, 2001.

He now lives in the village of Fearnan on the shores of Loch Tay, Perthshire, where he has a studio/gallery.

PHILIP BURTON

I studied Zoology at University College, London, and then taught for several years, carrying out my PhD study while doing so, finally gaining it in 1969. Two years before this, I joined the ornithological staff of the British Museum (Natural History).

I have participated in several expeditions as part of my museum work. I am a

Founder Member of the Society of Wildlife Artists, and have illustrated several books and other works.

JOHN BUSBY

Born in Yorkshire. Drew animals and birds from an early age. Studied at Leeds and Edinburgh Colleges of Art, then taught drawing and painting at ECA from 1956 to 1988. Has illustrated over 30 natural history books. Mainly interested in expressing the behaviour of birds, and the forms and inner meaning of landscape. Lives near the Firth of Forth and the Bass Rock and has studied seabirds in Shetland, New Zealand, The Falklands and Galapagos Islands, and shared an expedition to Aldabra Island with Bryan Nelson in 1974. His own books include *Drawing Birds* (RSPB 1987), *John Busby: Nature Drawings* (Arlequin 1996); and a new *Drawing Birds* (RSPB 2004). He has exhibited widely, with one-man shows at The Scottish Gallery, Edinburgh in 1997, a retrospective exhibition at Cartwright Hall, Bradford in 2000, and solo shows at The Wildlife Art Gallery, Lavenham in 2001 and at The Shire Pottery Gallery, Alnwick in 2003 & 2004.

He has been involved with the Artists For Nature Foundation since its inception in 1991 and taken part in projects in Poland, Spain, Portugal, India, and Ireland. He is an Associate of the Royal Scottish Academy and Founder Member of the Society of Wildlife Artists.

GER CLANCY

I was born in Ireland in 1980. I attended the National College of Art and Design in Dublin. Here, I specialised in fine art and sculpture. Since completing my studies, I have been working as a professional sculptor. My studio is in the Docklands area in Dublin port. I work with various materials. I am currently working on a commissioned piece and am building enough work for a solo show in Slovenia and Dublin for the end of the summer 2005. I have also worked in theatre and film-based work. At the moment I am lecturing in the IADT Dun Laoghaire teaching model making.

KATRINA COOK

With the dual occupations of bird artist and Bird Group Curator at the Natural History Museum's ornithological collection at Tring, I am often asked whether I'm an artist who became interested in birds, or an ornithologist who started drawing. There's no straightforward answer. A serious involvement in natural history has gone hand in glove with my art in a diversity of ways. My pictures are inspired by nature and strengthened by my knowledge of it. As a ringer, the opportunity to handle a variety of bird species has certainly given me a greater three-dimensional understanding – vital for any observational drawing – and a feeling for the weight and form of my subjects.

My 'finished' pictures were, for many years, predominantly drypoints, a copperplate engraving technique. I also etch and I am now concentrating on graphite drawings. I no longer have a studio to work in, but I take full advantage of residency and travel opportunities, producing my large work *in situ*.

My best-kept secret is the many volumes of sketchbooks and illustrated travel diaries I have amassed over many years of field drawing. I have seldom shown them and keep them strictly as personal raw material, which may be referred to later. I also try to keep my drawing skills sharp by attending regular life-drawing sessions – the ultimate workout for eye–hand co-ordination.

JOHN COX

As with most other bird artists, fieldwork is very important to John, and his sketchbooks have accompanied him to many parts of the world, from North America to Borneo. Although it is in no way possible to paint from life every bird that he is commissioned to illustrate, he believes that a good knowledge of as many species as possible in their natural habitat is essential to be able to create a lifelike image on the page.

John became a full-time wildlife illustrator in 1989, after winning *British Birds* magazine's prestigious Bird Illustrator of the Year award. He works mainly on illustrations for books, with his work appearing in, among others, *Handbook of Birds of the World* (Lynx Edicions), *Pigeons and Doves of the World* (Gibbs, Barnes and Cox), *Pheasants, Partridges and Grouse of the World* (Madge and McGowan), and *Petrels and their Allies* (Brook).

In 1993, John was elected a member of the Society of Wildlife Artists and wishes he could devote more time to producing 'gallery' paintings of subjects of his own choosing, especially from his many foreign trips. Born 9 April 1967 in Romford, Essex, England, John now lives with his family in Preston, Lancashire.

DUNCAN CURRIE

Duncan completed his secondary education on the Isle of Skye when his parents settled on the island. He grew to love the spectacular mountain and maritime scenery of Skye and north-west Scotland. As a keen painter, he expressed his enthusiasm for the natural environment of the islands: 'landscape' forming the dominant theme of his degree show at Edinburgh College of Art in 1985.

At about the same time, he became interested in the fishing boats of Cockenzie, a village just along the coast from Edinburgh. Fishing boats are a recurrent theme in his work today, their vibrant colours and lively compositions contrasting with the more subtle hues and fleeting light effects of his landscape paintings.

Nowadays his inspiration comes from hill walking and long fly-fishing trips. This enables him to find unfamiliar views of the well-known Skye hills and lochs. There is a unique light about the landscape of the island. This, together with the spectacular rock formations found in the Cuillins and the mountains and hills in the north of the island, forms the basis of his work.

Duncan specialises in mixed media painting, using a combination of oil and wax-resist materials overlaid with acrylics, inks and water-based media. He also produces traditional watercolour paintings and pen and ink illustrations of wildlife.

JOHN DAVIS

Born in 1956, John studied Wildlife Illustration at Dyfed College of Art in South Wales in the mid 1970s.

In 1987, he became a member of the Society of Wildlife Artists and also won the RSPB's Fine Art Award with a picture of a hunting Barn Owl. In 1991, he won the *British Birds*' Bird Illustrator of the Year award and the RSPB award again. More recently, he has won the black and white section of the *Birdwatch* Artist of the Year award.

Over the years his work has appeared in many books and journals, including RSPB's *Birds* magazine and *British Wildlife*, and he illustrated the 'new moon' page for *BBC Wildlife* magazine for several years. Books illustrated include *Downland Wildlife* with John Burton, *Badgers* with Ernest Neal, *Heathlands* with James Parry, and several field guides.

He is happiest in the field, painting either landscapes or wildfowl and waders at Pagham or Chichester harbours, or further afield such as Canada, Iceland, West Africa and lots of visits to Scotland. Paintings are often in watercolour, but increasingly in oils and acrylics. He has exhibited throughout England, and regularly at the Society of Wildlife Artists' annual exhibition at the Mall Galleries in London.

BRIN EDWARDS

I studied biology at Exeter University, followed by ecology at Durham University, with a vague idea that I would spend the rest of my life in scientific research. I soon realised that I was infinitely more interested in the way the natural world looks than in any theories about how it works. I had sketched and painted wildlife all my life, so it seemed a logical, if risky, step to continue doing that as a career.

My illustrations cover all aspects of natural history and wildlife and combine a passion for the natural world with my background knowledge of the subject. I now have more than 15 years experience working for a variety of UK and European book and magazine publishers.

When left to my own devices, I produce paintings of birds in their habitats, which are altogether looser and more expressive, and this is rapidly becoming an important part of my work. The resultant images have an emphasis on strong design and pattern.

In 2002 I moved from Bristol to a small village on the Suffolk/Essex border. This has provided me with a seemingly endless supply of inspiration for paintings; indeed much of my recent work is derived from the sights of the surrounding countryside.

CARL ELLIS

Since graduating from the Royal College of Art in 1994, I have been working as an artist, consultant and freelance illustrator, specialising in painting fish. I have worked with leading writers and artists on a variety of projects, such as John Bailey's *Freshwater Fishing*, Chris Yates' *The Secret Carp* and *The Wildlife of Britain* magazine.

In recent years my work has been selected for the Association of Illustrator's Images book and tour. My work has also been selected for the American Society of Illustrators Exhibition in New York and appeared in both their *Illustrators 40* and *Illustrators 41* annuals. Over the past few years I have been exhibiting my life drawings, studies and paintings of our British fish at galleries across the UK My work is also selected regularly for exhibitions organised by the Federation of British Artists, including the Pastel Society, the Royal Institute of Painters in Watercolours, the Royal Society of Marine Artists, and the Society of Wildlife Artists at the Mall Galleries in London.

My contribution to fish in art can be seen in a recent edition of *Wildscape* magazine. I am also excited about being included in the Febuary/March 2005 issue of *International Artist* magazine, for my fish work.

ROBERT GREENHALF

Born 1950. Trained at Eastbourne and Maidstone Colleges of Art.

A painter in watercolours and oils, and a printmaker producing limited editions of woodcuts and drypoints, mainly wildlife and landscape subjects. He has been a Member of the RBA (Royal Society of British Artists) and the SWLA (Society of Wildlife Artists) since the 1980s.

He was involved in Artists for Nature Foundation projects in Poland, Extremadura, Wexford, The Fens, and the Netherlands. He participated in the SWLA New Forest Project, and was Artist in Residence at the Parc des Ecrins in the French Alps for four years. His work is reproduced in the books connected to these projects, as well as in *Twentieth Century Wildlife Artists* (1986, Croom Helm) and *Modern Wildlife Painting* (1998, Pica Press), both by Nicholas Hammond. *Towards the Sea* (1999, Pica Press) is the first book devoted solely to his work.

PAUL HENERY

Born 1963 in Northumberland, Paul has studied Advertising, Graphics and Photography Illustration and Fine Art at the Newcastle College of Art and Northumbria University.

He was elected a member of the Society of Wildlife Artists in 2004 and has exhibited widely in galleries throughout Britain.

Paul has received a number of awards, including 1995 *Natural World* magazine readers' Award, 1997 Kittiwake Gallery Award, 1997 *British Birds*' PJC Award, 1998 *British Birds*' Bird Illustrator of the Year Award, 2002 BBC *Wildlife* magazine Art Award and, in 2004, the RSPB Fine Art Award.

Working in all mediums and outdoors in all weathers, Paul seeks to capture the essence of the elemental forces of nature and landscape.

ANNA KIRK-SMITH

Born in 1972. After initially studying veterinary science, Anna attended the Wildlife Illustration course at Carmarthen College and then gained a master's degree in Natural History Illustration at the Royal College of Art. She has exhibited with the SWLA in recent years and was awarded bursaries in 2002 and 2004, the latter for participation in the 'Aig an Oir' project. Anna also received the PJC prize for drawing in the 2004 exhibition. She now works as a freelance artist.

PETER MCDERMOTT

Peter entered the West Surrey College of Art and Design at the age of 15, becoming the college's youngest student. After 5 years of formal training, and following a period of 18 years spent in London, where he rose to the position of Creative Director within a highly respected agency, Peter felt the need to change direction, return to the country of his father, and pursue his first love, watercolours.

Now based on the Isle of Skye with his family, Peter has been painting professionally for just over 8 years, and in that time he has enjoyed several successful exhibitions. Peter's work is represented in private collections around the world.

As a child, landscape represented a connection to one's roots. Landscape evoked emotions of belonging and family. Later, the landscape became a demonstration of God's magnificent presence in creation, especially with the ever-changing light and dramatic weather patterns found particularly in the Western Isles. Because of this, my work is unashamedly representational, enabling everyone to recognise and react emotionally to the location and elements portrayed.

I draw my inspiration from James Fletcher-Watson, one of Britain's finest landscape watercolourists, Edward Wesson for his economy of brush strokes, and John Singer Sargent for his incredible ability to take the very ordinary and turn it into something beautiful.

DAVID GUY MEASURES

Brought up amid a wealth of wildlife on the banks of the Avon in Warwick, his enthusiasm for the natural world developed at an early age. He went on to study painting and printmaking at the Slade, before lecturing at Nottingham Trent University. His life has been divided between his enthusiasm for art and his deep love of natural history. He is an acknowledged expert on butterflies, having published two books on the subject and contributed to others. He has exhibited throughout Britain, won the BBC *Wildlife* magazine's major award and has had a television programme made about him. Fundamental to all his work are the diaries he has kept since his teens. He observes, writes and paints in the field. In the natural history work, he attempts that elusive quality – the life of the creature. In his landscapes, he is free to begin a dialogue with place, its changes and his medium when chance and inclination can prevail.

WILLIAM NEILL

William Neill was born in Middlewich, Cheshire, in 1943. He taught art in Britain and Australia, before moving to the Western Isles in 1980.

Since then he has worked as a wildlife and landscape artist and in nature conservation and biodiversity research. He is currently involved in a project to map the distribution of bumblebees in the Western Isles. He exhibits regularly at the Society of Wildlife Artists' exhibition at the Mall Galleries, London, where he was elected a member in 1990. He regularly facilitates courses in watercolour painting, wildlife art and natural history, both in the Western Isles and at the Nature in Art museum and art gallery, Gloucester.

LOUISE OPPENHEIMER

Louise studied Fine Art at Maidstone College of Art (1970–4). Here her close relationship with weaving and wool was founded, a medium which has continued to inspire her throughout her artistic development.

In 1985, a move to Argyll saw her childhood dream of living in a landscape of exposed rock fulfilled, and the rich and varied landscape of the area revealed subject matters that have never ceased to inspire her. The vibrancy of her colours and textures stems from both a broad understanding of her surroundings and a close observation of the influence of season, weather and light.

Drawing forms the backbone of Louise's creative process. However, whilst drawing is a relatively controllable process, Louise's style of weaving is much more organic and unpredictable, with finished weavings often evolving into something quite different from their original sketch.

Louise's methods in both weaving and drawing determine a slow process, which allows her to enjoy in her artwork a wealth of detail, and development of ideas as she creates. One weaving may take weeks to complete, and this scope of work and the solidity of the final piece are aspects which she particularly enjoys.

JANE LEYCESTER PAIGE

After studying botany, zoology and geography at A-level, Jane went on to do a Froebel teacher's training at Westhill Training College, Birmingham, taking art as her main subject.

From childhood, she was encouraged by her mother to identify and paint wildflowers and by her father to study and develop an interest in early English watercolours. These two interests continue to influence much of her work.

She was elected a Founder Member of the Society of Botanical Artists in 1982 and is a Fellow of the Chelsea Physic Garden Florilegium Society. She regularly illustrated gardening magazines as well as books for BBC Publications and the RSPB. Her work is featured in a new book, *The Watercolour Artist's Flower Sketchbook*, published by Quarto Publishing plc.

Her work has been exhibited with the RI and RWS and regularly with the SBA.

Jane and her husband, John Paige SWLA, run the Old Brewery Studios, King's Cliffe, Northamptonshire, where she teaches art generally and Botanical Illustration in particular. They are both involved with Artists for Nature Foundation projects, and for many years they led painting/birdwatching/botanising holidays for Wildlife Travel.

JOHN PAIGE

Trained in graphic design at Birmingham College of Art.

Member of the Society of Wildlife Artists. Work in the permanent collections of the Leigh Yawkey Woodson Art Museum, USA, and Nature in Art, UK. Participant in Artists for Nature Foundation in Alaska and SWLA Drawn to the Forest projects. Draws from life in the field, but most finished work now produced in the studio. A keen printmaker, as well as a painter in oil and watercolour.

PETER PARTINGTON

Peter grew up near Poole Harbour, which had a deep influence on his art. It was easy to escape from school and watch along the shoreline. He went on to art college, where he studied all aspects. He taught art students for many years, until demand for his work encouraged him to pursue painting and printmaking professionally. His preferred medium is watercolour, and more recently he has explored sculpture. He has had numerous one-man shows. He has written and illustrated many books on drawing and painting and writes regularly for art periodicals. He is currently illustrating for *BBC Wildlife* magazine; recent books include illustrations for the very successful *The Secret Life of Garden Birds*, published by the RSPB.

BRUCE PEARSON

As often as the opportunity arises I work out in the wild, where wildlife and landscape, and sometimes people, interact. A painting might be completed directly in the field, while other paintings and printmaking work results from re-working field notes and re-evaluating ideas in the studio.

Elected a member of the Society of Wildlife Artists in 1976, and its President from 1994 to 2004, I have painted professionally for almost 30 years. In that time I have been lucky enough to travel widely in search of subjects. However, much of my time is spent in East Anglia – either working out in the field or in my Cambridgeshire studio.

For the past 10 years, my work has largely involved private commissions from individuals, museums and institutions; and, by invitation from the Artists for Nature Foundation (ANF), I have participated in various international art events and exhibitions.

Some of my work has been used to illustrate various books, journals and magazines, including writing and illustrating *An Artist on Migration.* A BBC film was made about one part of the journey that I made. Other film projects include the six-part Channel 4 *Birdscape* TV series.

I have shown work in a range of group and solo exhibitions in a number of overseas countries and widely in galleries throughout the UK.

NIK POLLARD

Born 1970, England. Nik Pollard studied at the Royal College of Art, specialising in Natural History Illustration. He is a member of the SWLA and past winner of the Bursary for young artists. In 2001, he received the *BBC Wildlife* Art Award. He is a published author and illustrator of children's picture books.

Nik's work aims to convey a sensitive understanding of place, focusing on the inherent subtleties of landscape and natural history. Based in Kent, he spends most of the year painting on the Swale estuary, an area he has known since childhood.

GREG POOLE

Greg Poole became an elected member of the Society of Wildlife Artists (SWLA) in 1991 and a Council member in 1997. In 1993, Greg gained the *Natural World* art award and the Artists for Nature Foundation (ANF) Award and was subsequently involved in four of their projects.

Greg has had a varied career path, which began with a Zoology degree at Cardiff University, conservation work in Avon, and wardening at Bardsey Island Bird Observatory, Wales and Long Point Observatory, Ontario. He now divides his time between illustration (largely computer graphics) and more personal fine art work.

'Producing finished work is a juggling act between fieldwork (mainly in charcoal and acrylic) and the studio, generally using printmaking based on ideas derived from collage.

'I'm making pictures about nature, above all trying to celebrate appreciation of nature – to hear, smell, touch and see it, marvel at how it all fits together. I am upset about how a lot of it is getting ripped apart, but I don't feel inclined to express unhappiness in my art. It seems better to point out how great things are and to try to show the way I see things. I use artwork as a means of investigation, and this can go from micro to macro in microseconds.'

ALASTAIR PROUD

Alastair Proud was born and brought up in Co. Dublin. He went to Art College in Wales, leaving in 1978 to pursue a career as an artist. In 1985, he was elected to full membership of the Society of Wildlife Artists but had taken part in their annual exhibitions in the Mall Galleries, London, since 1976. The books he has illustrated include *Birds of Prey of the British Isles* and *Wildfowl of the British Isles*. His paintings are held in many private collections all over the world, including more than 50 works commissioned by the Sultan of Oman. He loves travelling and has been to both the Arctic and the Tropics in search of subjects to paint. His main venues for exhibitions are Dublin and London. Alastair lives in West Wales with his wife and two children.

DARREN REES

Darren Rees was born in Hampshire in 1961 and studied Mathematics at Southampton University, teaching the subject for a short time before pursuing painting full time. As an artist he is self-taught.

He uses a variety of media, most commonly watercolour in the field, and acrylic and oil paint for larger landscapes and studio works. He lists his influences as John Busby, Lars Jonsson and John Singer Sargent.

His work has attracted many awards, including *BirdWatch* Artist of the Year, *Natural World* Fine Art Award, RSPB Fine Art Award, and the Countryman Art Award at the Mall Galleries, London. His first solo book, *Bird Impressions*, as greeted by much critical acclaim and was a runner-up in the Natural History Book of the Year Award. He is a member of the Society of Wildlife Artists in London and is a regular writer with *Birds Illustrated* magazine.

He has been a contributing artist to the Artists for Nature Foundation/WWF projects in Holland, Poland, Peru and Ecuador.

He lives in the Forth Valley west of Stirling, Scotland, with his wife and two children.

PASCALE RENTSCH

Pascale was born and educated in Switzerland. She studied art at Brighton and Edinburgh. She has been a practising artist since 1999.

In July 2001, as part of winning the Artist for Nature Foundation prize in 2001, she was invited on to the ANF 'Spanish Pyrenees' project. In February 2000 she was invited on to the Society of Wildlife Artists' 'New Forest' project.

In October 1998 and July 1999 she was invited to work with seven other artists at the Minsmere RSPB Reserve, Suffolk, on two Society of Wildlife Artists' projects that involved screen-printing and hand designing two limited-edition handmade books, within the space of a week for each book.

She received the Isaac Howitt Award for the most promising Art and Design teacher, August 2003 – July 2004 and the Society of Wildlife Artists' bursary for travel and education in 1997 and 1998. She was elected as an associate member of the Society of Wildlife Artists in 2000.

Pascale was Artist in Residence at Edinburgh Zoo in 2000. She has taken part in several solo and mixed exhibitions and has exhibited annually at the SWLA exhibition at the Mall Galleries from 1997.

ANDREA RICH

Andrea Rich has an international reputation as a printmaker, working in multiple-colour woodcut prints. She produces her prints from personal observations of wildlife in their natural habitats. Madagascar, New Zealand, Costa Rica, Africa and Europe are some of the places outside North America that she has visited in search of interesting subjects. To create an image, she carves and prints a separate block for each colour, and then hand pulls each print. A typical print requires ten to twenty blocks. Because the process is very time consuming, editions of her work generally number 30 or fewer. Her woodcuts are represented in numerous museums and universities, as well private collections. As well as her fine original prints, she has published a limited-edition letterpress book of collected works. If you have a question or comment, she'd love to hear from you.

MARTIN RIDLEY

Upon completing the wildlife illustration course at Carmarthen in 1988, Martin was awarded course, faculty and college student of the year. May 2005 was his seventh Artist in Residency at The Society of Wildlife Art of the Nations at Nature in Art, Gloucestershire.

August 2003 saw his third successful exhibition at The Wildfowl and Wetlands Trust, Slimbridge. In 1999, a painting was selected for the prestigious Leigh Yawkey Woodson Art Museum *Birds in Art* exhibition in the USA.

A plethora of Martin's images have gone into printed circulation, including illustrations for books, prints, cards and calendar designs.

A painter of both mammals and birds, Martin has spent much time developing knowledge of the field, which is clearly reflected in his work. Combined with conceptual composition, his attention to animal behaviour, habitat detail and lighting creates an amazingly accurate and artistic record of his nature encounters.

CHRIS ROSE

Chris Rose was born in 1959 in Uganda, where he lived until the age of six. He was educated in Surrey and gained a degree in Biology at Nottingham University. On graduating in 1981, and initially unable to find work as a biologist, he was offered a post as illustrator for the Dorset Heritage Coast Project for one year. Drawing and painting birds and other wildlife had been a paid hobby since his early teens and the year with the Dorset Heritage Coast Project convinced him that this was the career for him.

Chris is an active member of the Society of Wildlife Artists and currently serves on the SWLA council and on the Board of Governors of the Federation of British Artists. He has exhibited widely in the UK and abroad and has won several awards for his work, including Bird Illustrator of the Year and European Bird Artist of the Year.

Chris has travelled widely and recently joined an Artists for Nature Foundation project visiting the endangered dry forests of north-west Peru and south-west Ecuador in order to highlight the conservation value of this area by painting its wildlife. However, most of the inspiration for his paintings comes from the countryside around his home in the Scottish Borders.

DAFILA SCOTT

After training as a zoologist, Dafila Scott turned to drawing and painting. Most of her work is inspired by wildlife and landscape, and features animals or places with which she has become familiar. As a member of the Society of Wildlife Artists, she has exhibited regularly at their annual exhibition at the Mall Galleries, as well as at regional shows. She has also illustrated books and articles.

Working mostly in oils, sometimes watercolours and more recently pastels, she paints either from life or from a combination of field sketches and memory. She has taken courses with painters and art teachers and is especially grateful for the inspirational teaching of Robin Child.

Recent work includes both figurative wildlife paintings and abstract landscapes inspired by visits to Wales and to the South African Kalahari. However, she is equally happy to gain inspiration at home in the garden or on the surrounding fenland. In 2003 she won the RSPB Fine Art Award.

ANDREW SINCLAIR

Andrew Sinclair was born in Garderen, Holland in 1975. He studied Fine Art, Drawing and Painting at Duncan of Jordanstone College of Art, Dundee.

In 1999–2000 he travelled in Western Europe, spending three months living in Barcelona developing range of arts practice, including animation. In 2000–1 he took part in Artist for Gaelic art workshops at Acharacle School, Ardnamurchan. From 2000–4 he designed and developed Resipole Studios, Ardnamuchan, which opened in July 2004. He is now a professional painter and owner–manager of Resipole Studios.

His work is held in private collections in New Zealand, Holland, Kenya and the UK.

JANE SMITH

After receiving a university degree in Zoology at Manchester, Jane became a researcher, producer and then photographer for the RSPB film unit. Jane was also Producer for the wildlife series *Operation Survival* for BBC Scotland. After a spell as a freelance camerawoman making films for the BBC and National Geographic (winning an Emmy for cinematography), Jane began to experiment with painting and printmaking.

With a young family, time is limited but she started painting for one day per week and says she is 'still feeling her way'. Jane has now stopped the constant travelling and is looking at her surroundings on a more intimate level. Regular walks in the Taynish oakwoods have given her much to look at and think about, which she is now expressing on paper.

ANDREW STOCK

Andrew is a self-taught painter and etcher and has been painting full time since 1978. Personally encouraged by the late Sir Peter Scott, he held his first one-man exhibition at the age of 21, at the Malcolm Innes Gallery in London. As well as participating in many joint shows, Andrew has held eleven solo London shows. He has won several awards, including *British Birds* magazine's Bird Illustrator of the Year in 1995.

Etching has formed an important part of Andrew Stock's creative repertoire since 1991, and printmaking now represents a significant portion of his portfolio. He was elected an Associate of the Royal Society of Painter-Printmakers (RE) in 2001.

Andrew was elected a member of the Society of Wildlife Artists in 1983 and has exhibited with them every year since 1981. Last year he was elected President of the Society, having served nine years as Honorary Secretary.

Andrew usually works in water-based media but he also paints in oils. Subject matter has primarily been wildlife, especially birds. However, in recent years he has been painting still life, landscape and figures with great success.

Andrew has lived in West Dorset for the last twenty years and now works from his studio in the hamlet of Ryme Intrinseca, near Sherborne

RICHARD TRATT

Richard Tratt was born in Enfield, North London, in 1953. As a young boy he developed a consuming interest in natural history, with a particular fascination for butterflies and moths. He began painting in his teens, and attended Northwich College of Art, Cheshire, and Dartington College of Arts, Devon (1970–4).

Richard spends a great deal of time observing and sketching his subjects in their environment. Most of his wildlife paintings are finished in the studio, but much of his landscape work is painted outdoors. He works mainly in oils or acrylics on canvas. Richard has been painting full time since 1979, and was elected a member of The Society of Wildlife Artists (SWLA) in 1981, and The Society of Botanical Artists (SBA) in 1986.

He exhibits at many galleries and venues throughout the country and shows regularly at the annual SWLA and SBA exhibitions. Richard has an international following. Recently his paintings have become popular in Japan, resulting in one-man exhibitions in Tokyo, in 1998 and 2000.

Work published by CK Art, Rosenstiel's, Medici, Reynard Fine Art, RSPB, and Sally Mitchell Fine Art. Paintings on permanent display at the International Centre for Wildlife Art, Gloucester. In 1996, first- prize winner of national competition 'Art in Nature', organised by *The Artist* magazine.

ESTHER TYSON

Born in 1973, Esther Tyson was brought up in a small town at the edge of the Lake District, Cumbria. She currently lives and works in South Wales. Esther studied at Carlisle College of Art and Design, Carmarthenshire College of Technology and Art and then London's Royal College of Art. Esther has exhibited widely in the UK, and her work has also earned acclaim in London, where she was shortlisted for the prestigious Hunting Art Prizes in early 2004.

Esther is a painter whose work reflects her deep feeling for the natural world, without being sentimental. Painting from life, she seeks to capture the essence of her subject. Her painting is a response to the smell, sights and sounds. It emerges from her reactions, feelings and thoughts toward both her subject and the marks she makes.

MATT UNDERWOOD

Matt was always curious about natural history as a child, and began drawing and keeping sketchbooks from an early age.

From school Matt went on to study art and art history at Salisbury College of Art, where his tutor provided him with many animal and bird skeletons to work from at weekends. Matt went on to study wildlife illustration at Carmarthenshire College of Art. After leaving college Matt began a career as a painter, his main subjects being landscapes and still life.

In recent years Matt has returned to his interest in natural history, producing eye-catching works in collage, mixed media and oil. Matt finds it is often a tiny piece of information, together with constant observation and drawing, which can trigger an idea for a painting; the real challenge for him is to convey his enthusiasm for the subject and to capture the feeling and wonder of seeing something for the first time.

Matt has exhibited his work at many galleries, including the Mall Galleries, where, in 2002, he won the RSPB Art Award at the Society of Wildlife Artists for his collage *Swallows over the dairy yard*. In April 2003 Matt had a very successful exhibition of his work in Amsterdam.

BARRY W. VAN DUSEN

Barry was born in 1954 in Portland, Maine, USA. He studied Visual Design at Southeastern Massachusetts University, graduating in 1977. Beginning his career as a graphic artist and designer, he soon narrowed his focus to natural history subjects. Barry's work has appeared in a variety of nature books and pocket guides, many as the result of a long and productive association with the Massachusetts Audubon Society. His articles and paintings have been featured in *Birder's World* and *Bird Watcher's Digest* magazines, and his bird illustrations have been published by the American Birding Association, HarperCollins and Princeton University Press.

In 1994, Barry was elected a full member of the Society of Wildlife Artists, and he is an annual contributor to their exhibitions. His work has been selected numerous times for the prestigious Birds in Art show (Leigh Yawkey Woodson museum, Wausau, Wisconsin) and has appeared in galleries throughout the United States and Europe. At the invitation of the Artists for Nature Foundation (the Netherlands), Barry has travelled to Spain, Ireland, England, India and Peru, working alongside other wildlife artists to raise money for conservation of threatened habitats.

Barry resides in central Massachusetts, USA.

MICHAEL WARREN

Michael Warren is a professional artist specialising in paintings of birds in their natural habitats. He has lived in Winthorpe, Nottinghamshire since 1975. His work has enabled him to travel widely, drawing and studying birds. These journeys have taken him to many European countries, all 50 American States, Micronesia, Peru, Ecuador, Africa and Australia.

His early training was at the College of Art, Wolverhampton. In 1972, on the offer of a one-man exhibition in Cork Street, London, he began to paint full time. Since then he has had numerous one-man exhibitions in England, New York, France, Spain and Mallorca. He is President of Nottinghamshire Birdwatchers and Treasurer of the Society of Wildlife Artists. He exhibits at their annual show at the Mall Galleries, London.

Michael has contributed to many publications and has had four books published. He has also designed postage stamps for the British Post Office and the Republic of the Marshall Islands and many conservation stamps.

All Michael's paintings are based on observations of birds in the field; immediate sketches provide the basis for paintings. Sometimes these are completed outdoors but more often in the studio. The paintings are done in watercolour and graphite on Arches or Fabriano paper.

JAMES WILLIAMSON-BELL

Born Wallsend-on-Tyne, 1938, James left school in 1954, and then worked as a shipbuilding draughtsman at Swan Hunter's Wallsend Yard. After twenty years in shipbuilding, James decided to paint full time.

In 1976, he was awarded a Silver Medal for watercolour at the Paris Salon, followed the following year with a Gold Medal, again for watercolour, and a Silver Medal for sculpture. He has exhibited widely in the UK and abroad, receiving several awards in the USA and Kenya for his wildlife work. James is a member of various societies, including the SWLA and Societe des Artistes Francais, the Bilan d'l'art Contemporain and the Royal Society of Miniaturists.

Apart from wildlife painting, James also paints industrial landscapes, originating from his time in the shipyards. Recently he has concentrated more and more on oriental work, woodblock printmaking and Chinese Ink painting. In 1989 he received a travel grant to study for 3 months in Taiynan, Shannstic Province. His work has also taken him to Cuba, Italy and Vietnam. In 1999 he participated in the SWLA and Forestry Commission project in the New Forest.

DARREN WOODHEAD

Darren was born in Leeds in 1971. After studying at Wakefield District College and Carmarthenshire College, he spent three years working on and around a small island off the Pembrokeshire coast, South Wales. He graduated with a Master's degree in Natural History Illustration at The Royal College of Art in 1997.

He has been a keen naturalist since a very early age, spending hours in his native Yorkshire Dales. Combining this interest with drawing was a natural step. All his work is produced in the field, trying to keep a sense of life and freshness in the images.

He has participated in several projects based on wildlife and conservation, including several Artists for Nature Foundation projects. He also participated in two handmade book projects at Minsmere RSPB Reserve, Suffolk, in October 1998 and July 1999.

Awards include: the Society of Wildlife Artists' bursary for travel and education, in 1994 and 1996; and the Artists for Nature Foundation Award 2000 at the SWLA Exhibition, Mall Galleries, London; *Birdwatch* Artist of the Year 1999. Elected a member of the Society of Wildlife Artists in July 2001, and currently serves on their council.

His first solo book of paintings and drawings is due to be published by Langford Press in October 2005.

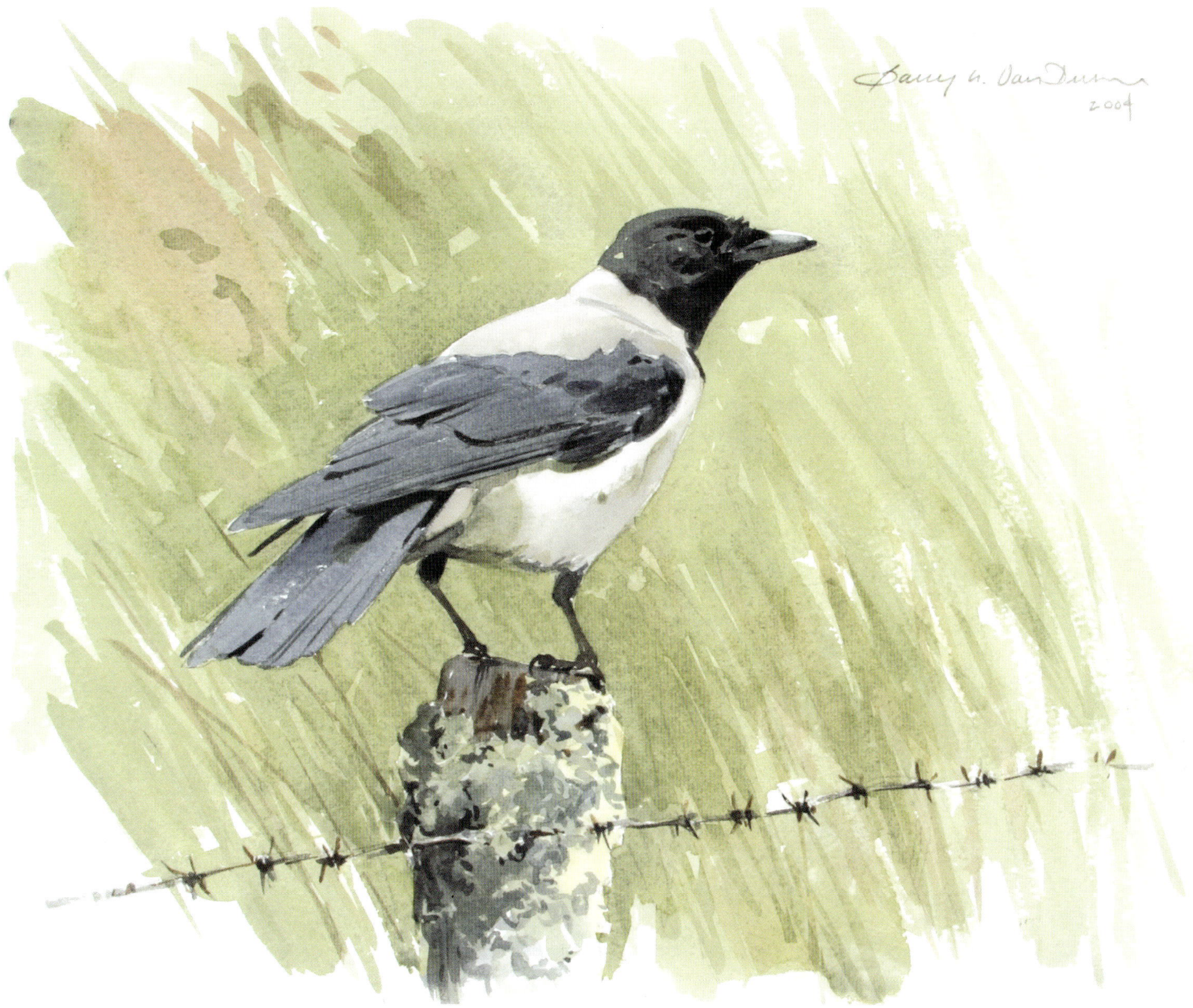

Barry W. Van Dusen *Hooded crow, Ariundle Reserve*
watercolour · 30 x 35.5 cm